Leo Laporte's Guide to TiVo

Gareth Branwyn

Leo Laporte

800 East 96th Street,
Indianapolis, Indiana 46240

Leo Laporte's Guide to TiVo

International Standard Book Number: 0-7897-3195-9

Library of Congress Catalog Card Number: 2004107054

Printed in the United States of America

First Printing: October 2004

07 06 05 04   4 3 2 1

Trademarks

All terms mentioned in this book that are known to be trademarks or service marks have been appropriately capitalized. Que Publishing cannot attest to the accuracy of this information. Use of a term in this book should not be regarded as affecting the validity of any trademark or service mark.

Warning and Disclaimer

Every effort has been made to make this book as complete and as accurate as possible, but no warranty or fitness is implied. The information provided is on an "as is" basis. The authors and the publisher shall have neither liability nor responsibility to any person or entity with respect to any loss or damages aris-ing from the information contained in this book or from the use of the CD or programs accompanying it.

Bulk Sales

Que Publishing offers excellent discounts on this book when ordered in quan-tity for bulk purchases or special sales. For more information, please contact

> **U.S. Corporate and Government Sales**
> **1-800-382-3419**
> corpsales@pearsontechgroup.com

For sales outside of the U.S., please contact

> **International Sales**
> international@pearsoned.com

Associate Publisher
Greg Wiegand

Executive Editor
Rick Kughen

Development Editor
Todd Brakke

Managing Editor
Charlotte Clapp

Project Editor
Dan Knott

Production Editor
Benjamin Berg

Copy Editor
Krista Hansing

Indexer
Ken Johnson

Proofreader
Elizabeth Scott

Technical Editors
Jeff Shapiro
Michael Adberg
weaKnees.com

Publishing Coordinator
Sharry Lee Gregory

Multimedia Developer
Dan Scherf

Designer
Anne Jones

Page Layout
Stacey Richwine-DeRome

Graphics
Mark Frauenfelder
Blake Maloof
Tammy Graham

Photography:
Jay Townsend/Primal Design

Contents at a Glance

Table of Contents

About the Author

Gareth Branwyn is a well-known technology journalist and self-proclaimed "reluctant geek." He is a contributing editor for *Wired* and writes for other national magazines such as *Esquire* and *I.D.* (International Design). He has written more than a half-dozen books on technology and technoculture, including *Mosaic Quick Tour* (the first book about the Web ever published), *Jargon Watch: A Pocket Dictionary for the Jitterati*, and Que's *Absolute Beginner's Guide to Building Robots*. Gareth is cyborg-in-chief at Street Tech (streettech.com), the "sucks-less" consumer electronics website.

About weaKnees.com

Michael Adberg and Jeff Shapiro are the co-founders of weaKnees.com (http://www.weaknees.com) and run a "how-to" upgrade site at http://www.upgrade-instructions.com. weaKnees is an online resource center and Internet retailer for all things TiVo. As an authorized DirecTV retailer, it provides complete satellite installation services throughout the United States. Running weaKnees has been a full-time job for these guys for years, but before TiVo, Michael was a computer consultant, and Jeff was a corporate lawyer. Both graduated from the University of California at Berkeley, and Jeff from the University of Chicago Law School. Now, Michael, Jeff, and the weaKnees staff spend their time getting high-capacity TiVo DVRs, upgrades, parts, and other information into the hands of fellow TiVo addicts.

Dedication

To Alberto Gaitán and Peter Sugarman. Your unwavering friendship, cosmic creativity, and unshakable spirit are awe-inspiring.

Acknowledgments

Friends. Gotta have 'em: Lewis Fulwiler, Cathy Fulwiler, Steve Wiggins, Sean Carton, Linda Lewett, Mark Frauenfelder, Nate Heasley, Tim Tate, John Bergin, Jay Townsend, Kate (my email muse) Ryan, David Pescovitz, and Virginia Vitzthum. You have to have great tech support too, and that means Jeff Shapiro and Michael Adberg of weaKnees.com. Their good humor, geekly wisdom, and tireless enthusiasm for this project was impressive. Also, I gotta give a shoutout to my boy, Blake Maloof. Papa's so proud. And then there's the Que crew: Rick Kughen, Todd Brakke, Dan Knott, Sharry Gregory—you guys rawk. And last but not least, we must give props where they're due, and big ones go to all of the participants at tivocommunity.com and dealdatabase.com/forum, especially the TiVo hackers who've coded open source apps for TiVo and who've created the tutorials, FAQs, how-tos, and hacks books from which we learned most of what we know about TiVo.

We Want to Hear from You!

As the reader of this book, *you* are our most important critic and commentator. We value your opinion and want to know what we're doing right, what we could do better, what areas you'd like to see us publish in, and any other words of wisdom you're willing to pass our way.

As an associate publisher for Que Publishing, I welcome your comments. You can email or write me directly to let me know what you did or didn't like about this book—as well as what we can do to make our books better.

Please note that I cannot help you with technical problems related to the topic of this book. We do have a User Services group, however, where I will forward specific technical questions related to the book.

When you write, please be sure to include this book's title and author as well as your name, email address, and phone number. I will carefully review your comments and share them with the author and editors who worked on the book.

Email: feedback@quepublishing.com

Mail: Greg Wiegand
            Associate Publisher
            Que Publishing
            800 East 96th Street
            Indianapolis, IN 46240 USA

For more information about this book or another Que Publishing title, visit our website at www.quepublishing.com. Type the ISBN (excluding hyphens) or the title of a book in the Search field to find the page you're looking for.

How to Use this Book

It is recommended that you read through all of the hardware and software hacking portions of this book first, before undertaking any of the procedures described therein. This book is divided into three sections, with Part 1, "TiVo Tweaking," being general and largely non-invasive tips, tricks, and hacks that any TiVo user can employ. Part 2, "Hardware Hacking," describes both the gory details of the TiVo hardware itself and then how to upgrade/improve upon it. Some of this will likely appeal to the average user, and other parts are here for the weekend widget warrior and the hardcore hardware hacker. Part 3, "Software Bashing," delves into how TiVo's software works, and then details how you can tweak the existing software, and for the more adventurous, how you can add on third-party apps (such as those found on the CD-ROM in the back of this book).

The linear progression of the chapters makes sense in terms of laying out a book, but in doing the upgrades/hacks on your TiVo, you'll likely have to use knowledge gleaned from different parts of the book, so be prepared to skip around. Also, when doing one procedure, it may be wise to perform another procedure at the same time. For instance: if you're upgrading your TiVo hard drive on a Series 1 TiVo (as detailed in Chapter 8, "Upgrading Hard Drives"), you might want to go ahead and open up the serial port for serial networking with your personal computer (as described in Chapter 10, "Quick n' Dirty Serial Networking") and while your drive is connected to your PC, you'll probably want to go ahead and move the bundle of Linux utilities from the CD-ROM included with this book onto TiVo for later use (as detailed in Appendix C, "About the CD-ROM"). And, if you don't know much about Linux, you'll probably want to read Chapter 13, "Touring Your TiVo: The Software," before doing any of this. See, we told you there'd be some jumpin' around. But hey, this is the age of hypermedia, so we bet your big 21st century brain pan is primed for non-linear media surfing.

Basically, before undertaking any of the hands-on projects in this book, you'll want to make sure you're patient, informed, and

(Boy Scout-level) prepared: with the right tools, having read the appropriate sections in this book and followed any cautions given in the chapters (about backing up data, not getting yourself electrocuted, and so forth). And then: Relax. If you're properly prepared, none of the projects are as hard as they may appear at first glance.

The Geekitude Indicator

Throughout the book, tricks, hacks, and projects have been given a "Geekitude" level of 1, 2, or 3. Level 1 means that anybody can do it, regardless of technical prowess or interest. Level 2 indicates a project that might require a bit more technical sophistication. If you

don't bat an eye at installing such things as a new CD-RW drive or video card on your PC, Level 2 projects will be no sweat for you. Level 3 projects are the most challenging. In this book, most of them are for hacking a Series 1 TiVo and involve both some hardware work

and some mucking around inside of TiVo using Linux. If this is your idea of a good time, you'll have one tricked-out TiVo box by the time you're done.

TiVo Is a Moving Target

During the time we were writing this book, the HD DirecTV DVR finally came out, DirecTV sold its interest in TiVo, Inc. (allegedly to make their own DVRs), and TiVo dramatically dropped its prices and began giving away the Home Media Option (redubbed the "Home Media Feature") for free. Also, an entirely new player entered the market, Humax, with an inexpensive line of both stand-alone TiVos and DVD/DVR combo units. Since this is such a fast moving market space, by the time you read this, things may have changed even further. One impact this has is on the TiVo user interface. Every time a new version of the software comes out, or a new player enters the game, they make subtle changes to the TiVo screens. The content of the menus in TiVo are different between Series 1 and Series 2 TiVos, between stand-alone and DirecTV DVRs, and between stand-alone and DirecTV DVRs and the newer DVD/DVR combo units. Throughout this book, we mainly used

How to Use this Book

the menu text/screens as they appear in version 4.0 of the stand-alone Series 2 TiVo software. Sometimes, when that text differs significantly from what you'll see if you're using a Series 1 machine (and likely the 3.0 TiVo OS), we included that text in parenthesis. If you're on an HD DirecTV DVR or one of the various DVD/DVR combo units, the screens may differ even more. Luckily, the functionality is basically the same, or given the user-friendliness of the TiVo interface, you should be able to figure out the difference between what we show in our examples and what you see on your screen.

What in Sam Hell Is a "TiVo"?

If you're new to TiVo—and the whole concept of digital video recorders (DVR)—we'd like to take a few minutes to enthuse over how much media-manipulating fun you're in for. If you already have a TiVo, you'll likely smile at the very question of "what is TiVo?" 'cause you know the discoveries that await the asker. You also know how challenging it can be to explain all facets of TiVo to the newcomer.

The unenlightened description of TiVo is that it's a digital answer to the VCR. With a few presses of a remote control while scanning an onscreen programming guide, you can set your TiVo to record your favorite TV shows and movies. No more entering in times, dates, or channels, and no more resetting that damn clock every time the power goes out (or watching it blink "12:00" for days 'til you get around to resetting it). Once programmed, TiVo will record desired programs to a hard drive (or drives) inside the TiVo unit. There are no more VHS tapes to buy, insert, eject, lose, or to pile up like plastic stalagmites in the corners of your family room.

But TiVo is far more than a tapeless video recorder. At its core, it is a dedicated audio/video computer, and that means it's much smarter and more versatile than a VCR. Using the onscreen menus, you can ask your TiVo to record as many episodes of a program as you like (from one to five, or all episodes, subject to your hard drive capacity) and tell it how long you'd like to hang on to these episodes before deletion.

NOTE

TiVo has become popular enough that most people know it by name and basically what it's for. But even the most evangelical user can struggle to explain *all* of TiVo's wonders in a casual conversation. TiVo, Inc. has answered the call with its "What is TiVo?" e-brochure for your Palm handheld. Okay, so whipping out your Palm and handing it to a friend across from you at Starbucks may seem silly, but how positively Star Trekkian: "I have the information you requested right here on my dataslate!" Make it so at www.tivo.com/4.3.7.2.asp.

Tip

If you'd like to take a peek at the fanatical TiVo community we're talking about, point your browser to—where else?—tivocommunity.com.

You can also create program-recording requests (called "WishLists") that will tirelessly hunt down shows in the program guide based on titles, actors, directors, and keywords that you've entered. This ability of TiVo to lie in wait for something good to capture is an eternal delight. You can see a trailer for the theatrical release of a film on TV, create a WishList item for it immediately, and then many months later, regardless of what channel it shows up on for its television premier (and whether you happen to catch it in the program guide or not), TiVo will remember and dutifully record it for you.

Then there's the ability to pause, rewind, and fast-forward through "live" TV. You can't imagine how spiffy this is! You know the drill: You're just sitting down to an episode of *Jeopardy* to impress your kids with your frightening intellect (who cares if they're still in diapers?), when the phone rings. Or you're about to marvel at the surrealist splendor of the so-not-funny-it's-almost-funny "Will it Float?" segment on *Letterman*, when baby wakes up wailing. Pre-TiVo? You missed out on the entire *Potent Potables* category on *Jeopardy* and you never found out that a 10-pound box of dog biscuits does, in fact, float. Post-TiVo? You just hit the Pause button, answer your phone, your baby, the call of nature, the siren song of the fridge, etc. and pick up right where you left off. The incoming TV signal is constantly being temporarily stored (buffered) to the hard drive, so when you come back to your easy chair, you can fast-forward through the commercials (or the next goofy Letterman bit), if you'd like.

And this is only scratching the surface! There are many more things that TiVo can do as-is (such as recording programs *it* thinks you might like) and many official and unofficial ways you can upgrade, add to, and improve TiVo to make it do even more. A vibrant community of users has arisen online and they love to share advice, tips, tricks, how-tos, and sophisticated hardware and software hacks for making TiVo the best darn TV computer it can be. Once you experience TiVo itself, the good vibes and great support of the online TiVo community, and the way that digital video recording can change your life (okay, your media life, anyway), we think you'll become as rabid a TiVo spokesbot as most other TiVo owners.

WE LOVE TIVO!

TIVO RULZ!!!

Why Are We Shouting?

We get worked up over TiVo (and DVR technology in general) because we think it's the greatest bit of lifestyle kit to come along since…what? The TV? The answering machine? The computer? The cell phone? All of these personal tech-tools seriously altered the way we live, work, socialize, get information, and communicate. TiVo is sort of like an answering machine for your TV. Before answering machines, you had to pick up the phone or miss calls. Answering machines suddenly gave you control. You could monitor calls, skip messages, save messages, and delete messages. It was "telephone your way" (to steal a slogan from TiVo, Inc.). A DVR gives you a similar type of control over television. You can store up the incoming messages…er…shows and watch them whenever you like. You can skip over the annoying parts (think of commercials as calls from your mother-in-law) or back up and relive those choice moments (think of Jessica Simpson's "Chicken *by* the Sea" comment as the TV equivalent of your uncle Louie's drunken New Year's Eve message).

And if you have a mixed marriage of a TV addict and a TV-phobe, TiVo can even help maintain marital harmony! Watch one (recorded) show while you record another. And who needs to know that you're watching half a dozen stored up episodes of *Elimidate* while nobody's around? "Honestly honey, I don't know *how* those got on there. They must be some of those misguided TiVo's suggestions. Frisky TiVo!"

Gareth On…

I was sent one of the first ReplayTV models to review on my hardware review website (streettech.com). I wasn't really sure what I was going to think of this odd gadget, but it didn't take long for me to fall madly in love with it. My wife, not a big TV watcher, fell for it too, especially its ability to pause a show to attend to the phone, laundry, going over junior's homework, etc. About two weeks into our new-found DVR bliss, in the middle of *Friends*, there was a knock at the door. She got up to answer it and said, "Pause it." "I can't!" I blurted in a panic, "we're live through the VCR!" I was recording something on the ReplayTV and so had switched over to watch live TV through the VCR's TV tuner. After my wife answered the door, we had a good laugh over our panicked reaction. Nearly overnight, pausing live television had become a birthright.

Why TV Will Never Be the Same Again

It is unfortunate that TiVo has been so slow in catching on. DVRs have been around since 1999, and yet, as of this writing, there are only a few million units in circulation. But this is starting to change. Every technology has a watershed moment, an event that widely demonstrates its usefulness and propels it into the mainstream. For the radio, it was FDR's *Fireside Chats* in the '30s. For the TV, it was the *Milton Berle Show* (when the nation would nearly shut down on Tuesday nights in the late '40s/early '50s). Many argue that the Internet came into its own with the online publication of the *Starr Report*. For the cell phone, it was probably the 9/11 tragedy, where cell phone calls from the doomed planes and struck towers became a central part of the drama (and cell phone sales spiked in its wake). For TiVo, its watershed moment may, unfortunately, be the Janet Jackson/Justin Timberlake "wardrobe malfunction" at the 2004 *Super Bowl*. The next day, everyone was talking, not only about the incident itself, but the fact that TiVo users had looked at the moment over and over again, making it the most rewound TV event since TiVo, Inc. began tracking anonymous viewer information in 2000. TiVo was even mentioned by FCC chairman Michael Powell (a devout TiVo fan) in discussing the incident and calling for an indecency investigation. Since then, it seems as though TiVo is suddenly on everybody's radar.

Gareth On...

In 2001, I was asked to speak at the annual NATPE (National Association of TV Production Executives) convention in Las Vegas. The panel was on the future of television and the Web. TiVo, Inc. had a booth at the convention, but in general, the TV execs seemed strangely unaware of this revolutionary new technology. During the talk, I told the audience that, since DVRs had entered my life, I hadn't watched a single TV commercial. There might as well have been fainting in the aisles and projectile vomiting; the looks on their collective faces were breathtaking. I was actually watching the captains of an industry being blindsided by the future. Many of them skipped the all-you-could-eat Krispy Kreme donuts and Starbucks coffee being served after the talk and made a beeline for the TiVo booth instead.

There is no doubt in the mind of anyone who owns a TiVo (or other DVR) that this is the future of television and that there's just no going back. DVR technology is unique in that it's hard to describe to someone who hasn't experienced it, and even harder to get that same person to shut up about it once they have. We've never heard of a single person who's tried a TiVo and decided that it wasn't for them. In fact, we've even heard of people so dedicated to the life-changing impact of TiVo that they buy and install units for their family and friends, promising that they'll take the TiVos back to the store within 30 days if they're unhappy. Nobody's ever unhappy. What other technologies can you say this about?

The Future of TiVo (and DVRs in General)

It's not a question of if; it's a question of when. Eventually, everyone will have a digital video recorder attached to his or her TV set. The future of all home media—TV, music, radio, gaming, photography—is digital. Hardware manufacturers and service providers are scrambling to try to create the technology that will serve as the conduit to this all-digital, all-networked home media future. So far, this has created a bloat of digital devices clustered around your TV set: game boxes, DVRs, DVD decks, set-top Internet devices, satellite radio receivers, cable boxes, MP3 players, along with various hybrid combinations of these. But still, the long-promised convergence has yet to materialize and it doesn't look like it'll be happening anytime soon.

There are glimmers, however, of what this future might look like in today's expanded TiVo functions. The current Series 2 TiVos have built-in network capabilities, and with the Home Media Feature, they can become part of your wired or wireless home computer network. From here, you can schedule TiVo recordings over the Internet, share TiVo programs between multiple Series 2 TiVos in your house, and view digital photos on your TiVo that are stored on your computer. You can also listen to digital music stored on your PC through TiVo and your home stereo system. And by using third-party software, such as the (free) JavaHMO, you can add other functions to TiVo, such as Internet radio and viewing local weather maps and movie listings.

Within the last year, TiVo, Inc. has made some announcements and created new partnerships that speak of their desire to stay competitive in a rapidly expanding DVR market:

- **HD TiVo**—The future of television is obviously high-definition (or HD) TV. For several years now, TiVo has been showing off a standalone HD TiVo prototype, but it's unlikely we'll see such a product anytime soon. TiVo needs a partner in crime to handle the development costs, and cable companies (now hawking their own DVRs) aren't interested. TiVo does now offer (through their partnership with Hughes) an HD DirecTV with TiVo, for DirecTV satellite subscribers who own HD sets.

NOTE

If you have a TiVo (or when you get one and start using it), you'll notice special programming showing up in your Now Playing program list under the curious name "TeleWorld Paid Programming." TeleWorld was the original name for TiVo, so it lives on in this content title. Thank goodness they changed it, or we'd be asking each other, "Did you TeleWorld last night's *Crank Yankers*?"

- **TiVoToGo**—As we write this, TiVo has just announced its TiVoToGo service, which will allow owners of Series 2 TiVos to send recorded TiVo programs to your desktop computer for viewing there or for burning onto DVDs for viewing on a laptop.
- **XM Satellite Radio**—While the details are currently unknown, a partnership with this satellite radio provider likely means that TiVo, Inc. plans to offer satellite radio as a future TiVo add-on service.
- **BravoBrava**—This partner has developed software that will allow owners of Series 2 TiVos with HMO to schedule recordings from cell phones and other mobile devices.
- **Adobe and Picasa**—Partnerships with these two software companies will allow TiVo Home Media users (Series 2 only) more tools for and access to their digital photo libraries across their home network.
- **Strangeberry**—The acquisition of this small Palo Alto, CA start-up by TiVo, Inc. in early 2004 created a flood of speculation and rumor online. The company, started by former employees of Sun Microsystems, was allegedly developing home networking applications (they had no actual products) when TiVo scooped them up (and their website basically went dark). The general speculation is that Strangeberry is developing plug and play tools that will allow more digital media devices to be effortlessly integrated into TiVo's growing Home Media network.

TiVo, Inc. stands at a critical juncture. Cable giants Comcast, Insight Communications, and Time Warner are now offering their digital cable customers DVR hardware and software built in to their cable boxes. While this technology has been nearly unanimously panned as inferior to TiVo, the massive subscriber bases of these companies and general public ignorance about the superior quality of TiVo could threaten its future. TiVo, now dominating the market, could quickly become the Macintosh of DVRs, superior (and more expensive) tech that's relegated to a small, fiercely devoted market.

TiVo, Inc. is aware of these considerable threats and is attempting to expand its partnerships with hardware companies as well as extend the functionality of TiVo itself. Some have even speculated that the company's recent business moves and public statements might signal that they're planning on turning TiVo into a full-blown digital hub, a dedicated computer that manages and serves up all forms of home entertainment, not just digital video recording (with a side order of family photos and MP3s). If that's the case, it would put TiVo in the direct line of fire of another corporate juggernaut, Microsoft, who's gunning for the anticipated home digital hub boom with their Windows Media Center technology.

If TiVo is to survive, they're going to have to leverage and license like crazy. Part of the reason why the cable companies' DVRs stink is that TiVo owns a boatload of patents related to digital video recording. The cable companies' DVR makers, such as Scientific Atlanta, have to skirt these patents, and that's led to bad interfaces and limited capabilities. Hopefully, TiVo will eventually be able to convince these companies to license their superior TiVo software. TiVo also has its name recognition going for it. *TiVo'd* has become a verb, for heaven's sake! And as someone pointed out on an online forum, "You don't hear Carrie and Miranda discussing their super-groovy Scientific Atlanta DVRs on *Sex & the City*." TiVo, Inc. should be able to use that household name recognition to its advantage as it moves forward.

Whatever TiVo's future, today's TiVo sets the standard for digital video recording. It is a consumer electronics device that, overnight, becomes an indispensable and fun-to-use entertainment tool, and takes something you've known all of your life—television—and drop-kicks it to a whole new level.

So Why This Book?

There are several TiVo books already on the market, but they're mainly targeted at hardcore hackers who already know a lot about computer hardware and software and want to delve deeper into TiVo's fiddly bits. We wanted to create a book that would appeal to a much broader TiVo audience, from the newbie to the "power user" to the dedicated gadgeteer. We wanted to create a book that was as user-friendly as TiVo itself that you could start utilizing right away, but that would grow in sophistication and detail as your mastery of TiVo grows.

We've tried to cover the range of what TiVo users might be looking for in such a guide, from basic advice on buying, setting up, and using your TiVo, to more in-depth coverage of advanced software features and the most popular hardware hacks (such as adding more storage space and networking your TiVo).

The book is divided into three main sections.

Tip

To find out more about Windows Media Center, check out www.microsoft.com/ windowsxp/ mediacenter/.

Part 1: TiVo Tweaking (Warranty-Friendly Fun)

Everything you ever wanted to know about what TiVo can do (but were afraid to ask), from the very basic to the most advanced. Remote control tricks and shortcuts, enabling hidden features, sophisticated WishList creation and management, getting the most out of TiVo's Suggestions feature: It's all here. Plus: a buyer's guide, a brief tutorial on understanding audio/video tech, how to set up multiple TiVos, useful accessories for TiVo, and more.

Part 2: Hardware Hacking (Machine-Monkeying Madness)

Here we'll help you gather up the chutzpah and arm you with the information you need to grab your tools, pop the hood on your Series 1 or Series 2 TiVo, and get to work: Adding more storage space, networking your TiVo, adding more cache memory, and more. Not only for the hardcore hardware hacker, we cover everything from doing it all yourself, to using a prepared upgrade kit (no computer required!), to even sending it to a service center and having them do all the heavy lifting.

Part 3: Software Bashing (Playing with Your Penguin)

In this section, we get all ones and zeros on you, heading down the rabbit hole into the heart of the TiVo OS. If you're on a Series 1 machine and want to add Internet-based scheduling and other third-party apps, here's where we show you how. If you have a Series 2 machine and want to add apps like JavaHMO, we'll show you, step-by-step, how to do that too. We'll also cover the many TiVo apps and utilities found on the accompanying CD-ROM.

The book also includes a Resources section, with details on the best TiVo-related books, parts and kit vendors, Web resources, and online communities, and a glossary of jargon and slang related to TiVo and digital entertainment tech.

This book is written by two guys who love technology…when it works. TiVo is technology that works. We're enthusiastic about this tech, what it can do now and what it promises for the future, and we hope some of this enthusiasm rubs off on you. If you're new to TiVo, this book will serve as a handy companion as you learn about and explore this innovative new technology. If you're an old TiVo dog, we still think we've got a few cool tricks to teach you that will allow you to maximize your TiVo experience.

So what are you waiting for, people? Those 200 channels aren't going to watch themselves!

Part I

Which TiVo Is Right for You?

Before we get into all of the fun stuff you can do with your TiVo, let's make sure you have one! If you don't already own a TiVo, this chapter will help with deciding which one to get, what service you'll need for it, and what accessories you might like (or need) to improve your TiVo experience. If you already have a TiVo, you might be ready for another one. Doesn't every TV in your house deserve its own dedicated show-hunting, digital recording computer?

TiVo Buyer's Guide

Luckily, there aren't too many knuckle-biting decisions to make before buying a TiVo. The choice mainly depends on what type of TV-delivery service you have (cable or satellite) and whether or not you want to tinker with your TiVo (hey that sounds dirty).

There are two main types of TiVos. The so-called stand-alone models (abbreviated "SA") can be used with either a cable service or with a satellite receiver. The DirecTV with TiVo (commonly known as the "DirecTV DVR" or "DirecTiVo") is a DirecTV satellite receiver with TiVo functionality built into it.

Let's run through the options for all available TiVo types and detail the benefits and trade-offs for each.

Series 1 Stand-Alone TiVo

As you might be able to guess, the Series 1 was the first generation of TiVo. They were manufactured from 1999 to 2001 and offered by Philips, Sony, and Thomson (in the UK). They came with between 14 and 60 hours of recording capacity (at the lowest quality, or "Basic," setting). They are no longer available commercially, but are still readily available through used channels, such as online auctions. The term "stand-alone" TiVo is used to differentiate it from so-called combo models, which combine a DirecTV receiver and TiVo DVR into a single device. We'll discuss these in the following pages (see Figure 1.1).

FIGURE 1.1

The Series 1 stand-alone TiVo.

NOTE

If you're uncertain about any of the audio/video input and output types discussed throughout this chapter, don't sweat it. We'll detail them all in the "Mini-Tutorial on Audio/Video Tech" in "Chapter 2, "Getting the Most Out of Your TiVo."

Series 1 models are built around the IBM PowerPC 403GCX processor running at 50MHz. All Series 1 models have one set of RCA-style composite audio left/right and video inputs and two sets of outputs, one each S-Video input and output, one each RF (Radio Frequency) coax cable input and output, serial control output (for connecting to a satellite receiver, some cable boxes, and external modems), and a standard RJ-11 telephone jack (for connecting the built-in modem). There is no USB port for stock networking of a Series 1 TiVo. All Series 1 stand-alone TiVos have a single built-in TV tuner. The operating system (OS) for Series 1 ran from versions 1.0 to 3.0.

So why would anyone want to buy a Series 1 TiVo? Several important reasons. The first is hackabilityThe Series 1 machines have been around for a long time now and lots of very smart and creative geeks have taken their S1 TiVos apart, found out what makes them tick, and have created all sorts of hardware and software to improve their functionality. Series 1

TiVos were not intended to be networked, but they can be, with a little hardware and software hacking. They were not intended to be accessible over the Web (as Series 2 machines are), but (free) third-party software has been created for that too. They were not intended to play music, display digital pictures, or stream Internet radio, but they can do all of these things as well—with the right amount of tinkering. They can also be upgraded with massive amounts of hard disk space, up to 344 hours of recording time!

The software for all TiVos is built upon a special version of the popular open source operating system (OS) known as Linux. Linux has taken the online world by storm and has become the preferred OS on many of the servers that link the computers of the Internet together. Unlike some other ubiquitous OSes that we won't bother to name, Linux is known for being tight, efficient code that is secure and crash resistant.

All of this had made Linux attractive to the digital appliance market, and there are increasing numbers of handheld devices, car computers, and digital home entertainment components that run on various specialized versions of Linux. The fact that TiVo is Linux-based instantly attracted the computer hacker community. They were delighted to find a system that was fairly easy to get into and play around with, and TiVo, Inc. seemed open to the hackers, as long as they didn't do anything to circumvent the paid TiVo subscriptions (where TiVo, Inc. makes most of their money).

Today, there are dozens of useful programs available for Series 1 TiVos that allow them to do nearly everything the Series 2 machines can do, and more. As TiVo has matured, and TiVo, Inc. has seen and heard what sorts of functionality subscribers are looking for, they've added these capabilities to their new machines and software upgrades. They've also progressively made new TiVo OSes much harder to hack (probably so that TiVo owners have to subscribe to a growing list of premium services, such as the once fee-based Home Media Feature [now offered for free] and TiVoToGo [the TiVo-to-PC sharing feature], both of which we'll get into in a minute). What this has done is to divide the TiVo community into two basic camps: the hardcore hackers/TiVo hobbyists (the so-called "TiVo Underground") and the more general TiVo consumer. If you're of the former bent, the Series 1 TiVo is for you. There are tons of great resources out there for adding hardware and software to your TiVo box, dozens of programs you can load, and even the capability of writing your own TiVo software.

NOTE

Most of the hacks mentioned here are outlined later in Parts 2 and 3 of this book.

NOTE

"Open source" means that the code is open to improvement, allowing others to add features and redistribute it, and hundreds of programmers worldwide are doing just that.

The other attractive thing about Series 1 TiVos is that, because they're no longer made, there are lots of used units available, on auction sites such as eBay and elsewhere. If you keep your eyes peeled, you can get a unit for as little as $50. At that price, it'll likely have a small hard drive, but if you're buying a Series 1, you're probably looking to hack it anyway, so adding more storage can be the first item on your to-do list. For a comparison of TiVo models (see Table 1.1, later in this chapter).

Series 2 Stand-Alone TiVo

The current TiVo model is the Series 2, first introduced in 2002. It has all of the software features of the Series 1 and it adds a number of new capabilities. It uses a NEC MIPS processor running at a much-faster 162MHz. This faster processor is far better suited to doing things such as playing digital music (which the Series 2 can do through the Home Media Feature). The Series 2 models have the same A/V inputs/outputs as the S1, with the addition of two active USB ports.

With an optional, compatible USB-to-Ethernet adapter or a wireless (WiFi) USB adapter, you can easily add a Series 2 machine to a home network. With this capability, you can use your broadband Internet connection to make TiVo's daily call to TiVo's central servers. With the now-free Home Media Feature, you also gain the ability to program your TiVo from any web browser in cyberspace, play digital music through TiVo and your home stereo system, and view digital pictures (stored on your PC) and run slide shows on your TV. If you have two Series 2 TiVos on your home network, you can watch shows on one TiVo that have been recorded on another. So, you can start watching a recording of *NYPD Blue* in the living room, and then, when you start nodding off, finish it in the bedroom (is it just us, or has that show "jumped the shark?"). All Series 2 stand-alone TiVos have a single built-in TV tuner (see Figure 1.2).

While Series 2 TiVos still use a version of the Linux OS, current versions of the TiVo software are much harder to hack into than Series 1. Doing things such as turning on "backdoors," a hidden mode that enables a number of undocumented, but useful, features, *can* be done, but it takes a lot of messing around with hardware and doing brain surgery on your TiVo (which can be hazardous to its health). Many of the features that TiVo users craved during the Series 1 era, and therefore coded software to create for themselves (such as networkability and Web-based scheduling), are now built into Series 2 machines (via HMF). This makes them

TiVo uses the same type of USB technology found on your home computer. "USB" stands for "Universal Serial Bus" and is a common standard for data transfers between computer devices. For more information, see the Glossary.

less attractive as a hacker's box and better suited for a consumer that's just looking for a satisfying "out of box experience" (that is, easy to set up and use) and a state-of-the-art digital video recorder that performs as advertised. That's the Series 2! With its networking capabilities, TiVo Series 2 also has an increasingly likely future as a more feature-rich networked home media server. New options such as TiVoToGo allow viewing TiVo programming on any computer on the network, or even on mobile computers.

FIGURE 1.2
The Series 2 Stand-Alone TiVo; this one is a TiVo TCD240040 with 40 hours of recording time.

Prices for new, stock Series 2 TiVo units run from around $100 to $350, depending on storage capacity (from 40 to 140 hours). Factory refurbished 40-hour units are currently being sold on TiVo's site for $49 (after a $50 rebate). By the time you read this, prices may have fallen and capacity increased. New, customized S2 TiVos with as much as 320 hours of record time can also be purchased (see "Customized Units," later in this chapter). For a comparison of TiVo models, see Table 1.1, later in this chapter.

Series 1 DirecTV with TiVo Combo Unit

Series 1 and Series 2 stand-alone TiVos can be used in conjunction with a DirecTV satellite receiver, but in 2000, Philips released a DirecTV receiver with a TiVo DVR built in to it. Three models of this combo satellite receiver and TiVo (popularly known as the DirecTiVo, but now officially called the DirecTV DVR) were produced: the Philips DSR6000, the Sony SAT T60, and the Hughes/DirecTV GXCEBOT. Like the stand-alone Series 1, it also used the pokey 50MHz IBM PowerPC 403GCX processor.

Besides combining the satellite receiver and DVR in one box, one innovation of the DirecTiVo was that it had two built-in TV tuners. One of the first questions that those new to TiVo often ask is "Can I record two things at once?" If you're talking about a stand-alone model, the answer is no. There is only one TV tuner available on the motherboard. But DirecTiVos

Tip

If you're somewhere in between a hardcore propeller head and an average consumer, there's still plenty of moderately geeky tinkering to be done on a Series 2. You can add networking hardware, upgrade your hard drive(s) to add more storage, and use third-party software such as JavaHMO (see Chapter 14, "Home Media Feature") to add more functionality to your machine.

15

(both S1 and S2) have two tuners built into them. This allows you to record two channels, while even watching a previously recorded program—how positively multi-taskstic! To make use of this feature, you have to have a dual-LNB (or triple-LNB) DirecTV dish. We'll discuss this more in the "Hardware Basics" section in the next chapter.

Series 1 DirecTiVos offer the same hackability as S1 stand-alones. Because the price of the DirecTiVo is so low compared to a stand-alone model (we'll discuss some of the reasons for this in the next chapter), there really is no reason to get a Series 1 unit unless you plan on hacking it. The Home Media Feature is not available for Series 1 (or Series 2) DirecTiVos. For a comparison of TiVo models, see Table 1.1, later in this chapter.

Series 2 DirecTV with TiVo Combo Unit

The current DirecTV DVR is also a Series 2 and is built around the same NEC MIPS 162MHz processor found in the Series 2 stand-alone models. DirecTiVos are now sold by Hughes, Philips, RCA, and Samsung. Stock recording capacity is 35, 70, or 105 hours on all models, but DirecTiVos can be upgraded to as much as 240 hours (see Figure 1.3).

FIGURE 1.3

The Series 2 DirecTV DVR, known to long-time TiVonauts as the DirecTiVo.

While stand-alone TiVos can be used in conjunction with a DirecTV satellite receiver, there really is little benefit to doing this (unless you must network your TiVo, which the DirecTV DVR does not offer). In fact, there are some downsides...namely the cost. The monthly charge for TiVo service purchased through DirecTV is considerably less than stand-alone service, which is purchased through TiVo, Inc. (see "Which TiVo Service to Buy?" later on in this chapter). DirecTV customers who subscribe to the Total Choice Premier package even get the TiVo service free of charge. Because of some hardware differences, which we'll discuss in the next chapter, DirecTiVos are also cheaper than stand-alone units. A new Series 2 35-hour DirecTV with TiVo can be had for as little as $99 with a DirecTV service installation.

For some strange reason, DirecTV does not yet offer the Home Media Feature (HMF). The hardware to enable it is on-board, but so far, there are no known plans to offer this service. If you're on a DirecTV system, not having the HMF is probably not a deal-breaker, just an unfortunate omission (which may or may not change in the future).

There is one circumstance where having a DirecTV DVR unit on a sat connection might be a significant problem. If you get your local channels OTA (off-the-air), or through a cable service, you will not be able to feed these signals into your DirecTiVo. It can only display signals coming from the DirecTV dish. If this is your situation, you'll have to settle for a stand-alone setup (or not have TiVo-control over local channels). For a comparison of TiVo models, see Table 1.1.

Series 2 DirecTV HD TiVo

Everyone who has a high-definition TV (or is thinking of getting one) is anxious to know when TiVo will have an HD model. For stand-alone users, the answer is currently unknown. TiVo, Inc. has been showing off a prototype for several years now, but they're still trying to find a partner willing to help them manufacture it. For DirecTV owners, the answer is *NOW!* In the second quarter of 2004, DirecTV released the HD-DVR250, the first DirecTV HD receiver with TiVo combo unit. It has a 250GB hard drive, which allows it to record up to 30 hours of high-def programming and up to 200 hours of standard-definition programming (or a combination of both). It has a whopping four TV tuners inside, two that can receive off-the-air signals (both standard and HD) and two from a DirecTV dish. This means that you can record two satellite programs simultaneously or two OTA, or one of each, all while watching a pre-recorded program! The DirecTV HD-DVR250 retails for $999 (see Figure 1.4). For a comparison of TiVo models, see Table 1.1.

Tip

DirecTV and authorized dealers offer a dual-LNB dish and professional installation free with the purchase of a DirecTV DVR with TiVo (and a one year subscription commitment).

FIGURE 1.4

The long-anticipated DirecTV HD TiVo, capable of recording up to 30 hours of high-definition television.

Table 1.1   Features Summary for All TiVo Models

Features	Series 1 Stand-Alone (SA)	Series 2 Stand-Alone
Processor	IBM PowerPC 403GCX processor @ 50MHz	NEC MIPS processor @ 162MHz
TV Tuners	1	1
Stock Recording Capacity	From 14 to 60 hours (Basic Quality)	From 40 to 140 hours (Basic Quality)
RCA-type Audio/Video Inputs	1	1
RCA-type Audio/Video Outputs	2	2
S-Video Input	1	1
S-Video Output	1	1
Satellite Inputs	None	None
ATSC OTA Input	None	None
RF Input	1	1
RF Output	1	1
Infrared Control Out	1	1
Serial Control Out	1	1
USB Port	None	2
Component HD Video Out	None	None
HDMI A/V Out	None	None
Dolby Digital Optical Audio Out	None	None
RJ-11 Phone Jack	1	1
Built-in Modem	36.6Kbs	36.6Kbs
Pros	Cheap. Hackable. Large community of hacker/hobbyists and lots of third-party software and hardware. Can be used as "dumb DVR" without a TiVo subscription. Can be used with all (and multiple) input sources (Cable, DirecTV, Dish Network).	Current stand-alone model. Networkable w/Home Media Feature. Future additions such as TiVoToGo.
Cons	No longer manufactured. Modems prone to failure. Can't use OS higher than 3.0. No Home Media	Harder to hack than S1. Most third-party apps are pay services.
Notes	Mainly of interest to DVR hobbyists/hackers.	Many of the third-party apps created for S1 are now found in S2's HMF.

Series 1 DirecTiVo	Series 2 DirecTiVo	DirecTV HD TiVo
IBM PowerPC 403GCX processor @ 50MHz	NEC MIPS processor @ 162MHz	Unknown
2	2	4 (2 for OTA broadcasts, 2 for digital satellite)
35 hours (Best Quality)	35 to 100 hours (Best Quality)	30 hours of HD, 200 hours of SD (Best Quality)
None	None	None
2	2	1
None	None	None
1	1	1
2	2	2
None	None	1 (split internally to 2)
1 (pass-through only)	1 (pass-through only)	None
1	1	None
1 (Future use)	1 (Future use)	1 (Future use)
1 (Future use)	1 (Future use)	1 (Future use)
2 (Future use)	2 (Future use)	2 (Future use)
None	None	1
None	None	1
1	1	1
1	1	1
36.6Kbs	36.6Kbs	36.6Kbs
Combines sat receiver and DVR into one unit. High quality incoming signal. Lower monthly fee than SA.	Combines sat receiver and DVR into 1 unit. High quality incoming signal. Lower monthly fee than SA.	Records TiVo programming record HD both in HD format, and can and OTA via DirecTV.
No longer manufactured. No HMF. OTA (or cable) signals cannot be run through DirecTiVo.	No HMF. OTA (or cable) signals, cannot be run through DirecTiVo.	An antenna hookup is required to receive local channels and OTA HD. No HMF service.
You need at least a dual-LNB dish and two lines from the dish to the TiVo to use the two TV tuners.	You need at least a dual-LNB dish and two lines from the dish to the TiVo to use the two TV tuners.	DirecTV intends to be the only brander of their HD TiVos

NOTE

By the time you read this, a third company, Humax (www.humaxusa.com) will have joined Toshiba and Pioneer in offering combo DVD and TiVo machines.

Other Devices with TiVo

TiVo, Inc.'s plan for world domination involves trying to get the TiVo software into other home entertainment devices. Toshiba and Pioneer now offer DVD players and recorders with TiVo built in to them. They ship with something called TiVo Basic, a free version of the TiVo software that only includes the basic pause, rewind, fast-forward, and VCR-like recording features. It does not have all of the full service's (now called "TiVo Plus") sophisticated search, scheduling, and recommendation features. TiVo Basic also only has TV guide data for three days, instead of seven days for TiVo Plus.

The **Toshiba SD-H400**, shown in Figure 1.5, is a DVD player with the TiVo Basic service built into it. The DVD player has some nice features, such as progressive scan component video output (for use with progressive scan-enabled TVs with component video input), 3D virtual surround-sound audio with Dolby Digital optical output, and the ability to play all formats of CDs and DVDs. But this is a DVD *player* only. There is no ability to burn TiVo content onto DVD-Recordable discs. The free TiVo Basic software can be upgraded to TiVo Plus at any time and there are all the hardware and software components available for adding the Home Media Feature and TiVo networking. It's a fully functional TiVo, with only some of the features enabled. The SD-H400 comes with 80 hours of recording time and can be found for as little as $300.

FIGURE 1.5

The Toshiba SD-H400 DVD player with free TiVo Basic.

When Pioneer released its **DVR-810H** (a.k.a. DVR-810HS), shown in Figure 1.6, it created quite a bit of excitement among TiVo users. You see, the Pioneer DVR-810H does something people have been dreaming about for years—it's a DVD-Recorder and it lets you burn recorded TiVo content onto blank DVD-Rs, so you can take your programming to other

DVD-enabled computers (laptops! You can watch *Survivor* on the plane!), DVD decks, and portable DVD players. While everyone who has a TiVo understands its superiority over analog VHS technology, users still sometimes miss the ability to record TiVo programs and move them to other playback devices. The DVR-810H gives you this flexibility.

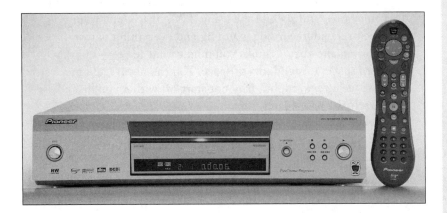

FIGURE 1.6
The Pioneer DVR-810H with free TiVo Basic.

NOTE

TiVo software does allow you to record programming from the TiVo onto VHS tape (if you have a VHS deck), but to do so is slow, clunky, and well, *SO* analog. We want *digital* recordability.

Like the Toshiba SDH-400, the DVR-810H comes with TiVo Basic, so you can start recording and burning shows (without having to subscribe to the TiVo service), right out of the box. Also like the SDH-400, upgrading to TiVo Plus is a phone call or Web visit away. It is set up to accommodate the Home Media Feature as well (which requires TiVo Plus). Unfortunately, if you do spring for TiVo Plus, set up the HMF, and have the DVR-810H networked with another TiVo in your house (using the Multi-Room Viewing feature), you cannot burn programs from your second TiVo onto a DVD-R in the DVR-810H. The DVR-810H ships with 80 hours of record time and has a street price of about $599. See Figure 1.6.

Customized Units

When buying a new TiVo, you don't have to settle for factory-installed storage capacities. There are a number of TiVo dealers that sell tricked-out TiVos upgraded with as much as 344 hours of recording time. Cracking the box and adding storage like this voids the manufacturer's warranty, but the dealers will usually match, or even exceed, the standard TiVo warranty. These customized TiVos are also available with extra cooling fans to help with the extra heat generated by maxing out the drive capacity. See the "Top TiVo Vendors" section in Appendix A, "Resources," for a list of recommended TiVo dealers.

Tip

If you already have a recordable DVD deck, it *is* possible to burn TiVo programming. You simply have to hook up composite audio/video cables to your TiVo's output and recordable DVD input, and follow the procedure for recording programs to videotape. Unlike with the DVR-810H (which takes about three minutes to burn a 1-hour show), this recording will happen in real-time.

TiVo Buying Tips

Here are a few things to keep in mind when buying your first TiVo (or in adding another to your collection).

- Buy as much storage capacity as you can afford (c'mon, you know you want to max out that plastic!). You'll see as you read the rest of this book, and spend time using TiVo, that you'll want your DVR tirelessly recording anything and everything you've requested and that it thinks you might want to see—and that means space, lots and lots of space. You can always add more storage space afterward, but why not start off with a bundle and save yourself the hassle later on?

- Don't sweat brands, most TiVos are made by the same manufacturer. Buy your TiVo based on price and manufacturer's or dealer's warranty (if you buy a dealer-upgraded unit).

- Don't be afraid to get a new or used unit at an online auction; just apply all of the same cautions you would while buying any high-ticket item this way. Be sure to thoroughly check out the seller (through seller's rating and feedback and their website if they have one), and the full details of the auction offer. Always read (and re-read) auction listings and bid with caution.

- When buying via online auctions, be especially careful of sellers offering "free lifetime service." Sometimes these are hacked boxes that are stealing the TiVo service. Email the seller and ask them directly if this is an unhacked lifetime service that they paid for. One clue of a hacked service is if they also claim that the TiVo is "privacy protected," which translates to mean that it doesn't do its normal daily call and the TiVo OS will never be upgraded. Series 2 DirecTV DVRs do not come with lifetime service, so any auction promising that service should raise red flags.

- Before you buy a stand-alone TiVo, you should check to make sure that your cable or satellite box is compatible. Most are, but you should still check to be sure. There is an excellent list of compatible (and known non-compatible) boxes at tivocommunity.com. Use the search feature on the site to look for the "Cable/Satellite Box Compatibility & Codes List."

Which TiVo Service to Buy?

The TiVo service is where TiVo, Inc. makes their money. Subscribing to the service (which you must do if you have any TiVo other than the TiVo Basic-enabled units described earlier in this chapter) gets you regular updates of the TV guide data, software upgrades, new TiVo Suggestions data, and everything else needed to make TiVo work.

There are two different service plan types, one for stand-alone TiVos, available through TiVo, Inc., and one for DirecTV customers, sold through DirecTV itself. Within these two types of plans, there are several options.

Stand-Alone Plans

You have two service plan options here: a monthly plan for $12.95, or a one-time lifetime plan for $299. "Lifetime" in this case, refers to the life of the TiVo unit, not you! This leads to anxiety for some buyers who are concerned that if they spend the $299 and their unit dies, they'll lose their investment (since subscriptions are not normally transferable to a new TiVo unit). This is not the case. If something goes horribly wrong with your TiVo, under warranty or not, and TiVo, Inc. (or a partner manufacturer or authorized repair shop) has to send you a new unit, they will transfer your account to the new machine. Even if you do a hardware upgrade yourself (such as adding or replacing a hard drive or replacing a modem), your subscription will remain intact after the upgrade. And there is value in your lifetime plan purchase. If you decide to get a new-model TiVo in the future, and you sell your old unit, the lifetime service plan goes with it. A used TiVo with a lifetime subscription is much more attractive to buyers so you'll be able recoup a fair amount of your investment. The only big drawback to the lifetime plan is that, if something does go wrong with your TiVo, it's past warranty, and the cost of repairs are high, you're stuck with fixing it. With a monthly plan, you could just cut your loses and buy a new unit.

For the stand-alone plans, you have to get a new service plan (either a monthly or lifetime) for each new TiVo you buy. There are no discounts for purchases of multiple lifetime plans, but monthly rates for additional TiVos has now been reduced to only $6.95.

DirecTV Plans

If you have a DirecTV with TiVo combo unit, there is only one method of payment, a $4.99/month plan. At this time, DirecTV does not offer a lifetime service plan. If you have the Total Choice Premier (TCP) package with your DirecTV service, TiVo service comes free with that. For each receiver you add to your system, regardless of whether it's a regular DirecTV receiver or a DirecTV DVR, you'll have to pay another $4.99/month. If you have two coax cables coming from your dish (through a Dual- or Triple-LNB), you don't have to pay an extra fee for using the second tuner on your DirecTV DVR unit.

Home Media Feature

With Series 2 machines, TiVo introduced the Home Media Option (HMO), a one-time-fee subscription service that moved TiVo beyond being just a TV tool and one step closer to being a digital home media server. HMO used to cost $99 for the first TiVo on the network and $49 for each additional unit. In mid-2004, TiVo changed the name of the service to Home Media Feature and is now offering it to all stand-alone Series 2 subscribers for free. When you set up and register your new unit, TiVo, Inc. downloads software to your TiVo to enable networking (with your home computer network), show scheduling over the Web, multi-room viewing (if you have more than one TiVo), digital photo viewing on your TV, and MP3 digital music playing through your TiVo and home stereo system. TiVo has also forged partnerships with digital media software makers such as MoodLogic, Picasa, Adobe, and others to add other digital photo-related features and capabilities to HMF. To use HMF, you have to either connect your TiVo to your PC via a USB-to-Ethernet adapter (and Ethernet cable), or via a Wireless USB adapter. The DirecTV DVRs have the hardware for HMF, but so far, there are no known plans to offer it. We'll discuss HMF in detail in Chapter 14.

TiVoToGo

Tivo, Inc is about to release (by the time you're reading this) an add-on service to HMF that will allow TiVo users to send TiVo programming over their home network to view shows on any PC or to burn shows onto recordable DVD for viewing on a laptop (hence the "ToGo" part). To view the programming on a computer, including one running a burned DVD, you'll likely have to use a device called a Content Security Key, a USB-based decryption device that you'll plug into a USB port. This key will, in essence, give you permission to watch the TiVo'd content. Without the key, you'll not be able to view the programming. The Content Security Key, along with special DVD burning and viewing software, will be included in the price of the TiVoToGo to service. No word yet on how much the service will cost. The Security Key, like many such copy-protection technologies of the past, could prove obnoxious to use. It is designed to prevent TiVo users from sending shows to their PC and then sharing them online with others.

Accessories

All you need to hook up and enjoy your TiVo comes with it, but there are some other fun toys you may want to consider. Toys!

Uninterrupted Power Supplies (UPS)

You're halfway through the weekly whack on the *Sopranos* when the power goes out. What's a goomba in the dark to do? Spring for a UPS, you knucklehead! An Uninterrupted Power Supply (UPS) is a battery backup (and surge suppressor) that will continue to provide power to your TV and TiVo for up to an hour after the lights go out. You might already have one of these on your computer. TiVo's a computer, too, so it feels left out. Get it a UPS and everyone's happy.

There is some confusion among TiVo users about what type of UPS to get. You don't need an expensive one with voltage regulation and other features designed to protect more sensitive electronic systems. All you need is at least a 350V (500V is ideal) UPS with surge protection and RJ-11 (phone) jacks. What most people don't realize is that any electrical pathway into your computer (in this case, your TiVo) is a potential threat if there's a power surge. That means the phone line and coax cables are vulnerable. Unfortunately, most reasonably priced UPSes don't offer coax protection, but often do have phone in/out jacks. We're big fans of the APC (www.apc.com) brand power management products. They offer low-end UPS for as little as $40 (see Figure 1.7).

Tip

A UPS isn't just for keeping couch potatoes growing into their seat cushions during a power outage. AC power fluctuations can cause a kind of frame stuttering on your TiVo known as "stopples." A UPS can help prevent minor occurrences of these. We'll talk more about stopples in the "Common Problems" section of the next chapter.

FIGURE 1.7
The affordable APC Back-UPS ES 350.

Which TiVo Is Right for You?

NOTE

We'll be discussing all things related to remotes and device control in the aptly named Chapter 4, "Remote Control Freak."

Tip

A great resource for everything having to do with remote controls for media devices is the website www.remotecentral.com. They offer reviews, how-to articles, a discussion forum, and more. One mistake that people frequently make is buying a universal remote before reading up on it and learning its strengths, weaknesses, compatibility issues, and so on. Thanks to this site, you don't have to make this mistake.

Universal Remote Control

It's called "remote bloat," and you're likely suffering from it. Every device in your home entertainment flotilla came with its own infrared remote control. Each likely offers to handle control of other devices (for example, the DVD remote might have buttons to control your TV and stereo on/off and volume). But for most media junkies with lots of gear, we still end up with a pile of semi-functional remotes: This one only does the TV, but can't talk to the stereo like it's supposed to; this one can turn the stereo on and off, but can't control the volume; and this one doesn't talk to anyone but itself. Sound familiar?

The answer is *supposed* to be the universal remote, a controller with bad button-acne that can talk to *everything*. We have drawers full of remotes, universal and otherwise, that testify to the sad failure of the Rodney King "Can't We All Just Get Along?" challenge of the media remote control. And then there's the issue, when talking about having one or two TiVos in the mix, of being able to have buttons like Thumbs Up and Thumbs Down.

The remote for the stand-alone Series 2 TiVo is designed to control two TiVos (it has a switch where you can select DVR 1 or DVR 2), your TV, and your stereo system. Instructions for how to set all of this up are in the TiVo *User's Guide*. If you're lucky enough, your television set and stereo receiver will be compatible with the TiVo remote. But you'll still need the stereo remote for other stereo functions, the cable box remote (if you're on cable), the remote for your DVD deck, and so on. Luckily, there are some inexpensive universal remotes that come close to being universal and include buttons for DVRs. One that comes highly recommended among TiVo users is the One for All 6-Device Universal Remote (a.k.a. the URC 6131, shown in Figure 1.8). It has DVR and DVD functions built into it (including Thumb Up/Down keys) and is fairly easy to program (even if the control codes for your devices aren't contained in the extensive code library that comes built into the device). The best thing about it (for all it offers) is that it only costs $18. Radio Shack also sells a decent universal remote called the 6-in-One Smart A/V Remote (15-1994).

FIGURE 1.8

The One for All 6-Device Universal Remote with built-in TiVo functions.

Tip

When you use S-Video for the video input/output, you skip plugging in the yellow composite video jack and just use the composite audio (red/white) jacks in conjunction with the S-Video cable. Series 1 TiVos came with one S-Video cable. Manufacturers got cheap and stopped including a cable in Series 2 machines, so if you want to use S-Video, you'll have to get at least two S-Video cables, so you'll have one from the TiVo to the A/V switch, and one from the output of the switch to the S-Video input on your TV.

A/V Switches

It's inevitable that you're going to run out of audio/video inputs on your TV set. Many TVs have only two pairs of composite A/V inputs; some have three. It's a rare TV that has four sets of inputs. If you have a TiVo, a DVD, a VCR, and a game box, you're already one device too many. The answer is an A/V switch (a.k.a. a "video switching box," a "video selector switch," a "signal switcher," nobody's sure what the heck to call this thing, but they all work the same way). Sophisticated electronic versions of such devices are usually called A/V Receivers (which usually offer signal amplification and other features).

A/V switches are very simple devices. They usually have one output to the TV and a number of inputs, from two to six. They always consist of a set of composite audio/video RCA-type jacks (red, white, yellow) for the output and each of the switchable inputs, and often, there's an S-video jack on each input/output as well. Definitely make sure to get a box with S-Video I/O, unless you're not planning on using S-Video in your A/V set-up (which you definitely should whenever possible).

Tip

One great thing about adding an A/V switch is that you're adding so many more input possibilities. For instance, if you have a 3-input TV and you add a 4-port A/V switch, you're adding three new inputs.

There are two types of A/V switches: mechanical and electronic. The mechanical ones work fine (and are much cheaper), but there's no remote control capability, so you have to get up from your chair (oh the humanity!) and switch from one input source to another. Electronic switches usually have a remote, which is very convenient if you plan on switching between TV inputs frequently.

We recommend just getting an el cheapo mechanical A/V switch (with S-Video). Radio Shack sells a 4-input switch with S-Video jacks for $30 (see Figure 1.9). The only circumstance under which you really need a higher-end electronic switch is if your TV only has two A/V inputs and you have a lot of devices you need to connect to your TV. That said, there are many different types of A/V receivers on the market (check out your local Circuit City, Best Buy, and so forth) that allow for tremendous flexibility for handling various types of inputs/outputs, not to mention support for Dolby Digital and DTS (Digital Theater Systems) audio formats (for DVD, satellite, and some/most digital cable receivers).

FIGURE 1.9

The Radio Shack A/V switch with S-Video.

Cable Splitter

All hail this cheap little widget that can send signals to all of your cable-ready devices. If you're on a cable service and have RF coax coming into your home, you've got a massive pipe of media that's squeezed off to a trickle (if you're just plugging that cable into a single device). A cable splitter will send that signal to everything with a TV tuner in it (DVRs, DVDs, VCRs, TVs). You have to split the signal before the cable box, so only one device will receive any premium content you subscribe to, but everything else will get all the other channels (including basic cable). Splitters have one input and two, three, or four outputs. Go ahead and get the 4-output splitter, so you're ready for any future devices. You'll need short runs of coax cable to go from the splitter outputs to each device. Radio Shack sells splitters and cables in 1, 3, 6-foot (and other) lengths.

Multiswitch

If you're on a DirecTV with a dual-LNB or triple-LNB dish and need more lines run than the dish itself will accommodate (for example, because you have multiple receivers and/or multiple TiVos), you have to use something called a multiswitch. These switches are designated by the number of their inputs and outputs. Common models are 2×4, 2×8, 4×4, 4×8. The first number refers to the inputs. If you have a dual-LNB dish, you have two outputs coming from the dish (and these are the two inputs to the multiswitch). The second number is the outputs you'll have available. So, if you have two DirecTiVo units that you want to connect to your dish, you'd get a 2×4 multiswitch and run two coax cables to the two TV inputs on each DirecTiVo unit.

There are three types of multiswitches: mechanical (unpowered), mechanical (powered), and electronic (powered). Unpowered mechanical switches are the cheapest, but also the least reliable. You should shy away from these unless you have very short cable runs from your dish to the switch (under 100'). The powered mechanical switches are likely what most users need. The popular Channel Master 6314IFD 3X4 (the third input is for a cable connection) can be found online for under $60. Solid-state electronic switches can be very expensive, running from $300 to $600. They have on-board power supplies, built-in signal amplifiers, and up to 16 outputs. This is overkill for all but media junkies with King Kong-sized monkeys on their backs.

A/V Wireless Transmitter System

If you'd like to have a cheap "multi-room viewing" solution, you can, thanks to a pair of devices called an A/V wireless transmitter and receiver. This wireless duo will let you send the TiVo output (from TiVo's second set of A/V outs) to any TV input source. That destination source can either be an actual TV or the inputs on your PC's TV card (if you have one). Cheaper versions of these systems do not let you control the signal from the remote viewing source, but others do. The remote-equipped models have an infrared detector on the wireless receiver. You point your remote at the receiver and it sends the control signals over the wireless link to its own infrared blaster (that you set up just like your TiVo's). This way, you can navigate TiVo's menus just as you would if you were at your primary television. The sound/image quality of these wireless units is good, but not great. They operate in the 2.4GHz radio band, which is shared by other devices, such as wireless Internet (Wi-Fi 802.11b and 802.11g), portable landline phones, and even microwave ovens. This can be a minor annoyance if you live in a house, but overwhelming if you live in an apartment or condo. Unfortunately, it's

NOTE

In shopping for a multiswitch, you'll likely see models with odd numbers of inputs (3×4, 3×8, or 5×8). In each case, the extra inputs are for over-the-air (OTA) antenna inputs, which can be passed through the multiswitch along with the satellite signals.

Tip

A couple of good online sources for multiswitches (and other satellite and cable components) are Future Home Systems (www.futurehomesystems.com) and HomeTech Solutions (www.hometech.com).

hard to know if the air around you is heavily radio trafficked until you set up a system to try it out (so save your receipt!). Some users have also reported big problems getting the remote to work over the Wavecom channel. If you have this problem, you may want to add a dedicated RF remote controller. Our esteemed tech editors, the WeaKness boys, sell them (www.weaknees.com). It will add another $50 to your wireless solution, but if you really want such a wireless setup, even with the addition of the RF controller, it's still cheaper than a second TiVo and service.

Gareth On...

I've been using the Wavecom, Sr. A/V wireless set for years and am basically happy with it. I do have a 2.4GHz phone system, but because of where the base station is set up, there is minimal interference. There is bad interference from the microwave oven, but I'm usually not cooking and watching TV at the same time. I use the Wavecom to send signals from my home entertainment system to the TV card on my PC. I can even switch sources if I want to (plugging the A/V cables from the Wavecom transmitter into any device's output). The drawback here is that you can only set up one remote control relay, so if I switch sources, I have to go into the living room to actually control the device (VCR, DVD, ReplayTV) from there.

Manufacturers of A/V Wireless systems include Wavecom, Terk, and RCA. All systems with the remote control feature cost just under $100 (see Figure 1.10).

FIGURE 1.10

The Wavecom, Sr. A/V wireless transmitter system, a great way to send TiVo recordings to your PC or another TV.

Wireless Phone Jack

TiVo needs a phone line to send and receive data. Most users are likely lucky enough to have a phone jack in the same room as their TiVo and it's simply a matter of using the dual phone jack that comes with TiVo to plug in both a telephone and TiVo's modem cable. If you don't have a jack nearby and don't want to have to manually hook up a lengthy cable to a remote jack on a regular basis so that TiVo can get its data fix, the solution is a wireless phone jack. This system consists of two AC-plug adapters, one that plugs into a wall outlet near your TiVo and another that plugs into an outlet near your phone jack. The TiVo modem cable plugs into one and a phone cable comes from the other and into the phone jack. The system actually uses your home's electrical wiring to transport the phone signals from the phone jack, through the wireless adapters, and into your TiVo. Wireless phone jack systems are sold by Radio Shack, RCA, GE, and others. They sell for between $60 and $90. Make sure the ones you get specify that they're designed to handle modem traffic (some aren't).

Media Carts

There is nothing more frustrating than having to wrestle a TV, TiVo, VCR, or other component off of a bookshelf, or from inside a fixed cabinet, to get to the inputs/outputs in the back. If the room where you have your entertainment system allows for it, put your gear on media carts or (backless) shelves on wheels. You won't believe the difference this can make. It will turn a new device hookup or system troubleshoot from a dreaded chore into a cakewalk. You just roll out the cart/shelf, turn it around, make your connections and roll it back into place. If you have existing shelves, you can easily add caster wheels, available at any home store.

Cable Organizing Systems

Ah…modern electronics and the wonders of cable…lots and lots of cable. Regardless of how well designed your home media system, how careful you are with keeping power cords and A/V cables to a minimum, everyone is going to end up with a giant pile of cable spaghetti heaped up behind their entertainment center. This creates not only an unsightly mess, but can also cause much frustration, confusion, and incorrect hookups when you, inevitably, have to change something (or add a component). This problem isn't specific to TiVo installation, but if you're installing a new TiVo, or you're reading this as a TiVo vet (whose media center is still an ungodly

Caution

Some home wiring systems are not wholehouse. If you have an addition on your home, or an older house that had its electrical system amended to deal with modern power needs, you may have two electrical wiring zones that are not connected to each other. If this is the case, and you try to use a wireless phone jack system, it won't work (if the signal is trying to go to outlets that aren't part of the same zone). Wireless jacks also cannot be fed through Uninterrupted Power Supplies (UPS). It will treat your datastream as noise and filter it out.

mess), why not use this as an opportunity to clean up your act? It'll make everything easier in the long run.

To keep your cables as neat and sorted out as possible, there are dozens of different organizing solutions. Go to your local electronics or computer superstore, see what's available, and choose the type that's right for your system setup. You'll find everything from color-coded Velcro cable-ties to wire guides (where the cables clip into channels that keep the cables side-by-side) to large-diameter flexible tubing that you can shove all of your cables into to create one big trunk cable in place of a dozen smaller cords. The TiVo upgrade and kit-seller, 9th Tee (www.9thtee.com), sells a nifty CordKeeper set that allows you to spool unused cable-lengths so that tons of excess cable isn't coiled up behind your gear. See Figure 1.11 for a selection of cable organizing technologies.

FIGURE 1.11

A sampling of cable management systems:
1. Channel wire guides,
2. Zip ties with label header,
3. wall-mountable ring clamps,
4. flexible plastic wire organizing pipe,
5. adhesive zip tie mounting pads,
6. purse-clasp cable rings,
7. zip ties,
8. wall-mountable cable organizer straps with Velcro.

Labels/Labeling Machine

When you're hooking up a new piece of A/V equipment, the last thing you want to do is a bunch of prep work. You want to plug it in, turn it on, and start enjoying it ASAP. But a few minutes with a pen and some tape, or better yet, a portable labeling machine, will pay off in the long run. It's inevitable that you're going to need to unplug components in the future and switch cables around, and if you have to trace each cable, it's going to become a huge hassle. Take the time to clearly identify each A/V cable ("TiVo L-Audio," "VCR Video Out," "TV R-Audio Out," and so on). Also, label the ends of your power cables (where they plug into the power bar or UPS). For many digital A/V devices, unplugging and replugging the power cable is used as a final means of rebooting after a hard crash or modem glitch, so making sure you're unplugging the right component becomes important. While a Sharpie and some masking tape are fine for labeling, nothing beats a handheld labeling machine. Brother makes a great line of labelers (see Figure 1.12). Keep an eye out for advertising inserts in the newspaper, as these devices are frequently on sale at office supply, department and drug stores. You can get a decent one on sale for under $20. Once you have it, you'll go nuts labeling all of your A/V cables, computer cables, wall warts (the AC power transformers found on the ends of many consumer electronics power cables), your offspring (it's so hard keeping their names straight), items in the fridge ("Touch? Die!"), and so forth.

FIGURE 1.12

Gareth's trusty Brother P-Touch PT-66 labeler. Remove this from his desk and he cannot be responsible for rude labels that end up on your back.

Wired/Wireless Networking Components

The other piece of add-on tech you'll need, if you're planning on connecting your TiVo(s) to your home computer network, is a wireless USB adapter or a USB-to-Ethernet adapter and Ethernet cable. We'll cover these accessories in much greater detail in Chapter 8, "Networking Your TiVo."

Tip

If you buy a stand-alone TiVo, as soon as you get it home, go ahead and call TiVo (877-BUY-TIVO) or go to their website (www.tivo.com) to sign up for the TiVo service. It can take a day or more before your service request is processed and your account is activated on your TiVo unit. All you need to sign up is your TiVo's 15-digit service number, found on a sticker on the TiVo box, sometimes in the back of your TiVo manual, on the back of the TiVo itself, or onscreen (TiVo Central -> TiVo Messages & Setup -> System Information). The most reliable source is the System Information screen. Some TiVos can end up in the wrong box, or with the wrong manual copy, so the on-screen service number is the safest to use.

You Say You Want a TiVolution?

With the information in this chapter, you should be ready to make an informed decision about which TiVo and TiVo service are right for you. Once you've purchased your DVR and any accessories you need or want, the standard setup is extremely straightforward. The manuals that come with TiVo are very good, as are the onscreen troubleshooting screens.

In the following chapters, we won't cover what's in the standard TiVo docs; we'll take you to the next level, sharing what we've learned in our own TiVo fanaticism and through the shared wisdom on the online TiVo community. There's so much you can do with TiVo right out of the box, but you'll be amazed at the number of nifty tips, tricks, and hacks that will allow you to get even more out of your TiVo experience.

Chapter 2

Getting the Most Out of Your TiVo

There are so many features to be found on TiVo that it can take awhile to get the hang of everything. Let's take a brief tour of TiVo's hardware and software and talk about how TiVo fits into the rest of your home entertainment system. Then we'll cover some of the common problems you might encounter when setting up or using your TiVo (that aren't covered in the TiVo manuals).

Understanding How TiVo Works

To get the most out of a piece of consumer electronics, it's often a good idea to know something about its capabilities and how it works. In Parts 2 and 3 of this book, we'll venture much deeper into the nuts, bolts, and bits of TiVo's hardware and software (for those who plan on more serious TiVo hacking), but for now, here's a quick peek at TiVo's inner workings.

Hardware Basics

One of the original terms for this type of digital recording device was a "hard disk recorder," and that's really what TiVo is: a big-boned hard drive that records TV signals. TiVo is a single-minded computer, what is known in the trade as an "embedded system." If you've ever taken the case off of your computer and had a look inside, you'll be right at home if you crack the case on your TiVo. Inside, you'll see familiar parts such as a motherboard, one or two hard drives, the familiar flat ("ribbon") cable, a power supply, and a cooling fan. What you won't see are the typical PC sound and graphics cards or a typical CPU package. These functions are all found on chips that are "baked" directly onto TiVo's motherboard. By engineering chips specific to a set function, in this case recording and managing TV signals, embedded systems can be mass-produced more cheaply than a PC that must be able to handle many different things and must be upgradeable. Figure 2.1 shows the insides of a stand-alone Series 2 Philips TiVo.

FIGURE 2.1

The inner workings of a Series 2 TiVo.

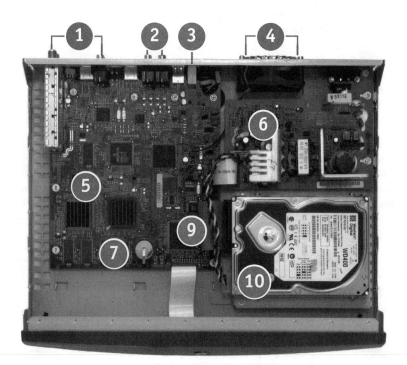

1. Inputs
2. Outputs
3. USB ports (S2-only)
4. Cooling Fan
5. Motherboard
6. Unshielded (read: shocking!)
   Power Supply
7. Backup Battery
8. Front Panel Control Cable
9. IDE Cable
10. Hard Disk Drive

There are currently two flavors of TiVo hardware: the stand-alone (SA) units and the DirecTV satellite receiver with built-in TiVo (DirecTiVo). Each type works slightly differently.

Stand-Alone TiVo

If your TiVo is hooked up to a cable service, the television signal comes into your house through the RF (Radio Frequency) coaxial cable provided by your cable company. Once inside, the signal (either analog or digital, depending on what service you have) usually goes into a cable receiver/descrambler before heading to other A/V devices, such as TiVo. After arriving at your TiVo (via coax cable, RCA cables, or RCA audio and S-Video), the signal is converted to a digital one via something called an MPEG-2 encoder. MPEG-2 is a digital compression standard, created by the standards organization known as the Motion Pictures Experts Group (MPEG). MPEG-2 is the same compression format found on commercial DVDs. During the encoding process, the program is compressed to varying degrees that the user can control, with four available levels of quality: Basic, Medium, High, or Best (or "Extreme" on Pioneer units). The less compressed, the better the sound- and image-quality, but the more space the programming takes up on your TiVo's hard drive(s). After encoding, the now-digital signal is sent to your hard drive for storage. If you're watching a TV that's hooked up to a TiVo, even if you're watching it live, you're not actually watching a "live" cable feed coming into the house, you're watching a signal that's being "written to" and then sent from TiVo's hard drive (see Figure 2.2). Before it leaves the TiVo, it has to be decoded again (via an MPEG-2 decoder) so that your television can display it (assuming you have an analog TV).

DirecTV DVR with TiVo

The DirecTV DVR with TiVo, or DirecTiVo, works a little differently than the stand-alone models. The signal coming down from the satellite dish has already been digitally encoded (using a high-quality MPEG-2 encoder on the transmission end) so there is no need to encode it before it gets sent to the hard drive. Skipping this analog-to-digital (A/D) conversion step results in a higher picture quality. Also because no encoding is required, there is obviously no need to include an encoder chip on the DirecTiVo motherboard (which saves some significant money, as an

NOTE

Because of the encoding process described here, if you have another TV in your house that's not hooked up to a TiVo and the two sets are running at the same time (and on the same channel), you can hear the slight delay (about a second) in the signal on the TiVo-connected TV.

MPEG-2 encoder is an expensive part). This means, however, that there is also no control over compression quality on a DirecTiVo machine; everything is recorded at what amounts to the "Best Quality" setting.

FIGURE 2.2

How a stand-alone TiVo works. This graphic is based on Series 1, but the functionality is basically the same for both S1 and S2 models.

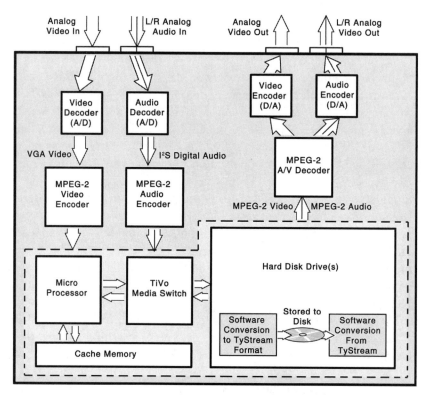

DirecTiVos also differ from stand-alones in that they have two TV tuner chips built into them instead of one. If you have two satellite inputs from a dual-LNB dish or triple-LNB dish, you can be recording two different channels at the same time while watching a previously recorded program. Unfortunately, you cannot split a DirecTV coax line coming from the dish like you can the coax coming from a cable service. You must have a multi-LNB converter on your dish with two cables coming from it (see Figure 2.3).

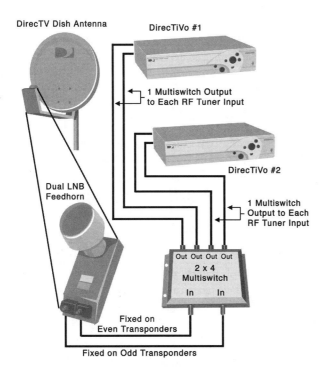

DirecTV Dish Antenna   DirecTiVo #1

1 Multiswitch Output
to Each RF Tuner Input

DirecTiVo #2

Dual LNB
Feedhorn

1 Multiswitch
Output to Each
RF Tuner Input

Out Out Out Out
2 x 4
Multiswitch
In   In

Fixed on
Even Transponders

Fixed on Odd Transponders

NOTE

Many cable subscribers
seem blissfully unaware
of the fact that cable is
actually satellite...sorta.
The service may come
into your house on the
end of a coax cable, but
most of the signals are
actually pulled down
from satellites to a cen-
tral location (called a
"head end") at your local
cable company outlet.
From there, they travel
through a network of
fiber optic cables, signal
amplifiers, and coax
cables to your house. So,
there may be some truth
to the cable companies'
claims that weather can
have a negative effect on
direct satellite dishes,
but if the weather gets
bad enough, all delivery
services suffer because
they're all satellite-
dependent.

TiVo's LBLs (A.K.A. "Little Blinking Lights")

Most TiVos have two lights located on the front of them that sometimes change colors. If you're wondering what the color states indicate, here's the rundown:

The light on the left has two functions (indicated by two colors):

• Green = TiVo is powered on
• Yellow = TiVo is receiving infrared commands from the remote

If this light is not lit, it means that TiVo is not powered on.

The light on the right has three functions (indicated by three colors):

• Red = TiVo is recording something
• Yellow = TiVo is making its daily call, processing data, or doing main-tenance
• Orange = TiVo is both recording something and making its daily call.

This light does nothing while watching live TV or playing back a recorded program.

Software Basics

TiVo's sophisticated software handles all of this encoding (on stand-alone units), decoding, storing, retrieving, and the various search and record functions. Obviously your TiVo comes with this software already installed, but it's not static. A built-in 36.6Kbs dial-up modem (and a standard phone line) are used to place a "daily call" to TiVo's central servers to download new TV guide data, to update your TiVo's software, and to upload *anonymous* information about your viewing habits so that TiVo can make better recommendations of what you might like to watch, and so TiVo, Inc. can create better hardware and software for the future. That's what they tell us, anyway [cue maniacal Big Brother-esque laughter].

One of the things that's made TiVo so popular is that it has an extremely easy-to-understand and operate user interface. When Apple was designing the Macintosh, they used the telephone "interface" as a model of user-friendliness. If you'd never seen a phone before and you were handed one and a phone number, you could probably, within a few minutes, figure out how to use this strange device to place a call. Apple engineers wanted to create a computer interface that, with obviously more than a few minutes, you could figure your way through. Even though TiVo's software is built on the rather gnarly Linux OS, it too has an intuitive user interface that even a child can figure out. The following sections explain TiVo's basic software components.

TiVo Central (or DirecTV Central)

This is TiVo's answer to your PC's desktop. Whenever you hit the TiVo (or DirecTV) button on the top of your remote (also referred to as the "TiVoGuy" on SA systems), you're taken to this TiVo Central screen. From here, using the Arrow and Select buttons on your remote, you can navigate your way through all of TiVo's functions, from Guided Setup and various utilities (such as system information, troubleshooting), to searching and scheduling, to viewing live and recorded programming (see Figure 2.4).

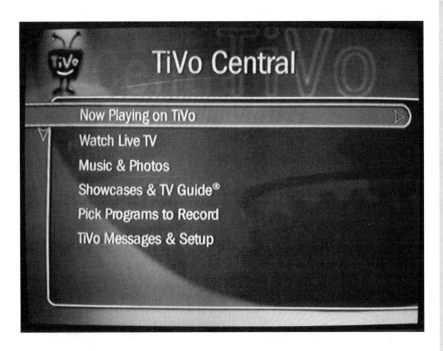

Now Playing on TiVo (Now Playing)

The first item on TiVo Central is Now Playing. A newbie might think that this was referring to live television, but calling it "Now Playing" says something very important about what TiVo is all about, and how it revolutionizes TV viewing. This is the area where all of your recorded programs are stored and accessed. When you first start using TiVo, the tendency might be to think of it as little more than a digital VCR, where you record shows that you can't watch in real-time, but otherwise, you watch TV live. Over time, and as you become more proficient at using TiVo's sophisticated search, record, and suggestion functions, you'll realize that watching TV in real-time is oh so 20th century. TiVo is a TV-dedicated computer that is constantly searching the TV schedule looking for shows you want to watch (or that it thinks you want to watch) and recording them for you. "Now Playing" soon becomes what *YOU* want to play now, not what the networks are playing at any given time.

Watch Live TV

If you *really* want to watch TV in real-time (shame on you—the TiVoGuy snickers in your general direction), you get there by choosing the Watch Live TV item from TiVo Central (or by pressing the Live TV button on your remote).

If you do want to watch live television, you still have some degree of control over the signal. When the doorbell rings or the dog spits up on your shoes, and you hit TiVo's Pause button, a "buffer" that is always being stored to the hard drive will hold your place. This buffer can store up to 30 minutes of incoming TV signals. When you come back to your easy chair and hit Play again, you pick up where you left off and now have up to 30 minutes of programming to view, fast-forward through, rewind, and so on. If you change channels, the buffer is always cleared.

From Live TV, if you press the Guide button (or press the LiveTV/Guide button again on the Series 1 remote), the TV guide data is laid over the TV signal. From here you can navigate through the channel line-ups to see what's on or upcoming and press the Record button on your remote to ask TiVo to record desired programs. Version 4.0 of the TiVo software offers two Guide view options: the traditional two-column TiVo menu guide, and a TV Guide-based grid layout (see Figure 2.5). The DirecTiVo also offers the Grid option.

Another cool Guide feature is the ability to filter the content of the Guide based on your interests. In the mood for a movie? Once in the Guide, you can select various content filters (movies, sports, animation, and so forth) via the Info/Display button. This highlights only the selected content in the Guide, graying out everything else so that you can quickly scan for a fabulous flick, any ballgames currently on, and so on.

FIGURE 2.5

The two types of Guide layouts (two-column and grid). The grid is available for Series 2 models only.

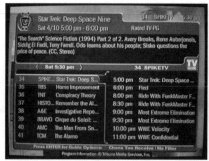 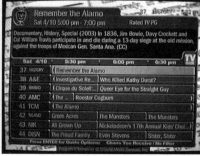

Showcases and TV Guide (Showcases)

The TiVo software offers you many different ways of discovering what's coming up on television. Showcases are suggestions that TiVo, Inc. bundles together to alert you to upcoming movies, specials, and themes (westerns, mysteries, sci-fi, and so on). Think of it as TiVo's answer to previews at the movie theater. You may or may not find Showcase's suggestions very helpful, but be sure to check it periodically because it sometimes features interesting exclusive TiVo content downloaded to your TiVo during the daily call. TiVo, Inc. now has a partnership with TV Guide and there is always a short TV Guide preview program (new every Monday) available in Showcases (see Figure 2.6).

FIGURE 2.6
TiVo's Showcases and TV Guide programming.

Pick Programs to Record

Besides this ability to cavort through "live" (or buffered) TV to your heart's content, the other big innovation of TiVo is the extensive recording and programming capabilities. In addition to using the onscreen Guide to select individual shows to record, there are a number of other ways to search through the guide data for the next two weeks, looking for upcoming shows and setting up TiVo to record them. These features are all found under this menu item:

- **Search by Title** allows you to scan through all of the upcoming programs, either in one big list or via show categories and subcategories.

Tip

While most items in Showcases are simple themed search lists, there are frequently exclusive video items to view (interviews with celebs, show previews, music videos, and so forth). On the Showcases screen, this video content is marked by a small movie slate icon.

For the free TiVo Basic service, you only get three days of Guide data.

The "To Do List" also includes a recording history, which will show what was recorded, what was not (and why), and what was deleted (and why). For those who want to spy on their kids, parents, the nanny, and so on, this is a great feature. Want to know whether the nanny records and deletes *The View* every day while she should be at the park with baby? Want to know if your teenager recorded a *Wild On* marathon while you were on vacation? This is where you can go to find out.

- **Search Using a WishList** is one of the most powerful features of TiVo. It's like a search engine for TV, allowing you to create search strings for titles, actors, directors, and keywords. Results can either be scanned and desired items can be set to record, or WishList items can be set up to Auto-Record.

- **TiVo Suggestions** will use the available space on your hard drive to record programs TiVo thinks you will like (based on your use of the Thumbs Up/Thumbs down buttons on the TiVo remote and on shows you've previously recorded). What TiVo plans on recording for you can be seen in this menu item.

- **Record by Time or Channel** is TiVo's manual recording feature. Ah...takes us back to those hazy, crazy days of the VCR!

- **Season Pass Manager** shows a list of all of the programs you've set up to record via the Get A Season Pass recording option or WishList items set up to auto-record. Season Pass items are marked with a double-check icon, auto-record WishList items with a star. Programs are recorded from this list based on their priority, so if there's a show conflict, the show higher on the list will be recorded. You can move items up and down the list by using the Arrow keys on your remote.

- **To Do List** is the master list of everything that TiVo plans on recording. Individual recordings are marked with one check, Season Passes with two checks, and WishList items with a star. You can edit and delete items from this list.

TiVo Messages and Setup

This area of TiVo's software is devoted to setting up your DVR, setting user preferences, and other utility functions:

- **TiVo Messages** are messages sent to you from TiVo, Inc. (about new local dial-up numbers, schedule changes, software upgrades, etc.) as well as alert messages from the TiVo software itself.

- **Preferences** contains parental controls, customizable channel listings, default recording quality, and other user-configurable options.

- **Recorder & Phone Setup** is where all of the utilities for setting up your TiVo and your phone connection can be found.

- **System Information** lists your TiVo service number, which version of the software your TiVo is using, your TiVo's maximum recording capacity, the date of TiVo's last call to TiVo HQ, and other important info about your TiVo.

- **Troubleshooting** contains help screens to various TiVo features.

- **Restart or Reset System** allows you to reset several types of stored data (such as your Thumb Ratings and your entire To Do List), go through Guided Setup again, or restart your TiVo.

- **Standby** puts TiVo in…well…a standby mode. The TV screen will turn gray and the lights on TiVo will go out. Shhh…it's sleeping… This feature can be used as a pass through video mode, allowing the signal to pass through the TiVo to your television. This is useful if you want to record something on TiVo while watching another live program through the TV's tuner. Putting TiVo in Standby mode will still allow it to record programs as scheduled, but will also pass the incoming signal to the TV's tuner so you can watch another program there while TiVo is busy recording.

Setting Up Your New TiVo

TiVo is known for its user-friendliness, both for its ease of setup and for its intuitive user interface. That said, it's still a piece of high-tech digital equipment, a computer with an operating system, a modem requiring a communications setup, numerous required cable connections, and more. This can all quickly become intimidating to some users. While the manuals that come with TiVo hold the newbie's hand as they set up and explore TiVo, there are some common problems and unexplained A/V concepts we thought should be explored in more detail. Understanding these can make your TiVo setup much smoother, especially if problems arise.

Media In/Media Out

TV out. TV in. TiVo out. TiVo in. S-Video or composite RCA out. RJ-11 jacks, USB, 75 Ohm RF coax with F-type connectors. It all sounds so geeky and complicated, but it's really not. To become a home A/V whiz, you only really have to understand two basic things: what all those initials stand for and the general concept behind A/V input and output (relax, this isn't going to be a birds and the bees lecture). We cover all of the cables and connector types in the "Mini-Tutorial on Audio/Visual Tech" that follows. The concept behind input and output goes something like this:

You're likely always going to have one primary A/V source coming into your house. This is going to be an RF (Radio Frequency) coax cable from a cable service, roof antenna, or coax cable(s) coming from a satellite dish. You can think of this main input as the media headwaters, the wellspring carrying all of that nourishing (or polluting, as the case may be) audio and video into your

Tip

The information in the Series 1 TiVo manuals is fairly out-of-date. To get the most current information, on both S1 and S2 set-up and operation, check out the Customer Support section of TiVo.com (customersupport. tivo.com).

home. If you have a cable service (whether analog or digital), this input will likely first be channeled (pardon the TV pun) into a set-top box. If you have a satellite dish, the signal will either go into a separate satellite receiver or into your DirecTV DVR. From these sources, the audio and video signals are then piped into the various components of your home entertainment system. The signal can be sent into and out of a number of devices (VCR, DVD, PVR, stereo amp, and so forth) and it can also be split (audio channels going to one device, video to another, for instance). This is where it can start to get confusing.

The first rule of thumb in A/V I/O is that if a signal goes into a device (via one or more of its inputs), it's likely going to be coming out of it again (via its outputs) until it gets to the TV (the final destination of the A/V signals). The main exception to this is if you're going to be feeding your audio signals to your stereo receiver. Here, in essence, you're splitting the signal one final time, sending the video to the TV and the audio to the stereo and its speakers. This can be done in a number of different ways. The main way is to use the Audio Out RCA jacks (or Digital Optical, if you have it) from your TV (or your TiVo's L/R RCA Out) to available auxiliary inputs on your stereo receiver. If you have an A/V Receiver, as discussed in the "Accessories" section of Chapter 1, "Which TiVo Is Right for You?" or even a mechanical A/V switch (which sometimes have audio output), you can send the audio to the stereo from there. The main thing to remember with TiVo in this chain is that the A/V signals *must* go into the TiVo unit together. If you send the audio signal to your stereo and the video to TiVo, the audio/video will not sync up properly.

NOTE

The exception to the main A/V pipe going directly into a cable box or sat receiver is if you're using a splitter (cable) or multiswitch (satellite). In these cases, the splitter/switch becomes the initial distribution point rather than the cable/sat box.

One problem with discussing A/V hookups is that there are so many different types of A/V devices and so many ways of connecting them that the possible combinations quickly become overwhelming. You need to figure out for your own setup what needs to connect to what. One great online resource for seeing diagrams of dozens of A/V variations is Richard Parker's "TiVo Wiring Guide" (www.electrophobia.com/tivo/). He shows simple, easy-to-understand drawings of both dish and cable hookups for TiVos in concert with a host of other devices such as DVD decks, VCRs, S-VHS, an A/V receiver, and more. Even if you don't see your specific setup there, the diagrams should help you in figuring out how your configuration should work.

If you just keep in mind the idea that the media is coming in through one pipe, splitting off into a number of devices that feed off that pipe, and then finally making their way into the inputs of the TV (and that you then use the TV Input button on your remote to switch between devices), you should be okay. But then there's the question of what kind of "pipe" is going into and out of all of your A/V gear? That's where our little tutorial comes in handy.

Mini-Tutorial on Audio/Visual Tech (or "How to Be an A/V Geek in Minutes!")

A/V geeks: You may have made fun of them in grade school—whoever would have guessed that you'd need to become one just to be able to watch TV? Just a few years ago, a "home entertainment center" was a piece of furniture your TV sat inside of (with maybe a VCR and some stereo components). Connecting this gear involved a coax cable connection, a few composite audio/video cords, and some speaker wire. Today's home entertainment centers incorporate computers, talk to home networks, access the Internet, and can deliver everything from high-definition TV to digital music to photo slideshows on the telly. And the cables that deliver this media have become a dizzying tangle of wires in half a dozen different formats. Regardless of how clear the owner's manuals for all your gear are (and they usually aren't), it's easy for the average user to quickly become overwhelmed. But once you know what the acronyms stand for, and understand some of the operating principles that underlie this tech, installation becomes much clearer. Figure 2.7 shows all of the main types of A/V cables and connectors you might encounter. Here's a rundown on how they work and what they do.

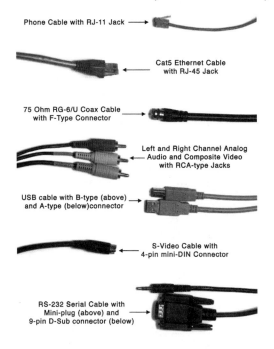

Phone Cable with RJ-11 Jack

Cat5 Ethernet Cable with RJ-45 Jack

75 Ohm RG-6/U Coax Cable with F-Type Connector

Left and Right Channel Analog Audio and Composite Video with RCA-type Jacks

USB cable with B-type (above) and A-type (below) connector

S-Video Cable with 4-pin mini-DIN Connector

RS-232 Serial Cable with Mini-plug (above) and 9-pin D-Sub connector (below)

FIGURE 2.7

Mmm. Spaghetti. The main types of cables and connectors encountered in home media systems.

The following sections discuss some of our favorite flavors.

Common Cable/Connector Types

One of the keys to feeling comfortable in the potentially confusing world of audio/video connectivity is knowing the different types of cables used, and what types of connectors are used to end ("terminate" in geekspeak) them. Here are the cable formats and connectors you'll encounter in TiVo setups and in most other A/V equipment.

Coax

"Coax," short for "coaxial cable," is a type of radio frequency (RF) carrying wire used for cable televisions, off-the-air (OTA) TV antennas, direct satellite connections, and ham radio hookups. Coax is a round two-conductor cable that consists of a central conductive wire surrounded by second braided or foil conductor (all covered by an insulated jacket). Both of these conductors share the same axis, thus the name coaxial. Coax cable is always designated with the prefix "RG" (old military jargon for "Radio Grade"), followed by the cable type (expressed in a number), and often, the suffix "/U" (for "Universal"). The type of coax you'll be using for home cable or satellite setup is known as 75Ohm "RG-6/U." You can get it at Radio Shack, any home store, or similar retailer. It's available in 1, 3, 6, 12-foot, and other common lengths. The connectors on the ends of the RG-6 coax are called F-type connectors. While coax is the most common way of getting the A/V signal into your home, and most A/V devices allow you to send signals to them via coax, once the cable gets to its first devices, it's preferable to use composite cables (good), S-Video (better), or component video/digital optical (best) for getting the signal into and out of the devices (refer to Figure 2.7).

Composite

Another common way of sending audio and video signals to and from consumer electronic equipment is via the composite cable. While they are frequently referred to as composite audio/video cables, only the video is actual composite. The term refers to the combining of three source video signal types: a luminance (or brightness) signal and two types of color signals. While the components of the video signal are combined, the audio signals are separated into left and right channels, giving you the three cables commonly found on home media devices. They are usually color-coded, with yellow for composite video, red for audio-right, and white (or sometimes green) for audio-left. This cabling is also often referred to as RCA cables, because of the RCA-type jacks on the ends of them. Like the coax cable's F-type connector, the RCA jack has a central male pin and a

Caution

The center pin on an F-type coax connector is very prone to being bent. Before pushing on and screwing in a connector, check to make sure that the pin isn't bent. If it is, gently straighten it before pushing it onto the RF jack.

surrounding ring, but unlike coax, the outer ring is not part of the electrical connection, it's simply used to hold the jack onto the corresponding RCA plug. The entire signal is carried through the central male pin. The RCA jack is also sometimes referred to as a phono plug. And as you might imagine, it gets its name from the fact that this jack/plug technology was developed by RCA (refer to Figure 2.7).

S-Video

One drawback to composite video is that, because the luminance and color information are carried on the same signal, there can be "crosstalk" (unwanted communication) between them, lowering the quality of the signal. S-Video sends the luminance and color signals through separate wires, which prevents this crosstalk, creating a higher-quality image. S-Video cables are connected using 4-pin mini-DIN connectors (refer to Figure 2.7). Like coax F-type connectors, the four pins are easily bent and need to be plugged /unplugged with care. Whenever possible, S-Video connections should always be used over composite (or RF coax) connections.

RJ-11

You probably know it simply as phone cable and phone jack, but its official name is RJ-11, "RJ" standing for "Registered Jack." The "11" refers to its registration number, not the number of wires it carries. RJ-11 can carry either four or six wires, often with only the center two (the red and green) used for carrying the phone signals. The outer two (or four) can be used for things such as powering lights on phones, or for carrying data around your house if you have a phone-based home network (refer to Figure 2.7).

Serial Cable/Connector

You are likely intimately familiar with the serial cable/connector (a.k.a. RS-232) technology (refer to Figure 2.7). Until recently, it was commonly used on computers to connect various peripheral devices, especially analog modems. On computers, this technology is being phased out in favor of the superior USB standard (see next section). Stand-alone TiVos come with an RS-232 cable (with a mini-plug on the other end) for connecting to a satellite receiver or cable box's serial control input (so that TiVo can send control signals to it). With the addition of some adapters, you can also turn this serial cable into a means of connecting a Series 1 TiVo to your PC (so that you can access TiVo's operating system). We'll discuss this in more detail in Chapter 13, "Accessing TiVo's Linux Bash Prompt."

Tip

Sometimes the connector ring on an RCA jack can be *too* snug, making it very hard to remove. Newbie medianauts will sometimes rock the jack back and forth while pulling on it. This is a no-no, as it can weaken the electrical contacts on the plug end. Using a twisting motion while pulling on a stubborn jack is much a safer way to remove it.

Tip

A common call into tech help lines dealing with TV, TiVos and any other A/V gear that uses S-Video goes *something* like this: "Help! My TV thinks it's in the 1950s and *Will and Grace* looks like *I Love Lucy*." A black and white picture often means that a pin on the S-Video connector is bent. Straightening that pin (with a pair of needlenose pliers) usually fixes the problem. If it's broken or too bent, you'll need to get a new cable.

Early Series 2 models (TiVo models TCD130040 and TCD140060) used the USB 1.1 standard, which has a data transfer rate of only 12 megabits per second (Mbits/s). Later models use the much faster USB 2.0, which is capable of speeds up to 480 Mbits/s.

USB

"Universal Serial Bus," or USB, is an upgraded standard for serial communications, allowing for much faster and easier connections and data transfer rates between computing devices and peripherals (refer to Figure 2.7). Besides faster data speeds (up to 480 Mbits/second for USB 2.0), USB adds some great features, such as the ability to hot-swap (plug/unplug while the devices are powered) and the inclusion of a power supply from the USB cable to the peripheral. For devices with low power requirements, a separate power supply is not required. All post–Series 1 TiVos have two USB ports, but they are only enabled on the stand-alone Series 2 models. On DirecTiVos and the new HD DirecTiVo, they are designated as being for "future use." On stand-alone Series 2, a wireless USB adapter or a USB-to-Ethernet adapter can be used in one of these ports to add your TiVo to a home network.

Ethernet

The most common wired communication technology for the home or local area network (LAN) is Ethernet (refer to Figure 2.7). There are many different types of Ethernet, with the most common being 10Base-T and 100Base-T, which have either two twisted wires, or four (two pairs) carried on what's called Cat-5 (Category 5) cable. Data transfer rates for 10Base-T are up to 10 Mbits/s, and up to 100 Mbits/s for 100Base-T. The connector for Ethernet is the RJ-45 jack. For TiVo, Ethernet is used (in both Series 1 and Series 2) for wired networking between TiVo and a home LAN. For Series 1, this is done by way of a plug-in Ethernet card and a cable run to the home network hub (discussed in Chapter 8, "Networking Your TiVo"). In Series 2, a USB-to-Ethernet adapter and Ethernet cable run are used (also covered in Chapter 8).

The "ether" in Ethernet pays homage to the 19th century scientific theory that light waves must have a substance to travel through. This invisible substance was called ether. The light-bearing ether theory has since been widely rejected by most scientists, but "ether" lives on as the medium through which datawaves travel around your home or office.

Other Cable/Connector Types

Beside the more common cable/connector types detailed previously, there are a number of other standards you may encounter on the back panels of your home media equipment, especially more high-end gear.

Component Video

If RF coax is the least desirable way of connecting home media components, followed by composite A/V, with S-Video being the most desirable (of connectors commonly available), component video is the best of the lot, at least for analog formats (see DVI and HDMI ahead).

Unfortunately, only some DVD decks, HD and progressive-scan TVs, and other high-end gear offer it. The HD DirecTV DVR has component video, as does the Toshiba and Pioneer DVD/TiVo combo units (for DVD output). Where S-Video sends its signal through two separate wires, component video sends its through three, one for luminance and two for color–related information. The result is an even cleaner, clearer image than with S-Video. The three component video cables are often combined with a digital optical cable to carry the audio information, as most devices that offer component video output have digital audio output as well. Component video cables end in a RC-style jack.

Dolby Digital Optical/DTS/TosLink

Dolby Digital Optical is the common audio technology found on digital home media devices. Dolby Digital can support up to 5.1 channels of sound: three front channels (left/right/middle), two "surround side" channels, and a low-range sub-woofer (the .1 part of 5.1). DTS stands for "Digital Theater Systems" and is the main competitor to Dolby. Dolby Digital is the more widely adopted technology and is part of the DVD standard, but DTS is widely found in home theater systems and is preferred by many audiophiles. Connections are made through a fiber optic cable that ends in a plug called a TosLink connector.

DVI-D

One of the problems with all of the preceding video connection formats is that they're all analog (with the exception of coax cable which can carry a digital signal). As increasing numbers of home media devices become digital, including TVs, you want the signal to stay in digital format, if it originates as digital and can be displayed as such. That's where the DVI-D (or Digital Visual Interface-Digital) comes in. It uses a computer-like cable with a familiar-looking 24-pin connector to link up devices such as DVD decks and HDTVs. Like component video, DVI-D is often teamed up with a fiber optic audio cable with TosLink connector to deliver CD-quality digital sound.

The "Tos" in TosLink refers to Toshiba, creators of the technology.

HDMI

Wires, wires, everywhere! Oh, if only there were one thin cable that could deliver the highest quality uncompressed digital images and sound, the back of my home media center wouldn't look like a gosh-darn weed farm! Hello High Definition Multimedia Interface! HDMI is the new standard, brought to you by the same corporate consortium that developed DVI. It promises to deliver digital audio and video on a single cable (see Figure 2.8). Imagine it: one cable from your DVR to your TV, one cable from your DVD deck, game console, and so on. Of course, with any new standard, HDMI will only stick if it's widely adopted. The good news is that consumer electronics giants such as Sony, Hitachi, Toshiba, and Philips are behind it. The first wave of HDMI-enabled devices was shown off at 2004's Consumer Electronics Show (CES). The HDMI cable terminates in something resembling a USB jack. The DirecTV HD TiVo has a HDMI connector for output to an HDMI-compliant display.

FIGURE 2.8
The HDMI cable and connector. Is this the cure for cable spaghetti?

Basic TiVo Troubleshooting

TiVos are known for their user-friendliness, for both setup and daily operation. But like any computer or consumer electronics device, problems can arise. What follows is a collection of the most common "challenges" one might encounter.

Hookup Troubleshooting

If you read through our Mini-Tutorial on A/V Tech, you shouldn't have too many problems at least understanding what should go where when hooking up your TiVo. The manuals that came with your TiVo describe most installation situations and problems you might encounter, but there are a few others worth mentioning.

- If you keep manually asking TiVo to make its daily call and it's still not downloading the TV guide data, don't worry. It could just be that your account has not been activated yet. It can take a few days (and even up to a week) before TiVo gets all of the information it needs from TiVo, Inc. (which is why you should register your account immediately after purchasing your unit).

- If your TiVo is having problems connecting to the TiVo servers, check to make sure that your RJ-11 cable is properly plugged into the modem socket on the TiVo and the phone wall jack. It should click when you plug it in. If it's still not connecting, hook a regular phone to the wall jack (using the same phone cable) to make sure there's a dial tone (and that the cable's not faulty). Try unplugging TiVo's power cable, waiting a few seconds, and plugging it back in again. This will reset the modem. You might also try turning off "dial tone detection" and "phone available detection" in the dialing prefix settings.

- If you have call waiting, it can interrupt TiVo's downloads. You can prevent this by adding the prefix *70,, (that would be Clear-7-0-Pause-Pause on your remote) in the Set Call Waiting Prefix menu item at TiVo Central -> TiVo Messages & Setup -> Settings -> Phone & Network Setup -> Edit Phone & Network Settings -> Phone Dialing Options (TiVo Central -> Messages & Setup -> Recorder & Phone Setup ->Phone Connection-> Change Dialing Options).

- If you're on a DirecTV DVR and you have a lot of telephone line noise, go to TiVo Central -> TiVo Messages & Setup -> Settings -> Phone & Network Setup -> Edit Phone & Network Settings -> Phone Dialing Options (TiVo Central -> Recorder & Phone Setup ->Phone Connection-> Change Dialing Options) and add ,#034 (Pause-Enter-0-3-4) to the Set Dial Prefix item. This causes the TiVo modem to try connecting at a lower transfer speed. This only works with DirecTiVo, not stand-alone units. If you need to slow the rate down even more, you can enter ,#019, or even further with ,#096. If you have excessive line noise, your first clue will be that your DirecTiVo has trouble making its daily calls. You can hear the noise yourself by picking up a telephone receiver and listening for static, pops, clicks, and so on as you're making calls. If your area suffers from line noise, you're likely aware of it already.

In some calling areas, the number to toggle off Call Waiting may be different. Check with your phone provider and enter the number given instead of "70").

Tip

In case you're wondering, it is okay to set your TiVo on its side. This can save some serious shelf space, especially if you have more than one DVR. Just make sure that there is space between (and behind) them to promote good air circulation, which will keep your TiVo(s) cool and happy.

Caution

Did you know that you can interfere with an audio or video signal by putting excess weight on A/V cables? If you use media carts/shelves/racks, make sure that you don't run over your cables with the caster wheels when you move your media center.

Common Problems

We thought it might be a good idea to run through some of the problems that may arise as you use your TiVo and how to address them.

- As you've undoubtedly heard, the first semi-serious question asked by computer tech support people is: Is it plugged in? In TiVo troubleshooting, one could ask a similar question: Did you unplug it and then plug it back in? For a number of TiVo ailments (freeze-ups, modem dialing problems, and more), a hard reboot like this serves as a quick cure.

- **Audio and Video are out of sync.** This happens periodically during normal operation. It is easily fixed by simply pausing whatever you're watching and then starting it up again. If this is a constant problem on a stand-alone TiVo, it could be that you have the video signal going from a sat receiver/cable box to TiVo, but the audio going directly to your TV or stereo. The audio *has* to enter the TiVo along with the video for them to be properly synced.

- If TiVo stops recording its Suggestions, try the following procedure:

  1. Turn Suggestions off by going to TiVo Central -> TiVo Messages & Setup -> Settings -> Preferences -> TiVo Suggestions (TiVo Central -> Messages & Setup -> My Preferences -> TiVo's Suggestions).

  2. Restart TiVo by going to TiVo Central -> TiVo Messages & Setup -> Settings -> Restart or Reset System -> Restart the TiVo DVR (TiVo Central -> Messages & Setup -> System Reset -> Restart the Recorder).

  3. Turn TiVo's Suggestions back on.

  4. Restart TiVo again.

  5. Make a manual daily call: TiVo Central -> TiVo Messages & Setup -> Settings -> Phone & Network Setup -> Edit Phone & Network Settings -> Connect to TiVo Service Now (TiVo Central -> Messages & Setup -> Recorder & Phone Setup -> Phone Connection -> Make Daily Call Now).

- If you turn your TV on and you see a blue screen where TiVo Central used to be, don't panic. First check to make sure that your cable box (if you have one) and VCR (if your TiVo's output is run to the VCR before being connected to the TV) are turned on. If there's a power outage (and you're not on a backup power supply), some cable boxes do not automatically reboot (a real drag if you lose power and you're at work or away on vacation). If that doesn't work, unplug TiVo for 10 seconds or so and plug it back in. Also: Make sure that the input control on your TV is set to the correct input (in this case, TiVo).

- If you still get a blue screen, try plugging your video source (cable or sat) directly into the TV to see if that gives you a picture. Often, especially after a bad storm, some channels may be too weak to constitute a signal. If you get the blue screen on only a few channels, this is likely the problem. If you get the blue screen after a storm, and you've done all of the above (as well as obviously checking all of your connections), wait a few hours (or call your cable or satellite provider to see if there are known service interruptions).

- If you start experiencing stuttering audio/video performance, where the sound/images freeze for a few seconds, you've got what are known to TiVo-types as "stopples." There can be several things wrong here, from the fairly benign to the far more malignant. One common reason is power spikes or fluctuations. You can deal with these by getting an uninterruptible power supply (see "Accessories" in Chapter 1), which will smooth out the power and stop the stopples. Also, check TiVo's internal temperature at TiVo Central -> TiVo Messages & Setup -> Settings -> System Information (TiVo Central -> Messages & Setup -> System Information). Scroll down to see the Internal Temperature entry. It should give the temperature and the status (which should read "Normal").

- If it's running hot (say, anything over 50 degrees F), first make sure that there's plenty of airspace around your TiVo. Some TiVo owners even raise their units up with plastic twist-off caps from soda bottles placed over each of TiVo's rubber feet (think of them as overshoes). This can give TiVo much more breathing space. If TiVo continues to run hot, you may have a blown cooling fan. Place your hand over the fan grill in the back. You should feel a slight breeze. If you don't, the fan is likely dead. This can easily be replaced. Parts vendors such as weaKnees.com sell new fans that can easily be replaced with a few screws. If it's not the fan, and the stopples continue, we hate to break it to you, but it could be a hard drive on death's doorstep. At the very least, you should record to VHS or DVD-R anything you want to keep, in case the drive suddenly tanks. To replace the drive, see our detailed instructions in Chapter 8, "Upgrading Hard Drives."

NOTE

Series 1 DirecTV DVRs do not have fan grills on the back panel. You have to put your hand underneath the TiVo and the airflow you can feel there will be slight even when the fan is functioning properly.

Tip

For more problems and solutions, check out the Weaknees Troubleshooting Guide (www.weaknees.com/repair.php) and the troubleshooting section of the TiVo FAQ (www.tivofaq.com).

Remote Control Issues

We'll get into all of the things you can do with your TiVo remote control (that we can discuss in a family tome) in Chapter 4, "Remote Control Freak." Here we'll only touch on problems related to setting up your remote control and common technical snags:

- If you're using a cable box or satellite receiver with a stand-alone TiVo, you're likely using TiVo's included IR blaster. This device sends the infrared remote control signals coming from TiVo's remote out of your TiVo, through a cable and then flashes them, via an IR emitter, in front of the IR receiver on your satellite or cable box.

- For most users, installing this system is simply a question of plugging the cable into the IR Out port on the back of TiVo and placing the blaster in front of the IR window on the sat/cable box. But depending on room conditions (lighting, reflections, proximity of devices), variations in cable boxes, and so on, there can sometimes be trouble with leaky IR signals messing up communication between TiVo and the cable box/sat receiver. To solve this problem, you need to build something known affectionately as a "fort," a little cardboard or thick cloth tent to enclose the IR blaster(s) and the cable box/sat receiver's IR window (see Figure 2.9). For information on building a fort/tent, see this TiVo.com troubleshooting page: customersupport.tivo.com/tivoknowbase/root/public/tv1069.htm.

FIGURE 2.9

An IR "fort" or "tent." Can be made of any material that is dark enough and that completely covers the IR window.

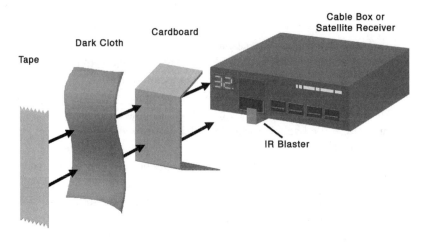

- Depending on the design of your cable box/sat receiver, it may be hard to see exactly where its IR window is and how big it is. It's usually covered by dark translucent plastic that's larger than the IR window itself. Knowing its exact size and location can help in placing the blaster or in building a fort (the fort should enclose the entire window). To see the actual window behind the plastic, shine a flashlight on it. You should be able to see the window inside and the lens of the IR receiver.

- If your TiVo IR blaster is constantly having trouble getting its point across to your cable/sat box, you may want to get a different type of blaster. The TiVo type sits in front of the IR window and beams its signal through the air. Other IR blasters have adhesive on them and are attached right over where the receiver's lens is (see Figure 2.10). You can get a blaster of this type at Radio Shack and online home electronics stores such as SmartHome.com. See the Appendix A, "Resources," for other sources.

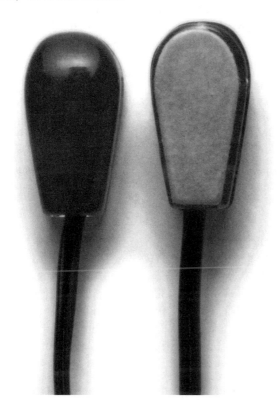

FIGURE 2.10
An adhesive-type
IR blaster.

- Your TiVo's IR blaster has two IR emitters. You can use both of them in front of the cable/sat box IR window or just use one (unless you need to operate a satellite receiver and cable box in tandem, in which case, you'd use one blaster on each device). If you use one, make sure the other one is hidden away behind your entertainment center, so that it doesn't send screwy IR signals all over your family room.

- If your blaster link from TiVo to your cable/sat box is causing an annoying delay in response time (for example, you change the channel on your remote and Simon Cowell has already liquefied the first contestant by the time the channel actually switches over to *American Idol*), you may want to change the control code. You can do this by going to TiVo Central -> TiVo Messages & Setup -> Settings -> TiVo DVR Setup -> Remote Control Setup (TiVo Central -> Messages & Setup -> Recorder & Phone Setup -> Cable/Satellite Box -> Cable Box Setup). Most cable/sat boxes have more than one control code listed in TiVo's control code libraries. Some will switch channels faster than others. Choose the fastest one that consistently changes the channels properly.

- If your blaster is consistently messing up sending channel changes to the cable/sat box, try switching to a slower control code. See the previous tip for accessing the control code menus. If all else fails, you can set your remote up to send a three-digit code (with a leading zero). You can also set it up to require a press of the Select button to send the code. This is useful if the cable/sat box insists on jumping the gun and starts heading off to channel 10 before you finish typing channel "101." These tweaks can be made in the Remote Control Setup (Cable Box Setup) menu.

Ganging TiVos

Some people get hit by the TiVo bug harder than others. Before they know it, one TiVo just isn't enough. It's dangerous once you realize that the cable signal coming into your house can be easily and cheaply split, or that a multiswitch is all that's needed to send the satellite signal to many receivers. All that luscious A/V bandwidth just being wasted, crammed into a single TiVo tuner card (or two). What you need is *ANOTHER* TiVo. Or two!

NOTE

Our esteemed tech editors point out that they've gotten calls from people who are unable to send a "6" to their box: 6, 16, 106, and so forth are all impossible to send. It seems that there was an issue with a change in the IR codes for a few mainstream cable boxes. TiVo addresses the issue here: http:// customersupport.tivo. com/tivoknowbase/ root/public/tv1552.htm.

How to Hook Up More Than One TiVo

The first thing that people ask when considering a second TiVo is: "Do I need to subscribe to a second TiVo service?" If you're using stand-alone TiVos on a cable service or Dish Network, the answer is, unfortunately, yes. You will have to pay another lifetime service fee for the second unit, or pay the $6.95/month. If you're buying a second Series 2 TiVo that you want to network for multi-room viewing, you'll have to buy and set up networking hardware (see Chapter 9). The good news here is that the networking service, the Home Media Feature, is now offered free-of-charge. If you're a DirecTV subscriber, you do not have to pay another fee. The $4.99/month covers as many TiVos as you can cram onto a multiswitch (and even that modest fee is waived if you have the Total Choice Premier package). You will, however, still have to pay a $4.99/month "receiver fee" for each DirecTV DVR or regular DirecTV receiver you add to your system.

If you have two TiVos connected to the same TV, you can program a Series 2 remote to recognize both of them (even if one of the TiVos is a Series 1). The Series 2 *Setup Guide* has the simple programming instructions. If you have two Series 1 machines (and two S1 remotes) in the same place, one remote is going to change channels on both TiVos. Not good. You can try orienting the two TiVo units and building little forts to shield the respective IR signals, but it's nearly impossible to isolate them (thanks in part to the fact that IR beams like to ricochet all over the place). Your best bet is to buy a Series 2 remote (which is completely backward compatible with Series 1) and program it with two separate IR channels. Or you can buy one of the universal remotes discussed in the "Accessories" section of Chapter 1 (and further discussed in Chapter 4). It is possible to program two separate Series 1 TiVo remotes so that each only controls one machine. It's not covered in the TiVo Viewer's Guide, but you can find details on how to do it at http://customersupport.tivo.com/tivoknowbase/root/public/tv1087.htm.

To split the signal on a stand-alone cable-connected TiVo, you need nothing more than a cable splitter and short lengths of coax cable for each output (see "Accessories," Chapter 1). For a DirecTV account (using either a stand-alone or DirecTiVo), you need nothing more than a multiswitch with the number of outputs for the number of TiVo inputs you desire and short lengths of coax cable for each multiswitch output. If you have a dual or triple-LNB converter on your DirecTV dish, but only one coax coming from it, you'll need to run a second line from the LNB. This can be a

NOTE

The Series 2 TiVo remote is not able to control either Sony-branded TiVos or the Toshiba DVD/TiVo combo units.

NOTE

While it's easy and cheap to split a cable service, the one thing you won't get on multiple lines is scrambled channels. If you want to get premium channels on more than one cable input, you'll have to get (and pay for) additional cable boxes.

pain, depending on how accessible your dish is, how comfortable you are scampering around on the roof, and so on.

A DVR by Any Other Name...

If you want to have more than one DVR but don't want to have to pay two monthly or lifetime TiVo subscriptions, consider a first-generation ReplayTV as your second recorder. ReplayTV also requires a subscription now, but early models accessed a free programming guide. Look for models in the 2000, 3000, and 4000 series. From models 4500 and higher, a service activation fee is required. You can get used units on eBay for under $150. One great feature of the RTV is that its "live" TV buffer is as big as the available recording space left on the hard drive, so you can pause live TV for hours.

Gareth On...

My old ReplayTV came in really handy during the recent Mars rover missions. NASA TV has hours with nothing on, followed by some live coverage and a few repeating segments, followed by a whole lotta nothin'. I was able to put the Replay on pause in the morning, then fast-forward during my lunch break, pause it again, fast-forward after dinner, and so forth. I never missed anything interesting.

Now the Fun Can Start...

In this chapter we took a look at TiVo hardware and software, how TiVo integrates into your home media system, and some common hookup and operation problems. For the next chapter, we recommend that you light up an expensive cigar, schedule a few power lunches, and sign up for some Tai Bo classes, 'cause you're about to become your very own TV programming executive, using the tools of TiVo to create the network of your dreams (or at least what you can stitch together from the cadaverous content you can drag into your house).

Chapter 3

DIY Network Programming

Wrapping your noggin around all of the things that TiVo can do is only the first step. The true "ah-ha" moment comes when you realize that TiVo is really like a search engine for your television. It constantly scans the TV guide listings for the upcoming two weeks, looking for the shows or keyword search strings that you've entered. It will then show you its search results, and/or record programs based on your choices (or what it thinks you'll like based on previous choices). Over time, as you get smarter about using TiVo, and TiVo gets smarter about understanding what you like, you'll start seeing an impressive list of shows in TiVo's Now Playing directory. It's kind of like Fantasy Baseball or Football, where gamers get to assemble their ultimate teams based on all available real-world players. With TiVo, you get to play Fantasy TV Network Executive, programming your own network with all of the available TV content. And what's so positively 21st century is that you not only have unprecedented control over what shows you watch and when, you also have control over how you move around *inside* of these shows.

Unless otherwise noted, all of the tips, tricks, and hacks in this chapter are Level 1.

TiVo Viewing Habits

Perhaps the greatest innovation of the digital video recorder is the ability to transcend the strict clock structure of real-time TV programming, offering the ultimate in what has been dubbed "time-shifting" or "time-shift viewing." Sure, people have been doing this for years with the VCR (for example, taping *The Late Show* at 11:30 p.m. and watching it over breakfast the next morning), but DVRs have taken this ability to a whole new level, with ease of recording and deleting, and greater control over the programs being recorded. This digital functionality is making time-shift viewing increasingly the norm. In this section, we'll look at some of the ways in which you can use your TiVo in creative ways to have a more enjoyable and time-saving TV experience.

Commercial Skipping

Ah...the joys of the commercial skip! Not since the advent of the mute button has a TV development been so welcomed by viewers (and so hated by advertisers). If you're watching a recorded program (or a live signal that's been paused for a few minutes), you can skip over the commercials when you get to them. The official way to do this is to use the Forward/Fast Forward button on your remote. There are three fast-forward speeds (3x, 20x, and 60x), so a quick triple-click of the Forward button will race you through the commercial block. The little green triangles on the TiVo Status Bar show you which FF mode you're in. When you see your program again on the screen, and press Play (or the FF a fourth time), the TiVo software does something called "overshoot correction" (a.k.a. "auto-correct"), an automatic rewind so that the 20x or 60x FF won't cause you to overshoot the beginning of show (the reflexes of even the most seasoned channel jockeys among us are not *that* fast). Using the Forward button and being quick on the Peanut, it'll take you only about five seconds to get through a 120-second commercial break.

But there's even a quicker way. All Series 1 and Series 2 TiVos (with the exception of Toshiba DVD/TiVo units) have an undocumented 30-second skip feature. This feature can be easily enabled using one of the Select-Play-Select (SPS) remote control tricks. We'll cover these remote hacks in more detail in Chapter 4, "Remote Control Freak," and Chapter 5, "I'm Your Backdoor Code," but in the meantime, here's how to enable the 30-second skip:

1. Start playing back a program that you've recorded.
2. Press the following sequence on your TiVo remote:

NOTE

You can change the values of the three fast-forward speeds that your TiVo uses. We'll discuss how to do this in Chapter 5, "I'm Your Backdoor Code."

3. Select-Play-Select-3-0-Select

4. Listen for the three system chimes (a.k.a. "dings") that tell you this feature has been enabled.

5. Try out the skip by pressing the Advance button (→|) on your remote. It should skip through the recording by 30-second jumps.

By enabling this feature, you will no longer be able to use the Advance button to skip to the end of a program, but that may not be a feature too many people will miss. The 30-second skip mode will remain in effect until you restart your TiVo (in which case, you'll have to redo the previous procedure) or until you enter the code again.

With the 30-second enabled, you can leap over drab ads in a single bound...okay, so it actually takes several bounds (clicks of the Advance button), but you get the idea. The 30-second skip is also handy when watching sporting events, where you can skip from play-to-play (leaping over the sometimes slow setups). The period between a tackle and the next snap in a football game and between pitches in baseball is often nearly perfectly attuned to the 30-second skip.

Gareth On...

As you might imagine, the networks and their advertisers are not happy about viewers being able to skip over commercials. The networks sued the makers of ReplayTV when they introduced a CommercialAdvance feature that allowed viewers to jump blocks of commercials altogether. It is probably this fear of litigation that has made TiVo, Inc. keep their 30-second skip mode an unofficial feature. One can hope that knowing viewers have this choice will only "inspire" advertisers to make more commercials that are actually worth watching. Let's face it, regardless of how anti-consumerist you profess to be, you likely still watch and enjoy commercials that are clever, funny, cinematic, and that don't insult your intelligence. Here's to seeing more of those. Go ahead, Madison Avenue, try and make me not dismiss you with a few well-placed clicks on my remote.

Must-Skim TV

In Raffi Krikorian's book *TiVo Hacks* (O'Reilly), he coined the term "must-skim TV" for those types of shows where you don't really need to watch the entire program to get the best of what it has to offer. If you're a fair-weather baseball fan (or have the attention span of a hummingbird), you might already watch the late-night highlight version of your home team's games (where the game is edited down only to the hits, runs, outs, and spectacular plays). TiVo allows you to create your own on-the-fly highlight show with any sporting event, home improvement program, reality show, or any other programming that may have a lot of setup time or segments that drag. When TiVo, Inc. coined their slogan "TV your way," they probably were thinking more about the ability to record at any time, watch at any time, and pause at any time when you needed to go to the can. They probably didn't realize to what extent TiVo users would actually change how they consumed the shows themselves. One can imagine that as DVRs become more common and time-shift viewing, program skimming, and other digital TV viewing behaviors become the norm, programming might actually change to reflect this.

10-FF40-10 Solution

One method of must-skim viewing offered is called the "10-FF40-10 solution." Many one-hour format reality shows, home shows, makeover shows, and similar programs rely on a tried 'n' true formula. The first 10 minutes or so of the show are devoted to the setup: introducing the characters, the challenges, the potential conflicts, and so forth. The next 40 are spent teasing out what was presented in the first 10 (fighting between characters, attempts at meeting the given objective, turning the pile of junk into the racecar, and so on). The last 10 minutes constitute "the reveal" (the bedroom wallpapered in wheatgrass, the limo turned into a fire truck, the ugly duckling nipped and tucked to reveal a swan). Applying the 10-FF40-10 solution yourself is easy. You simply record the program, watch the first 10 minutes, fast-forward through the middle 40 (stopping to watch anything that looks particularly interesting), and then watch the last 10. You'll be amazed how many shows you can watch this way and still feel like you're getting a satisfying viewing experience.

Half-n-Half Viewing

Even though you don't *have* to watch TV in real-time anymore (and you'll do less and less of it as you become more of a TiVo power user), there may be certain favorite shows, movie premiers, and sporting events that you want to watch as they happen (or at least close to it). Sure you could watch the *Super Bowl* or the *Academy Awards* later on in the evening or the next day, but it just wouldn't be the same. Such events have a sort of communal imperative. And who wants to not know what's going on when everybody at work is talking about a hysterical *Daily Show* skit that's sitting unwatched on your TiVo's hard drive? But watching anything in real-time means you sacrifice your control over the TV signal (what TiVo is all about). So, if you're planning on watching a half-hour show, start recording it (or just put the live feed on Pause when the show starts, if you don't care to record), let it run for 15 minutes or so (read a book, wrestle the cat, annoy your housemates) and then start to watch. This will get enough of the program written to the hard drive (or stored in TiVo's live TV buffer), so that you can then skip over all the commercials and still be done with the show on the half-hour. For an hour long show, wait about a half hour before starting. For really long special events, like the *Super Bowl*, you might want to delay viewing by a whole hour, or even more if you'd like to fast-forward your way through the Shania Twain and Sting tribute to the Captain and Tennille half-time spectacular. Of course, TiVo only stores up to 30 minutes of "live" TV, so if you are going to wait longer than that, you'll have to record the program, not just pause it.

Instant Replay (Not Just for Sports)

While we're talking about the *Super Bowl*, we should mention one of the obvious features of TiVo, the 8-second Instant Replay button. The slow-motion replay revolutionized sports broadcasting, allowing viewers to get another look at controversial plays and calls by officials. Digital video recorders give you the power to do this whenever you'd like. For sports fans, this is obviously great, but its use goes far beyond that. Forgot the final *Jeopardy* category? Hit the Instant Replay button a few times to find out. Did President Bush really just hold out his right hand while referring to his left and then his left while referring to his right? Instant Replay confirms that you just saw what you thought you saw. Hear a statistic on the evening news you want to write down? Instant Replay to the rescue. (Did you notice how we tactfully avoided mentioning the Janet Jackson/Justin Timberlake *Super Bowl* unpleasantries?)

Tip
If you happen to have something scheduled to record while you're pausing live TV, TiVo may automatically change channels while you're away and you'll lose the content saved to the buffer. It's usually better to just record whatever you really want to watch to avoid this problem.

Gareth On...
The TiVo has been a real boon to my job as editor of the "Jargon Watch" column in *Wired*. I'm always on the hunt for the latest jargon, slang, and technical and science terms. Sometimes a word or phrase will go by, barely noticed, on the evening

news, a talk show, MTV, and so forth. I'll hit Instant Replay to hear what I just missed. If the word is also defined, I can hit Instant Replay (and Back) over and over until I have the definition written down verbatim. Before TiVo, I'd have to jot down the word and then call the network and try to track down the reference. So, the DVR has saved me huge amounts of time.

Slow-Motion

Going hand and hand with the Instant Replay button is the Slow (a.k.a. slow-mo) button, which allows you to slow the video down to 1/4x speed. Again, this is thought of as largely a sports-friendly feature, but it can come in handy elsewhere. For movie fanatics, especially sci-fi, fantasy, and action fans, slow-motion offers a great way of seeing every last frame of a movie trailer. Ads for blockbusters are often crammed with action sequences, sometimes teasing the viewer with a special effects shot, a peak at a monster, or a shot of a spectacular vista that might only be a few frames long. In the trailer for *Lord of the Rings: The Fellowship of the Ring*, the Moria cave troll was only onscreen for a few seconds. Use of the Instant Replay and Slow buttons revealed what was barely seen at full speed. For *The Two Towers*, Treebeard was similarly teased (and revealed via TiVo).

Trying to figure out a dance step, an exercise routine, or a bit of handiwork that goes by too fast onscreen to figure out? You can use the Instant Replay, Slow, and Back buttons to your heart's content.

And then there's...let's call it "perv-mo." Want to draw out Halle Berry's jaw-dropping entrance on *The Tonight Show* as long as possible? Well, you should be ashamed of yourself. We would never recommend ogling the beautiful people at reduced frame rates. That's just...sad.

Fun at the Coliseum (Thumbs Up or Thumbs Down?)

One of the most innovative, controversial, and misunderstood TiVo technologies is the "TiVo Suggestions" feature. On the TiVo remote are two special buttons, a thumb pointing up (colored green on most remotes) and one pointing down (colored red on most remotes). As you watch live TV, record programs, and scan programs listed in the Guide, Now Playing, and elsewhere, you can tell TiVo which shows you like and which you

NOTE

It turns out that "perv-mo" viewing may be more prevalent than even we thought. After the Janet Jackson/Justin Timberlake "wardrobe malfunction" at the 2004 *Super Bowl*, TiVo, Inc. was widely reported in the news saying that their daily collected anonymous viewer data had shown that these few seconds were the most replayed since the company started keeping track of such data in 2000.

Leo Laporte's Guide to TiVO

Fun at the Coliseum (Thumbs Up or Thumbs Down?)   Chapter 3

don't by giving them the proverbial thumbs up or thumbs down. You can actually give up to three thumbs up or three thumbs down to communicate your level of interest (or not) in a program. The TiVo software uses these "Thumb Ratings" to suggest (and record) other programs it thinks you might like when there's free space on your hard drive. TiVo, of course, always gives preference to your recording desires and only records shows from its TiVo Suggestions list when there's free space (see Figure 3.1).

![TiVo Suggestions screen showing: Monster House Mon 4/12; Trauma: Life in the ER Mon 4/12; The Osbournes Tue 4/13; Animal Precinct Mon 4/12; Starting Over Tue 4/13; Fox Report Sun 4/11; The NewsHour With Jim Lehrer Mon 4/12; NBS 24-7 Tue 4/13]

FIGURE 3.1

The TiVo Suggestions List.

NOTE

We associate the thumbs up and thumbs down gestures with Roman emperors who would allegedly decide the fate of Coliseum gladiators by giving one of these signals. The problem is that historians have no proof that thumbs up actually meant spare him and thumbs down meant that the lion eats tonight (or whatever gruesome fate was in store). We've sort of decided by default which means good and which means bad because we tend to associate up with good things (heaven) and down with bad (hell).

As is often the case with high-technology, users of TiVo ascribe way too much intelligence to this function, thinking that TiVo, Inc. has developed some H.A.L.-like artificial intelligence that lives inside your DVR (or in some ominously large server farm someplace), constantly mulling over your viewing habits, trying to decide whether you only like dating shows with a hot tub segment or also ones where the contestants have to diss each other mercilessly to become the last dater standing. This technology is also controversial because there is an "upstream component;" in other words, some of your viewing data gets sent back to TiVo, Inc.'s central computers. There have been frequent outcries of invasion of privacy.

It's really not as exciting as all that. The TiVo Suggestions feature (sometimes referred to as the "suggestion engine") simply keeps track of show categories that you like (or dislike) and bases its choices for its own recording behavior on that. So, if you've given three thumbs up to two different makeover shows, for instance, given some free space on your hard drive, TiVo might record a third such program. It's really not sophisticated enough to discern likes and dislikes within a given show category. If you've given thumbs up to two different motorcycle-building shows, but one thumb down to a car building show, TiVo is still likely to record a second car building program if its stored keywords (the information that the suggestion engine uses to make matches) includes matches between the two types of shows (such as "how to").

Here are some tips for how to more effectively use the TiVo Suggestions feature:

- Don't be tempted to overuse the Thumbs Up/Thumbs Down buttons. It may be fun when you first get your TiVo, but you really don't have to sit there voting on every show in TiVo's various program lists. Keep in mind that every time you record a program, TiVo considers that a 1-thumb "vote" for it.

- To get TiVo started, give Thumbs Up to a few programs you really like. Give two thumbs to shows you especially like. Keep in mind that TiVo really thinks in terms of categories more than actual program content, so if you like reality shows, give Thumbs Up to a few and TiVo will likely start recording others. Most experienced TiVo users caution against the use of three thumbs. Give three thumbs to a couple of reality shows, and before you know it, you may have a *Surreal Life* marathon soiling your hard drive.

- Use Thumbs Down sparingly. If you don't like a category of show (say cop dramas), it's okay to give one or two thumbs down. Again, think in terms of genres (show categories). By "voting" negative on one such show (especially with more than one thumb), it will likely not record anything in the genre. Also, the suggestion engine doesn't just look at the show category, it also looks at actors and directors, so be careful about giving thumbs down to something you don't like if it features an actor, for instance, that you do. So, if you're a big Johnny Depp fan, but in your anti-cop-drama fervor, you give a couple of Thumbs Down to reruns of *21 Jump Street*, TiVo may not record another program starring Johnny Depp.

Leo Laporte's Guide to TiVO

Fun at the Coliseum (Thumbs Up or Thumbs Down?)   Chapter 3

- In general, it's best to vote far more frequently for what you *do* like. A few well-placed Thumbs Up to indicate your interest in a genre, say two thumbs for *Star Trek Enterprise*, is likely to also score you reruns of *Voyager*, *Deep Space 9*, and *Star Trek: Next Generation*, and also the *Battlestar Galactica* miniseries as well. And what geek wouldn't be happy with that? Okay, forget we brought up *Voyager* (just don't vote your conscience and give it Thumbs Down—that's what the "Delete Now" command is for).

- If you've scheduled a show to be recorded and then you see another show on at the same time that you like, give it a Thumbs Up. If the show is rerun, TiVo might record it. This, of course, is only worth doing on channels such as TLC, Discovery, Food Network, and others that frequently run new programming in multiple timeslots.

Questions over how the suggestion engine works, *where* it works, and what gets sent back to the TiVo Broadcast Center are frequently raised by TiVo users, especially newbies, in online forums. Most of the work is actually done within your TiVo. The TiVo software keeps track of your yay and nay thumb ratings (and what you've recorded) and correlates this information to make further suggestions (and "TiVo Suggestions" recordings). Where some users start to get fidgety is in knowing that this data heads upstream back to TiVo, Inc. during TiVo's daily call. What gets sent back is extremely detailed viewing behavior (right down to each click of your remote control), but none of this is attached to your personal TiVo account information (only to your ZIP code). TiVo, Inc. calls this "Anonymous User Information" and insists that it is in no way linked with your TiVo's serial number or any other specific user account information. Upstream viewing information is used, among other things, for correlating viewer preferences. So, TiVo, Inc.'s servers might say: Hey, look at this, a bunch of people who watch *Monster Garage* also like *Mythbusters*. These shows are not in the same show category, but they likely share an overlap in audience. So the software on TiVo Inc.'s end will change the information in every user's TiVo Suggestions database, so that if you start recording one of these shows, TiVo might record the other. At least it works something like this. Exactly how the suggestion engine works is something of a mystery, but TiVo, Inc. is clear that the viewing habits of specific TiVo households are not monitored in any way. They say that they also use the behavioral information (exactly how you're using the remote control) to better design

Tip

Don't forget, TiVo Suggestions is just one way of getting TiVo to record programs that you might like. There are also WishLists where you can specify categories, titles, actors, and so on for TiVo to be on the lookout for. See the WishLists section later in this chapter.

Tip

If you are interested in knowing more about TiVo's privacy policy and how and what it collects in terms of viewing data, check out the files on its Privacy Policy page (www.tivo.com/5.11.asp). The White Paper stored there goes into some detail about TiVo's privacy policies, data encryption methods, and how it uses collected viewing data.

Tip

If you want to completely put all of this silliness behind you, it's as easy as turning off the Suggestions feature. This is done in the Settings section of TiVo Messages & Setup.

future TiVo hardware and software. And, not surprisingly, they "share" this collected viewing information (a demographer's and advertiser's dream) with their partners (like Nielsen) to better target advertising, to instantly know what people have watched, and so forth. If this type of down-to-the-click monitoring (however anonymous) gives you a case of the Orwellian creeps, you can ask to opt out of such data collection by calling TiVo, Inc.

"My TiVo Thinks I'm Gay" (and Other Funny TiVo Suggestions Tales)

It's become something of an urban legend. Someone gets a TiVo, watches a few programs, plays with the Thumbs Up/Thumbs Down buttons, and before they know it, they're having to explain to their spouse why their new digital video recorder is filled up with dating shows, a *Queer Eye for the Straight Guy* marathon, and some softcore porn. This probably all got started with the publishing in the *Wall Street Journal* in 2002 of a piece by Jeffrey Zaslow titled "Oh No! My TiVo Thinks I'm Gay." The piece contained various humorous stories of TiVos recording shows of a certain genre and their owners trying to convince TiVo they were not who TiVo thought they were by giving many Thumbs Up to shows in other genres. In the example of the article's title, a TiVo owner started to fear his TiVo thought he was gay (recording many of what he considered gay-themed programs), so he started giving Thumbs Up to lots of "guy stuff," and before he knew it, his TiVo had him pegged as a crazed Nazi fan, recording the endless parade of documentaries and biographies of Hitler and his henchmen which the History Channel never seems to run out of. This same incident also became a subplot on *King of Queens*, securing the "My TiVo thinks I'm Gay" idea within popular culture. Other TV shows have run similar themes (the short-lived *Mind of the Married Man* on HBO had an almost identical plot line). Conan O'Brien has told the story several times on *Late Night* about getting a TiVo, hooking it up, playing with the buttons on his remote, and watching a few episodes of *G-String Divas* on HBO (that just *happened* to be on). Work took him away from TV-viewing for a few days, and when he and his wife finally sat down to watch TV, he had some explaining to do when he found his hard drive filled with softcore porn.

Leo Laporte's Guide to TiVO

Fun at the Coliseum (Thumbs Up or Thumbs Down?)   Chapter 3

Of course, most of these stories are silly. If you're imagining that your TiVo is *thinking* anything, you've got bigger problems than trying to convince it of your sexual preference. If your TiVo starts to record too much of one genre, give Thumbs Up to a few programs in other categories (don't overdo it). Since most TiVos are likely used by more than one viewer, each with different preferences, the TiVo Suggestions will likely be from a diversity of genres. TiVo may skew heavily toward one type of programming or another in the beginning, but over time, it should settle into offering enough desirable content to keep you (and other family members) happy.

And then there's the woeful tale: "My TiVo thinks I'm Hispanic (or Indian or Arab or...)!" We've heard stories about people's TiVos filling up with shows from Telemundo and other Spanish-speaking channels because they've given thumbs up to the Latin Grammys or other similar shows on English-speaking channels. This is easily corrected: If you don't speak Spanish and don't want all-Spanish channels (c'mon who doesn't like Mexican soaps and ribald game shows?), or other foreign language channels, simply remove them from your channel lineup altogether (see Figure 3.2). Here's how this is done:

1. From TiVo Central, go to TiVo Messages & Setup -> Settings -> Preferences -> Customize Channels (Messages & Setup -> Settings -> My Preferences -> Customize Channels).

2. From here, select Channels You Receive. (BTW: On TiVo Series 1 and Series 2 DirecTV DVRs, there is no Settings submenu; you go right from Messages & Setup to My Preferences.)

3. Now simply scroll through the channel list and deselect (by hitting the Select button to uncheck them) any channels you don't want, and TiVo will no longer consider anything on those channels when recording suggestions. Obviously this can be done for any type of programming. For instance, Gareth hates animals (well maybe *hate's* too strong a word), so he could easily nuke *Animal Planet* (if his son would let him). By removing all of the channels you don't actually watch, you not only prevent content from them being recorded, it also saves you time when scrolling through the Guide listings. Take *that* Home Shopping Network and CSPAN2!

NOTE

In discussing TiVo menus throughout this book, we've done our best to point out differences between series and operating systems. Exactly how the menus appear has everything to do with which version of the OS you have on your machine (and whether it's a standalone, DirecTV DVR, or a DVD/TiVo combo model). At a certain point, it becomes too confusing to point out every minor difference in menu appearance. Most of the differences are minor (for example, "Now Showing on TiVo" on Series 2 standalone versus "Now Showing" on Series 1).

FIGURE 3.2

Customizing your
channel lineup.

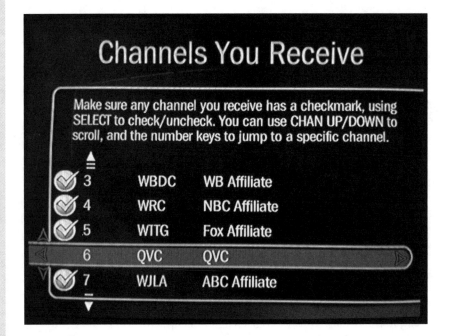

Tip

Grown-ups aren't the
only ones who *love* the
stand-alone TiVo remote
control ("The Peanut").
Little kids are drawn to
the cute shape of the
remote, the big colorful
thumbs, and the car-
toony "TiVoGuy" button
at the top. A few min-
utes of the neighbor
kids playing "What does
this button do?" with
your remote and your
carefully crafted Thumb
Ratings can be ruined.
Keep this in mind, and
keep your Peanut out of
reach of button-crazed
bambinos.

Thumbs Up for iPreview/TiVoMatic

One other use for the Thumbs Up button is called iPreview (previously
known as "TiVoMatic"), which is the ability to automatically enter the
Record Options screen with the press of the Thumbs Up button during a
commercial or show preview. If you're watching a commercial for an
upcoming program and you see an ovoid box in the upper right corner of
the screen with the Thumbs Up icon on it, pressing this icon on your
remote will take you to the Record screen and allow you to set this
upcoming show to record. When you see this iPreview icon, pressing
Select will work as well (see Figure 3.3).

FIGURE 3.3

The iPreview icon for
an upcoming show.

IPreview is also used in the "exclusive" preview programming that TiVo offers, such as through their partnership with TVGuide. The weekly *TV Guide Insider Picks* program (which shows up in Showcases every Monday) uses iPreview. TiVo, Inc. was hoping that more networks would be using this technology by now, but it does seem to finally be spreading. Eventually all previews for upcoming shows may offer this built-in easy recording feature. One can also imagine that advertisers might want to get in on the action too. Special ad content already shows up in TiVo Central and in Showcases, with offers to enter contests, send you product brochures, and so forth when you hit the Select button (in which case, you're agreeing to let your account information at TiVo, Inc. be accessed to fetch your address info). It seems only a matter of time before this type of "interactivity" comes to regular TV commercials where a press of the Thumbs Up is all you'll need to get "free" stuff from advertisers.

Gareth On...

When I spoke at NATPE in 2001 about TV and the Internet (see introduction) and told the TV execs I never watched commercials now that I had a DVR, I got a bizarre reaction from two of them. They came up to me after the talk, assured me that they knew all about DVRs and the future of TV advertising, and that it could all be summed up in one word: "coupons." Huh? "Here's how it'd work," said one confident exec. "You're watching TV through your TiVo and you decide to skip the commercials. All digital recorders would have a small built-in spool-printer, and for the commercials that you skip—maybe all of them— coupons would be printed out, and lottery-like tickets and stuff." I looked at him in disbelief and said, "Well, I just wouldn't keep paper in my printer." He thought quickly and added: "The recorder could be designed to not work without it." I thought about this conversation when I started to see TiVo pushing contests, brochures, and other ad-related "goodies" on TiVo Central. I thought this was a fine, non-invasive way of alternative advertising via TiVo. But something as obnoxious (maybe more so) is in the works as I write this. Advertisers and TV execs are bandying about the term "TiVo-proofing" to refer to ads actually embedded in shows and ads that pop up ON TOP OF shows. Please make it stop!!

Tip

The iPreview feature works in a recorded program or in live TV, even if the iPreview icon goes away and you have to back up the show to find it again. The iPreview code is actually embedded in the TV signal.

Tip

If you want the iPreview icon to go away during a show preview or commercial, just hit the Clear button on your remote. The Clear button can always be used to dismiss any information that's laid over the TV programming (Guide data, the channel banner, status bar, and so on).

WishLists, Advanced and Otherwise

One of the most powerful features of TiVo is its WishList capability (see Figure 3.4). Here you move beyond specific programs you know you want to record, and shows that TiVo thinks you might like, to creating search-based recording requests on show and movie titles, actors, directors, categories, and keywords. With these WishLists stored in the TiVo software, your TiVo will continue to look for matches and will record anything that fits your list criteria (for WishList where you've requested auto-recording).

FIGURE 3.4

The regular TiVo WishList screen.

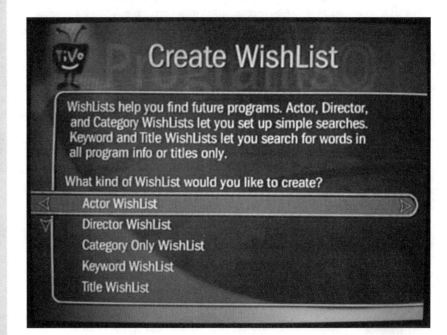

We won't go into the basics of creating and maintaining WishLists here; you can find that information in your *TiVo Viewer's Guide*. We'll only cover a few tips and tricks you may not know about.

- Think like an Internet search engine when you're creating your keyword-heavy WishLists. Try to guess which words and phrases will appear in show descriptions (pay attention to show descriptions as you use your TiVo to see how shows you like are usually described). As with most search engines, WishLists are very literal, so you'll get back good "hits" based on well-crafted search strings.

- Use the categories/subcategories in WishLists. Here's an example: The booted off *Survivor* cast members usually make the talk show rounds the day after their torch is extinguished for the last time. If you wanted to catch these appearances, and you entered in *Survivor* as a Keyword WishList, you'd scoop up everything on TV that has that word in the program title or description. By creating a Keyword WishList for the word "Survivor" and *then* choosing a program category "Talk Show" (which you are offered after you've created the keyword list), you'll get only talk shows in which the word "Survivor" appears in the show description. You may end up with a few shark bite and avalanche survivor segments on the *Today Show*, but you'll also get to see every appearance of what David Letterman likes to call "the parade of *Survivor* losers."

- Don't forget the special-use buttons when creating your keyword search strings in a WishList text-entry box: The Pause button on your remote is used for creating quotation marks (to constrain a search phrase), the Forward button enters a space, the Back button is used to delete characters one at a time, and the Clear button deletes everything in the box. The Slow button will create a "wildcard" asterisk (*). If you're a computer user (wait, who isn't a computer user at this point?), you're probably familiar with the use of the asterisk wildcard to find everything after a partial word (for example, *every** would find *everything, everybody, everywhere*, and so forth). Creative use of this wildcard can yield some interesting results. If you're an auto, racing, motorcycle nut, *moto** will hunt down *motocross, motorcycle, motorboat, Motorweek, MotoWorld, motor sports, motor racing*, and of course, the sledgehammered song stylings of hard rock anti-heroes *Motorhead*.

- Remember that hyphens (-), colons (:), periods (.) and slashes (/) are not used in search strings. If they're in a show title or keyword description, just enter a space where these characters would normally go. For apostrophes (') and ampersands (&), close up the space (the *11 O'Clock News* becomes *11 OCLOCK NEWS*).

- TiVo prioritizes what it's going to record next, working from your Season Pass Manager list, which includes auto-record WishList items. If there's a conflict, TiVo will go with what's higher on the list, *if* a WishList and regular Season Pass item conflict with each other. So, if you have a Season Pass for *Alias*, but have also created a Director WishList for Tim Burton movies, and *Alias* is lower in your SP queue, TiVo's going to record that *Edward Scissorhands* showing over your beloved *Alias*. To avoid this, make sure that your most desired programs are always at the top of your Season Pass queue.

- If you're big on movie premieres, preview shows, and TV pilots, create Keyword WishLists for these words ("premiere," "preview," and "pilot").

- Don't forget to set up keyword lists for all of your interests and hobbies. However obscure they are (model railroading, Hummel figurine collecting, Japanese gardens, sock puppetry). There are *lots* of channels these days. Eventually, TiVo may find a program that has what you're looking for.

- You're on the phone talking to someone, yammering on about films, and they say "Oh my God, I can't believe you've never seen <name of film goes here>!" Tell him he's a pretentious snob, hang up, and then make a Title WishList for the film in question. If it shows up on TV, it'll show up in TiVo. And then the next time you're on the phone with a different friend, you'll get to say, "Oh my God, you cultural wasteland. I can't believe you've never seen <name of film goes here>!"

- If there's a program that you're just crazy about and you don't want to miss it or anything associated with it, it's best to create an auto-record Title WishList rather than a Season Pass. For instance, if you had a Season Pass for *Survivor*, you'd get all of the regularly recorded episodes on CBS, but miss the *Survivor* MTV special. This feature becomes a "bug" if you only want first-run programs. For instance, if you create a Title WishList for *NYPD Blue*, it will record both the new episodes on ABC and the Caruso-era re-runs on FX.

- One of the great uses of Keyword WishLists is for recording performances by bands that you like. Create a WishList for each artist, and wherever they appear on TV (if they're listed in the show description), TiVo will show them in your WishList queue (or auto-record them if requested).

Enabling Advanced WishLists

WishLists are a wonderful TiVo feature, but they have their limitations. What if you want to search for a certain director AND a particular actor in a particular genre? With regular WishLists you can't do this, but TiVo has an undocumented feature called Advanced WishLists. Turning on this feature involves either a few carefully entered codes or a deep, slightly harrowing spelunk into the heart of your TiVo operating system, depending on which OS version you have.

Tip

All TiVo program listings include the first-run date of the shows. You can use wildcards on the dates to search for (or record) programming from a particular era. Let's say you're into suspense films from the 1950s. To find any that are scheduled, you would create a Keyword WishList for *195** under the Category *Movies* and the sub-category *Suspense*.

The first thing you'll need to do to activate Advanced WishLists is to enable what's called TiVo's "Backdoors" or "Backdoor Mode." How to do this is discussed in detail in Chapter 5, "I'm Your Backdoor Code." Skip ahead to that chapter and return here when backdoors are enabled. The "secret" codes for enabling backdoors are known for TiVo operating systems up to version 3.0 and are printed in Chapter 5. If your TiVo OS is 3.1 or higher (as with a Series 2), you've unfortunately got a lot of hardware and software hacking to do to unearth TiVo's hidden treasures. We won't be covering this procedure explicitly in this book, but we'll point you to the appropriate resources in Chapter 5.

Once you have backdoors enabled, to turn on Advanced WishLists, all you have to do is go to the regular WishLists feature: TiVo Central -> Programs to Record -> Search Using WishLists, select Create New WishList, and then press 0 on your remote. You will be taken to the Advanced WishLists screen (see Figure 3.5).

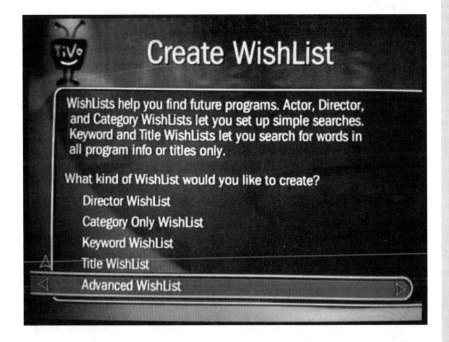

FIGURE 3.5
The Advanced WishList screen.

Caution

A little Que lawyer has just popped up on our shoulder to remind us to warn you of the dangers of traipsing around where you don't belong inside TiVo's sensitive bits. To be 100% safe, you really should do a backup of your TiVo software before cavorting about in the Node Navigator. If you don't, and your TiVo suddenly becomes a high-tech boat anchor, please don't send us threatening email.

Permanently Enabling Advanced WishLists

With backdoors enabled, you can always access Advanced WishLists by hitting "0" from inside the WishLists feature, but there's also a way of permanently turning this advanced feature on. This involves accessing something called TiVo's Node Navigator. The Node Navigator is a part of TiVo's software that you were never meant to see or mess with. Basically it's sort of like a backstage entrance to all of the menus in TiVo's software. Unfortunately, these back entrances are not labeled; they're simply a list of numbers. Mucking around in them can be extremely dangerous, so unless you have a complete backup of your TiVo software (see Chapter 18, "TiVo Utilities" for details), you want to be extremely cautious. If you are careful and follow these instructions to the letter, you should be okay.

1. To access the Node Navigator (after backdoors are enabled), press the following sequence on your remote control:

2. Clear -> Enter -> Clear -> 6

3. Once you see the Node Navigator menu (see Figure 3.6), scroll through the numbered list to item number 30. Press Select.

FIGURE 3.6

What the Node Navigator looks like.

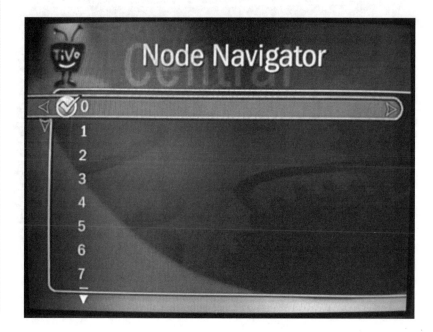

4. You are now looking at the Node Navigator's WishList Options menu (see Figure 3.7). Select Expert.

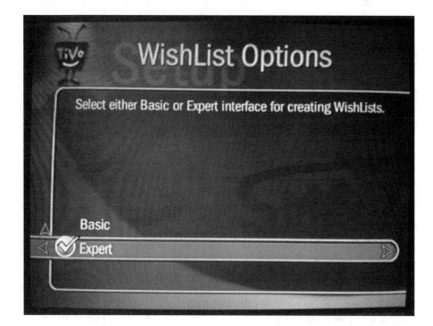

FIGURE 3.7
The WishList Options menu.

5. If you decide not to make changes to one of the nodes, simply press the TiVoGuy button to get out of the Node Navigator.

Now when you go to WishLists, the last item on the WishList screen should be Advanced WishList (you may have to scroll down the screen to see it in the menu choices).

Using Advanced WishLists

Basically the big benefit of Advanced WishLists is the addition of the AND and OR operators in search strings. Let's create an Advanced WishList item to show how this works. Let's say that we want to find all sci-fi/fantasy films directed by Tim Burton and starring either Johnny Depp or Christina Ricci (or both). Here's how we'd set that up:

1. From TiVo Central, we go to Pick Programs to Record -> Search Using WishLists -> Create New WishList.

2. From the Create WishList screen, we'd choose Advanced WishList (found at the bottom of the screen). If you don't have Advanced WishLists permanently enabled, you need to press "0" from within the Create New WishList screen to access Advanced WishList.

3. On the Advanced WishList screen, we choose Select Genre and scroll down to Sci-Fi/Fantasy. Under the Sub-Genre menu, we'd choose Don't Select Sub-Genre.

4. Back at the Advanced WishList screen, we'd choose Add Director, and then use the text-entry box (known among TiVo users as the "Ouija Screen") to find Tim Burton. Found and selected, we're taken back to the Advanced WishList screen (see Figure 3.8).

FIGURE 3.8

Entering the first search variable for our list.

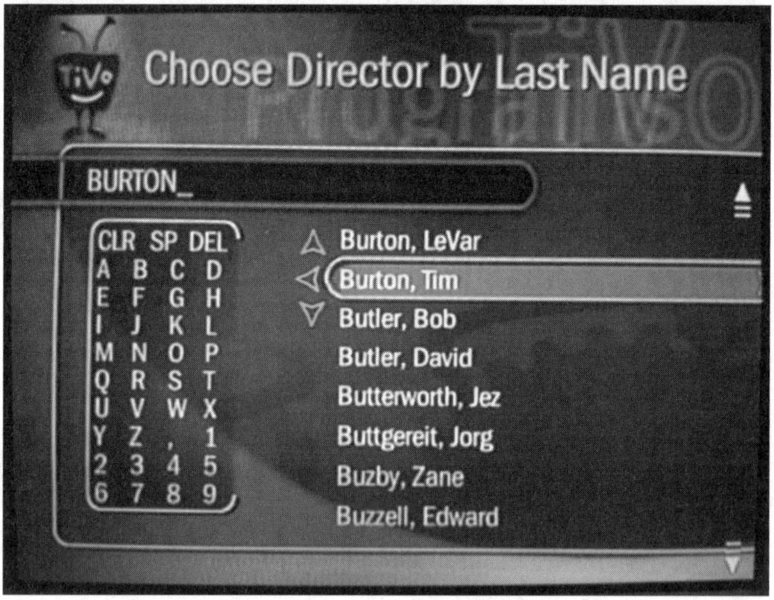

5. Selecting Add Actor takes us back to the Ouija Screen where we'd type out Depp, and select Depp, Johnny from the Actor list.

6. We'd repeat the process to find Ricci, Christina.

7. Back at the Advanced WishList screen, we'd choose Edit list, scroll down to Burton, Tim, and give him a Thumbs Up. What this does is make him required in the search results (see Figure 3.9). With this complete, we'd use the back direction arrow to return to the Create WishList screen and choose Done Creating WishList.

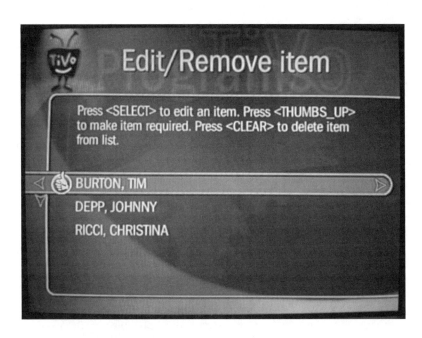

FIGURE 3.9

Making Tim Burton the required variable in our advanced search.

What we've done here is to create a search engine-like Boolean string that would look something like this if it was in a search engine:

Sci-fi/Fantasy AND "Tim Burton" AND ("Johnny Depp" OR "Christina Ricci")

Nifty, eh? Unfortunately, there isn't a NOT operator available in Advance WishLists, so you couldn't, for instance, add *NOT "Sleepy Hollow"* to this item.

Season Pass Management

What's so wonderful about TiVo's software is that there are so many different ways to get at the television content you're after. You can browse the Guide, look at TiVo Suggestions, create WishLists, and browse matches based on those. You can auto-record WishList items, and you can create very detailed search strings if you have Advanced WishLists enabled. And then there are Season Pass recordings and the Season Pass Manager. This feature allows you to auto-record all of the favorite shows you regularly view and to tell TiVo how many to keep and under what conditions (recording quality, show type [first runs, repeats, all], and when to delete them). We won't go into the basics of creating and managing Season Passes

Tip

Another cool feature of Advanced WishLists is that you can rename your list. If you create an AWL search string that's really long, it can look unsightly in your WishList and Season Pass lists. After creating your list, go to the main WishList screen, choose the WishList item, then "Edit Advance WishList" and "Rename WishList." Type in whatever title you like. In our case, we might say *Burton Depp Ricci*.

here (that's adequately covered in your *TiVo Viewer's Guide*), but here are a few more advanced considerations:

- When setting up a repeat recording, think about which recording technique is better: Season Pass or WishList. If you're only looking for first run episodes on the same network, then a Season Pass makes sense. Even if the show switches times or days of the week, TiVo will catch it. If you're looking to record a show that broadcasts several seasons on different networks (and you want to record them all), a Title-based auto-record WishList is what you want.

- For shows, such as the evening news, that you know you'll watch the same day they're recorded (or before the next viewing time), create a Season Pass, but only "Keep at Most" one episode, so TiVo will just record over the previous night's recording. Obviously, this is a question of personal preference (and disk space)—keep two if you like.

- If there's a show that you only like to watch now and again but don't really want your TiVo to fill up with multiple episodes (let's say *Dweezil and Lisa* on the Food Network), create a Season Pass but choose *Keep at Most = 1* and *Save Until I Delete*. That way, you'll always have one to watch when you're in the mood, and when you delete it, TiVo will go grab another one.

- Don't forget that conflicted recordings (two that are on at the same time) are prioritized based on where they're listed in the Season Pass Manager. Always make sure that your favorite shows are first in the list.

Padding

Padding is the fine art of adding extra recording time to the beginning or end of a show so that you don't miss anything. Some shows/networks are notorious for starting a few seconds off the hour/half-hour, or ending off-time. For instance, if you record *Friends* without padding, you will frequently miss the little ending punch line scene that runs alongside the credits. The official means of padding is done using the Record option called the Overtime Scheduler. This feature, found under Recording Options, lets you choose the Start Recording Time (from "on-time" up to 5 minutes) and Stop Recording Time (from a "on-time"

Tip

Tivocommunity.com has a very useful forum called Season Pass Alerts. Here TiVo users point out upcoming show conflicts, time changes, and other scheduling glitches that could mess us your Season Passes.

up to 3 hours after). This process has become known in the TiVo community as "hard padding." It's a wonderful feature, but it has its drawbacks. Adding one minute to the end of *Will & Grace* will let you have the last laugh, but if you have something else scheduled to record immediately after the show, TiVo will see this one minute overlap as a conflict and not record your next show. If you watch the show after *Will & Grace* on NBC, no problem; you just skip the padding, record the two shows as normal, and watch the last few seconds of *Will & Grace* at the beginning of *Scrubs* (or whatever). But if what you want to record next is on another channel, you're out of luck. This had led TiVo users to come up with all sorts of ideas for future padding options (and coined terms for them all: soft padding, semi-soft padding, negative padding, just-in-time padding, smart padding, and on and on). The idea behind soft padding is that TiVo would only record the requested x-minutes over if there were no conflict with another scheduled show. This is a much-requested feature, and hopefully something that TiVo, Inc. will add to future versions of the software.

The Semi-Soft Padding Hack

One of the Tivocommunity.com members (ccwf) came up with an ingenious method of pseudo-soft padding, dubbed "semi-soft-padding." Here's how it works:

Let's say, you like to watch *Survivor* at 8 p.m. on Thursdays, followed by *The Swan* at 9 p.m. on NBC. *Survivor* can sometimes run a few seconds over if the ousted person's final thoughts are long-winded. If you add five minutes of hard padding, you're not going to be able to record *The Swan* as well. To create semi-soft padding for this situation, you would:

1. Create a regular Season Pass for both *Survivor* and *The Swan*.

2. Create an auto-record WishList item for *Survivor* and set it to 5 minutes on the Ending Time selection in Recording Options. You have to use a WishList item for the second *Survivor* listing because you can't create more than one Season Pass for the same show on the same network.

Tip

Obviously, the handiest use of hard padding is to add space on the end of shows that traditionally run into overtime (such as the *Grammys,* the *Oscars,* the *Super Bowl,* and sports in general). For these special events, be safe and add at least an hour (if you don't have other must-view shows following on other networks).

3. In the Season Pass Manager, prioritize the three listings so that *The Swan* is first, followed by *Survivor*, with padding, followed by *Survivor* with no padding. This way, if both *Survivor* and *The Swan* are on, they will start recording at their normal times. But if NBC has monkeyed with its lineup, as they are wont to do, and *The Swan* is not on, *Survivor* will record *with* padding (see Figure 3.10).

FIGURE 3.10
What a semi-soft padding list looks like.

You can do a manual record semi-soft padding in situations where shows overlap a minute (such as *CSI* (9:00–10 p.m. on CBS) and *ER* (9:59–11 p.m. on NBC). Here, you'd create a regular Season Pass for both *CSI* and *ER* and a Manual Record for *ER* from 10–11 p.m. You would then prioritize them in this order (*CSI*, *ER*, Manual *ER*) in your Season Pass Manager. If both shows are on, you will get the full *CSI* and miss the first minute of *ER*, but if *CSI* is not on, you'll get every scalpel-wielding-minute of *ER*.

If you use these tricks too much, your Season Pass Manager will get very bloated, but luckily, there aren't too many instances where it is needed. We'll have to be satisfied with this little hack until soft padding becomes a real TiVo feature.

Other Types of Padding

So what about some of those other flavors of padding?

- **Negative Padding** is the ability to start and/or end a program within its timeslot (for instance, a minute into it or a minute before it ends). The only way to do this officially is to use the Manual Record feature. If you're on a TiVo using version 3.0 of the software, and have access to the TiVo's command prompt (see Chapter 13, "Accessing Your TiVo's Linux Bash Prompt"), there's a script (called *padhack.tcl*) you can install that will allow you to use negative padding. If you're interested in this script, go to tivocommunity.com and do a search on "negative padding" in the TiVo Underground forum.

- **Just-in-Time Padding** (a.k.a. "Smart Padding") is a requested feature for future TiVo software that would adjust the recording times dynamically if shows were running over. So, with JIT padding, you wouldn't have to try and guess how long the *Super Bowl* was going to run over the scheduled time. Your TiVo would be talking to the central TiVo servers, and if a show was going over, your TiVo would be told to automatically change the recording time.

Quality Versus Quantity

Series 1 and Series 2 stand-alone (SA) TiVos have four recording quality settings (Best Quality, High Quality, Medium Quality, and Basic Quality). As we discussed in Chapter 2, "Getting the Most Out of Your TiVo," DirecTiVo units don't compress their incoming signals, so programming always arrives as Best Quality and this cannot be changed.

On SA TiVos with the Premium service, you can set a default recording quality (under the Preferences menu). Your TiVo arrives defaulted to the Best Quality setting, which you'll likely want to change, as this level will quickly eat up hard drive space. (With the TiVo Basic service [on Pioneer and Toshiba DVD/TiVo combos, for instance], you can only set one quality level globally, and then all recordings are compressed to that level.) The amount of equivalent space usage between the four compression levels is as follows:

> 1 hour @ Best Quality = 1.5 hours @ High Quality = 2 hours @ Medium Quality = 3 hours at Basic Quality.

NOTE

Just to be contrary, the Pioneer DVD/TiVo combo units use different names for their recording quality levels: Extreme/Fine Quality (a.k.a. Best), High/Short Play Quality (a.k.a. High), Medium/ Long Play Quality (a.k.a. Medium), and Basic/ Extended Play Quality (a.k.a. Basic).

Unless you have tons of storage space on your stand-alone TiVo, it's best to keep it set to Basic or Medium Quality, and then you can change it up for specific programs. For most of what you watch, the two lower quality settings will likely be fine. It's really a matter of personal taste (and how good the signal is coming into your house). The only programming where you might want to go for less compression (that is, higher quality) is if there's likely to be fast-paced movement onscreen or numerous digital effects. It is in these situations where you get what is called "artifacting," where the low level of data compression can't adequately render the details of the scene and you see a pixilated, sort of painted-image effect for a few seconds.

In an image with a lot of quick movement, artifacting can get very distracting. If you see this sort of problem in a recorded program, note what type of program it is, and then up the recording quality the next time you set up to record a similar type of show. As you use TiVo, you'll come up with your own rule of thumb for what type of programming gets what level of recording quality. See Table 3.1 for ours.

Table 3.1 Recommended Recording Qualities per Program Type	
Recording Quality	**Program Type**
Best	Action Movies, Sci-Fi/Fantasy, and other special F/X-heavy fare, Concerts
High	Big Sporting Events (Super Bowl, World Series), Animated Films
Medium	Cartoons, Dramas, Reality Shows
Basic	News, Talk Shows, "Talking Heads" in general; anything where there's little camera movement. Do-it-Yourself Shows

Your recording quality choices will have a lot to do with your hard drive size(s). If you have precious little disk space, you'll probably rarely use the Best quality setting and just settle for sometimes-grainy images. The more space you have, the pickier you'll get. Hopefully, by the time you've finished this book, you'll be confident and knowledgeable enough to upgrade your TiVo with a giant honkin' hard drive (or two) and then you'll feel free to pick the optimal quality for a given show.

Miscellaneous Tricks

Here are a few more tricks we found up our sleeves that you may find useful.

Selective Manual Auto-Record

Don't forget to make use of TiVo's manual record feature (Record by Time or Channel). If you're only interested in parts of a show, such as the top of the news or the last 10 minutes of *The Apprentice* (where you get to see Donald Trump, and his increasingly Flock-of-Seagulls hairdo, fire that week's groveling trainee), you can create re-occurring manual recordings for these show segments.

Funky Space Figurin'

One of the great missing features on TiVo is a way to conveniently find out how much recording capacity is left on your drive(s). Crafty users have figured out one way of doing this. It's funky, but it works. If you have TiVo Suggestions turned on, TiVo will always try to record to fill the space left over after recording what you have requested. By going to Now Playing and adding up all of TiVo's Suggestions, marked by the round TiVo icon, you can roughly guess how much hard drive space is available (see Figure 3.11).

Tip

Help! My TiVo's haunted! One of the unfortunate things about TiVo is that, if you leave it on a menu screen and go away, it will eventually switch over to live TV. If you've gone off to do something else and not muted the TV, all of a sudden, you'll hear people talking in your house. This is particularly unnerving late at night, and depending on what TiVo tunes into, it can scare the bejezus out of you. So, if you leave your TiVo unattended, make sure to put the Mute button on.

FIGURE 3.11

This 14-hour hard drive has about 4 hours of recording time left (at Basic quality).

DIY Network Programming

Turning Your TiVo into a Channel-Changing Robot

Want to turn your TiVo into a very expensive robotic finger that changes channels? Let's say that you always get home a few minutes late for the news and miss the top stories. TiVo has likely been recording things all day and is not likely on your favorite news channel (where you could just back the broadcast up). You can fix this by creating a daily manual record for five minutes (the first five minutes of the news program). So, when you get home, even if you're 10, 15, 20 minutes late, TiVo will have changed to the news program and started buffering the telecast. You can then rewind to the beginning and you won't miss a thing. Why wouldn't you just record the full news program? You certainly could, but if you have limited hard drive space left, that half-hour (or hour) could be used by TiVo during the day to record something else. Make it a *Keep at Most = 1* so that it will record over the old recording each day.

Using "0" in Title/Category Searches

To go to the top of the list of programs in a Title search or within a show category/subcategory, enter a zero. Since numbers come before letters in the TiVo database, this'll take you to the top where you can scroll all upcoming offerings (see Figure 3.12).

FIGURE 3.12

Getting to the top of a Title Search.

Live TV: Bad/Now Playing: Good

As one person on the Tivocommunity.com put it: If your TiVo keeps telling you that it needs to change the channel to record something, you're probably watching too much live TV! TiVo is all about time-shifting your TV-viewing so you have much more control over the programming. If you've been good about setting up your Season Passes, WishLists, and giving TiVo good feedback with Thumbs Up/Down, you should have plenty of shows to watch in non-real-time. If something is on that you didn't know about/forgot to record, start recording it, then go to Now Playing and watch something else. If you're having to sit through segments of shows or commercials that you don't care to watch, you're not using TiVo to its fullest extent.

Using Closed-Captioning

One of the great benefits of TiVo and its Instant Replay and Back buttons is that, if you didn't catch a line from a speech, a movie, a game show question, and so forth, you can back the show up as many times as you like until you hear the missing line. But if after doing this, you *still* can't make it out, try turning on your TV's Closed-Captioning (CC) feature and then back up the show. If you have a universal remote (see Chapter 4, "Remote Control Freak"), you can even assign a button to your TV's CC feature so you can toggle it on and off at the touch of a button.

Playing *The Man Who Fell to Earth*: The Home Game

In Nicolas Roeg's 1976 sci-fi cult classic *The Man Who Fell to Earth*, David Bowie plays an alien (no typecasting there) who comes to Earth in search of water for his nearly dead homeworld. In a scene that has now become a cliché in sci-fi films, he quickly educates himself on everything having to do with Earth history and customs by watching dozens of TVs simultaneously. It's hard not to feel a little bit like this character after you've mastered all of TiVo's features and you find yourself with more must-watch programming than you know what to do with. With so much good stuff to watch, you'll find yourself wanting to accelerate everything, knowing that you can skip through whatever you're not completely enjoying. You'll learn how to apply the various viewing techniques outlined in this chapter to consume shows in at least half their broadcast times. You'll fast-forward through intros, setups, tired action sequences in movies (do we *really* need

NOTE

We'd like to think that all of the time saved not watching shows in real-time and skipping over commercials is being used for the betterment of humankind ("I've saved so much time with my new TiVo that I've started volunteering at our local senior's center!"). But in point of fact, it's probably just resulted in watching more TV ("Using my TiVo, I can now record and watch *all* of the dating shows that make me question my faith in humanity and my own self-respect!").

to ever see another long-winded car chase?), or other uninteresting parts. And if you have more than one TiVo, or an enabled dual-tuner DirecTiVo, you'll really feel "alienated" once you start doing two things at the same time (recording two shows while watching a recorded third show or jumping back and forth between two paused live shows). Our increasingly digital world allows us to pick and choose what bits we want and to skip the rest. TiVo brings this to television. Of course, you don't *have* to watch TV in such a hyper fashion; you can serve it up any way you like—that's the whole point (although we wonder if there's anybody that doesn't accelerate the TV montage once they have the tools to do so).

In Chapter 2 and in this chapter, we discussed TiVo's hardware and software and all that you can do with it. In the next chapter, we'll look at the critical link between you and your TiVo, namely the remote control.

Chapter 4

Remote Control Freak

If you're a media junkie (and you wouldn't be reading this book if you weren't), you likely have a disturbingly intense love relationship with your remote control. If you're really old (like us), you probably remember your family's first remote and how revolutionary it seemed. It was at this moment that the couch potato was born and America's backsides started expanding to fill the available space.

In this chapter, we'll discuss the three types of TiVo remotes; a few control tips, tricks, and advanced functions; how to get a stubborn remote to talk to other devices; and what you need to know about using third-party remotes with TiVo.

Unless otherwise noted, all of the tips, tricks, and hacks in this chapter are Level 1.

Found a Peanut

The most popular TiVo remote, affectionately referred to as the Peanut because of is distinctive shape, is arguably one of the nicest remotes ever designed. Those who design remote controls have a difficult task. The average remote has 30 to 40 buttons on it that have

NOTE

Paul Newby, TiVo's chief product designer who headed up the remote design team, designed something entirely different before joining TiVo, Inc. in 1998. He was a designer of construction machinery for Caterpillar. Talk about a change of scale!

Tip

The online TiVo store (store.tivo.com) sells Series 2 remotes (that will work with either stand-alone or DirecTiVo models) for $30. Designer models in clear or blue cases are also available (for $35). These replacement remotes will not work with Sony or Toshiba TiVos and don't have all the buttons for complete control of Pioneer combo units.

to handle a host of different functions, often more than one assigned to the same button, and be understandable to many different types of users. The remote needs to be sensibly laid out, comfortable to hold in your hand, and easy to navigate with a single thumb. Unfortunately, most remotes are poorly designed and suffer from "buttonitis," a profusion of buttons that always seem to be in the wrong place at the wrong time, or that, even after years of owning the device, you have no idea what they're for. In contrast, the TiVo remote is beautifully designed, is fun and easy to use, and has most of its well thought out buttons right where you need them.

There are three basic TiVo remotes: the Series 1 remote, the Series 2 remote (we could call 'em Peanut 1 and Peanut 2, respectively), and the Sony TiVo remote (sold with all Sony-branded TiVos). (There is also an entirely different remote that ships with the Toshiba DVD/TiVo units.) There are few differences between the S1 and S2 peanuts. The Series 2 is longer, separates a few functions that used to be combined on one button, and provides a DVR 1/DVR 2 toggle switch (stand-alone S2-only) so you can program and control two TiVos (either S1 or S2) from a single remote. The Series 2 remote also has a button called Window, which is marked for future use. (See Figure 4.1).

The Sony TiVo remote is more traditionally shaped, is much wider and flatter than TiVo, Inc.'s remotes, and its button arrangement is totally different.

Which remote is "best" is largely a matter of personal taste. Some people swear by the original Series 1 remote, claiming that its smaller size makes it more comfortable and the buttons easier to reach. Others like the more generous layout of the S2 remote and the addition of the separate Live TV and Guide buttons. And then there are those—even those who don't have a Sony-brand TiVo—who swear that the Sony remote is superior. Personally, we think they all have their strengths and weaknesses, and that any of them will serve your needs. If you have two TiVos you want to use in the same room, you'll want to buy a Series 2 remote to separately control both machines, or you may want to buy a universal remote to control both TiVos and most of the rest of your home media gear. We'll discuss universals later in this chapter.

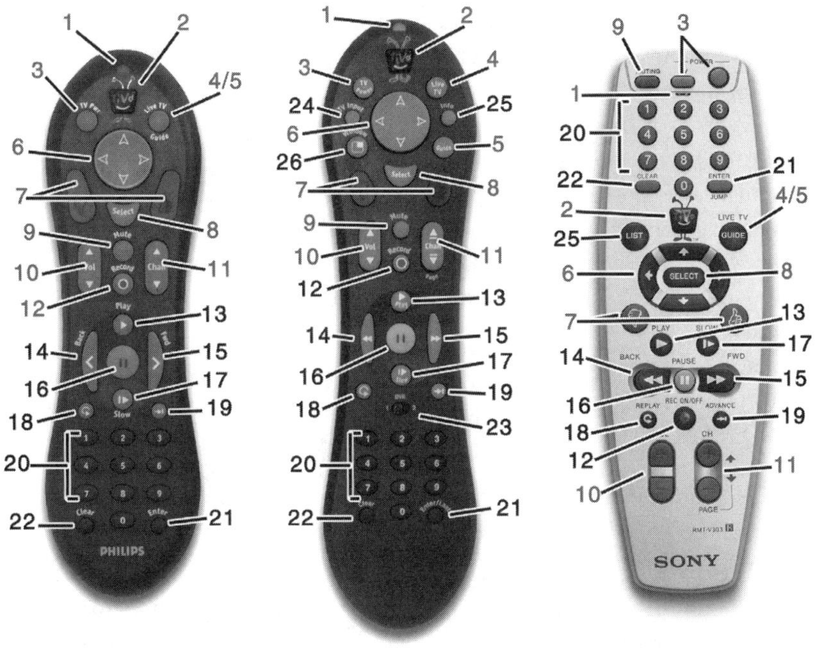

FIGURE 4.1

Anatomy of a remote.

NOTE

TV remotes really came into their own in the 1970s, at the same time that stretchable polyester was the reigning fabric. Coincidence? You be the judge.

Tip

If you have batteries that "go dead" in a device that uses a motor (say a toy or a CD player), those batteries may still have plenty of juice left in them to power your TiVo remote. There is still a fair amount of charge left in a battery that has stopped powering a high-demand device. TV remotes only need small amounts of power to operate, so you can get weeks, even months out of a couple of AAs that are no longer bringin' da noise (or da funk) to your CD player.

1. Activity Light
2. TiVo Button
3. Power
4. Live TV
5. Guide
6. Screen Navigation Arrows
7. Thumbs Up/Thumbs Down
8. Select
9. Mute
10. Volume
11. Channel Up/Down
12. Record
13. Play
14. Back (Rewind)
15. Forward (FF)
16. Pause
17. Slow
18. Instant Replay
19. Advance to Tick
20. Numeric Keypad
21. Enter/Last
22. Clear
23. DVR 1/2 Switch
24. TV Input
25. Info/List
26. Window

Controlling Other Devices with Your TiVo Remote

As we mentioned earlier, a Series 2 TiVo remote is designed to control two stand-alone TiVos (using the DVR 1/DVR 2 toggle switch located under the Slow button). The TiVo remote also has the ability to control other devices in your home media arsenal, namely the TV and a stereo receiver.

Chapter 4 | *Remote Control Freak*

Besides the DVR switch, the S2 remote adds a TV Input button. Once linked to your TV's IR receiver, this button lets you switch between all of the input sources going into your set (TiVo[s], DVD deck, VCR, and so on). The *TiVo Installation Guide* that came with your Series 1 or Series 2 TiVo describes how to access the control code lists on TiVo for many popular TVs and stereo receivers and how to program your remote to recognize them. But what if they don't work, or you have a piece of equipment that's not listed? Here's how to set up your remote so that it will signal you when it's stumbled upon the correct code.

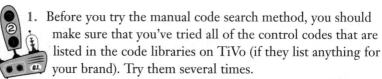

1. Before you try the manual code search method, you should make sure that you've tried all of the control codes that are listed in the code libraries on TiVo (if they list anything for your brand). Try them several times.

2. Point the remote away from your media center and place your hand completely over the IR window on the front of the remote.

3. Press the appropriate two buttons (see Table 4.1) simultaneously for a count of five. The red light above the TiVoGuy's head should light up and stay on to signal that the remote has entered Code Search mode.

Table 4.1   Remote Programming Entry Codes

To Program:	TV Power, Volume, Mute	TV Input	Stereo Power, Volume, Mute	Stereo Volume and Mute Only
Press These Buttons Simultaneously:	TV Power and TiVoGuy	TV Input and TiVoGuy (Series 2 remote only)	TV Power and TiVoGuy	Mute and TiVoGuy

4. Once the entry codes are engaged and the red light is on to indicate Code Search mode, you need to enter the beginning code to start the search. For TV controls, that number is 0999. For stereo controls, you'll want to enter 1999.

5. To start cycling through the control codes, point the remote at the target device (TV or stereo) and press the Channel Up button. Each time you press Channel Up, you're sending a new control code to the device. When the correct code is received, the target device will turn off. Stop! You've likely found the correct code! Try

pressing the Mute and Vol (+/-) buttons to see if they work. If they do, press the Enter button on your remote to lock in the code. You'll want to wait a few seconds between each Channel Up press before trying to send the next code. After you've found the correct code for the first device, if you want to program the second, go back to Step 1 and repeat.

If you go through all of these steps and the target device never turns off, and the red IR light on the tip of your remote finally winks out, unfortunately, your TV or stereo was probably made in some forgotten corner of the Earth under hellish sweatshop conditions and it has never met a manufacturing standard it cared to conform to. We kid! We kid the consumer electronics industry! Anyway, if you get to the end of the codes and it didn't find one for your device, you'll have to use that device's original remote to control it—or buy a universal remote.

NOTE

Cycling through the entire code list can take awhile, up to 20 minutes, so you'll have to be patient to do this operation.

Remote Control Shortcuts

Once you have the hang of all of the standard features on the TiVo remote, there are a few shortcuts you might like to know about. Pressing these button combinations will work from anywhere with the TiVo software.

- TiVoGuy + TiVoGuy—Takes you directly to the Now Playing menu.
- TiVoGuy + 0—Reruns the Introductory animation (great for entertaining easily amused children or the very elderly).
- TiVoGuy + 1—Takes you to Season Pass Manager (Ver. 3.1 or higher) or Now Playing (Ver. 3.0 or earlier).
- TiVoGuy + 2—To Do List
- TiVoGuy + 3—Search Using WishLists
- TiVoGuy + 4—Search by Title
- TiVoGuy + 5—Browse by Channel
- TiVoGuy + 6—Browse by Time
- TiVoGuy + 7—Record Time/Channel (a.k.a. Manual Record)
- TiVoGuy + 8—TiVo Suggestions
- TiVoGuy + 9—Showcases
- TiVoGuy + Slow—TiVo messages and Setup (only works in Ver. 4.0 or higher)

Area-Specific Button Functions

While the functions of the TiVo remote's buttons should be fairly obvious to you after spending some time with them, there are a few functions that change depending on what area of the TiVo software you're in. Let's run through some of these.

- **Program Listing Screens** (Now Playing, Season Pass, WishLists, To Do List).
  - **Chan Up/Chan Down** becomes a Page Up/Page Down button to jump through the list one screen at a time.
  - **Clear** takes you directly to the Delete Recording screen for the item you're on in the list.
  - **Play** starts playing the program selected in the list (Now Playing only).
- **Program Information Screens** (Now Playing, Season Pass, WishLists, To Do Lists).
  - **Chan Up/Chan Down** takes you to the previous or next program description in the list.
  - **Info (or "Display")** takes you to a second page of more detailed information about the program, including a full list of actors, episode number, and original air date (see Figure 4.2).

FIGURE 4.2

The Detailed Program Description screen.

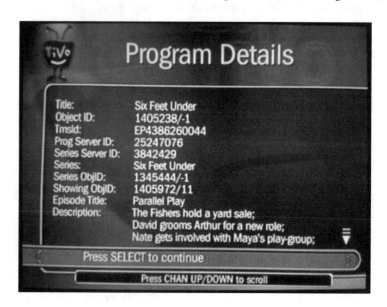

Program Details

Title:	Six Feet Under
Object ID:	1405238/-1
Tmsid:	EP4386260044
Prog Server ID:	25247076
Series Server ID:	3842429
Series:	Six Feet Under
Series ObjID:	1345444/-1
Showing ObjID:	1405972/11
Episode Title:	Parallel Play
Description:	The Fishers hold a yard sale; David grooms Arthur for a new role; Nate gets involved with Maya's play-group;

Press SELECT to continue

Press CHAN UP/DOWN to scroll

- **Clear** takes you directly to the Delete Recording screen for the program whose description you're looking at.
- **Play** starts playing the program whose description you're looking at (Now Playing only).

Live Television

While watching live television, using the following remote buttons causes the results described:

- **Live TV** (Series 1: LiveTV/Guide) brings you to live television from any TiVo menu. Pressing it while within live TV brings up the Guide screen. Pressing it again makes the guide go away and returns you to live TV. On DTV units with both built-in tuners connected to your dish, this toggles between the tuners.
- **Info (or "Display")** brings up the Channel Banner. If you press it again, the banner goes away. If you press the Right navigation arrow while the banner is displayed, it cycles through the three different channel banner designs. If you press Info/Display again to dismiss the banner (or otherwise go someplace else within TiVo), the last banner displayed becomes the default banner until you change it again.
- **Forward** (afterpressing Pause or Slow) triggers a single frame advance. Holding the Forward button down advances frame-by-frame until you let up.
- **Back** (after pressing Pause or Slow) triggers a few frames in reverse. Holding the Back button down reverses frame-by-frame until you let up.
- **Clear** dismisses any graphics laid over the live signal (Channel Banner, Status Bar, iPreview prompt, and so forth).
- **Enter/Last** (Series 1: Enter) takes you back to the previous channel you were on.
- **Record** pressed when you are already recording something stops the recording.

Program Guide

While within the Program Guide, pressing the following buttons on your TiVo will enable the features described:

- **Info (Display)** brings up Guide options. For stand-alone Series 2 TiVo with version 4.x of the software and DirecTiVo, this includes the option of switching between a TV Guide-style grid or the original TiVo two-column guide (see Figure 4.3).

FIGURE 4.3

The two different Guide options (ver. 4.x and DirecTiVo only).

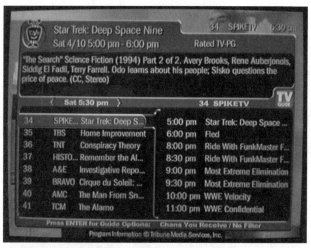

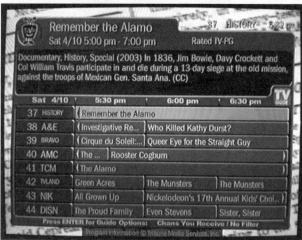

- **Forward** moves through the Guide one hour at a time (instead of the Right navigation arrow's one program at a time). (Grid-style Guide only.)
- **Back** moves through the Guide one hour at a time (instead of the Left navigation arrow's one program at a time). (Grid-style Guide only.)

Text-Entry Screens (Search by Title, WishLists)

On the TiVo screens that include a text-entry box (the so-called Ouija Screen), pressing the following buttons yields the described results.

- **Forward** inserts a space in the text-entry box.
- **Back** does a backspace.
- **Clear** erases everything in the text-entry box.
- **Pause** enters a quote mark (") in the text-entry box to enclose a phrase. This works in Keyword WishLists only.
- **Slow** generates an asterisk (*) that acts as a wildcard which will match any word that begins with the letter typed before the asterisk (for example, *tech** would find *technology*, *technical*, *techno*, *techie*, etc.)This works in Keyword WishLists only.
- **0** Takes you to the top of alphanumeric list (Search by Title only).

Undocumented Control Tricks

In the next chapter, "I'm Your Backdoor Code," we'll cover a number of nifty hidden features you can access after enabling TiVo's "Backdoors," or secret routes into the TiVo software. In this section, we'll cover a few hidden features that can be turned on without needing to enable backdoors.

A Word About Code Classes

The hidden TiVo control codes were found by obsessive TiVo users who've spent countless hours of their free time banging out different button sequences on their TiVos to see what the results might be. They invested all of this time getting thumb cramps so you don't have to. Let's all aim out remote controls in their collective direction and give them a big Thumbs Up!

One of the things that TiVo hackers discovered is that there are classes of these hidden codes. Each code class involves a set three- or four-button sequence and then a variable (such as a digit on the remote's number pad). There is only one major code class available outside of backdoor mode and it's known as Select-Play-Select (SPS).

Caution

These undocumented control codes were not designed to be activated by consumers. TiVo, Inc. does not officially support them. As such, you should undertake them at your own risk. We cannot guarantee that they won't make your TiVo start spewing smoke, making bad '50s sci-fi haywire computer noises, and finally expiring in a horrible digital heat death—though we can tell you that all this is highly unlikely.

Tip

These codes, because they are unofficial and unsupported, could go away at any time—or new code sequences may be discovered. To keep tabs on the latest, go to http://www.weaknees.com/links.php and take the link to Otto's "TiVo Codes List."

Tip

You'll know that you have successfully entered a remote control code when you hear three system chimes in response to your button sequence. Obviously, if you have disabled TiVo's system sounds (under Preference -> Audio Options), you won't hear the chimes.

Select-Play-Select (SPS) Codes

Each of the SPS codes are enabled by pressing the Select button, then Play, followed by Select, the specified code, and then Select one final time. All SPS codes should be done while playing back a recorded program (otherwise, when you press Select, it'll...well...select something). All of these functions can be turned off simply by re-entering the code (also while playing back a recorded program). SPS codes stay active until you re-enter them to toggle them off or you restart your TiVo (or if there's a power outage).

- **30-Second Skip** (S-P-S-3-0-S)—We already covered this one—perhaps the mother of all secret codes—in the previous chapter. This code changes the Advance button on your remote into a 30-second skip button.

- **Clock/Elapsed Time Indicator** (S-P-S-9-S)—This code sequence pops up a clock and an elapsed time display in the bottom-right corner of your TV screen. This clock/timer displays on both live and recorded programs. The elapsed timer is useful for remembering exactly where you were in a recorded program if you have to leave it and then want to return to where you left off. For instance, if you're watching a show with somebody else and you have to leave while they continue watching, you can use the timer to take note of where you were and then fast-forward to that exact spot when you return to the program. The elapsed time indicator has been removed and returned from TiVo's OS a number of times. It is not enabled in versions 3.0 and 3.1 of the TiVo software, but it is in versions 3.2 and higher. When you re-enter the code sequence to remove the clock, it doesn't actually leave the screen until you leave the program you're in (to go to a TiVo menu) and then return to recorded or live TV.

- **Speed Reader's Status Bar** (S-P-S-Pause-S)—TiVo's Status Bar is one of the cooler features that it lords over its competitor ReplayTV. It shows you where you are within a recorded or live program, whether the show is being recorded or not, what mode you're in (FF, Pause, Play, and so on), and other useful info. But if you find that the bar stays onscreen too long for your taste, you can accelerate its operation with this code sequence. And when we say "accelerate," we mean it. You'll have to have Superman-like visionary prowess to read the bar, as it'll only flash onscreen for about a half-second. If this feels like a perfectly reasonable amount of screen time, you may want to think about cutting back on the caffeine and all those all-night Xbox fragging sessions.

- **Status Message Display** (S-P-S-InstantReplay-S)—This one's probably for geeks only. Toggle it on and a status indicator pops up in the bottom left corner of the screen. It indicates the Input Type, the Channel (active in Live TV mode only), the episode ID number, as assigned by TiVo's internal "Media File System" (MFS) database (Live TV only), and the Mode ("COMPLETED: PlayRecording" or "RECORDING: WatchLive"). Here's what the status indicators would look like for a recorded and live show:

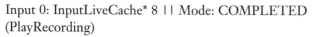

Input 0: InputLiveCache* 8 | | Mode: COMPLETED (PlayRecording)

Input 0: InputLiveCache* 4 FOCUS (1471410/155) | | Mode: LIVETV (WatchLive)

We can't think of anything terribly useful for this function, except to further disgust your friends with your Professorial level of Geekitude. Like the Clock code, you have to leave the program you're in and then return to recorded or live programming before the status indicator will disappear from the screen.

Miscellaneous Remote Tricks

Here are a few other useful things you can do with your TiVo remote. There are probably plenty of others. If you've gotten this far and are still hungry for more stuff to do with your remote, start hanging out on DVR-related bulletin boards, such as TiVoCommunity and AVSForum (see the "Resources" section). There are plenty of other TiVo inactivists there who, in lieu of having an actual life, are constantly thinking of new ways of using their remotes and other DVR gear. Relax! We're kidding the A/V geeks! Believe us, we're right there on the virtual couch beside them.

On some televisions, the clock/timer and status message readouts may be displayed partially off-screen or completely off-screen, depending on your screen size/design.

TiVo: Save My Place!

If you're watching a recorded show and aren't going to finish it, make sure to hit the TiVoGuy or the Left Arrow button before you leave; don't just turn off the TV. If you do, the show will continue running until the end, and you'll have to start from the beginning when you come back.

Scrubbing Buffers

If you're watching a show and you decide to start recording it, TiVo will start its recording from whatever's already been written to the live TV buffer (up to 30 minutes). If you don't want to record this buffered content, change the channel first (you can quickly hit the Enter/Last button twice to switch to a different channel and then back again). This clears the buffer, only recording the show from where you are at that moment.

Two-Fisted Deleting

If you want to delete a bunch of stuff from a program list (Now Playing, Season Pass, To Do List), you don't have to select each one and go to the Delete Now item for each; you can use the Clear button directly from the list. If you want to do a bunch of speed deleting, you can hold the remote in both hands with one thumb poised over the Clear button and one over Select. Pressing Clear/Select will quickly delete an item and move to the next item in the program list. Of course, there's really no need to delete all of the recorded TiVo Suggestions in your Now Playing list. TiVo will overwrite them with your requested shows or new Suggestions, but the anal compulsive among you might enjoy tidying up stuff you don't want.

Bouncing Beams

This one's for the desperately bored, the monstrously geeky, or those just looking for a cheap party trick. Infrared beams are tenacious little suckers (which is why they can cause the kinds of problems we talked about in Chapter 2's "Troubleshooting" section). They like to bounce all over the place, so much so that you'd be surprised where you can aim your remote and still have it send signals to your TiVo. Try it. Aim it off to the side, behind you, at the ceiling, the floor. Go into another room and aim the remote so that it'll bounce off the wall in front of the TiVo. It's hard to find a place to aim where the signal *won't* reach TiVo's IR receiver.

One of the few criticisms that users consistently have of the TiVo remote's design is that it's so symmetrical, it's hard, in the dark, without looking at it, to know which end is which. Luckily, when you're quickly grabbing the remote to pause it, it doesn't matter where it's pointing. The large, centrally located Pause button is easy to fumble for, and even if the hapless TiVoGuy ends up face-to-face with your intimidating beer belly, he's still going to go ahead and bounce the Pause signal off of you and send it to your TiVo.

My Peanut's Gone Rotten

It's amazing what kinds of abuse our remotes are subjected to. Computer geeks call the crud that builds up on computer mice and keyboards "hand salsa." On remote controls, it's often even worse because we're much more likely to be trying to negotiate a slice of stuffed-crust pizza while we channel surf. Over time, all sorts of disgusting goo, grease, and grim builds up on the remote and seeps between the buttons and into the electronics. Eventually, buttons will start sticking or stop working all together. Before you schedule a funeral for your beloved Peanut, try giving it a good bath.

1. Remove the batteries and unscrew the Philips head screw inside of the battery compartment.

2. Using a thin flat head screwdriver (or butter knife), run it along the seam between the two remote halves, starting from the back of the remote. Be careful not to "cut in" to the relatively soft plastic of the case. Working the seam will eventually pop the top off of the remote.

3. Peel off the rubber button pad and carefully remove the printed circuit board (PCB). Your remote should now be in five pieces: the case top, the bottom, the battery door, the rubber button pad, and the PCB (see Figure 4.4).

4. Wash all of the parts in warm, soapy water. Obviously, be especially careful with the PCB. If it's particularly grimy, use an old toothbrush to *gently* scrub it. Thoroughly rinse everything and leave it all out to dry overnight.

5. After you're certain that everything is completely dry, re-seat the PCB and the button pad, re-snap the cover on, and screw the case back together. Replace the batteries and try out your refurbished Peanut. It will often be as good as new.

FIGURE 4.4

A Series 1 TiVo remote: the "exploded" view.

1. **Case bottom with battery door**
2. **Printed circuit board (PCB)**
3. **Rubber key panel with separate TiVoGuy button**
4. **Remote case top**

Gareth On...

Most consumers seem aware of the fact that many electronics devices get wet (either on purpose or accidentally) and still work fine, as long as they are allowed to *thoroughly* dry first. I have a bad habit of dumping tall glasses of ice water onto my iMac keyboard. I simply shake it off, let it dry for a few days, then plug it back in and go about my business.

Several years ago I was at the beach when a giant, freak wave came up and thoroughly soaked everybody's stuff. The large family in front of me had CD players, digital cameras, and cell phones on their blankets, all of which suddenly became flotsam. So what did they do? Simultaneously, they all grabbed their gear in a panic and turned it on (while I did a slow-mo "NOOOOO!" in my mind). They likely fried the lot of it. They could have just taken the batteries out, rinsed away any sand, let it all dry for a few days, and everything (except maybe the cameras) could have been fine.

Universal Remote Controls

As we mentioned in the "Accessories" section of Chapter 1, "Which TiVo is Right for You?," some TiVo users ditch their TiVo remotes altogether and spring for a universal remote. As we also discussed, universals are not always so universal, with some functions or devices not being addressable by the remote, leaving the user to still need one or two other remotes around to control these stubborn devices. Also, there aren't that many remotes that have DVR buttons (especially TiVo's unique Thumbs Up/Thumbs Down buttons) built into them. All of these issues, as well as the exorbitant cost of many universals, have led many in the TiVo community to embrace a few specific low-cost remote models.

Universal Electronics (UEIC) Remotes

Universal Electronics Incorporated (a.k.a. UEIC) makes a number of reasonably priced (under $30) universal remotes. UEIC makes most of Radio Shack's multi-device remotes and remotes sold under the One For All (OFA) brand. The All-For-One 6 Device Universal Remote (URC 6131) is particularly popular among TiVo users because it has Thumbs Up/Thumbs Down buttons and comes with TiVo codes built into its code libraries (see Figure 4.5). The Radio Shack 6-in-One (RS 15-1994) remote does not have thumbs built in, but buttons can be assigned to create them. See Figure 4.5.

Besides the price, the relative ease of out-of-box operation, and the number of devices (and all their functions) that can be successfully controlled, UEIC remotes have two other huge benefits: They can be interfaced with your PC for custom button programming and there's a very large and active user community online.

PC Control of UEIC Remotes

Most UEIC universal remotes have something called the "JP1 Interface" pin available inside of them. This 6-pin jack is usually right above or below the battery bay, visible when you open the battery door. To interface with your remote using a PC, you need to either buy a JP1-to-parallel port cable or assemble one from parts. The cable will cost you $14, or you can get a parts kit for $9, both from JP1 Cables (jp1.filebug.com). Free software, available from JP1 Cables and the Yahoo! JP1 Users Group (groups.yahoo.com/group/jp1/), can then be installed on your PC to send customize button codes to your remote.

Tip

If you have a device that does not seem to be supported by a One For All Remote, fear not. If you call OFA (330-405-8655) and describe your setup, they'll research the proper code(s) for you. If they can't locate them, they'll tell you how to capture the control codes from your original remotes and how to enter the codes into your new universal.

FIGURE 4.5

The All-For-One 6
Device universal
remote (URC 6131).

Some UEIC manufac-
tured remotes don't
have the JP1 jack
installed, but they do
have pads on the cir-
cuit board to accept
the jack. The jacks are
readily available and
easily soldered on. If
you're not comfortable
soldering, get a friend
with soldering experi-
ence to do it. The URC
6131 only has the pads
to accept the JP1 jack,
not the jack itself.

If you'd like to learn more about JP1 remote control programming, check out Tommy Tyler's excellent "JP1 for Beginners" tutorial at www.lucindrea. com/jp1/. For a list of UEIC remotes with JP1 interfaces (check before you buy), consult this chart: jp1.filebug.com/remchart.htm. Also, check out the "Remote Controls" section of Appendix A, "Resources," in the back of this book for more JP1 vendors, tutorials, and discussion forums.

More Remote Control Alternatives

Of course, there are many other perfectly good cheapie universal remotes as well as very fancy high-end remotes. The Universal MX-500 is very popular, as is the Philips Pronto line. And there's the Harmony SST-659, billed as the first Internet-powered remote (see Figure 4.6). It connects to the Web via a USB cable for brainless device setup. It even has a TV schedule that can be downloaded to it: You can bookmark shows you're watching and the next time you connect the remote to your computer, it'll fetch information on the Web about the shows you've marked. Of course, all of these fancy remotes can cost a bundle, between $100 to $300, making them affordable to only the freakiest of remote control freaks.

Universal Remote Buying Tips

Regardless of whether you buy a modest universal remote or one that has delusions of world control, there are a number of…er…universal things to consider:

- **Number of Devices Controlled**—You want to make sure that the remote you buy will be able to control at least all of the home media devices you already have, with maybe room for a few more. You likely have at least a TV, VCR, home stereo, and of course, TiVo. Toss in a DVD, and that equals five devices already. So, you probably want to get a 6-in-1 or even a 7-in-1 remote.

- **Buttons Available**—Even though many remotes let you assign different functions to buttons (especially ones that can be JP1 interfaced), you ideally want as many buttons with the proper labels on them to begin with. You can spend all the time you want moving button functions around, but unless you're the only person using the remote, it's going to get confusing to other users. If you have a lot of buttons that mean different things in different devices, it's even going to get confusing to you. So try to get a remote that starts off with a lot of the proper button functions already designed in it.

By now, the lexically curious among you are probably wondering: "What does 'JP1' stand for?" It simply refers to the part location on the printer circuit board and stands for "Jack Port 1."

FIGURE 4.6

The Cadillac Escalade
of Universal Remotes:
The Harmony SST-659.

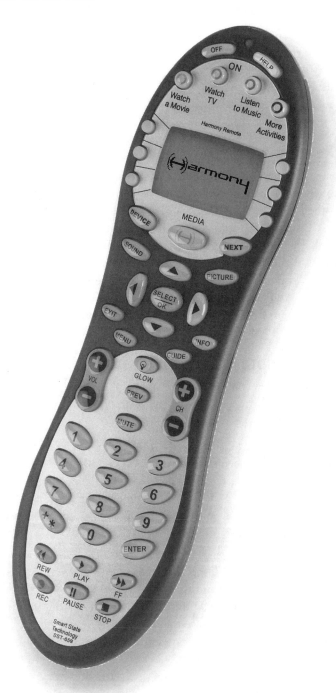

- **Large Built-in Code Library**—You want to make sure that the remote you choose ideally already has the control codes loaded onto it for the devices you'll be controlling, or that it can at least have them easily coded in. If you do your research ahead of time, you should know whether the remote you're interested in can control your gear or not. So-called "learning remotes" are good for this easy transfer of code data from your individual remotes to the universal.

- **Design Considerations**—There are many different opinions about what makes a good remote control design. A lot of it comes down to personal preference. You really have to see the remote in person (or see close-up images of it on the Web) to get an idea of whether you'll like the design, the button arrangements, and so forth. If possible, test drive the remote in person. Some remotes are wide and not comfortable to hold. Remotes with full touch-screen displays tend to be this way. Some are heavy, and if you like to hold the remote in your hand or lap while you veg out, a hefty remote can be a drag…literally. Most users are persnickety about button arrangements—the buttons have to make sense in how they're grouped and used. Some users don't mind buttons being small and close together; others can't stand it. One big complaint about the One For All URC 6131 is that its buttons are too dinky and tightly packed together. The TiVo remotes are widely praised for their superior layout and big, sensible buttons.

- **Use Considerations**—How you use the remote and who uses it needs to be considered too. If you tend to watch a lot of TV in the dark, in bed, for instance, you probably want a remote with glow-in-the-dark or lighted buttons, or with an LCD screen. If you have a large family with a lot of remote users, you probably don't want anything too complicated to use. And if the remote is going to be subject to a lot of abuse by family members and slipper-chewing pets, you probably don't want to invest in an expensive model.

- **Do Your Homework**—It pays to do research on universal remotes before you buy one. Each one has its strengths and weaknesses, and dozens of users are likely sharing their experiences of popular brands in online forums devoted to the subject. RemoteCentral.com is a great place to start your research. Also check out the Customer Reviews on e-tailers like Amazon.com.

NOTE

Some people love remotes with touch-screen displays. These let you customize many buttons (which appear as icons on the screen), have a backlit, and offer many programmable options. They're often "learning remotes," too, which means that you can transfer the codes from your old remotes to the universal with a few button presses. We're not so big on all touch-screen remotes. They're expensive, usually wider and heavier than other remotes, and can eat batteries. We also find it hard to locate the buttons on a touch-screen without looking down at the remote—there's no tactile feedback! Your mileage may vary, so try before you buy (if possible).

Remote Control Freak

They Can Have My Remote When They Can Pry It...

With the information in this chapter, you have hopefully brought your TiVo and other home media devices under your control and have learned a few remote control shortcuts and special functions you may not have been aware of.

In the next chapter, the last in Part 1, we'll get your feet wet with a little software hacking, peering down TiVo's secret passageways and opening up a few features and utilities that we mere mortals were never meant to see. Ew...we feel so wily...

Chapter 5

I'm Your Backdoor Code

If you saw *The Matrix Reloaded*, you'll likely remember the scene where Neo is within the Matrix and running down an endless white hallway, trying different doors. What you were looking at was a visual representation of something that every computer programmer and system administrator is intimately familiar with: a program's backdoors. Just as the name implies, a backdoor is another way into a program. It is usually set up as a secret entrance that programmers or administrators can use to access the system without having to go through the normal authentication process (the "front door"). In an embedded system with a simplified user interface, such as TiVo, backdoors often take programmers and technicians into parts of the system that the end user (that's you!) was never meant to see (for diagnostics, to access log files, and so forth). In TiVo, many of the utilities and undocumented features found behind these backdoors are really not useful and are accessed by hackers simply as a curiosity (or to try and piece together the details of how TiVo operates). The function of some of them remains a mystery. But there are a few hidden features that are very useful and worth the effort it takes to turn them on. That's what this chapter is all about. So let's get crackin'…er…hackin'…

Caution

Backdoor features are unsupported. While many of them perform as advertised, some can cause strange behaviors, and playing around trying to discover your own codes can incapacitate your TiVo. It is ideal that you make a backup of your TiVo drive(s) before attempting any of the codes, but it is imperative that you do so for any of the more mysterious codes or ones detailed in this chapter that are known to cause problems. See backup details in Chapter 8, "Upgrading Hard Drives."

NOTE

As of this writing, the current version of the software for SA Series 1 machines is 3.0. Because TiVo, Inc. has control over which software version gets downloaded to all TiVos on its service, this could change, although it's not likely to. S1 machines will likely stay at 3.0, while S2 machines continue to receive software upgrades.

Backdoor Codes in Software Versions 1.3 to 3.0

If you have a Series 1 stand-alone TiVo, its software version is going to be between versions 1.3, 2.0, 2.5, or 3.0. Because the central TiVo servers do updates of the software on all the machines that dial into them on a daily basis, regardless of what version your SA is using when you first hook it up, eventually, it will be upgraded to the "latest" version of the OS for Series 1, which is version 3.0.

The codes for enabling the backdoors in Series 1 TiVo software have been discovered by industrious alpha geeks who deserve their props. Again, tivocommunity.com is the place to go to see a running list of known codes and to find out when any new backdoor codes are discovered (always a cheap thrill).

Table 5.1 lists the known backdoor-enabling codes for all Series 1 machines. The mystical open sesame you'll likely be issuing is the one for the TiVo OS 3.0. To find out which software version you have, go to TiVo Central/DirecTV central -> Messages & Setup -> System Information. If you bought a Series 1 TiVo, have recently hooked it up, and it has an OS version other than 3.0, those access codes are provided in Table 5.1 as well. You can enable the backdoors now, but at some point in the near future, TiVo, Inc. will download a service upgrade to your machine (to bring it up to version 3.0) and you'll have to re-enable backdoors with the 3.0 code after that. The code for the stand-alone Series 1 DirecTiVo is also given in Table 5.1.

Table 5.1	Backdoor Codes for Series 1 TiVos	
Software Version	**Backdoor Code**	**Notes**
OS 1.3	0V1T	Also OS 1.50 and OS 1.51 in the U.K.
OS 1.5.2	10J0M	U.K. only
OS 2.0	2 0 TCD	
OS 2.5	B D 2 5	Also OS 2.5.5 in the U.K.
OS 2.5.2	B M U S 1	For DirecTiVo
OS 3.0	3 0 BC	Latest Series 1 backdoor code

How to Enable the Code

Once you know which code is correct for your OS, you need to issue it to your TiVo using your remote control. Since it's necessary to enter both letters and numbers, you'll need to use the text-entry (Ouija) screen in *Search by Title* (TiVo Central -> Pick Programs to Record -> Search by Title). Select All Programs, which will take you to a text-entry screen.

Using the Ouija screen, you need to carefully enter the numbers and letters *exactly* as they appear in Table 5.1. Pay special attention to the spaces in some codes and note that those are zeros (0) in the codes, not letter Os. Once you're confident the code has been entered correctly, press the Thumbs Up button (see Figure 5.1). You should hear five of the system dings, letting you know the code worked. The words "Backdoors enabled!" will also display in the text entry window. Now if you go back to the *System Information* screen (TiVo Central -> Messages & Setup -> System Information), shown in Figure 5.2, you should see a new item entry at the top that says Backdoors: ENABLED!

NOTE

Have a look at the codes in Table 5.1. They tell you something about how simple many such backdoor codes are (at least *after* you've figured them out). For 1.3, it's *TiVo* spelled backward (in alphanumerals), 1.5.2 is maybe *Mojo 1*(?), 2.5 is the no-nonsense *Back Door 2.5*, and how about 3.0? Talk about leaving the screen door unlocked!

FIGURE 5.1

The backdoor code for OS 3.0 properly entered.

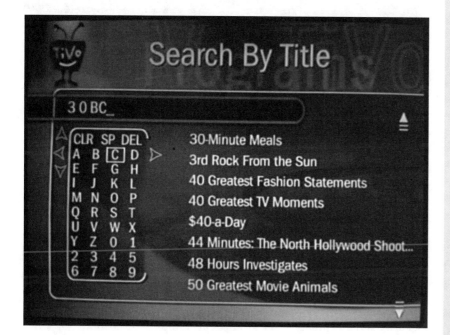

Tip

It is possible to hack your S1 TiVo so that it will no longer update its software version, or at least resist attempts by TiVo, Inc. to upgrade. Instructions for this hack are discussed in Chapter 14, "Accessing Your TiVo's Linux Bash Prompt."

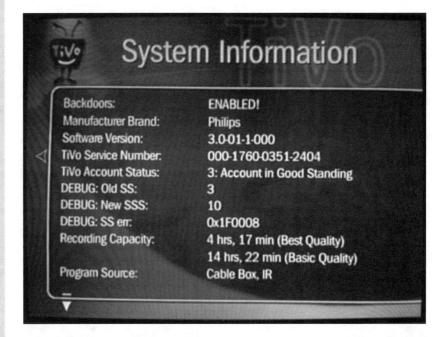

Once the backdoors are opened, you'll be able to enter any of the codes listed in Table 5.3 (that your TiVo's OS supports).

In the following section, we'll discuss in more detail those software features—available on the other side of backdoors —that a large percentage of TiVo users might find useful. For the deep geeks in the audience, we include a nearly complete list of currently known codes (whether useful or not) in Table 5.3.

Backdoor Codes in Software Versions 3.1 to 4.0

As we discussed in Chapter 1, "Which TiVo is Right for You?," Series 1 TiVos are much easier to hack. Part of that ease is due to the fact that all of the backdoor codes have already been discovered. With the introduction of Series 2 machines, and OSes from 3.1 onward, TiVo, Inc. has been tightening up its security and making it harder for diligent snoops to unearth the software's secrets. As such, the backdoor access codes are, as of this writing, still unknown. That means that there's no *easy* way of getting into the soft chewy center of a Series 2 machine, but there *is* a way.

I'm Gonna Yank That Drive Right Outta My Box...

To be able to access the backdoors in OS versions 3.1, 3.2, or 4.0, you have to actually remove the hard drive (or drives) from your trusty TiVo, hook it (or them) up to your PC, and replace some codes in TiVo's Linux-based OS. This will void the warranty and so discussing the procedure in this chapter would make us have to change the title of Part 1 (Warranty-Friendly Fun). We're lazy—we don't want to have to think up a new title. It's also a rather gnarly procedure (the hack, not the section name-change), requiring that you first back up your TiVo drive(s), so that if the backdoor hack goes awry, you can reinstall your TiVo's software.

Whether this will be worth it to you or not has a lot to do with what type of TiVo user you are. There aren't really that many critical features available through the backdoors that will make the process worth the effort for the average TiVonaut. All of the SPS-class codes, including the coveted 30-second skip, are accessible without having to hack backdoors. The main app that you'll not have access to on a Series 2 system running 3.1 to 4.0 is Advanced WishLists (discussed in Chapter 3, "DIY Network Programming"). If you think that this is a feature that you don't want to live without, then you may want to attempt the backdoor hack. Also, if you're already a seasoned computer geek who doesn't think twice about sticking your head under the hood of your PC to remove/install parts, and you already know your way around a hex editor (or are curious and patient enough to learn), the procedure should be straightforward enough. If, after reading the rest of this chapter and seeing what backdoor codes have to offer, you decide you want to do the hack, here's what you'll need to do next:

1. Read Chapter 6, "Touring Your TiVo: The Hardware," and Chapter 7, "TiVo Hacker's Toolkit," to familiarize yourself with TiVo's hardware and the tools you'll need to remove TiVo hard drives and install them on your PC. You'll also have to read the "How to Hook Up TiVo HDs to Your PC" section in Chapter 8, "Upgrading and Adding Hard Drives."

Tip

If you booted up your TiVo and you got nothing, or it won't work its way out of the boot sequence, we hate to break it to you, but you're probably going to have to send it back into surgery and put its old brain back. Thank God you made a backup! For the love of the TiVoGuy, please, tell us you made a backup! If you didn't, ask a geek friend if they have a disk image of the same TiVo OS as you have. Though TiVo, Inc. frowns upon it, there are also disk images to be found online. Do a search. You can also always send your drive(s) to an upgrade shop like weaKnees or PTVUpgrade and they'll restore the software (for a fee, of course).

2. Read Chapter 13, "Touring Your TiVo: The Software," and Chapter 14, "Accessing Your TiVo's Linux Bash Prompt," to familiarize yourself with TiVo's software and how to access it though your PC.

3. Read Chapter 8, "Upgrading Hard Drives," to learn how to back up TiVo drives and Appendix C, "About the CD-ROM" to learn about the included Linux HexEdit program (which allows you to search through and replace the hexadecimal code within Linux partitions).

If, after reading these six-plus chapters, you didn't

a) Fall into a deep and sonorous slumber,

b) Break out in a hideous case of hives, or

c) Cry out for your mommy like a night-spooked toddler,

Then, you may have what it takes to perform this hack. Congratulations. You're a tremendous geek! Unfortunately, we don't discuss the gory details of the hexcode hack in this book, since we didn't think that most of our readers will go through all the fuss. You can find the information you need for the hack by doing a search on dealdatabase.com/forum or tivocommunity.com. Search on your version of the Series 2 OS and "backdoors." You can also do a search on "hexedit," the name of the program you'll use to change the hexadecimal code in the TiVo software. Hexedit is included on the CD-ROM for your convenience should you decide to attempt the hack. You can also find detailed instructions for this hack in William von Hagen's book Hacking the TiVo.

When you're done with this procedure, and your TiVo is out of the recovery room and making unreasonable demands on the hospital staff, it's time to boot it out...er...up and see if you've lobotomized it or not. If all went well, you'll need to follow the steps in "How to Enable the Code" from earlier in this chapter to turn on the backdoors. When you hacked the passcode, you likely set it up to require the same backdoor code as used in version 3.0 (3 0 BC). So that's what you would enter to enable 3.1, 3.2, or 4.0 backdoors.

With backdoors enabled on your 3.1, 3.2, or 4.0 TiVo, you're ready to muck around with all of the hidden features that these OS versions support (see Table 5.3).

Hidden Treasures

As we've mentioned a number of times already, the Rosetta stone of hidden TiVo codes is the SPS 30-second skip code (described in both Chapters 3 and 4, "Remote Control Freak"). We'd love to be able to tell you that there are a lot of other gems like this one just a few Ouija screen sessions away, but there aren't. Most of the hidden features are little more than curiosities. A couple are also used by the TiVoWeb software (for Series 1) that we'll talk about in Chapter 16, "TiVoWeb." The features that *are* worth talking about are discussed in this section. Most known backdoor codes to date are listed in Table 5.3.

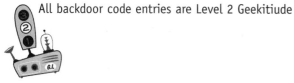

All backdoor code entries are Level 2 Geekitiude

TiVo Log Files

Clear-Enter-Clear-Thumbs Up

This one is a cool curiosity because it reveals what TiVo is doing behind the scenes. Pressing this sequence of buttons (Clear-Enter-Clear-Thumbs Up) on your remote control brings up TiVo's log files (stored in the var/log directory in the TiVo software), as shown in Figure 5.3.

```
                         /var/log/tvlog
Jul 31 21:18:45 (none) Promo[128]: Promo errNmNameNotFound: line 579
Jul 31 21:18:45 (none) Promo[128]: PromoRotation::NextValid cannot find valid promo
Jul 31 21:18:45 (none) Promo[128]: PromoRotation::SetupPromotion Could not find a
Promotion
Jul 31 21:19:00 (none) NowShowing[128]: Before DoEnterHelper
Jul 31 21:19:00 (none) snsl[128]: Dump: nRevisionDataM=63,
nRevisionCurrentRecordingM=63 nSortOrderM=0
Jul 31 21:19:00 (none) snsl[128]: FHasRevisionBeenBumped nRevision 63->68
Jul 31 21:19:00 (none) NowShowing[128]: DoEnterHelper Need to UpdateData
Jul 31 21:19:00 (none) NowShowing[128]: UpdateData Start
Jul 31 21:19:01 (none) NowShowing[128]: UpdateData End
Jul 31 21:19:01 (none) NowShowing[128]: After DoEnterHelper
Jul 31 21:19:03 (none) snsl[128]: Dump: nRevisionDataM=68,
nRevisionCurrentRecordingM=68 nSortOrderM=0
Jul 31 21:19:05 (none) VideoGuts[128]: PlayRecording for Proxy 86
Jul 31 21:19:05 (none) OutputState[128]: PlayRecording 0
Jul 31 21:19:11 (none) DbGc[110]: got EVT_DATA_CHANGED/DATA_PROGRAM_GUIDI
Jul 31 21:19:11 (none) DbGc[110]: got INDEX_SOON
Jul 31 21:19:11 (none) DbGc[110]:   setting action's timeout to INDEX_SOON
Jul 31 21:19:11 (none) DbGcBaseAction[110]: Background->SetTimeout( 2 )
Jul 31 21:19:40 (none) Recorder[121]: Adding check schedule task
Jul 31 21:19:42 (none) dbcache[122]: Couldn't find a pItemCachedData to MODIFY on
```

FIGURE 5.3
A TiVo log file.

The file shows a time-stamped log of all TiVo's communications, maintenance, errors, and other activity logs. To scroll through a log, use the Up and Down arrows (or Page Up/Page Down to move through the log a page at a time). To move to the next log, use the Right arrow button. The Left

See Table 5.3 for what areas of TiVo you need to be in before entering these codes. All code classes are entered in a specific area.

arrow (or the TiVoGuy) takes you back to regular TiVospace. While viewing the logs is mainly a geek pastime, you can learn some interesting things about your system. If you're having hardware or software problems, a quick scan of the log files may help you isolate where the problem is, if nothing else, so that you can alert the repair shop to what you found. See Figure 5.3.

Scheduled Suggestions in To Do List

Clear-Enter-Clear-2

In software versions 2.0 and 2.5, this code turns on a list of TiVo Suggestions in the To Do List. In these OS versions, Suggestions do not appear in the To Do List unless this feature is turned on. This code sequence does nothing after version 2.5.

Overshoot Correction

Clear-Enter-Clear-5

This code toggles off (and on) TiVo's "overshoot correction." As discussed in Chapter 3 when you're blazing along in Fast Forward at 2x or 3x speeds and you slam on the brakes when your show returns, TiVo does an "overshoot correction," rewinding the video back some frames (more at 3x, less at 2x), so that you hopefully don't miss anything. This code, when entered once, will turn overshoot off. Enter it again to turn it on again.

Enter the Node Navigator

Clear-Enter-Clear-6

As we discussed in Chapter 3, the Node Navigator accesses the backdoor entrances to the menu system of the TiVo OS. The functions of the different nodes (and what menus they're attached to) are not listed anywhere; they show up onscreen as nothing more than a numbered list. Mucking around in here can seriously mess with TiVo's head, so you shouldn't go down this rabbit hole unless you've made a backup of your TiVo software (see Chapter 8 and Appendix C).

If you're extremely cautious, you can go ahead and permanently enable Advanced WishLists by going into Node 30. The details of how to do this are discussed in the "Permanently Enabling Advanced WishLists" section in Chapter 3.

The other known node of note is Node 1 (see Figure 5.4). Going here will allow you to access a screen where you can change the overshoot correction values that TiVo uses (see previous entry on Overshoot Correction). The values as set by TiVo are shown in Table 5.2. Note that there is no overshoot value for 1x FF because TiVo doesn't do overshoot correction at 1x Fast Forward.

FIGURE 5.4
The Overshoot Correction screen.

Caution

Any flub-ups in the Node Navigator can cause your TiVo to go haywire, so it's ideal if you do a backup before doing *anything* here. That said, if you *carefully* follow the instructions in this section for working in Node 1 (Overshoot Correction) and Node 30 (Advanced WishLists), you *should* be safe enough. If you have any doubts about what you're doing: Get the heck outta there—she's gonna blow!

Table 5.2   Overshoot Correction Values and Corresponding Key Presses

Overshoot Speed Value	FF/Back Equivalent	Remote Keypad Equivalent
-6000	Speed3 (3x) Rewind	41000
-1800	Speed2 (2x) Rewind	14000
-300	Speed1 (1x) Rewind	01435
1800	Speed2 (2x) Fast Forward	15226
6000	Speed3 (3x) Fast Forward	48000

The overshoot value itself corresponds to a 5-digit number that is entered on the remote keypad to arrive at the overshoot value (we have no idea what the actual overshoot speed value refers to). So, for instance, 48000 would be entered on your keypad to arrive at an overshoot value of 6000 (if it wasn't already set to that value). For the numerical values you enter, every 1000 corresponds to one second of overshoot time. This would mean that 48000 is equivalent to 48 seconds of rewinding as you move ahead at 3x Fast Forward. With this information, you can experiment with entering numerical values to any or all of the overshoots. For instance, let's say you find that at 3x FF, the standard overshoot correction is consistently about 3 seconds too short for the speed of your trigger-finger. To change it, you would

1. (After entering Node 1 of the *Node Navigator*) Use the arrow buttons to scroll down to "Speed of 6000" in the Set Over Shoot Value menu.

2. Enter 51000 on your remote's keypad (which will be adding 3 seconds to the 3x FF overshoot correction).

3. Press Enter on the remote to send the new value to TiVo.

4. Change the values for any other overshoots you desire, and when you're done, hit the TiVoGuy button to get out of the Node Navigator.

These overshoot corrections are permanent (at least until you change them) and will even survive a reboot. If you decide to replace the original values, consult what numerical values to re-enter in Table 5.2.

Change Fast Forward Value for Speed1

Enter-Enter-1

Unfortunately, this hack only works in version 1.3 of the TiVo OS. It allows you to change the FF speed from its existing three times (3x) the normal speed to whatever you enter. After entering the E-E-1 code, at the prompt that appears, you'd enter a multiple of the FF speed you want times 100. So, the existing 3x speed would be 300. If you wanted to make it 5x, you would enter 500 at the prompt.

Change Fast Forward Value for Speed2

Enter-Enter-2

Works the same way as for Speed1 above, but here, the multiplier is 100. The default speed is 2000 (for 20x). Only available in ver. 1.3 of OS.

Change Fast Forward Value for Speed3

Enter-Enter-3

Works the same way as for Speed1 above, but here, the multiplier is 100. The default speed is 6000 (for 60x). Only available in ver. 1.3 of OS.

Scheduled Suggestions in To Do List

Thumbs Down-Thumbs Down-Thumbs Up-InstantReplay

If you enter this code while in the To Do List, TiVo's scheduled Suggestions are integrated into the list (see Figure 5.5). Normally, you have to go to the TiVo Suggestions screen to see what TiVo plans on recording for you. This code allows you to see all upcoming recordings combined in one list. Nifty! The TiVo Suggestions items are the ones in the list that have no check-mark icons in front of them. Re-entering this code turns the scheduled Suggestions off. This feature only works in OS versions 3.0 and 4.0.

FIGURE 5.5

Scheduled TiVo Suggestions revealed in To Do List.

Tip

Using the 2 on your remote in Ver. 4.0 while in the Now Playing list is a great way to switch between a list view and a folders view for quick navigation, especially handy if you have a big drive with long lists of recorded programming.

Scheduled Suggestions in To Do List

Thumbs Down-Thumbs Down-Thumbs Up-InstantReplay

When the same code sequence is used within Now Playing that was used in the To Do List in the previous entry, hidden TiVo recordings are revealed. TiVo records programming from the Discovery Channel early every Monday morning (usually between 4 and 5 a.m.). The program it records contains the various clips used on the TiVo Central menu (the so-called "Star item" on the menu list) and the video items in the Showcases menu. Turning on this feature reveals these clips in Now Playing as "Teleworld Paid Program." Turning on this feature in one area (To Do List or Now Playing) will not automatically enable it in the other. It has to be entered in each.

Clips on Disk

Thumbs Down-Thumbs Up-Thumbs Down-InstantReplay

As you may have noticed if you've looked at a Teleworld "program," it's actually a number of clips, all strung together, that are used in different places on TiVo (namely on TiVo Central and within various video offerings in Showcases). TiVo uses the VBI (Vertical Blanking Interval) part of the TV signal to send data related to where the clips within the Teleworld program will be used. Hitting this code sequence takes you to a special Clips on Disk screen where you can scroll through the various clips and watch them individually (see Figure 5.6).

FIGURE 5.6

The Clips on Disk menu.

In OS version 4.0, getting to this menu works a little differently. After back-doors are enabled, an item appears on TiVo Central called "Clip Lineup." Selecting this takes you to the same Clips on Disk menu as in OS 3.0.

Italic Font

Thumbs Down-Thumbs Up-Thumbs Down-Clear

When this code is entered on TiVo Central, it turns all of the onscreen text (in every menu, not just *TiVo Central*) to an italic font. Thumbing in the code again returns you to a normal font.

Sort the Now Playing List

Slow-0-Record-Thumbs Up

In version 3.0 of the software, if you press this code while on the Now Playing screen, a black bar appears on the bottom of the screen saying, "Sort: Press DISPLAY to Change." While in this mode, pressing 1 on your remote sorts the items in your Now Playing list by recording date (the default), selecting 2 sorts them by expiration dates, and 3 puts them in alphabetical order. Pressing Display (if your S1 remote has that button) or Enter takes you to a Now Playing Options screen where you can choose between these three sort types.

In version 4.0, a sort feature is built in. The Now Playing Options screen is accessed from the Now Playing menu by pressing Enter. From here, you can choose between Date Recorded and Alphabetical sorting (sorting by expiration date is no longer available). There is also a Groups feature. Turning this on organizes episodes of the same program (and TiVo Suggestions) into folders. From the Now Playing menu, you can also switch between the two sort options by pressing 1 on your remote, and toggle Groups on and off by pressing 2.

Free Space Indicator

0-Thumbs Up

Besides Advanced WishLists, this may be the one hidden feature worth going through all the hassle it takes to open backdoors on OS 4.0. Being able to tell how much recording space is left on your TiVo is something that TiVonauts have been asking for since 1999 when TiVo first hit the market. With OS 4.0 only, after backdoors are enabled, pressing 0-Thumps Up within the Pick Programs to Record screen brings up a Disk Space Usage screen.

Complete Code List

At long last, here is the much heralded (mostly) complete codes list for your tweaking pleasure (see Table 5.3).

NOTE

The "Vertical Blanking Interval" (or VBI) is a part of the TV signal that can contain text data. It is what's used to send Closed Captioning text. As you may or may not know, the image on an analog TV is rapidly "painted" on, line-by-line, by something called an "electron gun." When it gets to the bottom of the screen and has to move back to the top, that lag time (undetectable to us puny humans), is called the Vertical Blanking Interval. It is in these spaces that data can be transmitted.

Tip

See the "Funky Space Figurin'" item in the "Miscellaneous Tricks" section of Chapter 3 for a low-tech way of guestimating remaining disk space.

Table 5.3   Mostly Complete Code List

Code Class	Code Sequence	What it Does
Select-Play-Select (SPS) Note: Backdoors not required. These codes are best entered while playing back a recorded program.	S-P-S-3-0-S	Turns on 30-second skip
	S-P-S-9-S	Displays onscreen clock
	S-P-S-InstantReplay-S	Puts up Status Indicator
	S-P-S-Pause-S	Hyper-Fast Status Bar
Clear-Enter-Clear (CEC) Note: These codes are best entered while playing back a recorded program.	C-E-C-ThumbsUp	View TiVo Log Files
	C-E-C-ThumbsDown	Shuts down myworld program
	C-E-C-0	Transparent Clock
	C-E-C-1	Opaque Clock
	C-E-C-2	Scheduled Suggestions in To Do List
	C-E-C-3	Same as C-E-C-2
	C-E-C-4	Rebuild Suggestions
	C-E-C-5	Toggles On/Off Overshoot Correction
	C-E-C-6	Node Navigator
	C-E-C-Slow	Creates a myworld State file at /tmp/mwstate
	C-E-C-Fast Forward (or C-E-C-Back)	TiVo Reboot
	C-E-C-Advance	Boat Anchor Mode
Enter-Enter (EE) Note: All EE codes are entered from the Search by Title screen.	E-E-1	Change Fast Forward Value for Speed1
	E-E-2	Change Fast Forward Value for Speed2
	E-E-3	Change Fast Forward Value for Speed3
	E-E-4	Displays Rate1: prompt
	E-E-5	Displays Rate2: prompt
	E-E-6	Displays Rate3: prompt
	E-E-7	Displays Inter: prompt
	E-E-8	Displays Open: prompt
	E-E-9	Displays an int.disabled or int.enabled message
	E-E-TiVoGuy	Set Clock
	E-E-Back	Displays Offset: prompt
	E-E-FF	Displays Delay: prompt
Clear-Clear-Enter-Enter (CCEE) Note: All CCEE codes are entered from the System Information screen. Only worked prior to ver. 3.0.	C-C-E-E-2	Debug Mode
	C-C-E-E-3	Initiate Call to TiVo, Inc.
	C-C-E-E-7	Timestamp Problem in Error Log
	C-C-E-E-8	Empties the Channels You Watch Screen
	C-C-E-E-0	Change Dial-In Configuration Code
Thumb Codes (TTT) Note: Entered in various areas of software. See Notes column.	TD-TD-TU-IR	Scheduled TiVo Suggestions appear in To Do List
	TD-TD-TU-IR	Reveals hidden recordings in Now Playing
	TD-TU-TD-IR	Clips on Disk Menu
	TD-TU-TD-Record	MenuItem Backdoor
	TD-TU-TD-Clear	Displays Italic Font
	0-TU	Free Space Indicator
	TU	DirecTV Satellite Status Indicator
	0-TD	Advanced Troubleshooting
	Slow-0-Record-TU	Sort the Now Playing list

Notes

Works in all OS versions except 2.0.

Includes Elapsed Time Indicator in 4.0. Works in vers. 1.3, 3.0, 4.0.

May not show up completely (or at all) on some TV screens. Works in 2.0 through 4.0.

Now you see it…You did see it, did you? Works in 2.0 through 4.0.

Allows you to view TiVo's log files on your TV. Left arrow to get out. Vers. 1.3 and 4.0 only.

DO NOT use this code! This makes myworld, TiVo's user interface, shut down! Vers. 2.0 only.

Only works in ver. 2.0.

Only works in ver. 2.0.

Only works in ver. 2.0.

Only works in ver. 2.0.

Rebuilds TiVo's Suggestions based on recent Thumb Ratings. Works only in some versions.

When entered during 2x or 3x FF, causes the Overshoot Correction to be turned off. Works in Series 1 DirecTV DVR only.

Ver. 3.0 only. For setting Node 1 (Overshoot Correction) and Node 30 (Advance WishLists).

Dumps a snapshoot of the myworld program to a tmp file.

Actually useful! Does a full reboot of your system without having to unplug/replug your TiVo. Easier on your hardware.

Same as Messages and Setup -> System Reset -> Restart the recorder.

Makes TiVo thinks it has no Guide data. Very bad. **DO NOT try this at home!**

Known to work in vers. 1.3 and 3.0/.

Known to work in vers. 1.3 and 3.0/.

Known to work in vers. 1.3 and 3.0/.

Function unknown.

Function unknown.

Function unknown.

Refers to interstitial TiVoGuy animations that are long gone. Does nothing.

Function unknown.

See E-E-7 Note above.

Allows you to manually set TiVo's clock. An entry mistake here could be dangerous. Not advised.

Change Overshoot Correction "offset" for rewind. Default value is 2000. Works only in versions prior to 3.0.

Change Overshoot Correction "delay" for FF. Default value is 957. Works in versions prior to 3.0.

Sends debug files to var/log/tvdebuglog.

In versions prior to 3.0, this placed some sort of "special" call to Big Tivo.

Sends a timestamped debugging message to the log file /var/log/tverr

Takes you to the Channels You Watch screen but displays no channels. Can cause problems. Best avoided. Only works prior to 3.0.

Only worked prior to ver. 3.0.

Only works in vers. 3.0 and 4.0. Entered in To Do List.

Only works in vers. 3.0 and 4.0. Entered in Now Playing.

Reveals components of the Teleworld program. Entered in Now Playing.

Reveals menu code for TiVo Central promo items. Entered in TiVo Central.

Turns all text throughout TiVo to italic. Entered in TiVo Central. Only works in vers. 3.0 and 4.0.

Only works in ver. 4.0. Much appreciated feature.

On DirecTiVo startup, single Thumb Up displays sat data, including which transponder (TX:) is being used.

Backdoors not required. DirecTiVo only.

On Series 2 w/HMF, entering this in Now Playing brings up an "Advanced Troubleshooting" screen for HMF. Use unknown.

Allows you to sort Now Playing list by date recorded, expiry date, and alphabetically. Only works in 3.0. Entered in Now Playing.

Tip

To learn more about the codes in Table 5.3 and other codes not listed here, search for the "Almost Complete Codes List" on tivocommunity.com. The discussion attached to the list is where any new code discoveries will likely be posted. Who knows, you may have one or two of your own.

Tip

You'll notice that this Easter egg makes a reference to *Austin Powers: The Spy Who Shagged Me*. Now, remember earlier in this chapter, in Table 5.1, that the backdoor code for the UK OS 1.5.2 was MOJO1 spelled backward. And why did Austin Powers go back in time in the film? To get his mojo back! Someone at TiVo obviously has a keen interest in Austin Powers. Could this hold a clue to the backdoor codes of OSes 3.1, 3.2, and 4.0? You won't know until you try.

Other Codes

There are a number of other code sequences that have been found, but they do nothing except trigger the system dings (the Thumbs Up sound). They may be doing something unseen, but no one has yet figured out what. With your TiVo OS safely backed up, feel free to while away the hours, thumbs racing across your remote like you're playing some geeky instrument, in search of fame and fortune through the discovery of more hidden features. (Okay, we're lyin' about the fortune part.)

Thumbs Up for Team TiVo!

The term "Easter egg" is used in computer circles to refer to hidden messages, features, jokes, pictures, and so forth that are left behind by rascally programmers for the overly curious to discover. They are not only found in computer programs, but DVDs and computer/video games as well. Some people are starting to widen the usage of the term Easter egg to apply to *any* hidden anything—in this case, all of the codes in this chapter—but we'd like to maintain the tradition of only calling the more frivolous, fun stuff Easter eggs. And TiVo does have such a hidden treat. If you turn on Closed Captioning on your TV set, then go to *Search by Title* in TiVo and type in SHAGWELL (as in Felicity Shagwell from *Austin Powers*) and give 'er the ole Thumbs Up, you can watch the credits roll (literally) for the TiVo developers. Yah, baby!

Hittin' the Hard Stuff

In Part 1, we covered most of the cool things you can do with TiVo without having to crack the case. As you've seen (if you were paying attention and applied what you learned), there are a ton of features (both overt and covert) and tips and tricks to make TiVo do your media-obsessed bidding.

In the next section, we'll take the top off your TiVo and have a look around. We'll cover upgrading and replacing hard drives for all levels of TiVo users (so, you non-techies can relax), how to network both Series 1 and Series 2 TiVos, and some other common hardware add-ons and fixes. So grab your tools, roll up your sleeves, and let's do some hardware hacking!

Part **II**

Chapter 6

Touring Your TiVo: The Hardware

In this chapter, we pop the top on TiVo and take a tour of its internals. If you want to, you can play along at home by removing the lid on your own TiVo and having a look around, or you can just take the virtual tour via the following text and images. For most users, there isn't much you can do with the information in this chapter in terms of upgrading or replacing components. But knowing how TiVo works and what component does what will give you a better understanding what might be at fault should something go wrong.

 This entire chapter is Geekitude Level 3

Getting on TiVo's Case

The first thing that you need to do before you crack the case on your TiVo is to unplug it from the wall and wait at least five minutes for it to discharge. This will *not* provide a complete power discharge; you could still be in for a serious shock inside. Read the "Power Supply" section later in this chapter if you're actually planning on taking your TiVo apart now. The first thing you'll need to do is do is remove the T-10 Torx screws found on the back most TiVo cases (not SVR-3000, Samsung 4040, or the Toshiba and Pioneer DVD/DVR combo units) See Figure 6.1. For information on Torx drivers, see Chapter 7, "TiVo Hacker's Toolbox."

FIGURE 6.1

The Torx screws that hold TiVo together. Depending on your model, there will be three to five of them.

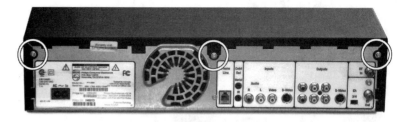

With these screws removed, you need to slide the top back and then pull upward. In TiVo hacking circles, partitioning a new TiVo hard drive is called "blessing the drive." So, we decided to call the popular maneuver for removing the case the "hardware blessing." See Figure 6.2.

FIGURE 6.2

The TiVo "hardware blessing." Incense and incantations are optional.

Leo Laporte's Guide to TiVO

Look at All Them Cool Shiny Parts!   Chapter 6

To perform the blessing, put the TiVo on the floor and kneel in front of it with your knees about 6" from the front of the case. Get out your incense, prayer beads and...okay we're kidding about this part. Place the palms of your hands on the back edges of the top (on some units, such as the HDR and SVR-2000 series, you really have to put your weight into it). Push toward the back of the box. The case will finally slide back and then you can lift it up and off and take a gander at your TiVo's guts (see Figure 6.3). Again, you want to give the open power supply area a wide birth.

FIGURE 6.3

The three main areas of TiVo's Internals: 1) The motherboard, 2) The drive(s), 3) The **unshielded** power supply. Area 3 will try to bite you if you go near it.

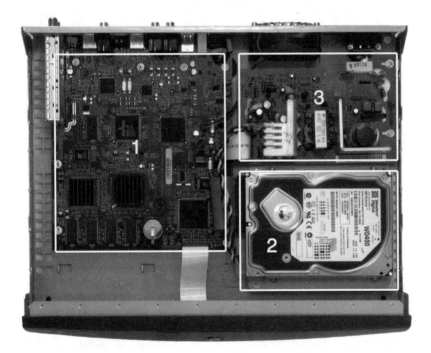

Look at All Them Cool Shiny Parts!

With the lid off, you can finally see all of the baked-in (and bolted on) electronic goodness that makes your TiVo so delicious. Let's take a look at the main components, one at a time. We've reprinted the figure that we used in Chapter 2, "Getting the Most Out of Your TiVo," but here have detailed more of the components (see Figure 6.4).

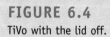

FIGURE 6.4
TiVo with the lid off.

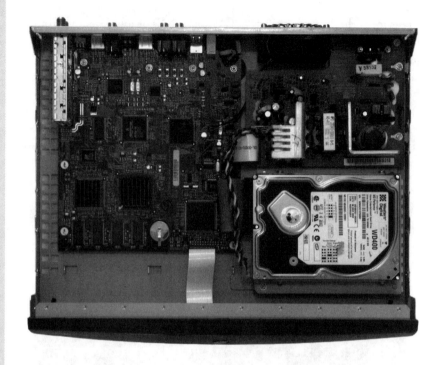

Tip

Trying to keep track of all these parts and what they do can get a little dizzying. It may be helpful to refer back to Figure 2.2 in Chapter 2. This diagram shows the flow of A/V signals through the various components detailed here.

Motherboard

Like any computer, everything springs from TiVo's motherboard (or "mobo" for short). While there are many similarities to a PC's board, since this is an embedded system, there are a few distinct differences. The main difference is that many more of the components, from the central processing unit (CPU) to the video processor to the TV tuner, are not "socketed," they are hardwired (or "baked") right onto the board. On a PC, these components are designed to be replaceable and upgradable, so they (and other key components) are on circuit boards that plug into sockets on the motherboard. On a digital home appliance such as a TiVo, keeping the manufacturing costs down is critical, so using chips instead of plug-in boards and socketed processors saves a lot of money. There is one socketed connector on TiVo's mobo (Series 1 only) that looks like the standard PCI (Peripheral Component Interconnect) slot found on a home computer (see Figure 6.5). Unfortunately, it is not. It is a proprietary connector. We'll discuss it later in this chapter (see "Edge Connector").

Leo Laporte's Guide to TiVO

Look at All Them Cool Shiny Parts!   Chapter 6

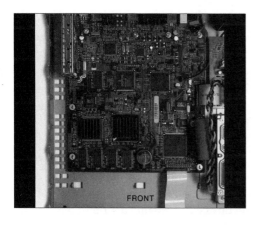

FRONT

FRONT

FIGURE 6.5

Close-up of the TiVo motherboards. The left image is a stand-alone Series 1; the right image is from a SA TiVo-branded Series 2. Your Series 2 mobo might be slightly different.

The Not So Central Processing Unit

In most computers, the CPU is just as its name implies, a central fetcher, decoder, and interpreter of all of the instructions sent to it by the computer's operating system and other loaded software. The CPU also serves as the chief data traffic controller, transferring information to and from the other hardware components over the computer's main data transfer path, called the "system bus." On TiVo, the CPU is not really that "central"; it works in concert with a proprietary processor called the TiVo Media Switch (see the next section). It is not known exactly how these two work together, but based on comments made by TiVo representatives in the past, it sounds as though the Media Switch does more of the heavy lifting and the CPU is dedicated more to the traffic cop functions of such a processor, passing the data back and forth between TiVo's filing/database system, other hardware components, and the Media Switch.

All Series 1 TiVos, both stand-alone and DirecTiVos, used the IBM 403GCX PowerPC as the CPU (see Figure 6.6). The PowerPC chip was first developed in the early 1990s by AIM (an alliance of Apple, IBM, and Motorola). PowerPC uses what's known as a RISC (Reduced Instruction Set Computers) design. This refers to the way the processor is streamlined to reduce the number of memory accesses and to simplify instruction sets in the processor so that they all execute faster (and all take the same time to execute).

NOTE

The "Power" in PowerPC is borrowed from IBM's earlier POWER chip architecture (which allegedly stands for "Performance Optimization With Enhanced RISC"). And while you might think that the "PC" stands for "Personal Computer," it actually stands for "Performance Computing." So that gives us "Performance Optimization With Enhanced RISC Performance Computing." We guess that they were so busy simplifying the instruction sets that they didn't have time to simplify the horrific geekspeak!

NOTE

In case you're interested, here's a processor stats datadump from an S2 MIPS R5432 processor:

cpu	: MIPS
cpu model	: R5432 V3.0
system type	: TiVo UMA P0 board
BogoMIPS	: 161.38
byteorder	: big endian
unaligned accesses	: 8198
wait instruction	: no
microsecond timers	: yes
extra interrupt vector	: no
hardware watchpoint	: yes
spurious interrupts	: 55745
cycle counter frequency	: 81003906

Here's a link to the datasheet on the processor at NEC's website http://www.necelam.com/docs/files/1375_V1.pdf

For Series 2 machines, both stand-alone and DirecTiVos, the NEC MIPS R5432 processor is used. This CPU uses another type of RISC design. "MIPS" stands for "Microprocessor without Interlocked Pipeline Stages." Without getting too geekitudinal on you, besides the shorter, same-length instruction sets used on other RISC architectures such as PowerPC, MIPS processing uses instructional pipelines where a CPU instruction is divided into smaller steps and a successive step starts to execute even before the preceding step is complete. In contrast to this, previous architectures executed one instruction at a time, leaving a lot of the CPU's available processing power idle. MIPS allows the processing to be spread out and get a jump on itself by using multiple "pipelines" for each instruction. The MIPS design has proven to be extremely popular, especially in the embedded systems market. Besides current TiVos, Windows CE handhelds, the Sony PlayStation 2, and Sony's new PSP handheld game machine all use a MIPS processor.

FIGURE 6.6

The Central Processing Units. Left: The IBM PowerPC for Series 1, Right: the NEC MIPS CPU (hidden under a heat sink).

Leo Laporte's Guide to TiVO

Look at All Them Cool Shiny Parts!   Chapter 6

Media Switch

The square chip on the mobo with the big smiley TiVo face on it is called the TiVo Media Switch (see Figure 6.7). It is TiVo's proprietary audio/video processor and it works in concert with the CPU to control the A/V encoding and decoding, and manage TiVo's file system (called the *MFS* for *Media File System*) and other processing tasks. In the embedded system world, the Media Switch is referred to as an *ASIC* (or *Application-Specific Integrated Circuit*). This additional chip makes TiVo into something of a dual-processor, which allows it to handle such multi-tasking as recording a program, sending an already-recorded program to the screen for you to watch, and dialing into TiVo's remote servers, all at the same time, without dropping any frames of video or bits of audio.

FIGURE 6.7

The mysterious TiVo Media Switch. It does most of the work while the "central" processing unit gets all the credit.

Random Access Memory (RAM)

Series 1 stand-alone TiVos had 16MB of RAM built into them (DirecTV DVRs came with 32MB). There are pads on S1 SA motherboards for an additional 16MB. Some brave geeks have soldered on additional RAM chips to bring the total up to 32MB. Early TiVo hackers hoped that boosting the RAM would improve TiVos ability to sort data, load menus, and execute other software activities that can sometimes be frustratingly slow (especially if you have a lot of Season Passes, Wish List items, recorded shows, and so on). Performance does increase a small amount with added memory, but not by enough to be worth it to most users. The sluggishness in TiVo's software operation is not due to RAM access issues but is caused by disk access slowdowns. TiVo's Media File System database can cause bottlenecks as it gets bigger and needs to fetch more data, all of which is stored on the hard drive(s). Accelerating this process has been addressed by the creation of a third-party CacheCARD, designed specifically to more deftly juggle all of the database transactions in the MFS. We'll discuss the CacheCARD in Chapter 11, "Adding a CacheCARD."

Series 1 DirecTiVos, Series 2 stand-alone, and DirecTV DVRs come with 32MB of RAM. There are no means of adding more RAM, and because there's no edge connector on S2 models (see the "Edge Connector" section later in this chapter), there is no way of adding database cache memory either. Refer back to Figure 6.4.

Video Decoding and Encoding

In this section, well take a look at the chips that do the amazing silicon hat trick of decoding the incoming analog signals, prepping them for conversion to MPEG-2 digital, encoding them for storage, and then re-encoding (or decoding again, depending on how you look at it) for transfer to an analog display. Of course, this is only on regular TiVos. Something entirely different happens on HD DirecTV DVRs, where the signals (the high-def ones, anyway) arrive in digital form and head to the digital display as digital output.

Video Decoder Chip

Of course, the CPU and the Media Switch wouldn't have any A/V to play with if it wasn't for the video and audio encoders and decoders that are working feverishly to convert the incoming signals from analog to digital, into the MPEG-2 format for storage, and then back into analog signals for outputting to your TV. On DirecTV systems, the signals come down from the heavens already in a high-quality MPEG-2 format (heaven can afford a much better MPEG-2 encoder than you can), so no A/V decoding from analog to digital and no MPEG-2 encoding are required (Decoding, from MPEG-2 back to analog is, of course, required on the output end).

On stand-alone TiVos, the first thing that happens to the video signal coming in is that it needs to be converted from analog to digital. This conversion happens so that the video signal can then be sent to the MPEG-2 encoder. The encoder can only handle digital input, so this analog to digital (A/D) conversion needs to happen first. The format it's converted to is VGA. This is the same VGA (Video Graphics Array) computer display standard that's been found on most computer monitors for decades. Because it's been around for so long and the chips are so cheap, it's a convenient format that TiVo's on-board MPEG-2 encoder can accept.

Leo Laporte's Guide to TiVO

Look at All Them Cool Shiny Parts!   Chapter 6

MPEG-2 Video Encoder

Now that the graceful, undulating waves of analog radio signals have been mercilessly reduced to the stair-step conformity of digital ones and zeros, they can enter the MPEG-2 encoder where they are subjected to a dizzying array of channel separations, division into coding blocks, transforms, encoding schemes—and other stuff that people much smarter than we are fully understand—until the signal is further compressed for efficient transfer and storage on the hard drive. As you might imagine, all of this mathematical wizardry and image processing doesn't come cheap. The MPEG-2 encoder remains the single most expensive component on the stand-alone TiVo. Thanks to the popularity of PVRs, DVD decks, and other media appliances that require real-time MPEG-2 encoding, the price has rapidly fallen on this component. When Sony first released its CXD1922Q encoder, later used on S1 stand-alone TiVos, in 1997, the chip sold for $600!

MPEG-2 Audio/Video Decoder

After the MPEG-2 encoder has had its way with the now-digital data stream, software within TiVo translates the compressed MPEG-2 data (both audio and video) into a proprietary TiVo format called TyStreams. It is these TyStreams (stored as .ty files) that end up getting parked on your hard drive. We'll discuss the software process (what happens within TiVo between the MPEG encoding and decoding) in Chapter 13, "Touring Your TiVo: The Software." When you ask TiVo to play you something from the hard drive, it starts its circuitous journey to your TV by splitting the combined audio and video TyStream files back into separate audio and video channels. The video is sent to video side of an MPEG-2 decoder and the audio is sent to the audio side of the same chip. Just as the incoming analog signal had to be converted to VGA digital before it could be MPEG-2 encoded, it now needs to be un-encoded from the MPEG-2 digital format before it gets passed to an analog encoder that will then ready the audio and video signals for display on your TV. The MPEG-2 A/V Decoder chip serves this function (refer back to Figure 6.4).

Video Encoder

Finally, the still-digital but now un-MPEG-ified video arrives at its final processing plant on the motherboard, the Video Encoder chip. Here it is converted from a digital to an analog signal, into NTSC format, the display standard that your TV understands (in North America, anyway). Once converted to analog, the video stream finally makes its way to the TV display via composite video or S-Video cable. The stand-alone S1 TiVo uses the Philips SAA7120H encoder chip. Series 2 models use the Broadcom BCM7020 chip, which handles both digital to analog (D/A) video encoding and audio encoding. See "D/A Audio Converter" later in this chapter. Refer back to Figure 6.4

Audio Handling

The decoding, encoding, storing, decoding, and re-encoding we've just discussed (whew!) is on the video side of the signal. The audio signals have to make their own epic journey across TiVo's mobo. Let's chart the way-points on the journey.

Sound Processor

The audio input first enters a signal processor that converts it from analog to digital (A/D). The signal is then output from this chip as an I^2S Digital Audio stream. "I^2S" stands for *Inter-IC Sound* and is a digital audio format commonly used on CD players, digital TVs, and other digital consumer devices. The sound processor used on Series 1 stand-alone TiVos is the Micronas MSP340Ga4. For the Series 2, the MSP4448G chip is used. This latter chip was specifically designed for digital set-top boxes such as TiVo. Refer back to Figure 6.4.

MPEG-2 Audio Encoder

Suitably one'd and zero'd, the audio enters an MPEG-2 audio encoder and is compressed for storage using the MPEG-2 audio compression standard. Once compressed, it gets converted through software to the TiVo tyStream format (.ty files), where it is combined with its video counterpart and written to the hard drive. When you request a file, the stored .ty object (otherwise known as that episode of *The Honeymooners* you recorded from TVLand) heads to the MPEG-2 A/V Decoder where both audio and video signals begin the process of being converted back to analog. Refer back to Figure 6.4.

D/A Audio Converter

The last step for the audio part of the signal is to be converted from digital to analog. This is done on a stereo D/A audio converter chip. Once converted, the sound signals head out of the left and right RCA audio jacks on their way to your TV's audio inputs or to your stereo system. On Series 1 TiVos, the Cirrus Logic CS4333 D/A Stereo Audio Converter was used. On Series 2, the Broadcom BCM7040 chip is used, which combines audio and video D/A conversion functions on one chip. Refer back to Figure 6.4.

Hard Drive(s)

The heart of a TiVo is its hard disk drive (or drives). In the Series 1 era, some models came with one drive; others came with two (see Figure 6.8). Some came with brackets already built in to accept a second drive; some did not. For Series 2, manufacturers stuck with a single drive and more models now come with a bay for adding a second drive. Table 6.1 lists all the Series 1 models, how many drives that came standard on them, and their size(s) and recording capacity. Table 6.2 details the same information for Series 2 machines. If you want to see which TiVo models require brackets for adding second drives, turn to Table 8.1 in Chapter 8, "Upgrading Hard Drives."

FIGURE 6.8

TiVo Hard Drive. Here is a Quantum Fireball CX 13.6GB.

Touring Your TiVo: The Hardware

Table 6.1   TiVo Series 1 Models

Brand	Model	Type	No. of Drives
Philips	HDR110/HDR112	Stand-alone (SA)	1
	HDR212	SA	1
	HDR310/HDR312	SA	2
	HDR3120x	SA	1
	HDR612	SA	2
	DSR6000 DSR6000R DSR6000R01	DirecTV DVR	1
	DSR6000 DSR6000R DSR6000R01	DirecTV DVR	2
Sony	SVR2000	SA	1
	Sat-T60	DirecTV DVR	1
	Sat-T60	DirecTV DVR	2
Hughes	GXCEBOT GXCEBOTD	DirecTV DVR	1

** For stand-alone TiVos, storage capacity hour figures are for Basic Quality recordings.
For DirecTV DVRs, all recording is one quality setting (equivalent to "Best" on SA TiVos).*

Table 6.2   TiVo Series 2 Models

Brand	Model	Type	No. of Drives
TiVo	TCD130040	Stand-alone (SA)	1
	TCD230040	SA	1
	TCD240040	SA	1
	TCD140060	SA	1
	TCD240080	SA	1
	TCD240140	SA	1

Leo Laporte's Guide to TiVO

Look at All Them Cool Shiny Parts!   Chapter 6

Storage Capacity*	Notes
13.6GB HD 14 hrs	
20GB HD 20 hrs	
Two 13.6GB HDs 30 hrs	
30GB HD 30 hrs	
Two 30GB HDs 60 hrs or One 40GB and One 20GB HD	
40GB HD 35 hrs	For Serial #s 4704xxx & higher. Not a hard and fast rule; the only way to be certain is to check. You can also turn on backdoors and look in the log files (see Chapter 5).
One 30GB and One 15GB HD 35 hrs	For Serial #s 4703xxx or lower.
30GB HD 30 hrs	Also some 40GB models.
40GB HD 35 hrs	For Serial #s 801xxx & higher.
One 30GB and One 15GB HD35 hrs	For Serial #s 800xxx & lower.
40GB HD 35 hrs	

Storage Capacity*	Notes
40GB HD 40 hrs	
40GB HD 40 hrs	
40GB HD 40 hrs	Also model TCD24004A.
60GB HD 60 hrs	
80GB HD 80 hrs	Also model TCD240080A.
120GB HD 140 hrs	

Touring Your TiVo: The Hardware

Table 6.2 TiVo Series 2 Models

Brand	Model	Type	No. of Drives
AT&T	TCD130040	SA	1
	TCD230040	SA	1
Sony	SVR3000	SA	1
Hughes	HDVR2	DirecTV DVR	1
	SD-DVR40	DirecTV DVR	1
	SD-DVR120	DirecTV DVR	1
	HR10-250	HD DirecTV DVR	1
Philips	DSR7000	DirecTV DVR	1
	DSR704	DirecTV DVR	1
	DSR708	DirecTV DVR	1
RCA	DVR39	DirecTV DVR	1
	DVR40	DirecTV DVR	1
Samsung	S4040R	DirecTV DVR	1
	S4120R	DirecTV DVR	1
Toshiba	SD-H400	SA	1
Pioneer	DVR-810H DVD	SA	1
	DVR-57H	SA	1
Humax	T800	SA	1
	T2500	SA	1
	DRT800	SA	1
	DRT2500	SA	1

* For stand-alone TiVos, storage capacity hours are for Basic Quality recordings. For DirecTV DVRs, all recording is one setting (equivalent to "Best" on SA TiVos). For HD DirecTV DVR, capacity ranges from 30-200 hrs, depending on quality setting.

Leo Laporte's Guide to TiVO

Look at All Them Cool Shiny Parts!   Chapter 6

Storage Capacity*	Notes
40GB HD 40 hrs	Current versions of this unit now say "Comcast" on the System Info screen.
40GB HD 40 hrs	See previous note. The box for this model does not say AT&T on it like the 130040 does.
80GB HD 80 hrs	
40GB HD 35 hrs	Some models of this unit are known as the HDVR3. Same unit, different name, depending on which version of software it is using. This often confuses people.
40GB HD 35 hrs	
120GB HD 100 hrs	
250GB 200 hrs SD/30 hrs HD	High-Definition Model.
40GB HD 35 hrs	
40GB HD 35 hrs	
80GB HD 70 hrs	
40GB HD 35 hrs	
40GB HD 35 hrs	
40GB HD 35 hrs	Uses Philips-head screws on drive mount
120GB 100 hrs	Uses Philips-head screws on drive mount.
80GB HD 80 hrs	With DVD Player.
80GB HD 80 hrs	With DVD Recorder.
120GB HD 120 hrs	With DVD Recorder.
80GB HD 80 hrs	
250GB HD 250 hrs	
80GB HD 80 hrs	With DVD Recorder
250GB HD 250 hrs	With DVD Recorder. As of this writing, details on this model are not known.

RF Modulator

If you've ever looked inside of a VCR, game machine, or other device that's intended to talk to a TV set, you've likely seen a slender silver box with F-type coax cable connectors poking out of the back. This is the RF modulator, the device that takes the signals coming out of the unit and converts them to the radio frequency (RF) modulated signals that your TV expects (see Figure 6.9). Many of these RF devices, like the one on your TiVo, are actually demodulators, as well.

FIGURE 6.9

RF modulator. You could call it a "modem," 'cause modulation and demodulation of radio signals is what it's all about.

If your signal comes into the TiVo from some other source than a coax cable (such as from a set-top box equipped with S-video and/or composite output), the RF demodulator/tuner on your TiVo will not be used. That's because the set-top box has already done the demodulation/tuning for you, allowing the signal to enter your TiVo through a different input pathway (such as S-video and RCA audio L/R, or RCA composite video and audio L/R).

As you can see by looking on the back panel of your TiVo, there is an RF input and an RF output. Incoming signals over coax cable (coming from a cable or satellite source) enter the "demodulator block" of the device (the RF input) and are stripped of the radio carrier waves they traveled in on. From here, they enter the system (as analog audio/video input) on their way to video and sound decoders (see previous entries earlier in this chapter). If you connect a coax cable to the RF output, the signal is converted (frequency modulated) back into NTSC output (in the US) for sending to your TV. When people talk about the TV tuner inside a TiVo, they're really talking about the RF demodulator/modulator. A chip on the circuit board inside of this device tunes the incoming signal to a particular frequency; whatever frequency the channel is that you (or your TiVo) has selected. It is this tuned radio signal that enters the encoding/decoding process we described earlier in this chapter.

Leo Laporte's Guide to TiVO

Look at All Them Cool Shiny Parts!   Chapter 6

Modem Chips

All Series 1 and Series 2 TiVos have chips on their motherboards, as shown in Figure 6.10, that serve as the modems used to make TiVo's daily calls (unless your TiVo is networked, which we'll cover in Chapter 9, "Networking Your TiVo"). Series 1 TiVos used the V.90 standard. V.90 refers to the standards number used by the ITU (International Telecommunication Union). The "V" stands for the series designation (A–Z) and the "90" part is the specific standard's serial number. V.90 modems are capable of data transfer rates up to 33,600Kbits/s upstream (that is, from you to TiVo, Inc.) and 56,600Kbits/s downstream (from TiVo, Inc, to you). Since most of the traffic is downstream, these modems are usually listed as 33.6. Series 2 TiVos use chips designated as "V.34 bis" or "V.34+". This standard defines modems that operate up to 33.6Kbits/s in both directions.

These modem chips are a highly integrated solution that compresses all of what you'd normally find on a modem card or external modem (various specialized controllers, transformer, relays, ROM chips, support electronics, and so forth) into two very small surface-mounted chips. One chip serves as the modem itself; the other, a modem controller. See Figure 6.10.

Backup Battery

Every TiVo model has a backup battery on the motherboard (see Figure 6.11). This battery is used to retain the current date and time information and other settings held in a static RAM chip if there's a power outage or other sudden interruption of power (or if you turn your TiVo off).

FIGURE 6.10

TiVo's teeny modems chips on the motherboard (here on an S1 SA).

Tip

The modems used on the Series 1 TiVo were prone to breakdown. If your TiVo is not connected to a home network, a broken modem means that you lose your link to TiVo's remote servers (which means no Guide data or software upgrades). In Chapter 12, "Dark Hardware Hacking Arts," we'll discuss how to troubleshoot and replace a broken modem chip or how to use an external modem to replace a dead internal one.

The RAM chip used has extremely low power requirements, so it can hold this information for a long period of time.

FIGURE 6.11

TiVo backup batteries: SA Series 1 (left), SA Series 2 (right).

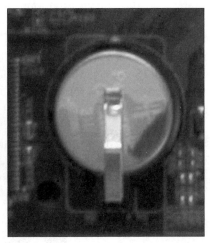

All TiVo models use the Sharp C2032 disk-type Lithium-Ion battery that connects to the motherboard via a slide-in holder. This particular battery and holder type is common on many computer motherboards and serves a similar function. Under normal operation, for most TiVos, this battery will never need to be replaced. If the battery goes dead, you will only know it when TiVo is powered down and powered back up again. Without a battery to maintain time and date information, your TiVo will think it's 1998 (Hello Bill and Monica!). As far as we know, no other critical data is lost, and at the next daily call, the date will correct itself and new Guide data will be downloaded. Everything will work fine again until the next time TiVo is powered down. Obviously this situation is not ideal and we have heard reports of a bum battery causing strange operating behaviors, so if a battery goes bad, you'll want to replace it.

The Fan

Every TiVo has a single cooling fan, the same type of small, direct current (DC) fan found in computer cases (see Figure 6.12). Fans from several manufacturers have been used in TiVos over the years. Most are either 60mm or 80mm in size, with some of the newer chassis using a 70mm fan.

Tip

In Chapter 12, we'll show you how to replace the motherboard backup battery. On S2 machines, this is a trivial matter, but on S1 models, a poor location for the battery holder requires that you remove the motherboard to get at it. Turn to Chapter 12 to see how it's done (for all TiVo types).

Leo Laporte's Guide to TiVO

Look at All Them Cool Shiny Parts!   Chapter 6

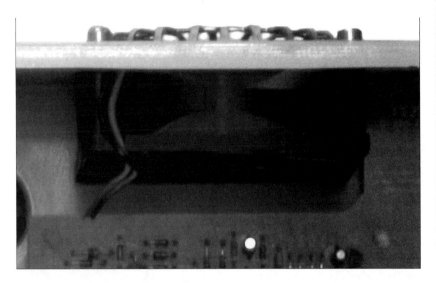

FIGURE 6.12
TiVo's cooling fan. This one's from a TiVo-brand Series 2.

The fan is usually located in the back of the TiVo box, and intake grills are usually located underneath. Under normal circumstances, TiVo doesn't tend to run too hot and doesn't require any special maintenance or treatment to keep things cool (besides making sure there's adequate airspace around the TiVo case). But fans, like any components, can sometimes fail, or after adding a second drive, things can start to heat up. In Chapter 8, we'll cover some extra cooling options. See Figure 6.12.

Edge Connector (Series 1 Only)

The edge connector (also called a "header"), shown in Figure 6.13, is found along the front of all Series 1 TiVo motherboards, and looks like a typical PCI (Peripheral Component Interconnect) slot, as seen inside any home computer (used for plugging in peripheral devices). It isn't. It's a proprietary header that's used in the manufacturing of TiVo and for hardware debugging at the plant. Industrious hardware hackers pieced together information on what the pins on this connector do, and armed with that information, developed Ethernet adapter cards and other add-on hardware that plug into this slot. This has led to the unsupported (by TiVo, Inc.) ability to connect Series 1 machines (both stand-alone and DirecTiVos) to a home network. We'll discuss these third-party networking add-ons in Chapter 9.

FIGURE 6.13

The proprietary TiVo edge connector, found only on all Series 1 TiVos.

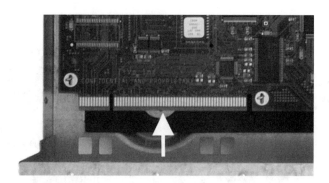

Power Supply

Your PC's power supply is safely stored away in a shielded enclosure that prevents you from frying off parts of that skin-encased bag of water you call a body. The TiVo supply does not offer such protection (see Figure 6.14). Its shocking components are right out there in the open, just waiting for you to touch 'em. Don't make their sick little electron wishes come true. Obviously, always unplug your TiVo before opening it up, let it discharge for a few minutes, and always stay well clear of the entire power supply area as you muck around inside. It's also a good idea to wear a static electric wrist strap, but even with that, you should be extra careful. That unshielded power supply can deliver quite a wallop.

FIGURE 6.14

The open-to-the-world TiVo power supply. This part wants to bite you. For the love of TiVoGuy, don't let it!

Leo Laporte's Guide to TiVO

Look at All Them Cool Shiny Parts!   Chapter 6

The Back Panel

If the TiVo Central screen is your software interface to TiVo, the back panel is the hardware interface. Here you'll find all of the inputs and outputs that TiVo uses to communicate with your A/V source(s) and the other devices to which you output TiVo. We covered all of the input/output types in the "Mini-Tutorial to A/V Tech" in Chapter 2.

Figure 6.15 shows the back panels for Series 1 and Series 2 stand-alone TiVos. The only thing we didn't talk about in Chapter 2 that you can see in these images is the Channel 3/4 selector switch for the RF cable output. This is normally used only in situations where you don't have a cable box and want to run a cable service into your TiVo and then from TiVo to your TV set. Ideally you would use S-Video and RCA left/right audio, or composite video and RCA left/right audio. But if your TV does not have either of these connection technologies, you can use the RF output from TiVo to TV.

The Channel 3/4 selector switch is used to tune the frequency output to either channel 3 or channel 4. You'll then need to tune your TV to that channel and use TiVo's tuner to navigate the channels. This is the lowest-quality option for TiVo output, so you only want to use it if no other options are available on your TV. Oddly enough, this option is not available at all on the Pioneer DVD/DVR combo unit.

NOTE

The power supply for the stand-alone S2 TiVo is 38 watts, while the S2 DirecTV DVR runs at 78W. The S1 (both SA and DirecTiVo) used a 61W supply. All are what's known as switching power supplies. Replacement power for the SA S1s is reasonably inexpensive. Replacement power supplies for the S1 DTVs are very expensive. As far as we know, weaKnees.com are the only parts supplier who carries them.

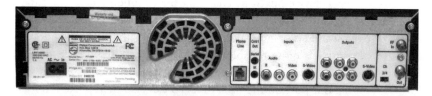

FIGURE 6.15
The back panels on TiVo Series 1 and Series 2 stand-alones.

Other Miscellaneous Parts

Obviously that's not every component found inside your TiVo. There are a few more worth mentioning:

- **Cryptographic Chip**—All TiVos have a cryptographic security chip on their motherboards. These chips are OTP (One-Time Programmable), meaning that data can only be written to them once—in this case, during the manufacturing process. It's not entirely certain what's stored on these chips, but it's widely believed that each TiVo's unique serial number is stored here.

- **MPEG Clock Chip**—In A/V, as in life, timing is everything. The MPEG clock synthesizer makes sure that the MPEG audio and video signals stay in sync. There are actually several other clocks on the motherboard dedicated to keeping various signals on track as they move through the inputting, decoding, encoding, storing, re-decoding, re-encoding, and outputting process.

- **Infrared (IR) Receiver**—The ribbon cable coming from the front of your TiVo to the motherboard is the connector for the IR receiver on the front of your TiVo. This is your IR input. On the back panel of your TiVo is a mini-plug out port for IR. This is used for outputting IR signals (via the IR Blaster that comes with your TiVo), so you can relay the IR commands you enter via your remote to whatever device might be changing the channels (such as a cable box or satellite receiver). Every TiVo also provides a serial (RS-232) control output (via a mini-plug jack found just above the IR port). Serial control is more reliable than IR output, so if you have a serial control jack on your set-top box, use it instead of the IR blaster. The serial out port on the back of TiVo can also be repurposed for use as a low-tech network connection between TiVo and your PC (see Chapter 10, "Quick n' Dirty Serial Networking").

- **Parlex Ribbon Cable**—On Series 1 DirecTV DVRs, the white ribbon cable that connects the power supply to the motherboard is notorious for causing problems due to corrosion on its contacts. If an S1 DirecTiVo unit goes from powering up to "Almost There…" and then restarts, there's a good chance that this cable is to blame. "Brightening" the contacts on the plug (where it attaches to the mobo) with a pencil eraser will often solve the problem.

Leo Laporte's Guide to TiVO

That Concludes Our Tour. Please Exit the Chapter in an Orderly Fashion.   Chapter 6

That Concludes Our Tour. Please Exit the Chapter in an Orderly Fashion.

This chapter should have given you a basic understanding of how TiVo's hardware works and what components are tasked with doing what. While most of this information falls into the category of geek curiosity only, some of it will come into play as we start doing some actual hardware hacking (adding hard drives, adding networking capabilities, doing some troubleshooting and repairs).

In the next chapter we'll gather together the tools needed to do some hardware hacking. Then, in Chapter 8, we'll finally roll up the sleeves on our mechanic's overalls and get down to business, tricking out that DVR with more TV show storage capacity than any human being should rightly possess. Couch potatoes of the world, relax!

Chapter 7

TiVo Hacker's Toolbox

Before you start wailin' away on that poor, defenseless TiVo (who's never done anything bad to you), you're going to need some proper tools [Cue: Unsettling mad scientist laughter]. Which tools you need depends a lot on what hardware hacks you're planning on implementing. If you're just going to open your TiVo to have a look around, or if you plan on, say, simply installing a prepared hard drive upgrade kit (see details in the next chapter), you're really not going to need much more than a Torx driver (or two). Cheap versions of these drivers even come with some kits. If you plan on doing more serious hacking, such as installing an Ethernet card on a Series 1 stand-alone, you'll need a few additional tools. In this brief chapter, we'll look at the tools you need, and some tools you might want to make your hacking exploits a little easier, safer, and more productive.

Hand Tools

Here are a few tools that are worth tossing in your box. They'll not only come in handy for TiVo hacking, but will be useful for any sort of media equipment work.

Torx Drivers

You're likely familiar with flat-head (a.k.a. "slot-head") and Phillips-head screwdrivers. Flat-head used to be the most ubiquitous of screws, but the single slot makes it prone to slippage while turning it. The four "pointed" Phillips-head screw was designed to help provide more secure contact between screw and driver (though its "dished" points can cause slippage under some circumstances). Well, just like in the shaving razor wars—where, if three blades give you a close shave, four have *got* to shave you even closer!—imagine how secure a driver head with six points would be? That's a Torx.

Torx screws are found on many types of consumer electronics, including TiVo, so you'll need a couple such drivers to open up your case. Nearly every TiVo model has its lid held in place by three to five T-10-size Torx screws (the new Pioneer and Toshiba combo units use Phillips). Most TiVos also require a T-15 driver for removing hard drives from their mounting brackets. As stated above, some TiVo drive kits come with cheapo L-shaped Torx drivers. These are all you need if you're only planning on a one-time upgrade. But if you think you're going to be doing a lot of hardware hacking, on your TiVo and other devices, you may want to invest in a decent set of drivers. But before you go buying anything, check first to make sure that you don't already have a set. If you have a bit set for your electric drill/driver, it likely has T-10 and T-15 bits (see Figure 7.1). Also, if you have a hand driver with a bit set, it likely has these common Torx sizes as well. If you don't already have Torx drivers, and plan on buying some, don't get individual drivers or a Torx-only set; you might as well spend the money on a decent driver set that includes Phillips, flat, and Torx bits. One helpful thing about the L-key drivers is that the L-shape is required to access some drive mounts attached with a T-15 Torx screw. If you get a Torx set, make sure it has an extension that can handle right angle situations.

FIGURE 7.1

An assortment of Torx-type drivers and bits.

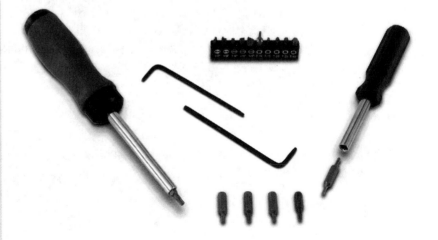

Screwdriver Set

Anybody who's courageous enough to crack the top on his or her computer or home media appliances needs a good, versatile set of screwdrivers (see Figure 7.2).

FIGURE 7.2
An inexpensive, but well-stocked driver set.

NOTE

When buying Torx bits, you'll likely encounter regular Torx and "security Torx" (sometimes referred to simply as "security drivers"). These are a special type of Torx that have a hole in the middle of the bits to fit into a pin in the middle of special Torx security screws. These pins prevent regular Torx drivers from being used. TiVo does not use these security screws, so you don't need to buy this type, but if they're available in a set that you can afford, the security version of the bits are nice to have (and they can be used on "non-secure" Torx screws as well).

You can get either a set of fixed drivers or a set with a driver handle and a collection of bits. The latter is more versatile and gives you many more bit options, and there are often extra components, such as an extender for getting the driver into those hard to reach places. If you're a tool freak, you might want to invest in a fancy set of drivers made by high-end tool manufacturers such as Excelite (www.excelite.com) and Wiha (www.wihatools.com). If you're not that...er...freaky, your local electronics or home store should have decent driver/bit sets for less than $20. Obviously, make sure that the kit has T-10 and T-15 Torx bits and a decent range of small-to-large Phillips and flat-head bits. If the set has other specialty bits such as security Torx, Posidriv (a common Euro standard), square recess, and hex-head: bonus, dude! You won't encounter these in TiVo hacking, but you might while deconstructing other gadgets around the house.

Needlenose Pliers

When doing any sort of electronics work, you'll likely end up needing the services of needlenose pliers (see Figure 7.3). The nose of these pliers tapers to nearly a point (hence the name), allowing you to get it into tight spaces. Needlenose pliers are also great for twisting wires together and bending electronic component leads. See Figure 7.3.

FIGURE 7.3

A trusty pair of needlenose pliers.

Tip

So, what do you look for in a screwdriver set? First you want a nice range of sizes for Phillips-head, flat-head, and Torx screws. You also want comfortable handles on the drivers, which will allow you to apply the most amount of torque. Also, the better the brand, and the more expensive the set, the higher the quality of materials and machining (in general).

FIGURE 7.4

Tab A in Slot B: The tabs that hold TiVo's lid on.

Tack Puller

In Jeff Keegan's book *TiVo Hacking*, he recommends using a tack puller (an expensive tool available at any home store) to pry the TiVo case top off. In Chapter 6, "Touring Your TiVo: The Hardware," we showed you the "Hardware Blessing" method of muscling the lid off. The TiVo case is held in place (besides Torx screws) by a series of tabs around the lid that fit into slots around the back panel of the case bottom (see Figure 7.4). Using the tack puller method, you can gently pry next to the tabs to pull the lid away from the back panel (and then off).

Anti-Static Wrist Strap

If you've ever had a tech repair dude (or dudette) come to your home or office to fix any electronics equipment, you likely saw him or her wearing a strange-looking bracelet with a wire attached to it. That wasn't the latest in geek chic, that was a grounding, or anti-static, strap (see Figure 7.5).

This is a handy bit of kit that electrically grounds you to the device you're working on so that you don't discharge static electricity into sensitive components that can be damaged if you and the shag carpet build up too many free electrons.

FIGURE 7.5
A cheap anti-static wrist strap. It's trés geek!

The strap usually consists of an elasticized wrist strap with a metal grommet on it that makes contact with your skin. This grommet is attached to a wire that usually has an alligator clip on the other end. To use it, you simply attach the alligator clip to the metal frame of the device you're working on. Being thusly attached to your work, you won't be able to build up static electricity, which can damage sensitive chips. Some fancier straps have a snap where the grounding wire attaches to the wristband, so that if you need to fetch a tool (or a Big Mac), you can just disconnect yourself (leaving the band on your wrist) and snap back in (to the wire/alligator clip) when you return. Antic-static straps are available at any electronics shop.

Caution

An anti-static strap protects the components from *YOU*, not you from them. The open and unshielded power supply (as discussed in Chapter 6) is still a danger to you even with the wrist strap on.

Dust-Off

We love this stuff so much, we've written odes to it. Okay, so it's a little sad to be writing enthusiastic effusions about an overpriced can of compressed gas, but it's just so handy to have on hand. If your TiVo has been around for a while, you'll see when you open it that dust has likely collected inside the case, especially on and around the cooling fan. There are air intake vents underneath the TiVo, and the cooling fan is in the back. This fan draws up air through the vents, across the motherboard and drives, and out the fan itself. This process also draws in dust. Spraying the insides of your TiVo with the Dust-Off removes any build up. Under normal conditions, your TiVo won't likely build up enough dust to cause any real problems, but removing what dust has accumulated while you're mucking around inside your box can't hurt. Think of dust on electronic components as a blanket. Blankets keep you warm. Electronics don't like warm. They're much happier with the air conditioning turned on high, no covers, sans P.J.s; you get the idea—the cooler the better!

Gareth On...

When I wrote a piece on the pleasures of blowing stuff away with Dust-Off several years ago for the *Baltimore Sun*, Falcon Safety Products took notice. The makers of this fine, but staggeringly overpriced product (a 10 oz. can of air for $8!) sent me a case of it in gratitude. I'm now on my last can. Falcon: are you listening? Send more Dust-Off!

Parts/Inspection Mirror

If you do a lot of futzing around with media equipment and computers, a parts mirror (also called an "Inspection Mirror") is a handy thing to have around (see Figure 7.6). It's basically a small (usually) rectangular mirror on an extendable rod. Some even have super bright LEDs on the ends that direct some light on the subject. This tool is great for quickly checking the back panels on components without having to drag them out. It's also handy for looking behind hard drives, under raised motherboards, and so on.

FIGURE 7.6
A parts mirror.

Other Miscellaneous Tools

The following aren't tools you need, but tools that can help make your hardware hacking life a little easier.

Labeling Machine

We already covered our labeling machine fetish in the Accessories section of Chapter 1, "Which TiVo Is Right for You?" This is obviously not a critical tool to have, but if you do have one, it's very handy for neatly labeling your primary and secondary master and slave IDE connections on your PC and the A and B drives on your TiVo (if you have more than one drive). As we'll discuss in the next chapter, it is extremely important to keep your drives straight when you are hooking your TiVo up to your PC to partition new drives or to load software onto your TiVo.

Computer Repair Kit

One way of getting a nice complement of tools for TiVo hacking and other hardware projects is to buy a computer repair or computer technician's toolkit (see Figure 7.7). These kits vary in size (and cost) and can include everything from a few drivers and pliers to kits complete with soldering tools and digital multimeters.

Tip

Many computer repair toolkits come with a "parts tube," a handy plastic tube with a lid on it. This is used to safely store screws, nuts, bolts, and other small, easily lost components while you work. If you don't have a parts tube, keeping a couple of extra 35mm film canisters in your toolkit for the same purpose is a great idea. You remember 35mm film, don't you?

FIGURE 7.7
An inexpensive, but indispensable computer repair kit.

You want to make sure that your kit at least includes a decent assortment of screw and nut bits, a crimping/wire gauge/stripping tool, needlenose pliers, diagonal cutters, and tweezers. Chip manipulating tools are nice too (extractor, inserter, desoldering pump), if you plan on doing any of this type of work.

Gareth On...

I've had the same trusty computer repair toolkit for nearly 10 years. I got it from JDR Microdevices (www.jdr.com) for $40. They still sell the same 26-piece kit, now for only $20. I use it on a nearly daily basis and a tool has yet to break or fail me. These aren't the best-made tools in the world, but for basic, light repair and hardware hacking, they're perfect, especially for the amazing price. This kit comes with a driver and set of bits (including T-10 and T-15 Torx), a wire guage/cutter/crimper, chip tools, needlenose pliers, side-cutters, a desoldering pump, and other useful tools. It also includes a 30-watt soldering iron and basic soldering tools. Everything is neatly stowed away in a zippered case. Other electronics vendors, such as Jameco (www.jameco.com), sell similar kits in a similar price range.

Serious Hardware Hacking Tools

If your idea of fun is spending a weekend with your precious PC, home stereo equipment, DVRs, and other media appliances deconstructed on your dining room table, the heady aroma of soldering wire wafting through the house ("I love the smell of solder in the morning"), then these tools are for you (but then, you likely already have them).

Soldering Tools

Actually firing up the ol' soldering iron and going to town on your TiVo's motherboard is obviously not for the weak of heart, or the poor of soldering skill. Soldering, especially on tightly populated motherboards and surface-mounted components, is best left to skilled wireheads only. But if you already have such skill, or are willing to spend the time to learn, there are a few repair projects you can do on TiVo. These projects are briefly discussed in Chapter 12, "Dark Hardware Hacking Arts," "dark" as in the mood you'll be in if you accidentally fry your TiVo's mobo.

If you do decide to rise to the challenge, you'll need a decent soldering iron and some support tools (see Figure 7.8).

FIGURE 7.8
Solder iron and miscellaneous tools.

Here's a brief rundown:

- **Soldering Iron**—Irons have different wattages, usually from 20 to 45-watts. A 30-watt iron, like the one found in the JDR Microdevices computer repair toolkit, is a common type. We like the variable wattage irons, such as the Xtronic 16-30-watt iron. For sensitive electronics soldering, you want it hot enough to quickly and thoroughly melt solder, but not so hot that you bake components. A variable iron allows you to dial up the level that attains this correct heat balance.

- **Conical Tips**—You want the sharpest, smallest soldering tips you can find. A common type is sold as a "Conical Sharp" tip and comes in a 1/64" size.

- **Holder and Sponge**—Don't rely on that goofy little stamped metal stand that comes with many irons. Do so, and you may end up with a very geeky tribal tattoo on your thigh that you didn't get on purpose. You want a proper solder stand that has a place to holster the iron. These stands also come with a sponge and sponge holder. Keeping a soldering iron hot and clean is a key to soldering success. The sponge is used for cleaning the tip between soldering.

- **Desolder Pump or Wick**—To remove old components, you need to desolder and remove them. This is done by heating the old solder with an iron and then sucking away the molten material before it solidifies again. For this, you need either a desoldering pump or a product called a desoldering wick. The pump is a reusable mechanical device that, when triggered, sucks the molten solder into the barrel of the pump. A soldering wick is braided copper material on a spool that you use to "wick up" the solder as it melts. Which one you're comfortable using depends a lot on your soldering style, so as you're learning, it's a good idea to try both. A pump and wick are cheap and can be had at any electronics store. For motherboard work, most people prefer the wick, as the pump can be a bit unwieldy in the tight spaces of the board.

- **Solder**—To attach electronic components with a soldering iron, you need, can you guess? Solder. It comes in various alloy mixtures, the most common being 60% tin, 40% lead. For motherboard work, it is better to use a rosin-core 63/37 formulation, which is less prone to cold solder joints (that is, a less than adequate weld). Radio Shack sells this as "High-Tech Solder." You also want to make sure to use the thinnest-diameter solder you can find. Most everything on a PC or TiVo motherboard is extremely close together, so to get in there and solder only what you need to, you want the tiniest iron tip and thinnest solder wire.

- **Liquid Flux**—Flux is a material used in soldering to help prepare the metals being soldered together by cleaning their surfaces of any impurities that might hinder bonding. Flux comes in different varieties and forms. For close in, surface-mount soldering, liquid flux is best. It can be found in pen-type dispensers, which allow you to apply the flux right where you need it.

- **Flux Remover**—This chemical is used to remove any residue left over from the soldering process that could interfere with the components' proper functioning. It can be found as aerosol spray and other forms. There are special formulations for printed circuit boards that are a little gentler on the components than a heavy-duty flux remover.

Digital Multimeter

Again, a digital multimeter (DMM) is more of a general hardware hacking tool than one you need for the majority of TiVo hacks, but it's an excellent tool to have in your kit. With it, you can do everything from checking to make sure that a wall socket is getting power (or safely powered off), to measuring the amount of juice left in batteries, to testing

Caution

Solder contains lead. Lead makes you stupid. Always make sure to have adequate ventilation when using solder.

electronic components to see if they still have a heartbeat. In Chapter 12, we'll talk about how you can use a DMM to troubleshoot a misbehaving TiVo modem.

There are many different types of DMMs on the market and they range in price from under $20 to hundreds. Stores like Radio Shack frequently have decent models on sale. Make sure you get one that at least offers these features:

- Direct Current (DC) and Alternating Current (AC) voltage measuring (expressed in *Volts/V*)
- DC and AC current measuring (measured in *amps/A*)
- Resistance (measured in *ohms/Ω*)
- *A* Continuity Test (lets you know if an electrical connection exists between two points)
- A Diode Check (for testing the health of diodes, transistors, and other semiconductors)

As shown in Figure 7.9, most DMMs come with needle probes, which is what you use for motherboard testing, but if you're planning on other hardware hacking and electronics work, you'll want a set of hook and clip probes (both of which allow you to fasten the probes to components for hands-free testing). See Figure 7.9.

FIGURE 7.9
A digital multimeter and needle probes.

Gareth On...

Caution: Shameless Plug Ahead: In my book *Absolute Beginner's Guide to Building Robots* (Que), I have short "Thumbnail Guides" to soldering, digital multimeters, beginning electronics, breadboarding circuits, and more. I've gotten many emails from readers saying that in reading these sections, they finally "got it," and are now soldering, metering, and electrifying with the best of 'em. If you're interested in getting into basic hardware hacking (and have an interest in robots), you might want to check out this book.

PC Parts

If you're going to do any TiVo drive backup and restore, planning on networking a Series 1 TiVo, or fixin' to load third-party programs onto it, you'll need a computer handy, along with the proper cabling for attaching your TiVo drive(s).

IDE Cable(s)

IDE (or EIDE) is actually ATA; no wait, it's *really* P-ATA. Okay, if you want to be a stickler about it, it's ATA/ATAPI. No, we haven't been smoking anything funny; these are all of the initialisms associated with those flat ribbon cables found inside your computer (and your TiVo). *IDE* stands for *Integrated Drive Electronics* (man, do geeks ever come up with some strange names for things!). IDE is actually a brand name for the *ATA (Advanced Technology Attachment)* standard used for connecting storage devices (hard drives, CD drives, tape drives) inside a computer. ATA cables are spec'd to be no longer than 18" (though cables up to 36" do exist), so they are best suited for internal connections only. ATA is a parallel data transport technology, so when a serial version was introduced, the parallel flavor became known as P-ATA. In the beginning, it was only used for connecting hard drives. As the standard expanded to include other storage devices, the name was expanded too, now known as *ATA/ATAPI (Advanced Technology Attachment/Advanced Technology Attachment Packet Interface)*. Not surprisingly, it's still commonly revered to as IDE (or *EIDE*, for *Enhanced IDE*).

So what does this all have to do with TiVo tools? If you're planning on attaching your TiVo drive (or drives) to your PC to back them up, partition new drives, hack the OS for serial networking over the serial out port, and so forth, you're going to need an IDE cable. You may already have what you need inside your computer, but you'll have to check. A PC usually has a

You may or may not need a new IDE cable for the TiVo itself if you are adding a second hard drive. Some models have a second connector on the cable; some do not. We'll discuss this further in the following chapter. A regular IDE cable will not work, as designed, within TiVo. You'll need to flip it around so that the master drive is attached to what normally would be the mobo connector. Our tech editors, weaKnees.com, also sell custom IDE cables that fit most TiVo models.

primary and a secondary IDE cable attached to controllers on the motherboard. These cables usually each have two available connectors on them (to connect two storage devices). There are instances, however, where the hard drive will be on a cable with only a single connector. In this case, you'll have to get a new IDE cable with two available connectors on it. What you'll be looking for is a 40-pin ATA/66 cable (see Figure 7.10). It will likely be 18" with connectors spaced at 0" (the motherboard connection), 12", and 18".

FIGURE 7.10
A 40-pin IDE/ATA ribbon cable.

A PC

Your final required tool for doing many of the deeper geek hacks later in the book is a Windows (or Linux) PC (see Figure 7.11). In Chapter 8, "Upgrading Hard Drives," we'll discuss all of the different methods of supplementing or replacing the storage space of your TiVo. This can be as painless as sending your beloved box off to have someone else do it (oh the horror!), using a prepared upgrade kit, or the grow-hair-on-your-chest DIY method of buying your own drives, backing up your existing TiVo drive(s) onto your PC, and partitioning a new TiVo drive (or drives). For this latter operation, and a bunch of other hardware and software hacks discussed throughout the rest of this book, you'll need access to at least one IDE connector on your PC.

FIGURE 7.11
Look what we found in the basement—an old PII ready to do our TiVo's bidding.

Caution

Don't head too far back into computer history when repurposing an old PC for doing TiVo work. We don't really recommend anything older than a Pentium II. The more antiquey you get, the more problems you're likely to have with proper BIOS settings, suitable drive partitions, file system (must be FAT32), and so on.

Caution

It goes without saying (but we're fixin' to say it anyway): Back up your PC before attaching TiVo drives to it or otherwise messing with attached devices! The rule of thumb is simple: If you can't afford to lose it, back it up. The corollary to this rule is that the *ONE* time you risk violating the rule is when something really ugly is going to happen. Conduct yourselves accordingly.

As we discussed in the previous chapter, some TiVos have more than one drive already installed, or you might wish to add a second drive. See Tables 6.1 and 6.2 in Chapter 6 to determine how many drives your TiVo model has installed. If it has two (or you plan to add a second drive), you'll need a PC with two open IDE slots. If the PC you're going to be using only has one connector available, you'll need to remove a device (such as a Zip drive) to make room for the second TiVo drive. Keep in mind when checking your PC for available slots that you'll need to keep your CD-ROM drive connected, as you'll be using the CD that came with this book to run installation utilities and to install additional software on your TiVo.

Chapter 8

Upgrading Hard Drives

If you've read the first part of this book and applied a number of the searching, recording, and remote-controlling techniques described there, you might have engineered too much of a good thing. You might constantly find yourself filling up your hard drive and having to call in sick to run a TiVo marathon, or TiVo might be recording over a bunch of shows before you've seen them (depending on how you have your Save Until option set up).

There are two fixes for this: First, put down the remote and back out of the living room! Take up a sport, play in the yard with the kids, or pick up litter in your neighborhood. Or, second, add a buttload more storage space! If you decided on course of action no. 1, we can't help you. Say hi to the sunshine and fresh air for us. If you want to go with fix no. 2, you're in luck! In this chapter, we'll help you trick out that DVR with so much TV recording space, you'll never see sunshine again!

What Kind of Geek Do You Think You Are?

Exactly *how* you're going to replace your existing hard drive or add another one to your TiVo has a lot to do with how tech-savvy you are and how dirty you want to get. Let's first look at the different options available to you (after you're done with the list, check out Table 8.1):

- **Mail it to a *real* geek**—If the idea of whipping out hand tools, cracking the top on your TiVo, and sloshing through its entrails makes you break out in a clammy sweat, this could be the route for you. TiVo e-tailers and upgrade/repair shops like weaKnees.com and PTVUpgrade.com will install new hard drives for a $50 fee (which includes return shipping costs). You just select the upgrade size you want and send them your TiVo, and they'll do all the work. This is especially recommended if you want to replace your existing drive (instead of adding one) and you want to retain all of your TiVo settings and recorded programming. To do this yourself involves either using a product like InstantCake or taking on a complete do-it-yourself installation (see details later in this chapter). Getting the pros to back up and reinstall your existing TiVo recordings will cost you extra.

- **Use a prepared upgrade kit**—There was a time when, to upgrade a TiVo yourself, you had to start with a blank hard drive, back up your TiVo's existing drive to a computer, partition the new TiVo drive, load everything back on, reinstall it in your TiVo, and pray for the best. Now upgrade shops will send you a TiVo drive (or drives) already prepped with the TiVo OS for your specific model. Installing the kit involves little more than opening your TiVo, unscrewing and unplugging the old drive(s), and plugging in and screwing in the new one(s). The only big drawback to this method is that, if you *replace* the existing drive, you'll lose any recorded programming that you haven't saved to tape or recordable DVD. If you add a second drive, your settings (Season Passes, WishLists, Suggestions, and so on) and your already-recorded content will be preserved. BTW: In case you're wondering, upgrading drives does not impact your lifetime TiVo service (if you have this).

Table 8.1   Comparison of Different TiVo Upgrade Options and Their Trade-Offs

	Mail It to a Real Geek	Use a Prepared Upgrade Kit
Adding a 160GB drive to a Series 1 TiVo	Cost $238*	Cost $189*
How it works	Disconnect and send in your TiVo. It'll come back to you with the upgrade drive installed and fully tested. Your settings and recordings are just as you left them.	You get a preformatted drive, custom drive bracket, Torx tools, and instructions with pictures. No PC is required. Physical drive installation is the same as with the next two options.

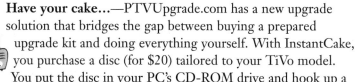

- **Have your cake...**—PTVUpgrade.com has a new upgrade solution that bridges the gap between buying a prepared upgrade kit and doing everything yourself. With InstantCake, you purchase a disc (for $20) tailored to your TiVo model. You put the disc in your PC's CD-ROM drive and hook up a blank hard drive (or drives) to your PC, and the CD walks you through the installation process (which is only a couple of steps). You still have to do all of the basic work required for a do-it-yourself upgrade (as detailed later in the chapter), but you can save a couple of bucks (over an upgrade kit) if you're comfortable doing this type of work and have access to a spare hard drive.

All of the available upgrade options are explored in more detail throughout this chapter.

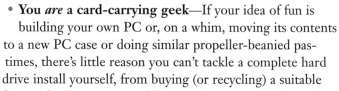

- **You *are* a card-carrying geek**—If your idea of fun is building your own PC or, on a whim, moving its contents to a new PC case or doing similar propeller-beanied pastimes, there's little reason you can't tackle a complete hard drive install yourself, from buying (or recycling) a suitable hard drive to backing up your old TiVo drive onto a PC, partitioning the new hard drive, and moving TiVo software (and recorded programming) onto the new drive.

Table 8.1 looks at two different storage-increasing situations (adding a 160GB drive to a Series 1 TiVo and replacing a 160GB drive on a Series 2 TiVo) and the relative costs and merits of each upgrading method.

Have Your Cake...	You Are a Real Geek
Cost approximately $185 Maxtor drive: $149* (QuickView) or similar Instant Cake CD: $19.99 Bracket: SA-$14* (not needed for DirecTV DVR)	Cost approximately $165 Maxtor drive $149* (QuickView) or similar Bracket: SA-$14* (not needed for DirecTV DVR)
Connect the blank hard drive to your PC, boot the CD, and follow the onscreen prompts. Verify size, shut down the PC, and install the drive in the TiVo.	Use an online guide (www.upgrade-instructions.com) to burn a CD. Follow the online instructions step by step: Boot the CD and the drive in a PC. Type two lines of code, verify size, shut down, and install the drive in the TiVo.

169

Table 8.1   Continued

	Mail It to a Real Geek	Use a Prepared Upgrade Kit
Ease	No-brainer. The hardest part is packing the TiVo well in a box and remembering where the cables go when the unit comes back. Label them!	Not too bad. Even Grandma could probably handle this level of geekitude.
Pros	Completely hands-off. You don't touch a thing inside the TiVo; no PC is required.	No PC is required. Everything you need (except a Phillips-head screwdriver) is included. You'll never be without the TiVo. This option is less expensive than sending in your TiVo. It has no big cost disadvantage over the next two options, all things considered.
Cons	Your TiVo has gone on vacation! You lose the will to live until it returns. This is the most expensive option.	You have to open your TiVo and muck about inside.
Conclusions	If you have no interest in popping the top on TiVo and you can stand being without your TiVo for a while, this is your best option.	This is the most popular option by far. It's not hard for even the tech newbie, it's quick, it's relatively cheap, and so on.
Replacing a 160GB drive on a Series 2 TiVo	$238* (standard)/$268* (deluxe). The deluxe option includes moving settings and recordings to the new replacement drive.	$189*.

Have Your Cake...	You Are a Real Geek
Only slightly less gnarly than the next option.	Takes a bit of knowledge, reading, and some patience. For a newbie, installation could take about 1.5 hours.
You don't need to actually burn your own CD.	This option costs the least. You get a nice satisfaction of doing it yourself and earn street cred with the propeller beanie/Penguinhead crowd.
This option costs basically the same as with a prepared kit (unless you already have an available HD). You have to hook up both drives to your PC. You have to find or buy a bracket and tools separately.	Time is money, and actual time requirements vary depending on abilities, unknown snafus, and other considerations. Make a mistake, and your TiVo (and your marriage) could be toast. You need two IDE ports free on your PC, if you're backing up TiVo content (or you need to free up two temporarily), and you have to partition both drives together.
It doesn't make much sense with an add-on situation (you won't lose recordings and settings by using a prepared kit).	It's not a bad idea if you're a techie or are into an interesting learning experience. This option is especially recommended if you already have a suitable hard drive lying around.
$149* (QuickView). $19.99 CD. (Plus the cost of tools.)	$149* (QuickView) (Plus the cost of tools.)

Table 8.1   Continued

	Mail It to a Real Geek	Use a Prepared Upgrade Kit
How it works	Pack up and send off TiVo. The upgrader installs a new drive, adds swap, tests it, and sends it back. With Deluxe, settings and recordings also are copied to the new drive. General turnaround is the same or next business day.	Take out the old drive and put in the new prepared drive. Kits come with a prepared drive, instructions, and all tools (except a Philips-head screwdriver).
Ease	This couldn't be simpler, especially if you want your settings and recordings preserved.	It's quick and dirty. Pop the top, unplug, unscrew, replug, and rescrew. Done.
Pros	It's easy and hands-off.	You achieve a cost-to-effort balance. You don't have to be without your TiVo.
Cons	You have no TiVo until it's back. Extra expense is involved, especially with the Deluxe option.	You lose your settings and all recordings. You have to start over with TiVo's Guided Setup.
Conclusions	If you're a nontechie and want to save your TiVo settings and recordings, this is the safest bet (with Deluxe handling).	If you don't care about losing settings and recordings, this is probably the way to go.

Pricing based on products and services from weaKnees.com

Have Your Cake...	You Are a Real Geek
Boot the CD and drive in your PC. Follow the prompts. Choose your path. Shut down and install.	Get customized directions (www. upgrade-instructions.com). Burn a CD. Boot the PC with the CD and drives connected. Type a few lines of code. Shut down and install.
Read menus and answer questions. You need to plug the hard drive into the PC.	Type a few lines of code, given to you on the Web. You need to plug the hard drive into the PC.
No CD burning is necessary. You read menus instead of issuing Linux commands. You can retain your TiVo settings and recorded programs.	You earn big-time tech cred. Be the envy of all your geek buds. You can retain your TiVo settings and recorded programs.
Weight cost vs. benefits. Time is involved here. You have to hook up the drive to the PC.	Time and risks are involved here—so is the geek factor.
If you don't have a TiVo disk image but you want to do some of the work yourself, this is the next step beyond a prepared kit.	This will put geekly hair on your chest. It's best for complex situations with very specific needs. Here are a few such examples: (1) You have already upgraded your TiVo and want to copy settings/programming onto a larger A drive; (2) You have a two-drive TiVo, want to save recordings, but don't want to send it to an upgrade shop; (3) You're making your own backup on CD, with your own settings rather than a generic backup.

My TiVo Done Left Me

If you decide to mail your TiVo to the pros, you have little to do but properly pack it safely for mailing. In Chapter 1, "Which TiVo Is Right for You?", we extolled the virtues of labeling machines and cable organizing tech. This is a time when such Martha Stewart tech comes in handy. Before you unplug all of the cables in the back of your TiVo, label each for easy hook-up. If you have a giant tangle of wires behind your media center that your TiVo cables are likely to get lost in, labels or not, bundle the whole lot of them with a zip-tie (or twisty tie) before unplugging.

You likely still have your TiVo box with its foam inserts. Most consumers these days are in the habit of saving consumer electronics packaging for repair and return purposes (and for making bigger bucks when finally unloaded on eBay). If you don't do this, start! It's really a good habit to get into. Yeah, we know it's a hassle to save all of these giant boxes and packing, but it really does make it easier and safer when you have to return a device or send it in for repairs.

If you don't have your original packaging, here's how to prepare your TiVo for safe shipping:

Tip

By all means, insure the package, and include your lifetime service fee (if applicable) in the insured amount. Also make sure to save your tracking number.

1. Unplug everything, including the power cable. You do not need to send any cables, the remote, or anything else—just the TiVo (and the access card for DirecTV DVRs for test purposes).

2. Wrap the unit in at least 3 inches thick of bubble wrap. Use the wrap with the large-diameter bubbles, not the type with small bubbles. Make sure all sides, the top, and the bottom of the unit are covered in wrap.

3. Ideally, you want a box that the wrapped TiVo fits into snuggly. If the box you have has some slop room in it, pack the spaces with more bubble wrap until the unit is secure in the box.

4. Make sure the flaps on the box are securely fastened with wide packing tape. If you need to, reinforce the seams of the box with more packing tape.

5. After clearly labeling (and return-labeling) the shipping box, find a box of tissues in the house. Dab liberally under eyes as the UPS driver walks away with your little TiVoGuy.

Leo On...

Our gearheaded tech editors, Michael and Jeff (a.k.a. the weaKnees boys) tell great stories of clueless customers who send in their TiVos for upgrades and repairs under the worst possible packing conditions. One lady took the 12 reams of paper out of a Xerox box, tossed in the TiVo, and slapped a label on it. No padding, no peanuts, no nothin'. The TiVo was left to rumble and tumble in the box all by itself. Other customers have sent TiVos wrapped in grocery bags and their underwear, padded with bed pillows (sleep tight, my fine digital friend), buttressed with bath towels, and secured inside a box with empty plastic water bottles or rolls of toilet paper used like bumpers on a boat dock. Creative? Yes. Safe shipping conditions? Heck, no! Another customer did a fantastic packing job with one horrific exception: He left the two hard drives disconnected inside the TiVo itself. They played demolition derby with each other (and the rest of TiVo's sensitive bits) on their way to the repair shop. Obviously, the TiVo needed a few more repairs once it arrived.

Upgrade shops can usually turn your TiVo around in 24–48 hours, so if you spring for quick shipping to the shop (next day or two day) and you pay extra on the other end, they'll return it the next day or two days after the upgrade. So, your TiVo shouldn't be gone for much more than a week under these circumstances.

WeaKnees.com and PTVUpgrade.com are the most popular professional upgrade houses. See "Upgrade Kit Suppliers" in Appendix A, "Resources," for others.

It Came from a Kit

With the current availability of prepared TiVo hard-drive kits, complete with quiet-running drives (optimized for multimedia content), preinstalled software, simple installation instructions, and even required tools (all at a very affordable price), it's no wonder that this has become the upgrade path of choice for most TiVonauts. Hard-drive prices, which used to be prohibitively high, have dropped dramatically in the last decade. For less than $200, you can replace your current drive with 165 hours of storage capacity (via a 160GB drive) or add 160GB in a second drive for the same price. Hardware installation, including unhooking your TiVo, opening it up, removing the old drive (if applicable) and installing the new one, takes much less than an hour.

To Replace or to Add? That Is the Upgrade Question

Replacing an existing TiVo hard drive or adding a second drive to your existing one brings advantages and disadvantages. Table 8.2, kindly provided to us by weaKnees.com, explains the various trade-offs involved.

Tip

Don't forget, you don't have to buy a new stock TiVo and then wait to upgrade it with a bigger drive. TiVo and DirecTV DVR dealers offer new TiVos already loaded with monster drives. Again, whether you "need" hundreds of hours of record time has a lot to do with what kind of TV consumer you (and your household) are. If you're already thinking that a 40- or 80-hour drive seems puny by your media-hungry standards, you might as well invest in a bigger capacity up-front.

Tip

TiVos that have two factory-installed drives cannot use an add-on kit (as we said previously, the drives are a married pair, so you can't just replace one of them). Your best bet here is to replace the two drives with a single (or two) large-capacity drive(s).

Table 8.2   Trade-Offs Involved in Adding Versus Replacing a Hard Drive

	Replacing Existing Drive(s)	Adding a Second Drive
Programming/Settings	You will lose your TiVo settings and recorded programming.	You will retain all of your TiVo settings and recorded programming.
It's a Hard Drive Life	Hard drives have a limited work life. As TiVos age, the drives generally become less reliable (and, in some cases, quite noisy). Depending on your TiVo's vintage, you might benefit by removing an older, factory hard drive and replacing it with a new one. Replacing your factory drive(s) is like replacing the batteries in an appliance. In addition, replacing your drive(s) will enable you to retain the factory drives as a backup if you need your new drives repaired or replaced down the road.	You will end up with two drives—one brand-new drive and one factory drive. When you add a second drive to your TiVo, they become a married pair. In other words, once a second drive is added to your TiVo, the two drives act as one and cannot be separated if one of those drives fails down the road. If a drive failure occurs, the good drive can be reused if it is reformatted and reconfigured (but you'll lose settings and recordings). By keeping an old factory drive, you increase the chance for failure.
Storage Space	If you purchase a prepared kit, you will remove your old drive and retain it as a backup drive. You will not be able to use that drive space together with your new drive's capacity. For example, if you currently have a 30-hour TiVo and you purchase an 80GB replacement kit, you will end up with approximately 90 hours and will use only the 80GB drive (storing the 30GB drive as a backup).	You will be adding the kit's drive capacity to your existing storage. So, if you currently have a 30-hour one-drive stand-alone TiVo and you purchase an 80GB add-on kit, you'll add approximately 95 hours to your 30 hours, giving you a grand total of 125 hours (at Basic quality on an SA TiVo).
Capacity Options	Remove your existing drive(s) and replace with: • One 80GB drive • One 120GB drive • One 160GB drive • Two 80GB drives • Two 120GB drives • Two 160GB drives Notes: Actual capacities and drive options vary, depending on the unit being upgraded. Pioneer DVD/DVR units accept only one drive. Newermodel S2 units and the HD DirecTV DVR can handle drives up to 300GB.	Keep your existing drive/capacity and add: • One 80GB drive • One 120GB drive • One 160GB drive Note: Actual capacities and drive options vary, depending on the unit being upgraded.

TiVo DVR and TiVo Upgrade Kit capacities are at Basic Quality (DirecTV DVRs have only one quality level) and might vary due to hard drive models used.

Here's the bottom line:

- If you have a Series 1 TiVo (Philips HDR series, Sony SVR-2000, Sony SAT T-60, DSR6000, or Hughes GXCEBOT), we strongly recommend that you choose a replacement drive kit.

- If you have a middle-aged Series 2 TiVo (TiVo 60-hour or AT&T 40-hour), you should take into account the preceding mortality factors.

- If you have a newer Series 2 TiVo (less than 18 months old), we recommend an add-on kit, unless you are interested in replacing your existing drive with two new drives for maximum capacity.

If you decided to replace a drive with a newer, bigger one, go to the following "Replacing a TiVo Drive" section for instructions. If you decided to add a drive to your existing setup, go to the "Adding a Second TiVo Drive" section, later in this chapter.

Replacing a TiVo Drive

If you decide on this option, the first thing you have to do is order up the drive. We recommend getting the biggest drive(s) you can afford. At $189 for a 160GB drive kit, there's little reason to go smaller (unless you're really strapped for cash). While you're waiting for the drive kit to arrive, you can have a TiVo viewing marathon to watch the recordings you'll otherwise lose. You can also take the time to offload to VHS or burn to DVD-R (if you have such capability) any shows you want to save. You might also want to take the time while you're waiting for your upgrade kit to label all of the cables going in and out of your TiVo, if you haven't already.

When the kit arrives, make sure it has all of its parts, as listed on its installation instructions, and that you have the tools that you need. You likely won't need more than T-10 and T-15 Torx wrenches (included in most kits), a Phillips-head screwdriver, and maybe a can of Dust-Off (see Chapter 7, "TiVo Hacker's Toolbox") to remove any dust build-up inside your box.

Your installation might involve some variations, depending on what type of TiVo you have (Series 1 or Series 2, stand-alone or DirecTV DVR), but a drive-replace installation usually follows the basic procedures outlined here. All TiVo upgrade kits come with installation instructions, so default to those when you're actually ready to get your hands dirty. The following

NOTE

WeaKnees sells dual-drive upgrades with up to 320GB (344 hours). If you have a Series 1 standalone TiVo and want even more capacity, PTVUpgrade will sell you a dual-drive kit with up to 640 hours of recording time. So what's the downside to a 640-hour beast (beside $650 leaving your wallet)? Well, first, you'll have to wave goodbye to that thing called a life. Second, the legal TiVo software in these units has a capacity limit built into it of 137GB. Certain vendors get around this by using a software patch called LBA48. The risk here is that, if TiVo, Inc. downloads a software upgrade, you'll lose your tricked-out storage capacity (requiring a reinstallation of LBA48), the money you spent to get it, and possibly all that you have recorded on the drives. This is less risky on S1 machines, where an OS upgrade at this point is unlikely, but it's very risky with S2, where such an upgrade is inevitable.

Tip

Full-color instructions for all of the upgrade kits that weaKnees.com and PTVUpgrade.com sell are available on their websites. Black-and-white instructions come with all kits. These instructions are specific to your TiVo model and upgrade kit, and you should refer to them before doing your upgrade.

FIGURE 8.1

The two hard-drive bracket screws (on an SA S1) that attach the bracket to the drive platform inside your TiVo.

Caution

Don't forget the dangers of the unshielded power supply located directly behind the hard-drive platform. Stay well clear of this area. Refer back to Figure 6.3 in Chapter 6, "Touring Your TiVo: The Hardware."

shows you the basics and gives you an idea of just how easy it is. For purposes of this demonstration, we're upgrading a Series 1 standalone TiVo-branded unit. It came with a single 13GB HD. We're replacing it with a single 80GB drive.

1. Remove the lid screws on the back panel that attach the lid to the chassis. Note that the Pioneer DVD/DVR combo unit and the SVR-3000 have side screws as well.

2. Perform the hardware blessing, as described in Chapter 6, to remove the lid of your TiVo.

3. Using the T-10 Torx driver (T-15 on S1 DirecTiVos and models 130040/140060), unscrew the two bracket screws located on the front of the hard drive bracket (see Figure 8.1). Note that some TiVo units use Phillips-head screws. Use a Phillips driver if you encounter these.

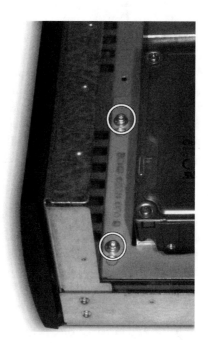

4. Grasp the drive and its drive bracket, and gently move it toward the back of the TiVo (so the drive bracket can clear the two mounting pins on the back edge of the drive platform). Pull the drive/bracket away from the drive platform (see Figure 8.2).

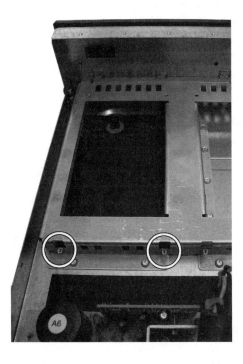

FIGURE 8.2
The two pins that help hold the hard drive bracket to the drive platform.

NOTE

Step 4 does not apply to the Series 1 DirecTiVos or stand-alone models 130040/140060.

5. With the drive/bracket in one hand, grab the black connector on the IDE cable where it plugs into the back of the hard drive, and gently pull it loose.

6. Now you need to remove the power cable connector that's plugged into the back end of the hard drive. This is the smaller plastic white connector (called a Molex connector). These types of plugs can sometimes be stubborn to remove. Grab it from the sides and gently wiggle it from side to side; it will eventually come loose. Be patient.

7. With the drive/drive bracket free from the TiVo, it's time to remove the old drive from the bracket and attach the bracket to your new replacement drive. Remove the four drive bracket screws that attach to the hard drive using a T-15 Torx driver.

8. Line up the screw holes on the bracket with the threaded holes on the replacement hard drive, and screw in the four T-15 screws. Make sure you orient the bracket so that the right-angle part of the bracket (the part that slots into the pins on TiVo's drive platform) is facing toward the back end of the drive (see Figure 8.3).

Tip

When trying to remove an IDE connector, grasp the connector from the top and bottom (not from the two ends) and gently pull. You can rock it up and down a little to help dislodge it, but go easy. There are 40 pins inside there that you don't want to loosen or bend.

FIGURE 8.3

Proper orientation of the drive and bracket (so that the bendy part of the bracket is on the same end as the IDE port and power jack). A stand-alone TiVo-branded Series 1 is shown.

Back End
of Drive

Mounting
Pins

Front End
of Drive

[Drive and Bracket
Shown Upside Down]

NOTE

Step 10 does not apply to Series 2 TiVos.

Caution

Although there's the "key" on the IDE connector, it is possible to jam it in upside down. Pay attention and be careful.

9. With the new drive connected to the drive bracket, carefully reconnect the IDE connector and the power plug into the back of the new hard drive. The IDE connector has a "key" on it so that it can be attached only one way. The power connector also has a special shape, so it, too, goes in only one way.

10. Reseat the drive bracket, making sure that the holes on the right-angle part of the bracket slot into the pins on the drive platform. If it's seated properly, the two screw holes on the front end of the bracket should once again line up with the screw holes on TiVo's frame (refer back to Figures 8.1 and 8.2). Screw in the two T-10 screws that you removed from the bracket in step 3.

11. Before you close up your TiVo, make sure that the IDE connectors are well seated (on both the hard drive and the motherboard) and that the power plug is pushed in all the way. It's easy to think that these are properly plugged in when they aren't. Double-check. Also make certain that the ribbon control cable from the front of your TiVo that plugs into your motherboard did not get dislodged while you were rampaging inside TiVo. Even a partial unplugging can actually damage your DVR.

12. Place the lid back on your TiVo. Place it so that several inches of lid overhang from the back. When the inside of the lid comes to rest against the side frames, slide the lid forward (toward the front of the TiVo) until the tabs along the back lock into place. Use your T-10 driver (or Phillips on some models) to replace the case screws on the lid back.

Your hardware installation is complete. Congratulations! You're a wily hardware hacker now. All you have to do is reconnect all of your input/output and power cables (connect the power cable last) to the back of your TiVo. Because you replaced the existing drive and are starting with a new drive with nothing on it but the TiVo software, you'll have to go through TiVo's Guided Setup procedure again. As we discussed in Chapter 6, the crypto chip on the TiVo motherboard is where your TiVo ID is kept, so your TiVo is still connected to your TiVo account even though you have to re-enter all of your cable/satellite information, remote control codes, and so on. This is one of the negative trade-offs of going with a drive replacement (as opposed to an add-on). In terms of TiVo settings and preferences, you have to go back to square one.

As with your initial setup, it will take several hours for TiVo to complete its connections with the remote TiVo servers and to index the guide data and other information that it downloads. When the system is done, you can verify the upgrade by going to TiVo Central, Messages & Setup, System Information. Page down to see the Recording Capacity entry. Woo-hoo! Look at the hours and hours (and hours) of brain-wave-flattening fun in store for you!

Adding a Second TiVo Drive

The steps involved in using a hard-drive add kit are basically the same as those in installing a replacement kit, but here, you have to new-mount the drive in a second drive bracket, plug in the second connector on the IDE cable, and use the second power plug that's stowed away inside the TiVo.

If you decide, after consulting Table 8.1, that you want to add a second drive, the first thing you'll want to know is what the provisions are for a second drive inside your TiVo.

- **Series 1**—Some Series 1 machines have a second space for a drive on the units drive platform; others require a third-party bracket kit. If you have one of the following units, you will have to install a special

Caution

Always be careful when powering up your TiVo after it's been disconnected and reconnected. Plug the power cable in last and do not move the machine while the hard drive is spinning up. Drives are most venerable at this point.

NOTE

Not all TiVo models come with a second plug on the power cable and second connector on the IDE cable. If you buy an add-on kit from a vendor such as weaKnees.com, you will get the parts you need to make the second connection.

bracket as part of your upgrade procedure: Philips HDR112, HDR212, or HDR3120X, or Sony SVR-20000. Luckily, most drive-add kits include a bracket kit, if it's required for your model TiVo (see Figure 8.4).

FIGURE 8.4

The weaKnees bracket kit used for adding a second drive to a Series 1 TiVo.

- **Series 2**—If you have one of these Series 2 machines, you'll need to install a special bracket as part of your upgrade procedure: DirecTV DVRs: Hughes HDVR2, SD-DVR40, SD-DVR120, or HR10-250; Philips DSR7000, DSR704, DSR708, RCA DVR39, or DVR40; Samsung S4040R and S4120D; or the Series 2B stand-alones TCD230040, TCD240040, TCD24004A, TCD240080, TCD24008A, or TCD540140. Luckily, most drive-add kits include a bracket kit, if it's required for your model TiVo (see Figure 8.5).

FIGURE 8.5

The weaKnees bracket kit used for adding a second drive to a Series 2 TiVo.

While you're waiting for your kit to arrive, you can go ahead and label all of the input, output, and power cables on the back of your TiVo. This makes reinstalling your TiVo much easier after the upgrade. Because you're adding a drive and not replacing your existing drive, you don't have to marathon-watch or offload to tape or DVD-R already-recorded programming. That said, we are talking about a computer parts replacement, and we all know how pernicious computers can be. The rule on TiVo's hard drives is the same on any other computer drive: If you can't afford to lose it, back it up! If you have something precious (your mom's hysterical appearance on the *The Price Is Right*, your kid's play on the local educational access channel, a nonstop *Joanie Loves Chachi* marathon) that you can't risk losing, definitely dump it down to tape or DVD-R.

When your kit arrives, make sure it has all of its parts. If the kit comes with a drive bracket, it might have numerous small parts. Make sure everything's there as listed or pictured on the installation instructions. Also make sure you have all the tools. Most kits come with the T-10 and T-15 Torx wrenches that you need. You'll also need a Philips-head screwdriver, if your kit includes a bracket. With everything present and accounted for, you're ready to get started.

Adding a Second Drive to a Series 1 TiVo

For purposes of this demonstration, we're going to be installing an add-on drive that does require a bracket. Your kit will come with specific instructions addressing your model TiVo, and you should default to that. The following instructions show you the basics and give you an idea of how easy it is.

1. Remove the lid screws on the back panel.

2. Perform the hardware blessing, as described in Chapter 6, to remove the lid of your TiVo.

3. Go ahead and prepare the bracket kit (if applicable). If a bracket kit is not required, proceed to step 4.

    The first thing you want to do on the bracket kit is install the four blue rubber grommets inside the four hard drive mounting holes. These rubber pieces act like shock absorbers for your hard drive. To get the grommets into the notches next to the drive screw holes, you'll need to squeeze them into an oval shape (see Figure 8.6).

This is a genericized set of instructions. Your mileage may vary depending on your S1 (for instance, if you have an S1 DirecTiVo). When in doubt, default to the instructions that came with your kit.

With the grommets in place, insert the four white nylon spacers
into the grommets (see Figure 8.7). Turn the bracket upside down
(so that the right-angle bend is facing upward) and insert the four
hard drive mounting screws (with built-in washers) into the screw
holes. They don't screw in here; they just pass through these holes.
They'll be threaded into the screw holes on the hard drive.

Now with the screws slotted into the holes on the bracket, align the
screws over the four screw holes on your new hard drive. Attach
the bracket to the drive using your Philips-head screwdriver. Make
sure that the bracket and drive are attached so that the back of the

hard drive (with IDE and power connector sockets) is facing the same direction as the right-angle part of the bracket. Your bracket and drive are now ready to install on the drive platform of the TiVo chassis.

4. The second power connector that will be used to power the second hard drive is inside the TiVo but is often tucked underneath the motherboard and the cable, zip-tied to the other power cables (or to a little loop on the base of the TiVo's housing). To use it, you'll have to clip off the zip-tie and pull out the plug from under the mother-board (see Figure 8.8). Diagonal-cutting pliers (see Chapter 7) are the best tool for the job. You can also use an X-acto knife or other cutting tool. Be extremely careful that you cut only the zip-tie, not any of the wires! With the cable unbundled, you can pull it free from the mobo, and it's ready to plug in.

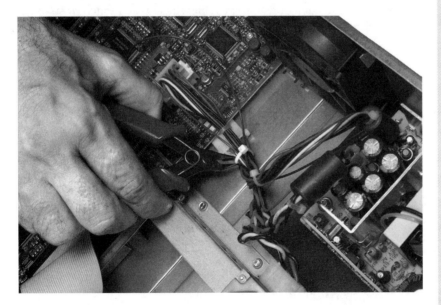

FIGURE 8.8

Free the power! Free that power that be! Snip carefully, or you might power something that wasn't meant to be powered.

5. To connect the second IDE connector to your new drive, it's a lot easier if you first disconnect the IDE connector where it plugs into the motherboard.

6. With the power and secondary IDE connector free, you're ready to plug them into your new secondary drive. Make sure both connectors are seated fully and properly on the back of the new drive. It's easy to make the mistake of not plugging them in all the way.

185

IDE connectors can plug in only one way. They have a little notch key in the center of the top. Make sure this lines up with the keyhole on the receiving end, and you should be fine. It is still possible to plug it in upside-down, so pay attention.

7. If you have a bracket kit type of installation, make sure the mounting holes on the right-angle part of the bracket slot into the pins on the hard drive platform. Properly seated, the two screw holes on the front end of the bracket should line up with the two threaded holes on the front of the TiVo chassis. Use the two Phillips-head screws that came with your bracket kit to fasten it down to the hard-drive platform. If you have a TiVo with a built-in bracket, use the four screws provided with the hard-drive-add kit to fasten the drive to the secondary drive bay. If the bracket doesn't fit, you may have to move the other drive bracket over a notch; the brackets have two sets of holes.

8. Replug in the IDE connector that attaches to the motherboard. Double-check to make sure that it—and all of the IDE and power connectors on both drives and the mobo—are properly seated.

9. Place the lid back on your TiVo. Place it so that an inch or so of lid overhangs from the back of the chassis. When the inside of the lid comes to rest against the side frames, slide the lid forward (toward the front of the TiVo) until the tabs along the back panel lock into place. Use your T-10 driver to replace the case screws.

The hardware installation is complete. Congratulations! You're a wily hardware hacker now. All you have to do is reconnect all of your input/output and power cables (connect this cable last) to the back of your TiVo. Plugging in the power turns on your TiVo. Because you added a drive rather than replacing one, all of your TiVo settings and recordings should have been preserved. To check that the installation was a success, go to TiVo Central -> Messages & Setup -> System Information. Page down to see the Recording Capacity entry. Look at those oodles o' hours that await your viewing pleasure. Spudville, here we come!

Gareth On...

When I added a second drive to my Series 1 TiVo, the pins on the drive platform would not accept the holes on the drive bracket. I tried bending the pins, but that didn't work, so I used a metal file to enlarge the holes a bit; then everything fit fine. If you have to do this, remove the bracket from the drive and work away from the TiVo so that you don't get damaging metal filings on any other components.

Adding a Drive to a Series 2 TiVo

Some models of Series 2 TiVos have a dual drive bracket built into them, even if they have only one factory-installed drive. As with Series 1 upgrade kits, the S2 add-on kits that require a bracket come with one. For purposes of this demonstration, we're going to trick out our TiVo with a weaKnees hard-drive-add kit, which includes a TwinBreeze bracket, cables, tools, and the optional Advanced Cooling Pak. In addition, weaKnees kits for most Series 2 stand-alone units include the PowerTrip, a special power cable that staggers the startups of the drives by a few seconds. This is an issue only on TiVo-branded TCD240040, TCD24004A, TCD 240080, and TCD24008A, and the AT&T-branded TCD230040 and 240140. These models have a smaller power supply (of 38W instead of 61–78W in other models), and the big power draw from two drives on startup could cause problems. weaKnees ships the PowerTrip only in those models that have the smaller power supplies. PTVUpgrade sells its own product, SmartStart, as a separate component (for $24.95). We're also going to use the weaKnees Advanced Cooling Pack, which is available when you buy the S2 add kits, for an additional $9 or $19, depending on your model. This kit adds a small cooling fan to a special bracket on the Twin Breeze and provides an upgrade to TiVo's factory-installed case fan (if your model has the older, noisier Series 2 fan). If you don't spring for the Cooling Pack, you can just skip over those steps (steps 15–21) in the following instructions.

Before you get started, be sure to inventory all of your parts, to make sure you have everything. The Twin Breeze Complete package contains a lot of parts, so make sure they're all in the box as listed in the parts list found on the instructions that came with the kit (see Figure 8.9). We're doing our add-on drive upgrade on a TiVo-branded TCD240040. Your installation procedure might be slightly different, depending on your model, so default to the instructions that came with the kit, when in doubt. The kit comes with T-10 and T-15 Torx wrenches. You will also need a Philips-head screwdriver.

1. Remove the lid screws on the back panel.
2. Perform the hardware blessing, as described in Chapter 6, to remove the lid of your TiVo.
3. With the lid safely off, you'll see the single hard drive on the raised drive platform in the right-front corner of TiVo's insides. You'll need to remove the drive from the platform. Find the two drive-attachment screws at the top edge of drive bracket, and remove these using the T-10 Torx wrench (see Figure 8.10).

FIGURE 8.9

The weaKnees Twin Breeze Complete Drive Add Kit with Advanced Cooling Pack.

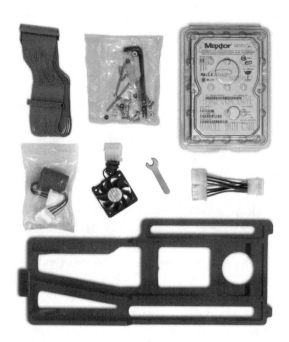

FIGURE 8.10

The two drive-mounting screws attached to the hard-drive platform.

4. With the drive/bracket detached, push the bracket slightly back toward the unshielded power supply (don't touch any of the supply components!) until the bracket clears the two mounting pins that help hold it onto the drive platform. With it free from the pins, lift up the drive and bracket and flip it over (see Figure 8.11).

FIGURE 8.11
The drive and drive bracket removed and ready for disassembly.

5. With the drive and bracket in one hand, grab the white power connector that plugs into the back of the hard drive, and gently wiggle it out. Now grab the IDE connector (the wide black connector on the end of the flat gray ribbon cable), and gently wiggle it out as well from the back of the drive. Also remove the IDE cable entirely by unplugging the other end of it from the motherboard (see Figure 8.12). You won't need this cable anymore. You'll be replacing it with the IDE cable that came with the kit.

FIGURE 8.12
Removing the connections from the factory-installed drive.

6. Now the hard drive and its bracket should be free from the TiVo. Using the T-15 Torx driver, remove the four screws that hold the hard drive to the drive bracket (see Figure 8.13). The hard drive should now be free and ready to install on the Twin Breeze bracket (along with your new add-on drive).

Tip

Besides staying clear of the power supply parts behind the drive platform, you want to take care not to dislodge the ribbon cable that runs from the front of your TiVo to the motherboard. Powering up your TiVo with this connector even slightly unplugged can damage your system.

7. Before you go any further, you want to make sure that the little plastic jumper(s) are set properly (following the instructions that came with your kit). In our case here, we're making sure that the existing drive is set to be a master drive and that your new add-on drive is set to a slave setting. With IDE computer technology, there is always this master/slave relationship. Little pins on the back of the drives enable you to select which drive leads and which drive follows by connecting the pins with a little widget called a jumper (see Figure 8.14). The bank of jumper pins is located on the back of the drives between the IDE connector port and the power-connector jack. For the master drive (the one you just took out of your TiVo), you want to make sure that the little plastic jumper is on the two vertical pins all the way to the left (with the label of the hard drive facing up).

FIGURE 8.14
The jumper (the white plastic bit) on a 40GB hard drive installed a Series 2 TiVo.

How your jumpers should be set depends on what brand of hard drive is in your TiVo. They might already be properly set, but on some drives, such as the Western Digital brand, you'll have to move the jumper to a special "master with slave present" setting. Consult Table 8.3 for some help with setting up jumpers for your particular drive.

Table 8.3   Proper Jumper Settings for Common TiVo Hard Drives

Drive Brand	No. of Jumpers Used	No. of Pins in Jumper Bank	Proper Master Jumper Setting(s)	Notes
Quantum	1	4	Leftmost vertical pins	Ignore the single leftmost pin
Maxtor	1	4	Leftmost vertical pins	Ignore the single leftmost pin
Maxtor	2	5	One on leftmost vertical pins, one on second and third horizontal pins (creating an L-shape of jumpers turned 90 degrees clockwise)	Two-jumper configuration required to make this drive function as a master
Western Digital	1	5	Center vertical pins	Position indicates "master with slave present," so if you have a WD drive, you will have to move the jumper to this position

In the above examples, "left-most" refers to the jumper orientation while looking at the drive from the back, with the label-side up.

Tip

To learn more about master/slave connections, jumper settings, and other aspects of IDE technology, see "Hardware Concepts" in the "Do-It-Yourself Upgrading" section, later in this chapter.

8. With the settings verified (and changed, if needed), you're ready to attach the two drives to your new drive bracket. Using four of the drive screws that came in your kit, attach Drive A, or the master drive (your original hard drive), to the Twin Breeze drive bracket (refer back to Figure 8.9). Now attach the new drive, Drive B, or the slave, to the bracket, as shown in Figure 8.15.

FIGURE 8.15

The proper drive arrangement of the original hard drive (left) and the new added drive (right).

Caution

The hard drive in a kit should come with its jumpers already set properly. In Maxtor drives, the jumper position for slave is usually horizontal, or no jumpers present (the slave jumper is in a "park" position). While the instructions for the kits usually say not to bother with the jumper settings, if you see a jumper on a Maxtor slave that's vertical, you might want to contact the kit vendor before continuing with the installation.

9. Find the new IDE cable that came with your kit, and, holding on to the gray IDE connector, pass the blue connector through the hole in the bracket between the two drives. With the blue connector in the pass-through holes, plug the gray connector into the IDE port on the Master/A drive. Now connect the black IDE connector to the Slave/B drive.

10. Holding the drive bracket on the end with the circular (fan) hole, bring the Twin Breeze back onto the drive platform. Find the tab on the end opposite the one you're holding. Tuck this tab underneath the frame onto which the original drive was mounted (see Figure 8.16).

11. With the drive bracket still in your hand and slotted into the drive frame, reach underneath the bracket, grab the blue IDE connector, and plug it into the IDE port on the motherboard (see Figure 8.17). With this connector plugged in, lower the bracket so that the end you were holding comes to rest on TiVo's frame on the side opposite of the hard-drive platform and power supply.

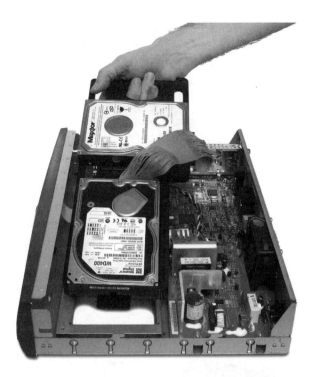

FIGURE 8.16
Slotting the Twin Breeze hard-drive bracket into the TiVo chassis.

FIGURE 8.17
Reaching underneath the new drive bracket to plug in the blue IDE control connector.

Upgrading Hard Drives

Just to confuse you, the color-coding on the IDE connectors (blue/gray/black) on the cable provided in your kit does not conform to the usual IDE arrangement. Ultimately, the colors don't matter; it's the jumper settings that tell the computer which drive is which.

FIGURE 8.18

Installing the screws and spacers from the Twin Breeze Accessory Kit (required only on some TiVo units).

12. If your weaKnees kit came with two self-tapping screws and did not include a supplementary instruction sheet labeled Twin Breeze Accessory Kit (along with two long screws, nuts, bolts, and nylon spacers), all you have to do is use the two self-tapping screws to attach the bracket to the TiVo frame (on the end where the fan hole is).

If your kit did come with the Twin Breeze Accessory Kit, it's because your TiVo cannot accept the two self-tapping screws and, therefore, needs a set of stand-offs that attach the new drive bracket to the TiVo case by way of two washers and nuts threaded onto the screws from underneath TiVo's frame. This is simply a matter of threading washers onto the long screws, slotting the screws into the two holes on the mounting bracket, putting two of the nylon spacers onto each screw, and securing the spacers in place with nuts (see Figure 8.18). Now slot the ends of the screws through the two vent holes directly underneath the screws, and use your last set of washers and nuts to secure the bracket to the TiVo chassis.

13. (If your kit came with a PowerTrip, skip to step 14.) Connect the red/yellow/black Y-power splitter that came with your kit to the connector on the existing TiVo power cable (see Figure 8.19). Next, connect the shorter cable/connector to the Master/A drive power jack and the longer cable connector to the jack on the back of Slave/B drive. If your kit uses the PowerTrip, the Y-splitter's cables will be of the same length. If the kit does not require the PowerTrip, one power cable will be longer so that it can reach the power jack on the slave drive. See Figure 8.19.

NOTE

The stand-off spacers kit for the Series 2 weaKnees bracket are included only in the Twin Breeze kits for the TiVo models TCD24004A, TCD24008A, and other newer-architecture TiVo units. Other units come with and use the two self-tapping screws.

14. (If you installed the Y-power splitter only in step 13, skip this step.) Connect the red/yellow/black Y-power splitter that came with your kit to the connector on the existing TiVo power cable (see Figure 8.20). Now connect one end of the splitter to the PowerTrip included in your kit, and connect the other end of the PowerTrip to the Master/A drive power jack. Now connect the remaining end of the Y-power splitter to the jack on the back of the Slave/B drive.

FIGURE 8.20

Your TiVo's on a PowerTrip, man! Plugging the PowerTrip into the Y-power splitter.

NOTE

The weaKnees PowerTrip and the PTVUpgrade SmartStart products are designed to stagger the start-up of a dual-drive system, spinning up the slave drive a few seconds behind the master. There is debate in the TiVo community about whether this is necessary, but it certainly doesn't hurt. weaKnees ships only the PowerTrip destined for TiVos that have the lower-wattage power supplies (where a big power-draw at start-up might make your TiVo have an aneurism).

FIGURE 8.21

Attaching the hard-drive cooling fan to the Twin Breeze bracket. On the fan itself, note the arrow pointing out the airflow direction.

If you are not installing the weaKnees Advanced Cooling pack, you are done with the hardware installation process. Skip ahead to step 22.

15. Find the smaller of the two cooling fans that came with your kit (if your kit came with two). That's the drive bracket fan. The first thing you need to do is determine the direction of the airflow. Look around the edges of the fan case. On one edge, you'll see two arrows. The one that points front to back indicates the direction of the airflow. The one pointing from one side to the other shows the direction in which the fan blades spin (see Figure 8.21). Insert the four self-tapping screws that came with your kit into the fan-mounting holes with the points of the screws going in the same direction that the airflow arrow is pointing. With the screws in the holes, put the rubber washers on the screws (on the other side of the fan). Just screw them on a few turns to get them started.

16. With the screws and rubber washers in place, attach the fan to the drive bracket over the fan hole. The airflow arrow on the fan should be pointing in toward the hard drives (see Figure 8.21).

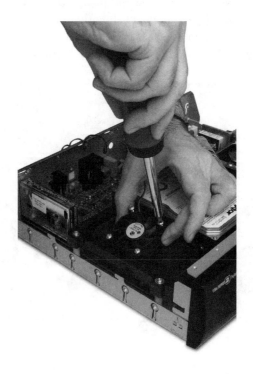

17. Unplug the power connector that's going into the Slave/B drive, and plug it into the male connector on the fan's power cable. Now plug the female fan connector into the B drive's power jack (see Figure 8.22).

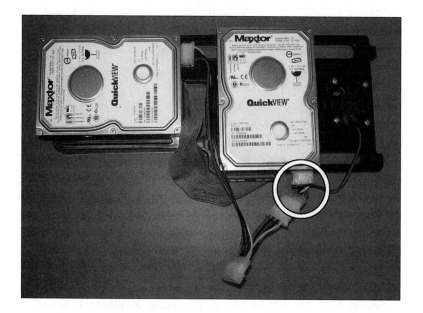

FIGURE 8.22

TiVo feels cooler already. Bringing power to the fan.

Some Advance Cooling Paks come with a replacement fan for the one in the back of your TiVo. The factory-installed fan on these models is actually more powerful than the Cooling Pack fan, but it is also noisier. Because you installed a fan on the drive bracket, the two kit fans should at least equal the cooling power of the old fan (and make less noise). If you want max cooling power and don't care about the noise, you can leave the original fan in place. But if you want to replace the existing fan, proceed with step 18. (On models that already have the newer, quieter fans, weaKnees does not include a replacement case fan.)

18. Remove the existing case fan's power connector from the motherboard. This is the plug on the mobo that's connected to the fan in the back of the case (see Figure 8.23). Pull straight up and away from the board.

19. Using a T-15 Torx wrench, remove the four screws that hold the case fan in place and remove the fan completely from the TiVo.

FIGURE 8.23

The existing fan power connector that needs to be disconnected to make way for the new fan.

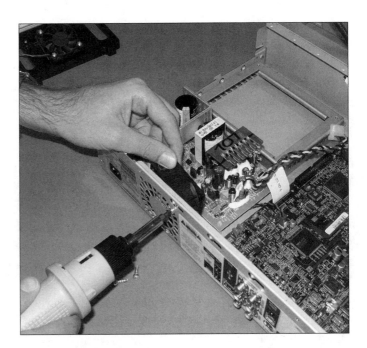

20. Replace the screws you took out of your old fan into the mounting holes on the new fan. Once through the holes, place the rubber washers that came with the fan onto the opposite side of the fan frame. With these washers in place, screw the new fan into the TiVo case (see Figure 8.24).

FIGURE 8.24

Shhh...quiet fanning coming soon. Screwing in the new weaKnees fan.

21. Your replacement fan might have three power wires: red, black, and yellow (or sometimes white). You'll notice that the power connector on your mobo has only two pins. Plug in the fan so that the red and black wires are connected to the motherboard pins and the yellow (white) connector hangs over the edge (plugged into nothing). (See Figure 8.25.)

FIGURE 8.25
Attaching the three-holed power connector to the two-pin jack on the mobo. Note that the yellow (or white) wire doesn't connect to anything (how existential).

22. Place the lid back on your TiVo. Place it so that about an inch of lid overhangs from the back of the chassis. When the inside of the lid comes to rest against the side frames, slide the lid forward (toward the front of the TiVo) until the tabs along the back panel lock into place. Use your screw driver to replace the case screws.

The hardware installation is complete. Congratulations! You're a wily hardware hacker now. All you have to do is reconnect all of your input/output and power cables (connect this cable last) to the back of your TiVo. Plugging in the power turns on your TiVo. Because you added a drive rather than replacing one, all of your TiVo settings and recordings should have been preserved. To check that the installation was a success, go to TiVo Central -> TiVo Messages & Setup -> System Information. Page down to see the Recording Capacity entry. Look at all that TV show parking space. Grab some bed pillows, a few takeout menus, the telephone, and a credit card. You're going to be here for a *very* long time.

Caution

Double-check to make sure that the power connector for the new fan is properly plugged in (with the red and black wires connected to the pins on the motherboard). If it is not properly connected, the fan will not power up and your TiVo might overheat.

Do-It-Yourself Upgrading

As you can see from consulting Table 8.1, a DIY upgrade is not going to save you a lot of money. At the most, if you don't already have a spare drive, you're going to save yourself around $20. The only situations in which DIY upgrading makes sense these days is if you do already have a spare big-gigabyte hard drive lying around and have the technical confidence to hook up the drive to your PC to prepare it for installation in your TiVo. A home-brew upgrade is also worthwhile if you want to replace an existing drive, have a lot of recorded programming and meticulously crafted settings that you don't want to lose, and if you don't want to part with the unit for the time it takes to have the recordings transferred by the pros.

Using InstantCake

PTVUpgrade's InstantCake software is an attempt at offering something in between buying a prepared upgrade kit and doing everything yourself. You buy a $19.99 CD-ROM from PTVUpgrade tailored to your TiVo model. You search on your model and order a CD that contains a disc image of your TiVo's software and special upgrading software. To use the product, you hook the hard drive (or drives) you want to install onto IDE connectors on your PC, set your PC to boot from the CD-ROM drive, and then choose which drive setup you're doing (single or dual). That's basically it. InstantCake does its thing and tells you when it's done, and you remove the TiVo drive(s) and install it in your box. The software process couldn't be easier, but the hardware setup is the same as if you're doing a full DIY install. If you're doing a dual-drive installation, this can get fiddly because you need two free IDE connectors in your PC and you need to properly set your jumpers on the drives. If you are comfortable with this sort of hardware installation but are a little nervous working in Linux (which you'll have to do for a full DIY install), InstantCake is a good way to go. For more information, check out instantcake.com.

If you decide to use InstantCake, you'll need to do the installation of the new TiVo drive (or drives) in your PC as described in the following "DIY Drive Upgrading" section. While you're waiting for your InstantCake CD to arrive, you can read this section to prepare yourself for labors ahead.

DIY Drive Upgrading

Although do-it-yourself upgrading couldn't really be called "easy," it's actually not as difficult as you might think. It does involve some hardware work inside your PC (along with inside your TiVo, obviously) and working within the less-than-user-friendly Linux OS, but it's really all about patience and understanding a few basic hardware and software concepts. Let's take 'em one at a time.

Hardware Concepts

It's all about IDE, my friend. Integrated Drive Electronics, or IDE, is the common internal connection standard used for storage drives in PCs (and TiVos). The typical configuration of the connecting cable used is a flat 40-pin so-called ribbon cable. Inside Series 1 TiVos, this ribbon cable is usually sliced in places between each of the internal wires to make them more flexible for connecting drives in tight places. The IDE connectors are narrow plastic rectangles with 40 square holes that plug into the male pins on the IDE sockets found on the back ends of drives and on motherboards. One standard feature of the IDE connector is a key, a raised piece in the center of the top of each connector that slots into a notch at the top of the IDE socket. This notch (called a key cutout) helps prevent you from plugging in the connector upside down. Another feature of IDE cabling is a blue/gray/black color-coding standard on the connectors, with blue indicating the connector that plugs into the motherboard, gray indicating the secondary/slave drive connector (always in the middle of the cable), and black indicating the primary/master drive connector (see Figure 8.26). This standard is not always followed. Some (often older) IDE cables have all-black connectors, for example. In the end, it's the jumper settings (see later in this chapter) that matter, not the color of the connector. See Figure 8.26.

NOTE

We gave a little more background on the IDE standard when discussing the IDE cable as a needed "tool" in Chapter 7. Refer back to that for more information.

FIGURE 8.26

A ribbon-sliced IDE cable designed for tight, twisty fits. The color-coding is not always followed but is likely what you'll find inside your PC.

The concept of master and slave in communicating electronic devices has been around for decades. It comes from the telecommunications industry, in which phone switches (slaves) were set up to follow instructions from other switching stations up the line (masters). Many technologies use the term *slave* to refer to a secondary device that's set up to dutifully follow another primary device. As you might imagine, some people take offense at the terms and would like to replace them exclusively with *primary* and *secondary*.

You need to understand three main concepts to safely and easily use IDE technology: master/slave relationships, primary and secondary IDE channels, and jumper settings. Let's take these one at a time:

- **Master/slave relationships**—IDE connections allow for two devices to be attached to a single IDE port on the motherboard. The first of these devices, usually attached to the end IDE connector (generally colored black) is the master device. If there's only one device on the cable, it will usually be on the end. This is not always true in TiVos, where sometimes, the drive is set to master and is connected to the middle connector. If you add a second device, it gets attached to the connector in the middle (usually colored gray), and it becomes the slave (or second in the line to the master). This relationship is defined more by jumper settings than by drive placement on the cable (see the following item).

- **IDE channels**—Most modern computers have two IDE ports on the motherboard. One is known as the primary IDE channel; the other is known as the secondary. The ports themselves are usually labeled on the mobo itself. The labeling is tiny, so you may need a magnifying glass to read them. The primary channel typically has the main hard drive on its master connector and a secondary device (often a CD-ROM drive) on the slave. Other devices, such as CD-RW drives and Zip drives, are found as the slave on the primary slave connector or the master and slave connectors on the secondary IDE cable. Again, these relationships are kept straight by jumper settings and (usually) by drive placement on the cable.

- **Jumper settings**—The storage drives on an IDE channel are identified to the computer motherboard and processor by means of little pin connectors called jumpers (technically known as jumper blocks), found on the back ends of the drivers. A jumper is simply a little plastic-covered metal connector that electrically connects the two pins that it fits over. Pins that have no jumpers on them are considered off, and pins with jumpers attached are on. The pins are connected to the drive controller inside the drive in such a way that turning a jumper set on identifies that drive as either a master (the primary drive on the channel) or a slave (the secondary drive). There are other jumper setting configurations, and they can get confusing; for the sake of simplicity, we don't go into all of them here. Most hard drives have a jumper settings map on the top of their case that shows you what each pin set controls. For purposes of TiVo drive formatting, master and slave settings are all you need to worry about.

Software Concepts

As we mentioned previously, TiVo is built upon the Linux operating system. To do a total DIY TiVo hard-drive backup to your PC and then partition a new TiVo drive (and reload your TiVo OS and recorder shows), you have to use Linux tools. Don't worry, you don't have to install Linux on your PC. This book comes with what's called a minidistribution (or minidistro) of the Linux OS. This is a version of Linux that includes only the basic components required to boot the OS and some support utility applications (such as the TiVo backup/restore program, called MFS Tool 2.0). The idea of a minidistro is to keep out anything unessential so that the OS can all fit on a floppy disk—or, in our case, a single CD-ROM (with plenty of room to spare).

If you are unfamiliar with Linux, how to use Linux, and basic Linux concepts and commands, see our "Minitutorial on the Linux OS (or 'You'll Be a Penguinhead in No Time!')" in Chapter 13, "Touring Your TiVo: The Software." When you've finished that section, you can come back here, and you'll be ready to do the hard drive installation.

One Drive or Two?

As we mentioned in Table 8.1, adding a second drive to your TiVo requires that you hook both the existing drive (or the replacement drive) and the add-on (second) drive to your PC at the same time. This requires that you have two IDE connectors free (or that you temporarily free up two). This is not a huge deal, but working with the two drives just makes everything more cumbersome. Make sure that you don't put anything on the primary IDE channel's master connector (that's where your PC's boot hard drive is connected and needs to stay), and make sure you keep your CD-ROM drive connected (it does not matter where—just leave it where it is). You'll need to boot from the CD drive to run the Linux on the disc (more on this later). As we said previously, with the cost of drives so low, and with the official limitation of 137GB built into the TiVo kernel, we suggest going easy on yourself and getting a single 160GB drive. This will give you 165 hours, give or take, of viewing time (in stand-alone units) at the Basic setting. If you need more TV time than that, you might want to think about seeking out a good therapist, getting a little fresh air, or taking up a hobby (other than cataloging continuity problems in '60s sitcoms for TV fan sites).

Caution

When working with prepared hard-drive kits for TiVo, *never* move the jumpers on the drive(s) unless instructed to do so. For drives that you are preparing yourself for TiVo, you'll need to set the pins appropriately for the relationship that the to-be-formatted drive needs to have on your PC. For example, if you're installing the drive as the slave on the primary IDE channel, you'll have to set the jumper to the slave position before installing it on the PC.

NOTE

Another software consideration you need to keep in mind is that, to back up TiVo files to your PC, your hard drive must be formatted with the FAT32 file system (not NTFS). To check your formatting type, right-click on the hard drive icon on your desktop and look under Properties. The file type is listed under the General Properties tab. All Win9x/Me-based OSes are FAT, while Windows 2000/XP installations are usually NTFS. If you have an NTFS-system on your primary drive, you're outta luck as far as TiVo drive-handling is concerned. Better check the recesses of the basement (or a friend's basement) for an older box.

What You'll Need for a DIY Upgrade

When you decide whether you want to go with one drive or two, you're ready to get the tools and parts you'll need to perform the upgrade.

You need these tools:

- A PC with one IDE port and a power plug free (single-drive replacement), or two IDE ports and two power plugs (dual-drive upgrade). The PC also must have its drive partitioned using the FAT32 file system. About 1.5GBs of free drive space is a comfortable parking area for your TiVo backup files.

- If either of your IDE cables has only one connector on it, you'll need to buy a 40-pin IDE ribbon cable with two available connectors (three total).

- T-10 and T-15 Torx wrenches.

- Philips-head screwdriver.

- The CD-ROM from this book.

You need these parts for a Series 1 TiVo:

- When replacing your TiVo's existing drive, all you'll need is the hard drive itself. The power and IDE cables and mounting hardware are already there. We recommend the Maxtor QuickView drives. These drives are manufactured specifically for the DVR market. They are optimized for audio/video streaming and for running quietly. These drives are not sold in retail stores and are available only through select licensed Maxtor resellers. weaKnees is such a reseller.

- If you're adding a drive to your TiVo, you'll need a second hard drive. We recommend the Maxtor QuickView drives. These drives are manufactured specifically for the DVR market. They are optimized for audio/video streaming and for running quietly. These drives are not sold in retail stores and are available only through select licensed Maxtor resellers. weaKnes is such a reseller. Depending on your model, you might also need to get an IDE cable with a second drive connector and a Y-power splitter to deliver power to the second drive.

- Finally, when adding a second drive, you need a mounting bracket kit for the second hard drive (required on Philips HDR-series and Sony SVR2000 only). For S1 DirecTV DVR units, you need drive mounting screws too.

You need these parts for a Series 2 TiVo:

- For a simple replacement job, you need just the new hard drive that will replace your TiVo's original drive. The power and IDE cables and mounting hardware are already on-board. We recommend the Maxtor QuickView drives. These drives are manufactured specifically for the DVR market. They are optimized for audio/video streaming and for running quietly. These drives are not sold in retail stores and are available only through select licensed Maxtor resellers. weaKnees is such a reseller.

- When adding a drive, you'll need to pick up a second hard drive. We recommend the Maxtor QuickView drives. These drives are manufactured specifically for the DVR market. They are optimized for audio/video streaming and for running quietly. These drives are not sold in retail stores and are available only through select licensed Maxtor resellers. weaKnees is such a reseller.

- Finally, when adding a second drive, you'll need a mounting bracket kit (required only on the following models:

  DirecTV DVRs: All units except SAT-T60, GXCEBOT and DSR6000 require an S2 bracket.

  Stand-alone: All units that start with TCD2 or TCD5 require a bracket.

  You will also need to get an IDE cable with a second drive connector and a Y-power splitter to deliver power to the second drive. You might also want a power delay device, such as the PowerTrip, to stagger the startup of your drive. If you buy the TwinBreeze Complete bracket kit from weaKnees, it comes with all the parts you need (minus the second drive) for your particular Series 2 TiVo model.

Connecting the Drive(s)

When you have all of your tools and parts in hand, you need to pull the existing drive(s) from your TiVo. For basic instructions on opening up a TiVo and removing the drives, refer back to the "Replacing a TiVo Drive" section, earlier in this chapter. Basically, after the TiVo is opened, you need to remove the screws that hold the drive bracket(s) to the hard-drive platform, and disconnect the IDE cable(s) and power connector cable(s) from the drive(s). If you have dual drives and they're not labeled A (master) and B (slave), mark them as you remove so that you don't get them confused later.

Upgrading Hard Drives

Tip

On most PCs, the boot sequence is set in the BIOS so that the A: drive boots first (if there's something in the floppy drive). You can go ahead and keep A as the first boot drive (but keep the drive empty on bootup). Just make sure that the CD-ROM is in line before the hard drive.

Tip

If your PC is massively dusty inside, now might be a good time to drag out the vacuum and do a little digital house cleaning. PCs can suck in a lot of dust (especially if you haven't cleaned out that bad boy in a while). It's best to use a vacuum instead of Dust-Off (which will just blast up mushroom clouds of debris that'll settle back down on everything, including you!). Use the plastic crevice tool on your vac, and be careful not to disturb anything inside your box. And, obviously, you should have your PC unplugged while doing this.

You can usually determine which is which by looking at the jumpers and the jumper diagram on the drive label, or in most cases, by noting which drive was at the end of the IDE cable when you pulled the drives out.

With the drive(s) removed, move over to your PC. Insert the CD-ROM that came with this book into your CD-ROM drive, and restart your PC. Before it launches into Windows, head into your Setup/DOS BIOS settings. On most PCs, this is done by hitting the Delete key or F2 right as DOS starts its boot-up sequence. The first screen tells you what key to press to enter setup. BIOS menus are different, so you'll want to consult the manual that came with your PC; basically, however, you're looking for the menu item for changing the boot disk (usually a screen called Boot, Boot Sequence, or something similar). You want to change the first boot device from C or Hard Drive to CD-ROM.

How you change the boot sequence differs from BIOS to BIOS, but the instructions are right there on the screen. When you're resetting the sequence, press F10 or whatever the Save and Exit command is. Your computer restarts itself and boots into the Linux OS on the CD. When you know that the CD-ROM booting is working and that it's launching the Linux minidistro, press Ctrl+Alt+Delete to quit Linux and shut down your PC before it restarts.

With the Linux disc bootable in your CD drive, it's time to install the old TiVo drive(s), copy all the files (but not recordings) to your PC, and then partition/restore to a new drive (or drives).

Open your PC to gain access to the IDE cables. Connect your old TiVo drive(s) to your PC's available IDE ports. If possible, hook the drive(s) to the secondary IDE cable. As stated previously, you can hook the drives to any free port(s) except the primary master. The important thing is to make sure that the jumpers indicating master and slave are correct for each IDE cable and that you know which drive is which after you boot into Linux from the CD-ROM. Table 8.4 shows the Linux naming conventions for hard drives.

Table 8.4   Linux vs. DOS Drive Name Conventions

IDE Location	Linux Naming Scheme	Known to Your DOS PC As
Primary/master	hda	Device 0
Primary/slave	hdb	Device 1
Secondary/master	hdc	Device 2
Secondary/slave	hdd	Device 3

To dizzy you even further, "hda" is known to you as your C: drive in Windows. Are we confused enough yet?

Looking at Table 8.4, let's say you have a dual-drive TiVo that you want to back up to the PC, and you have the entire secondary IDE channel free. After hooking up your TiVo master (or A on TiVo) drive to the secondary master and the slave (or B on TiVo) drive to the secondary slave IDE ports, you would have this:

- **hda**—The PC's hard drive (to which you're going to back up your TiVo files)
- **hdb**—The CD-ROM drive (which you're using to boot into Linux)
- **hdc**—Your original TiVo A/master drive (The contents of which you're going to back up to your PC HD)
- **hdd**—Your original TiVo B/slave drive (The contents of which you're going to back up to your PC HD)

This might all seem a little confusing at first, but as long as you double-check what you're doing, keep track of which drives are where, note what they should be called in Linux, and make sure that the jumpers are properly set, you should be fine.

Also remember that, when hooking up drives to your PC, you have to power them, too! You should have a free four-pin power connector for each IDE port in your PC. If you never had devices on the secondary channel, the connectors might be bundled to other power wires by zip-ties. Carefully cut the zip-tie to free the connectors. If you need to, you can unplug a device (say, a Zip drive) that's not going to be used during the TiVo backup/upgrading process and use its power connector. Just be sure to plug it back in when you're done with your TiVo hacking.

NOTE

Factory-installed IDE cables can be a huge pain. The connectors never seem to be in the right place. For example, the CD-ROM drive is often on the secondary master; the primary master IDE cable has a slave connector about 2" away (meant for stacked hard drives), but the CD-ROM is never installed that close. This is one of the many sources of frustration that DIYers may encounter. You may just want to go ahead and buy a longer IDE cable that allows you to comfortably and safely attach the drives.

Backing Up Existing TiVo Drive(s)

With the hardware properly installed and the PC set to boot off the CD-ROM drive, you're ready to power up and hope for the best! Start up your PC. It will boot into your Linux disc, and you'll see the "Leo Laporte's Guide to TiVo" start-up screen. If you're backing up a Series 1 TiVo, press Enter at the Linux prompt (#). If you're backing up a Series 2 machine, type in `series2` and then press Enter. The system displays screensful of gobbledygook before stopping at the Linux command prompt. Use the Shift+PageUp keys to shift through the previous screens. You're looking for evidence that Linux found and properly identified your TiVo drive(s).

Let's say that you hooked up a single 13.6GB drive from a Series 1 TiVo to your secondary master drive (known to Linux as hdc). Paging up several screens, you should find something like the following:

```
hda: _____, ATA DISK drive
hdb: IDE/ATAPI CD-ROM 48X, ATAPI CD/DVD-ROM drive
hdc: QUANTUM FIREBALL CX13.6A, ATA DISK drive
ide0 at 0x1f0-0x1f7,0x3f6 on irq 14
hda: _____ sectors (YYY MB) w/___KiB Cache,
CHS=1111/222/33, UDMA(33)
hdb: ATAPI 17X CD-ROM drive, 128kB Cache, UDMA(33)
hdc: 26760384 sectors (13701 mb) w/418KiB Cache,
CHS=1665/255/63 UDMA(33)
```

Here you're looking to verify that your three plugged-in drives (your PC HD on hda), your CD-ROM drive (on hdb), and your TiVo drive (on hdc), are all being properly recognized. You're also looking at the sectors reported for hdc (your TiVo drive, in this case), to make sure that all 13.6GB (shown here as 13701MB) are being recognized. If everything checks out (your drive locations and drive sizes might vary, obviously), you can move on to the "Back That Thing Up" section. If not, read the next section, "Picking Locks."

Picking Locks

When you boot from the CD-ROM included with this book and choose "Series1" or "Series2" from the main menu (with your TiVo drive(s) attached, it will automatically unlock your TiVo's hard drive(s)—or, it should. If your TiVo drive size is being grossly underreported, the drive is likely locked and you'll need to unlock it using a special utility, such as DISKUTIL.EXE (included on this book's CD-ROM). To run it, you'll have to copy it over to a bootable floppy disk and boot into your PC through the floppy drive.

After booting from the floppy drive (BTW: You may have to change your BIOS to boot from the floppy), issue the following command at the A:\ prompt:

```
diskutil /PermUnlock 2
```

As you can probably figure out, this is asking diskutil.exe to permanently unlock the disk on device 2. In DOS device naming (refer back to Table 8.4), the main hard drive is device 0, followed by device 1 (primary slave), device 2 (secondary master), and device 3 (secondary slave). So, in this case, you'd be unlocking the TiVo drive on the secondary master IDE connector. If your drive is on a different connector, you'll have to change the command accordingly. Diskutil will give you confirmation (or not) on the unlocking, in case you make a mistake.

With the command executed and the drive unlocked, completely power down your PC (Ctrl+Alt+Delete will not do), pull out the floppy, and boot back in through the CD-ROM drive again. You're now ready to back up the contents of your TiVo HD to your PC.

Back That Thing Up

To back up the software and settings (but *not* programming) of your TiVo drive to your PC's hard drive, the first thing you need to do is mount your PC's hard drive. (All right, smart aleck, get off the desk—you know we didn't mean it like *that*.) The mount command in Linux is used to make a hardware device accessible to Linux. Issue the following command:

```
mount /dev/hda1 /mnt
```

This command assumes that the target location for your primary PC hard drive is hda. It mounts it into the Linux directory /mnt. By the way, the 1 following hda in the command refers to the first partition on the A: drive. Obviously, if you have a FAT32 partition that you created someplace else (such as at hda2), you'll need to mount that partition instead of hda1.

With the PC hard drive ready for action, tell Linux to use the MFS Tool 2.0 backup utility to create a backup of your entire TiVo hard drive on the mounted PC sector by typing in the following command:

For a single-drive backup, type this command:

```
mfsbackup -f 9999 -1so /mnt/backup.bak /dev/hdX
```

Tip

If you need help remembering how to create a boot floppy for your PC, get thee to bootdisk.com, where you'll find instructions and boot disks for various PC OSes available for download.

NOTE

You'll need at least 300MB of free space on your FAT32 PC's hard-drive partition to store the compressed TiVo backup file you're going to create.

Tip

You can actually call the backup file anything you want. Just change the name in the command from /mnt/backup.bak to /mnt/[Anything You Want].bak.

For a dual-drive backup, type this:

```
mfsbackup -f 9999 -1so /mnt/backup.bak /dev/hdX /dev/hdY
```

Important: In these commands, X and Y are in place of the actual hard-drive letters (hdb, hdc, hdd) where your TiVo drive(s) are installed. Change this accordingly before issuing the command.

The previous command creates a compressed backup of your TiVo drive and stores it at C:\backup.bak.

If you are familiar with DOS, Unix, Linux, or other OS command-line interfaces, you know about options (also known as switches) that are entered along with commands. Table 8.5 shows the mojo we applied to the backup command.

Table 8.5   Command-line Options Used in TiVo Backup Procedures

Option/Switch	What It Does
-f [value]	This backs up all video streams with an fsid (File System ID) of less than [value].
	The -f 9999 is a universal value that works with all versions of the TiVo OS. For some backups, the toggle can be left out completely; in others, the precise minimum number will likely be less than 9999 (for example, 4138). By entering a number such as 9999, you increase the backup file size a little but save yourself a lot of heartache by ensuring that the correct files are backed up. The default value is 2000, which is too low for Series 2 TiVos.
-1 (or 0 to 9)	A compression level indicator. This can be anything from 0 (no compression) to 9 (max compression). The more compression you use, the longer it takes. The less compression you use, the bigger the backup file is. The safest bet is to use 9999. You increase the backup file size a little, but save yourself a lot of heartache by ensuring that the correct files are backed up.
-s	This option shrinks down the backup volume to as small a size as is possible, given the data being backed up.
-o [file]	This switch indicates that the backup is headed to a file, as well as where that file is to be written.

You should use these options as is, with the exception of the compression level, which you can set to whatever level you desire.

With the command given, you're presented with status indicators on your screen showing you the backup in progress, and you're told when the backup is complete. Be sure to park the heads on your TiVo drive by shutting down Linux (with a Ctrl+Alt+Delete), and then turn off your PC. You are now ready to remove the old TiVo drive(s) and hook up the new one(s) to prep and restore your TiVo contents.

Bless You, My TiVo

With MFS Tool 2.0, you don't have to do a separate partitioning (called a "blessing"), and then, a separate procedure to move your TiVo's backup contents from the PC to your new TiVo drive(s). It's all done in one step with the `restore` command.

To set up your new drive(s), make sure the jumper settings are set appropriately to where the drive(s) will be in your PC, and go ahead and install it. Start up the computer (still booting into the CD-ROM drive). At the Linux command prompt, the first thing you want to do is mount the PC hard drive again:

```
mount /dev/hda1 /mnt
```

With partition 1 on the hard drive present and accounted for, you're ready to bless and restore (genuflect, genuflect).

If you are restoring to one new drive, issue this command:

```
mfsrestore -s 127 -xzpi /mnt/backup.bak /dev/hdX
```

The X refers to the location of your TiVo drive (on hdb, hdc, or hdd). Change accordingly. If you used a different name for the TiVo backup file, change accordingly.

If you are restoring to two new drives, issue this command:

```
mfsrestore -s 127 -xzpi /mnt/backup.bak /dev/hdX /dev/hdY
```

The X and Y refer to the locations of your TiVo drives (on hdb, hdc, or hdd). Change accordingly. If you used a different name for the TiVo backup file, change accordingly.

You might be curious what all the options in this command string are for. Table 8.6 details them.

Table 8.6   Command-line Options Used in MFS Tools's Restore Process

Option/Switch	What It Does
-s [value]	Defines the size of the swap space on the drive(s). With nothing entered here, it defaults to 64MB. Here we're asking it to create a 127MB space. Don't ask for more.
-x	Expands the TiVo MFS volume to fill the available space of the new drive(s).
-z	Zeroes out inactive partitions.
-p	Optimizes the drive partitions for better performance (for example, the .ty streams will be stored on the outside of the drive, meaning less seek time).
-i	Indicates what file to read from—in our case, /mnt/backup.bak.

The partitioning/restoration process takes some time. Be patient. Go do something else. A watched restoration process never successfully completes! When it's done, MFS Tool reports the size of your new drive(s). Yay! Press Ctrl+Alt+Delete to stop all processes, and shut down your computer.

You are now ready to install the drive(s) in your TiVo. Don't forget to reset the jumpers to the appropriate settings for master (single drive) or master/slave (dual drives).

If you started with a single drive (or dual drives) and are replacing it with a single drive, attach the original drive bracket to your new drive and install it following the appropriate instructions earlier in this chapter, in the section "Replacing a TiVo Drive." If you started out with dual drives and are using two new hard drives, attach both new drives to the original drive bracket in the same manner that they were in before you removed them. If you started with a single drive and are upgrading to a dual-drive system, you might need to add a drive bracket. Both weaKnees.com and PTVUpgrade.com sell drive brackets (and other parts, such as power splitters and IDE cables) for both Series 1 and Series 2 upgrading.

With the drive(s) properly installed, the jumper setting(s) correct, and power and IDE cables properly connected, you're ready to close up your TiVo and reattach all the cables. Hold your breath and plug it in. With the machine powered up, go to TiVo Central -> TiVo Messages and Setup -> System Information. Under Storage Capacity, you should see big,

Caution

Be sure to put your PC back the way you found it, reconnecting all IDE and power connectors, before you close it up and turn it back on.

splendid numbers. Go forth and vegetate, my spudly friend. You did it all yourself. You deserve a break (and you earned really geeky bragging rights).

Upgrading: It's the Right Thing to Do

With so many options for upgrading, and with hard-drive (and TiVo upgrade kit) prices so low, there really is no reason not to upgrade, unless you already have beaucoup amounts of storage (or are happy with the limited amount you have). We hope this chapter has inspired you to roll up your sleeves and do some hardware hacking (or, if that's not your speed, to toss that TiVo in a box and send it to a geek who'll be happy to do it for you). Now, if you'll excuse us, we have two maxed-out TiVos with about two weeks' worth of 24/7 viewing. Note to our editors: We *had* to watch it all to make sure that every sector of the hard drives were partitioned properly. We wouldn't want to be giving people bad upgrading advice now, would we?

Chapter 9

Networking Your TiVo

Next to adding more hard drive space on your TiVo, the upgrade most users are interested in is networking. The home network, linking together a growing population of computers and digital appliances (digital stereo systems, Internet picture frames, and, of course, DVRs), has become a staple of life in the early 21st century. With everything talking to everything else, you can trade files, print documents from any computer on the network, send your MP3 collection to the home stereo, and so on. With TiVo(s) on the network, you can do things such as schedule shows for your DVR(s) from any computer in cyberspace, play your PC's MP3 collection through TiVo, view your digital photo library on your TV, and, on Series 2 machines, record a program on one TiVo and then send it to another one over the network for viewing on a different DVR.

With TiVo Inc. now offering the Home Media Feature (for networking Series 2 machines) for free and dropping the price of service for additional SA S2 TiVos down to $6.95 (from $12.95) a month, lots of TiVonauts likely will want to get into the networking game. If you're one of these home network converts, read on....

In this chapter, we cover the hardware aspects of networking both Series 1 and Series 2 TiVos. Later, in "Part III, Software Bashing," we cover the software involved in home networking in two chapters: Chapter 16, "TiVoWeb" (for Series 1), and Chapter 15, "Home Media Feature" (for Series 2).

Networking Your Series 2 TiVo

At this point, more people likely have Series 2 machines than Series 1, so we cover networking these DVRs first. It's also much easier to network Series 2 machines. Because they were intended to be networked from the start, they have much of this capability already built in. When we started writing this book, the Home Media Feature was a separate service you had to buy; after purchase, TiVo would "turn on" the required software components on your DVR(s). Now TiVo, Inc. does this automatically, so your TiVo is ready when you are set to add the networking hardware. You have two networking options available to you: wired or wireless. Let's take a look at each.

Wired TiVo Networking (S2)

If you have an Ethernet-based wired network at home and can add TiVo to the Net with little disruption (for example, you don't have to snake Ethernet cables through the middle of the dining room or punch too many holes through ceilings, walls, floors, and so on), this is definitely the way to go. Wireless networking is a great convenience because, well, there are no wires—you can set up anywhere. But over-the-air (OTA) radio communications always comes at a price. There can be interference from other devices, security concerns, and slower data-transfer rates. Ethernet has none of these drawbacks. If you can discretely run an Ethernet cable from your TiVo(s) to the router/gateway on your home network, do it! It's your most "robust solution" (as the IT geeks would say).

To connect TiVo to an Ethernetwork, you need to buy (for each Series 2 TiVo you want to connect) a device called a USB-to-Ethernet adapter. TiVo doesn't have Ethernet RJ-45 jacks on it; it has only two USB ports. The USB-to-Ethernet adapter plugs into one of the USB ports and then has a jack on the other end of a dongle that accepts an RJ-45 Ethernet plug. Some adapters have a short USB cable built in; others are only the adapter box itself, and you have to provide both a short USB cable and the Ethernet cable run. We're big fans of the Linksys product line (as is TiVo Inc.) and recommend the EtherFast 10/100 USB Network Adapter ($39 on Amazon.com), shown in Figure 9.1. It does require that you buy a separate USB cable, but because so many devices use USB at this point, you might have a USB cable lying around.

Tip

Besides the network adapter, the other item of hardware that you'll need is the Ethernet cable run itself. You can get bundles/spools of Ethernet Cat5 cable just about anywhere these days. It comes in everything from 3-, 5-, and 10-foot bundles to 25-, 50-, 100-foot, and 1000-foot spools. Usually the spooled versions require that you install your own connectors, so you'll need connectors and a special crimping tool (sold where the cable is sold). At the larger prepared lengths, it can get rather expensive, so it's best not to by it at your local "radio store." Home stores, which now often carry parts for home networking and home automation, often have long-length bundles (25 to 50 feet) and spools for cheaper prices. You can also search Froogle.com and buy it online.

FIGURE 9.1

The Linksys EtherFast 10/100 USB Network Adapter. BYOUSB (bring your own USB).

Numerous other wired network adapters can be used with the Series 2 TiVo. See Table 9.1 for some other models that are known to work with TiVo.

Table 9.1   USB-to-Ethernet Network Adapters Known to Work with Series 2 TiVos

Manufacturer	Adapter Model	Notes
Linksys (www.linksys.com)	Linksys 100TX	Recommended by TiVo, Inc.
	Linksys USB200M	Recommended by TiVo, Inc.
	Linksys USB100M	Requires no USB cable (plugs directly into USB port) .
NETGEAR (www.netgear.com)	NETGEAR FA101 NETGEAR FA120	Another established name in home network tech.
Belkin (www.belkin.com)	Belkin F5D5050	Slightly expensive relative to some others here.
D-Link (www.d-link.com)	D-Link DUB-E100	We haven't had the greatest success with D-Link products (in general, but your mileage may vary).
	D-Link DSB-650TX	At $50 (and no USB mini-cable), not worth the money.
	D-Link DSB-650	Need to provide both USB and Ethernet cables.
Siemens (www.siemens.com)	Siemens SpeedStream SS1001	Users have reported some problems with this unit.
3Com (www.3com.com)	3Com 3C460B	Need to provide both USB and Ethernet cables.
Microsoft (www.microsoft.com)	Microsoft MN-110	Also known as the M53-00001.

Table 9.1   Continued

Manufacturer	Adapter Model	Notes
Hawking Technology (www.hawkingtech.com)	UF200 UF100	Expensive, at more than $50.
	HUF11	Requires no USB cable.
SMC Networks (www.smc.com)	SMC2208USB	Requires no USB cable.
SOHOWare (www.sohoware.com)	NUB100 Ethernet	
Compex	Compex UE202-B	Requires no USB cable. Steal of a deal at less than $20.

TiVonauts have had success with some other Ethernet adapters as well. To see a current list of known compatibles, search on "Series 2 networking" at tivohelp.com.

The hardware installation for Ethernet networking on a Series 2 TiVo couldn't be easier. All you have to do is plug the USB-to-Ethernet adapter into one of the USB ports on your TiVo, plug your Ethernet cable into the other end, and then plug the Ethernet cable into a free RJ-45 Ethernet jack on your home network router/gateway.

That's it. You're done! Now you can turn to Chapter 16 and follow the instructions for setting up the networking software on your TiVo(s) and your PC.

Gareth On...

Built-in home networking and home-automation technology have really been slow in catching on. Even though the "smart house" has been hyped since the 1980s (that's right, the '80s!), few new homes—except for high-end ones—have such technology built into them. That said, the components needed to build your own "smart walls" for delivering computer and multimedia connectivity to outlets in every room of the house are as close as the shelves of your local Home Depot, Lowe's, or other home store. There you'll find all of the cabling, wall jacks, media-distribution boxes, backup power supplies, and everything else you need. It takes a fair amount of monkeying in the rafters of your attic, under the floors, in the walls, and other places to run all the wiring, but once it's done, you can have a media-distribution center in your basement that consolidates all of your coax, phone, Ethernet, fiber optic, whole-house audio, and other incoming media sources and feeds it to multiport wall outlets all over the house. See what's available by checking out Leviton's website (www.leviton.com). It's one of the bigger manufacturers of built-in home-networking systems (Home Depot carries this line of products).

Wireless TiVo Networking

Setting up a Series 2 TiVo to talk to a wireless home network is done much the same way as a wired network—er, minus the wire. In this situation, you also need a special network adapter that connects to one of the two available USB ports. For this, you need a USB-to-wireless adapter. This gizmo sends the signal through the USB port to a small radio transceiver and then over the 2.4GHz WiFi radio spectrum (also called 802.11b) to the antenna on your router/gateway. Again, we like the Linksys products, especially the WUSB11 Wireless-B USB Network Adapter (see Figure 9.2). It sells for less than $50. There are cheaper options as well (see Table 9.2).

FIGURE 9.2
WUSB11 Wireless-B USB Network Adapter.

Table 9.2   USB–to–WiFi Wireless Network Adapters Known to Work with Series 2 TiVos

Manufacturer	Adapter Model	Notes
Linksys (www.linksys.com)	Linksys WUSB11 version 2.6	Works on all S2 TiVo models.
	Linksys WUSB11 version 2.8	Works on all S2 TiVo models.
	Linksys WUSB11 version 3.0	Works on models with service numbers starting in 230, 240, 264, or 275.
	Linksys WUSB12	Works on models with service numbers ending in 230, 240, 264, or 275.
NETGEAR (www.netgear.com)	NETGEAR MA101 V.B	Works on all S2 TiVo models.
	NETGEAR MA101 V.A	Known to work with service numbers ending in 110, 130, or 140.
	NETGEAR MA111	Known to work with service numbers ending in 230, 240, 264, or 275.
Belkin (www.belkin.com)	Belkin F5D6050	Works on all S2 TiVo models.
	Belkin F5D6050 v2000	Works on all S2 TiVo models.
D-Link (www.d-link.com)	D-Link DWL-120 V.E	Works on all S2 TiVo models. Do not use model DWL120+.
	D-Link DWL-120 V.A	Known to work with service numbers ending in 110, 130, or 140. Do not use model DWL120+.
	D-Link DWL-120 V.D	Known to work with service numbers ending in 230, 240, 264, or 275. Do not use model DWL120+.
	D-Link DWL-122	Known to work with service numbers ending in 230, 240, 264, or 275.
SMC Networks (www.smc.com)	SMC 2662W V.2	Works on all S2 TiVo models.
Hawking Technology (www.hawkingtech.com)	Hawking WU250	Known to work with service numbers ending in 230, 240, 264, or 275.
Microsoft (www.microsoft.com)	Microsoft MN-510	Known to work with service numbers ending in 230, 240, 264, or 275.
Dell (www.dell.com)	Dell True Mobile 1180	Known to work with service numbers ending in 230, 240, 264, or 275.

Wireless adapters are a bit more finicky in terms of compatibility than their Ethernet siblings, so we do recommend either that you get one of the adapters listed here or that you check out known compatibility/incompatibility by doing a search on tivocommunity.com. Do a search on an adapter you're interested in; if you don't find any mention of it, ask in the TiVo Help Center forum. There's a topic there called "Read This If You Want to Use Your Series 2 DVR with a Wireless Adapter."

When you have the wireless adapter plugged into one of the USB ports, you're basically done with the hardware part—at least, on TiVo's end. For purposes of this chapter, we're assuming that you already have a wireless home gateway/router setup. Chapter 16 walks you through the instructions for setting up the networking software on your TiVo(s) and your PC.

Networking Your Series 1 TiVo

The Series 1 TiVo was never intended to be networked. By the time TiVo Inc. got around to thinking about plugging TiVo into the rest of your electronic cottage, the company was already knee-deep in developing the Series 2 machines. It was here that the TiVo folks decided to put their networking energies. But that didn't stop enterprising hackers from poking around inside S1 TiVos and figuring out how they could use the edge connector pins (see Chapter 6, "Touring Your TiVo: The Hardware") to create a data-communications channel in and out of TiVo.

When it was clear what the pins did, it was simply a matter of creating an add-on circuit board that could plug into this connector. Then all you had to do was connect an Ethernet cable or WiFi card. Given the open-source spirit around the Series 1 TiVo, numerous software applications were created that would enable you to do most of the media options (and then some) that Series 2 HMF offers. In this section, we look at the two most popular products available for S1 TiVo networking. We cover the software side in Chapter 16 and Chapter 17, "Other TiVo Apps." First up: wired networking.

Wired TiVo Networking (S1 Stand-Alone)

Several third-party products are available for connecting your S1 TiVo to a home network. They are sold by 9th Tee (9thtee.com) and manufactured by Silicondust Engineering (www.silicondust.com). The currently available Ethernet-only card is called the TurboNET Ethernet Adapter, and it sells for $69.25.

Tip

It's certainly not a requirement, but it's often a nice convenience if you get the same brand of wireless adapter as your home network router. It can make things a little easier, especially if something goes wrong and you need to call on tech support to troubleshoot your network. These folks obviously know their own hardware and software better than anyone else's (and they can't blame the other company for the problem, as they are often want to do). There's a similar benefit in getting the hardware that TiVo recommends (in this case, Linksys): If you have to go through tech support for a TiVo networking question, they're likely to have more experience with the hardware they recommended in the first place.

Unlike the Series 2 networking solutions, which work only with stand-alone TiVo models, all Series 1 TiVos, both SA and DirecTiVo DVRs, have the edge connector and can therefore be networked (see the DirecTV DVR installation discussion later in this chapter).

When you have your TurboNET card in hand, installing it is a cinch. Follow these steps:

1. Remove the cover on your TiVo (refer back to the images in Chapter 8, "Upgrading Hard Drives") for instructions on opening TiVo (a.k.a. the hardware blessing).

2. Locate the edge connector on the front edge of your TiVo's motherboard (see Figure 9.3).

FIGURE 9.3

The Series 1 Edge Connector, your gateway to, well, your gateway.

9th Tee, the manufacturer of TurboNET, also offers an add-on board called the CacheCARD with Network Interface ($99.95). This wonderful widget combines the TurboNET features with a slot for a 512MB SDRAM module (which you have to supply). This added memory allows TiVo to cache its entire database, improving its performance speeds. Check out Chapter 11, "Adding a CacheCARD."

3. Hold the TurboNET card in front of the connector so that the printed circuit board part of the card is perpendicular to the mobo/edge connector (see Figure 9.4).

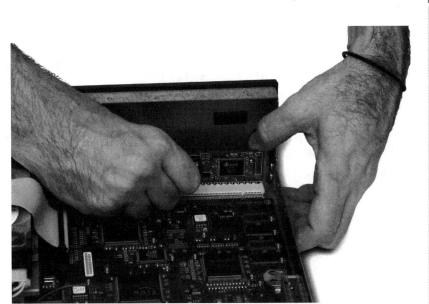

FIGURE 9.4
Installing the TurboNET
card. Go gentle on
TiVo; this is its first
network connection.

NOTE

You will sometimes see
the initials JTAG associ-
ated with the edge con-
nector used on TiVo
mobos. JTAG stands for
Joint Test Action Group
and refers to a standard
for test access ports
found on embedded sys-
tems, such as TiVo. On
the TiVo connector, the
JTAG part is the left-
most set of pins (look-
ing down from the front
of TiVo). On the 9th Tee
TurboNET board, there's
actually a pad for sol-
dering on a JTAG socket
(because the JTAG on
the mobo edge connec-
tor is part of the
TurboNET attachment).
It's unlikely you'd be
reading this book if
you're *that* geeky—we
just thought you might
be curious.

4. Press the white header socket on the card onto the connector pins.
   You might have to rock it back and forth and really push to get it on.

5. With the TurboNET installed, plug your RJ-45 jack from your
   Ethernet cable onto the RJ-45 port on the TurboNET.

6. When you have the card and cable installed, you need to figure out
   some way of getting the cable out of your TiVo box. The easiest way
   to do this is to simply use a hacksaw or Dremel tool to cut a notch
   into the back panel of your TiVo near the fan that you can use to
   pass the cable out. Some hackers also run the Cat5 cable out of one
   of the holes found on the bottom of the TiVo case. These holes are
   too small to run the cable out with an RJ-45 jack attached, so you
   can do this only if you have unterminated (as we geeks like to say)
   cable. In this case, you need a cable-crimping tool and RJ-45 jacks to
   attach on both ends of the cable after you run it.

7. That's it with hardware. You're done! It's a good idea to hook up the
   cable and power up your TiVo with the top off, to make sure that the
   connection is working. The TurboNET card has a little activity light
   in the upper-left corner (marked LINK on the PCB). It glows green
   when there's a connection established and flickers when there's data
   traffic over the line. Cool!

Caution

Any time you power up your TiVo with the lid off, you want to be extremely respectful of the unshielded power supply area.

FIGURE 9.5

The motherboard locks on TiVo. Twist and lift to make space for the TurnoNET connector.

Tip

If you want to get all fancy-schmancy, 9thtee.com sells an RJ-45 Ethernet jack kit for attaching onto the back of your TiVo. You just double-stick it to the back, run the wires out of any available (or created) notch or hole, and then attach it to the terminals inside the jack box. It's not necessary, but it's nice and neat. These jacks are available at radio and home stores, too.

To find out about how to set up the networking software for your wired Series 1 TiVo connection, turn to Chapter 16.

And now a word about annoying rubber parts:

On some models of S1 TiVos, a piece of rubber underneath the edge connector socket and motherboard can make it impossible to plug in the TurboNET card. In this situation, you need to twist the motherboard locks (with a needle-nose or other pliers) located near the front of the TiVo (see Figure 9.5). This will give you just enough play to socket the board.

Wired TiVo Networking (S1 DirecTV DVR)

If you're installing the TurboNET card in a Series 1 DirecTV DVR, follow the same installation instructions as with stand-alone models (see "Wired TiVo Networking [S1 Stand-Alone]," earlier in this chapter), except that you need to remove the hard drive bracket that's installed over the motherboard to gain access to the edge connector underneath (see Figure 9.6). For information on how to uninstall and reinstall drive brackets, refer back to Chapter 8.

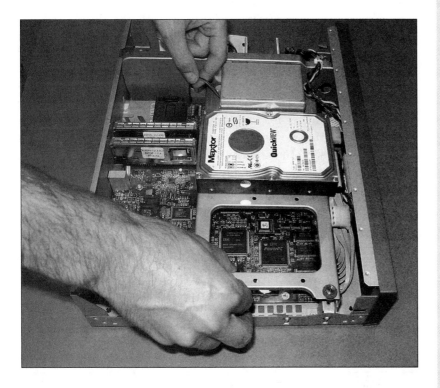

FIGURE 9.6
The hard-drive bracket removed from a DirecTV DVR.

After you've installed the card onto the edge connector, you need to reinstall the hard drive(s) and hard-drive bracket in the case. Run the Ethernet cable underneath the drive bracket. It's a tight fit, so be careful.

With the TurboNET card installed and the Cat5 cable running out of the box and connected to your LAN gateway/router, it's time to check that ye ol' data pipe is connected properly. Power up your TiVo with the top off, to make sure that the activity light (the teeny-weeny LED) in the upper-left corner (marked LINK on the PCB) is lit. It glows green when there's a connection established and flickers when there's data traffic over the line. For now, it should be glowing green.

That's it for the hardware part. You're done! To find out how to set up the networking software for your wired Series 1 TiVo connection, turn to Chapter 16.

Wireless TiVo Networking (S1 Stand-Alone)

Although wired (Ethernet) networking is great for those who can snake wires from wherever their TiVo happens to be to wherever their computers are (and, for many of us, that's several rooms away), wireless networking gives us far more flexibility. The TiVo and the PC can be rooms or floors away and still talk to each other. For S1 TiVos, this is where the 9th Tee AirNET card comes in. This is a plug-in board that has a slot that accepts a WiFi/802.11b wireless card. You have to provide the wireless card yourself. See Table 9.3 for a list of WiFi cards that are known to be compatible with the AirNET.

Table 9.3   WiFi Cards Known to Be Compatible with the 9th Tee AirNET Card

Manufacturer	Model(s)	Notes
Linksys (www.linksys.com)	WPC11	Integrated antenna.
D-Link (www.d-link.com)	DW-655H	Integrated antenna. Has antenna connector.
	DWL-650	Integrated antenna. Known hackable.
Proxim (www.proxim.com)	RangeLAN-DS 8434-05	Has detachable antenna.
	RangeLAN-DS 8433-05	Detachable antenna.
SMC Networks (www.smc.com)	SMC2532W-B	Integrated antenna.
	SMC2632W	Integrated antenna. Known hackable.
Zcomax (www.zcomax.com)	XI-300	Detachable antenna.
	XI-300B	Integrated antenna.
	ZFE-300	Integrated antenna.
	XI-325	Detachable antenna.
	XI-325H	Detachable antenna.
	XI-325H1	Detachable antenna.
Belkin (www.belkin.com)	F5D6020 (Version 1)	Make sure it's version 1. There's an F5D6020 that uses a non-PRISM chipset. Integrated antenna. PCB has mount for adding connector. Hackable.
Compaq (www.compaq.com)	WL100	Cannot use the WL110. Different chipset. Integrated antenna.
	HNW-100	Exact same card as D-Link DWL-650. Hackable.

Table 9.3   Continued

Manufacturer	Model(s)	Notes
ZoomAir (www.zoomair.com)	ZOOM4105	Detachable external antenna and 20-inch extension cable. Recommended (and sold) by 9th Tee.
Teletronics (www.teletronics.com)	WL-11000	Looks like it could be the same hardware as the XI-300. Models with and without detachable antenna available. Model without still has connector for antenna.
Addtron	AWP-100	Integrated antenna.
	AWP-101	Integrated antenna.
Demarc (www.demarctech.com)	Relia-Wave DT-RWZ-200mW-WC	Detachable antenna, two high-gain antenna connectors.

"Integrated antenna" means that the antenna is part of the WiFi card itself.

"Detachable antenna" usually means that it has a small rubberized antenna (called a "rubber ducky" antenna) that can be disconnected. With the proper cable, you can extend the antenna to the outside of your TiVo.

"Hackable" means that there are pads on the cards PCB where coax cable or an antenna connector can be soldered on to create your own external antenna.

Installing the AirNET Card (on an SA S1 TiVo)

Installing the AirNET card is done exactly the same way as installing the TurboNET (refer to those instructions earlier in this chapter). Basically, you need to do the following:

1. Open the case (perform the hardware blessing).
2. Plug the WiFi card into the slot on the AirNET.
3. Plug the AirNET card onto the TiVo mobo edge connector.

You're done with basic hardware installation.

Installing the AirNET Card (on an S1 DirecTV DVR)

The AirNET card that 9th Tee sells is designed so that you can plug in the card over the top of the hard-drive bracket, which is found over the mobo. If you can get the AirNET card onto the edge connector pins without removing the hard-drive bracket, go ahead and do it. It'll save you some time and effort. Here's how the standard DirecTV DVR installation would go:

1. Open the case (perform the hardware blessing).

Tip

The AirNET adapter is designed to work with WiFi cards that employ the PRISM2 (or PRISM2.5) chipset in their internal electronics. Luckily, the majority of cards on the market use this chipset. If you have access to a WiFi card that's not listed here and you do a search and see that it's PRISM based, it'll likely work with the AirNET. Avoid Cisco Systems cards (and Dell cards, which use Cisco parts) because they use their own set of chips.

2. Plug the AirNET card onto the TiVo mobo edge connector.

3. Plug the WiFi card into the slot on the AirNET.

You're done with basic hardware installation.

And now a word about annoying rubber parts:

On some models of S1 stand-alone DirecTV DVRs, a piece of rubber underneath the edge connector socket and motherboard can make it impossible to plug in the AirNET card. In this situation, you need to twist the motherboard locks (with a needle-nose or other pliers) located near the front of the TiVo. This will give you just enough play to socket the board. If you're installing the AirNET card on a DirecTV DVR, to do this operation, you have to temporarily remove the hard-drive bracket to get to the motherboard and the mobo locks (refer back to Figure 9.6).

Options for Improving AirNET Reception

The astute among you might have noticed that on either the stand-alone or DirecTiVo DVR AirNET cards, the arrangement of the WiFi card with its built-in antenna means that, when you close up the TiVo case, your antenna is trapped inside your TiVo box. Now, you're also probably thinking: Is that really a big problem? WiFi radio waves go through floors, walls, and so on, so why not TiVo cases? The answer is "yes and no." You can get reception from the integrated card antenna with a closed-lid TiVo (depending on where your TiVo and home router are located), but you'll get much better reception by using an external antenna or by doing a few cheap tricks described here.

- **External antenna**—By far the best way to go is to get a WiFi card that has a detachable antenna. Some of these even come with an antenna extension cable that attaches where the antenna normally attaches to the card; then you attach the antenna onto the other end. This way, you can run the antenna out of your TiVo box (by cutting a notch or hole in the case with a hacksaw or drill) and attach it to the outside of your media center, bookshelf, or other structure.

If your WiFi card has a connector on it for attaching an external antenna, you need to get the appropriate cable. Some connectors used on cards are proprietary, so you have to get a special cable that has the proprietary connector on one end and a common antenna connector (such as a N-type connector) on the other. This type of cable is called a pigtail adapter.

If the connector on the end of your cable is not compatible with the antenna that came with your WiFi card (assuming that one did), you have to either buy an antenna, too, or buy an adapter that can be attached to the common connector on the business end of the cable you bought to attach to the WiFi card. Confused yet? Don't be. All you need to do is find out the name of the connector type used on your WiFi card, buy a cable that plugs into that connector, find out the name of the connector on the other end of the cable, and see if it connects to your antenna (if you have one). If not, buy the appropriate adapter.

Tip

Two good sources for all types of radio connectors and cables for WiFi networking are JEFA Tech (www.jefatech.com) and HyperLink Technologies (www.hyperlinktech.com). You can also do a Google search on the type of WiFi card you have; you'll likely find discussions and how-tos on antenna connecting, signal boosting, and more.

- **Couch potato antenna hack**—The easiest, and downright laziest, way to get a better signal on your AirNET/WiFi card is to leave the top off your TiVo altogether, or place the lid on the TiVo but leave a large (say, 5-inch) gap in the front (don't slot the lid in all the way, and don't attach it). The gap should leave enough space for decent radio wave dispersion. Leaving the top off or with a wide crack might seem wrong (what about the dust and the tacky look of it?), but it might also raise your geek cred. It is a true testament to the depths of your geekitude how many devices you have around the house with the lids off so that you can hardware-hack at will. We have PCs that haven't seen a lid or a side panel in years. Many of our digital devices seem to think they're nudists. And if your TiVo is shelved on a home entertainment rack, people are going to see mainly the front panel anyway.

- **Handyman (or woman) antenna hack**—If a nude TiVo strikes you as a little unseemly, you can just cut a rectangular hole in the lid above the WiFi card instead (see Figure 9.7). The easiest way to do this is to use a Dremel-type rotary tool and a metal cutting blade. Obviously, this won't appeal to a large number of users. If literal hardware hacking is not your cup of mocha latte, a card with a detachable antenna is the way to go.

FIGURE 9.7
Careful with that hacks, Eugene. Cutting an antenna opening for the AirNET card.

Caution

Obviously, when cutting metal with a Dremel or any other type of power tool (or even with a hacksaw), it's really important that you take all safety precautions, especially wearing goggles or safety glasses.

- **Deep geek roll your own antenna hack**—If you don't want to spend the bucks on a proprietary connector and cable for your WiFi card, you can make your own, if you're handy with a soldering iron. This works only on some WiFi cards. In Table 9.3, cards with known hackability (and online instructions) are listed in the Notes column. Here are links to several antenna-hacking how-tos:

  Adding an antenna connector to the D-Link DWL-650: c0rtex.com/~will/antenna/

  Adding an SMA-type antenna connector to an SMC-2632 WiFi card: http://www.guerrilla.net/ reference/80211_mod/SMC2632_antenna_mod/

  Basically, the deep geek antenna hack involves removing the case on the integrated antenna, desoldering and moving a capacitor to a different pad on the printed circuit board, soldering on the wires from a coax cable or the pins from an antenna connector, and cutting a hole in the case for the cable or connector. If this sounds like no big deal to you, check out the two previous how-tos or do a Google search on the card you have to see if it's hackable.

In the end, it's probably just easier to get a WiFi card such as the ZoomAir, which comes with the detachable antenna and extension cable. You can find the ZoomAir card online for as little as $45.

Installing the Drivers for the AirNET

Unlike the TurboNET card, which is unofficially supported by version 3.0 of the TiVo OS, the AirNET card requires the installation of drivers (which means hooking up your TiVo drive[s] to your PC, as described in Chapter 8). To ensure reliable operation of the WiFi card, you should also make sure that the latest version of the card's firmware is installed. As mentioned previously, all of the WiFi cards that are compatible with the AirNET use the PRISM chipsets by Intersil, so the good news is that the same firmware upgrade works on all Intersil-based cards. The bad news is that performing the firmware upgrade involves plugging your WiFi card into the PCMCIA (PC Card) slot on a laptop and loading the firmware onto the card. If you don't have a laptop, you'll have to borrow one to do this. For instructions on where to get the latest firmware and how to install it and the AirNET drivers onto your TiVo, check out the AirNET Software page at www.silicondust.com/airnet/install_software.html.

Have Your Machine Call My Machine

If you've read this far and geeked out with us along at home, you should now have your Series 1 or Series 2 TiVo talking to the other devices on your home network (unless you have an S2 DirecTV DVR, which is a snob and doesn't give other gadgets the time of day). So now you'll want to know what cool things you can do with TiVo on the network. For Series 2 stand-alone TiVos, turn to Chapter 15. There you'll learn how to do everything from scheduling recordings over the Web to playing music and sending recorded programs between TiVos. If you've just networked a Series 1 TiVo (either stand-alone or DirecTiVo), you'll want to check out Chapter 16. It covers installing and using the TiVoWeb software that's included on the CD-ROM in the back of this book. There are also additional apps (mainly for Series 1 machines) in Chapter 17.

Before moving on, you can do one software twiddle to assign your new network node its first task. You can configure TiVo to make its daily call over the local area network (and through your cable or DSL modem, over the

Internet). It's like opening the gates at SeaWorld so the dolphins can head out into the great Atlantic: Swim TiVoGuy, *swim!*

- **On Series 2 TiVos:** Go to TiVo Messages, Setup, Settings, Phone & Network Setup, Change Connection Type. Select Network. That's it! Now TiVo will use the Internet to make all calls to TiVo servers, and your phone line will never suffer another squealing modem call.

- **On Series 1 TiVos:** Before version 3.0 of the TiVos OS, you had to fiddle around in a Linux TCL script to get a networked S1 TiVo to make its daily call over the Net. With 3.0, all you have to do is the following: Go to Messages & Setup, Recorder & Phone Setup, Phone Connection, Change Dialing Options. Under Set Dialing Prefix, to enter ,#401 (use the Pause button to create the comma and the Enter button to create the # sign). That's it! Now TiVo will use the Internet to make all calls to TiVo servers, and you can disconnect the RJ-11 phone jack and cable from the TiVo.

Chapter 10

Quick 'n' Dirty Serial Networking (Series 1)

Ah, the forgotten but not gone (RS-232) PC serial port. We computer old timers remember it fondly. Your authors are so crusty and ancient (in computer/Internet years, anyway), that we remember when the RS-232 serial communications standard was pretty much the only way that PCs talked to each other, either directly (from serial port to serial port) or through serially connected modems over a phone network. You ungrateful whippersnappers today, with your fancy USB 2.0, and your Ethernet, and your FireWire. Why, when we were first computer cowboys, we had to sit at a green screen and a command prompt and—oh wait, we're getting a little off-track here.

Although the RS-232 serial port might be legacy tech accumulating dust on your PC, it can still be called into service for allowing your PC and your TiVo to talk to each other. With the two devices connected directly through their respective serial ports, you can use a terminal program on your PC to view the contents of your TiVo's drives, transfer files, load programs onto your TiVo, and do other cool stuff. "Retro computing" is all the rage these days, so let's get a little nostalgic for RS-232 technology and make it work for us in tricking our DVRs.

Tip

This chapter takes us knee-deep into the Linux OS. If you're unfamiliar with Linux, you'll want to read Chapter 13, "Touring Your TiVo: The Software," and Chapter 14, "Accessing Your TiVo's Linux Bash Prompt," before attempting the software side of serial networking.

FIGURE 10.1

TiVo's serial cable, included with all SA models. If you don't have one, you can buy one from weaKnees.com.

Some Hardware Required

You might not be aware of it, but your TiVo likely came with a serial cable. If you've had your TiVo for a while, the cable could still be in the box, stored away in the attic or basement, or wherever you stashed it in case you ever had to send back the TiVo for repairs. All Series 1 and Series 2 stand-alone machines come with a serial cable (DirecTiVos do not) (see Figure 10.1). The serial cable that ships with TiVo has the typical nine-pin D-sub (short for "D-shape subminiature") connector on one end and a miniplug on the other. The official purpose of this cable is to connect a satellite receiver's serial control data port (used for sending channel control signals) to your TiVo. The nine-pin D-sub goes into the sat receiver, and the miniplug goes into the Control Out serial port on the TiVo. That's the *official* use, but with a little software hacking, you can open up the serial port so that it'll share data streams with your PC.

The TiVo serial cable is the main piece of gear you need to connect TiVo to PC, but you're going to need a few other items. The first component you need is called a null modem adapter (see Figure 10.2). In this case, you want a DB9 female to DB9 male null modem adapter. You can buy one at many electronics and computer stores, both online and off. They sell for about $8–$10. A null modem is a device that allows two computers to talk to each other over a serial line without having to use modems.

FIGURE 10.2
A DB9 female to DB9 male null modem adapter.

The next bit o' kit you need is what's called a gender changer (or "gender bender"). Our null modem adapter has a female end that we plugged the male end of TiVo's serial control cable into. That leaves a male end available on the null modem. But, unfortunately, our PC's serial port has pins (that is, it is male), so we've got a problem. Enter the gender changer. It's a little adapter that has the same plug "gender" on both sides (see Figure 10.3). In our case, we're looking for a DB9 female-female gender changer. This enables us to plug one end of it into the pins of the null modem adapter and plug the other end into the pins of our PC's serial port. You can get the appropriate gender changer for about $8 at many electronics and computer stores, both online and off.

NOTE

The instructions given in this chapter refer to Series 1 TiVos only. It *is* possible to set up a Series 2 machine for serial networking, but it's much more complicated, and honestly, we think that the payoff is not worth it for most users. There really aren't that many open-source "killer apps" for S2 TiVo. If you're on a Series 2 machine and want to set up serial networking, William von Hagen does an excellent job of describing the process in his book *Hacking the TiVo* (Premier Press, 2003).

FIGURE 10.3
"Turn and face the strange ch-ch-changes...."
The trusty gender changer.

Attention Macheads:
You can make a serial connection between your Mac and TiVo, but you need one other widget: a serial-to-USB adapter. It has a DB9 male serial connector on one end and a USB connector on the other. You'll obviously need to load the appropriate Mac drivers to enable RS-232 serial communications through the USB ports. And, yes, unfortunately, you will likely find only a male connector, which means that you'll still need the gender changer in addition to the serial-to-USB adapter.

Tip

For more information on TiVo's software, the underlying Linux OS, and the command-line interface called Bash, check out Chapters 13 and 14.

That's it for hardware. All you have to do now is to plug the miniplug from the serial cable into the Serial Out port on your TiVo and plug the null modem/gender changer end into the serial port on your PC. But to get them to talk to each other, you've got some "splainin" to do (to your TiVo's software). Unfortunately, this requires installing TiVo's drives directly to your PC again. The good news is that, after this is done and you have the serial networking figured out, you can use it to talk to TiVo without having to remove the drives again.

Open the Serial Port Doors, Hal!

To get your TiVo to talk to your PC over a serial connection, you need to do a little twiddling in TiVo's system scripts so that it will automatically enable the Linux Bash shell each time TiVo boots up.

Performing this hack involves attaching your TiVo drive(s) to your PC again. When you have the drive(s) installed (as detailed in Chapter 8, "Upgrading Hard Drives") and have booted into the Linux mini-distro on this book's CD, you need to edit the rc.sysinit script. This system-initialization script controls the processes and program loading in Linux on bootup. First, though, being good little geeks, we'll want to make backup copies of the files we'll be editing.

To create a backup copy of rc.sysinit, issue the following commands at the Bash (#) prompt:

```
mkdir /mnt4
cd /mnt4/etc/rc.d
cp rc.sysinit rc.sysinit.orig
```

As you can probably figure out, the first command makes a directory at /mnt4, and the second changes directories and mounts partition 4. Then we use the cp command to make a copy of initialization file.

Now, with the backup safely stored, it's time to put on your pointy wizard hat and issue arcane commands to be added to the end of the active rc.sysinit file. At the Bash prompt, type this:

```
echo '/bin/bash < /dev/ttyS3 >& /dev/ttyS3 &' >>
➥rc.sysinit
```

The echo command is used in Bash to write the strings listed in the command to standard output. In this case, we're asking Bash to take any input (<) from /dev/ttyS3 and send its output (>) and any error messages (&) to /dev/ttyS3. /dev/ttyS3 is also known as our serial port, so we're telling Linux/Bash (through our amended sysinit script) to talk to the serial port (is that anything like talkin' to the hand?) .

In case you're curious, TiVo actually has either three (Series 2) or four (Series 1) serial ports onboard. Table 10.1 lists their Linux device names and what each of them does.

Tip

If you're reading through this book before doing any of the actual hardware or software hacks (always a smart idea), you might want to plan what software you want on your TiVo and what script changes you need to make (to do things such as access TiVo's Bash prompt) and to do all of this loading and script hacking while you have the drives hooked up for backup or drive upgrading, as described in Chapter 8.

Table 10.1 TiVo Serial Ports and What They Talk To

Serial Port Address	What It Talks To
/dev/ttyS0	The IR output (IR Blaster) on the back and the IR input on the front of TiVo.
/dev/ttyS1	TiVo's built-in 33.6 analog modem.
/dev/ttyS2	The debug port located on the edge connector of S1 TiVos. The Serial Out (Serial Control) port on the back of Series 2 TiVos.
/dev/ttyS3	The Serial Out (Serial Control) port on the back of Series 1 TiVos.

Geek Etymology Note: TTY stands for Teletypewriter and refers to the first device to make use of RS-232 serial communications technology. TTY has come to indicate any serial communications terminal or RS-232 serial technology.

Don't Blow the Dismount!

Any time you make changes to configuration files in Linux, you want to unmount the TiVo partitions and shut down your PC. This ensures that the changes are clean and properly saved. Never just turn off your PC after making conf file changes because you risk leaving the files in a corrupted state, which can, well, corrupt everything. To unmount the partitions you mounted for the script tweaking, issue the following at Bash (#):

```
cd /
umount /mnt4
```

If you mounted more than one partition during your Linux session, you can unmount all of them at once by saying umount /mnt4 mnt7 mnt9, and so on. Note that the command is umount (*not un*mount, as you might expect—silly geeks!)

Caution

It's possible that your TiVo does not have an active partition 4. If you get an error message while trying to mount it, it simply means that partition 7 is active instead. Make a dir (mkdir /mnt7) and change the cd command to mnt7, and you should be fine. TiVo switches between these two drive partitions.

NOTE

Unfortunately, easy access to the Bash prompt over a serial port is only available on stand-alone S1 machines. On S1 DirecTiVos, you have to do a procedure called "flashing the PROM" to make this work hack stick. TiVo, Inc. frowns on this practice, so we're not covering it in this book, but if you do a search on dealdatabase.com/forum, you'll find the information you need.

Tip

As you'll discover in Chapter 13, TiVo always has an active partition and a backup partition, usually partitions 4 and 7. So, if you make changes to the active partition, it's a good idea to make those same changes to the backup. To do this, you issue the cd, cp, and echo commands that you did earlier, replacing mnt4 with mnt7. This ensures that if TiVo switches partitions, your open serial port stays that way. Unfortunately, if TiVo, Inc. does a software update, all of your hacks will be toast.

With the TiVo partitions safely out of the running, so to speak, you can exit the Bash shell by giving this command:

```
exit
```

Now press Ctrl-Alt-Delete to reboot your PC, and at the first signs of booting back up, turn off the machine. You're now free to remove the TiVo drive(s) and restore them to your TiVo, as instructed in Chapter 8. As always, don't forget to reset the jumpers properly for TiVo.

Talk to Me, TiVoGuy!

With the TiVo drive(s) back home, it's time to try to get a conversation going over your new serial communications channel. Now that the script hack has opened the serial port to two-way traffic, you need a program to connect to it. You need (retro-futuristic drum roll, please) a terminal emulation program! Again, we aging meatbots remember when a terminal program window was what the Internet used to look like. Hell, we remember back before it was even called the Internet, but that's just making us look sad, so let's move on.

A terminal emulation program is a little app that, in essence, turns your expensive, tricked-out Pentium whatever into a mid-20th-century dumb terminal—basically, a monitor and keyboard that can peer into the innards of a remote computer (in this case, your TiVo). Terminal emulators that use a graphical user interface are often called terminal windows. Let's look at a few common emulators:

- **HyperTerminal**—You've probably seen this app on your Windows desktop and wondered, "What the heck am I ever going to do with *that*!" This is what you're going to do with it. You're going to launch this Microsoft app that came with Windows and use it to poke around inside TiVo (see Figure 10.4).

- **SecureCRT**—Another popular Windows-based program, SecureCRT offers encrypted communications through its terminal window software (see Figure 10.5). It's not free ($99), and its encryption features are overkill here. If you already own it, it's a good program to use, but otherwise, for what you're going to do over your serial network, HyperTerminal is just fine. If you want to check it out, the maker is VanDyke Software (www.vandyke.com).

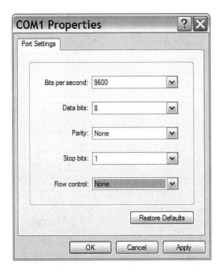

FIGURE 10.4
Look kids, it's the network wayback machine! MS's HyperTerminal finally earns its disk space.

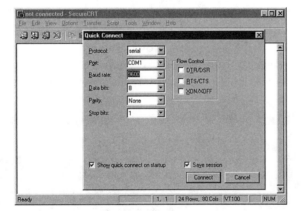

FIGURE 10.5
SecureCRT. Cause geeks *love* encryption.

Tip

While you have your TiVo drive(s) hooked up to your PC, now is an excellent time to load the package of Linux utilities included on the CD-ROM in the back of this book. These utilities will help you navigate inside TiVo's file systems when you get the serial connection established. If you want to do this, turn to Chapter 14 and follow the instructions in the "Installing Bash's Little Helpers" section. The utilities themselves are described in Appendix C, "About the CD-ROM."

- **ZTerm**—Every veteran Machead knows ZTerm, the terminal emulator that has been around forever (see Figure 10.6). We could easily go all nostalgic on you, regaling you with tales of using ZTerm to hop around from one bulletin board system (BBS) to another. But we'll save that for chat over cocktails (you're buying, right?). ZTerm has several things going for it: It's free to try ($20 to buy), it works on both pre-OSX and OSX, and, as we said, it's venerable. Respect your elders! It's available direct from the geek who makes it (how DIY is that?): Dave Alverson, at homepage.mac.com/dalverson.

FIGURE 10.6

Mac users can go back in time, too. Straight from the '80s: It's ZTerm!

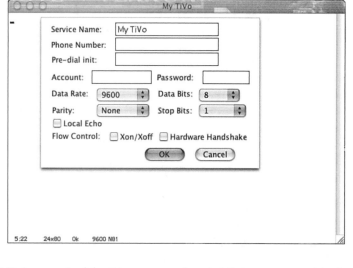

- **Minicom**—And for Linux users, there's Minicom, a surprisingly sophisticated terminal emulator that has all sorts of nifty features (see Figure 10.7). If you're on a Linux box and you don't have Minicom on it already, get thee to ibiblio.org/pub/Linux/apps/serialcomm/dialout/ and help yourself to a download. It's free.

FIGURE 10.7

And for Penguinheads, there's the ubiquitous (and powerful) Minicom.

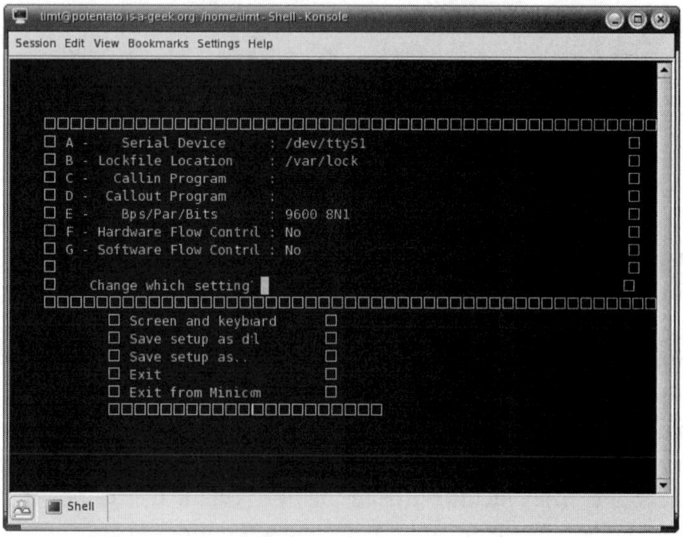

Establishing a Comm Session

With your serial cable installed, your TiVo's sysinit script tweaked so that it's bit-spittin' Bash commands against the serial port, and a terminal window running on your PC, you're finally ready to chat up your DVR.

Again, we hate to belabor the serial communications reminiscences, but does 8N1 mean anything to you people? It certainly did in the days before the Web. It refers to the common terminal emulation settings 8 data bits, no parity, and 1 stop bit. We won't go into what this means here—just make sure your TTY program is set to 8N1 in the appropriate preferences/settings/setup area. It should also be set for a 9600-baud rate. Also check to make sure that flow control (both hard and soft) is turned off (or set to "none").

With the terminal window running and set up as discussed, restart your TiVo. When TiVo is running, your terminal window should display the Bash prompt, which will likely look like this:

```
bash-2.02#
```

If you don't see this right away, hit Return/Enter a few times; hopefully, TiVo will respond.

You're in like Flynn, baby! So what can you do over a serial connection? Plenty. It's not the fastest networking you'll ever do (in fact, it's probably the slowest), but with it, you can look around inside TiVo's file structure, transfer programs onto TiVo, and even move copies of files from TiVo onto your PC. On the CD-ROM included with this book, we have a suite of common Linux utilities that TiVo Inc. didn't bother to install 'cause TiVo didn't need them. You do! We discuss how to install these utilities, and the various things you can do over a serial network connection, in "Part III, Software Bashing (Playing with Your Penguin)."

Chapter 11

Adding a CacheCARD (Series 1)

TiVo has a lot going for it. Peppy process handling ain't among them. Get a bunch of programs in your Now Playing queue, have a lot of WishLists and numerous Season Passes, and you're going to get intimately familiar with TiVo's "Please Wait" screen. Color us cranky, but this is *not* TV our way!

Performance was improved on Series 2 machines, but neither S1 nor S2 TiVo is going to win any speed demon awards. Performance can get so slow on Series 1 machines that hackers quickly strapped on their battery-operated propeller beanies and started looking for solutions. Upgrading the 16MB of motherboard RAM (by adding 8MB chips into the two available slots) did little to help. Enter the trusty (and versatile) Series 1 edge connector. 9th Tee and SiliconDust Engineering, makers of the TurboNET Ethernet adapter and AirNET cards, also offer the CacheCARD with Network Interface (see Figure 11.1). This card plugs into the Series 1 edge connector and provides both an RJ-45 connector for an Ethernet cable and a slot for adding 512MB of SDRAM.

FIGURE 11.1

The CacheCard, produced by SiliconDust Engineering, can improve the performance of your Series 1 TiVo.

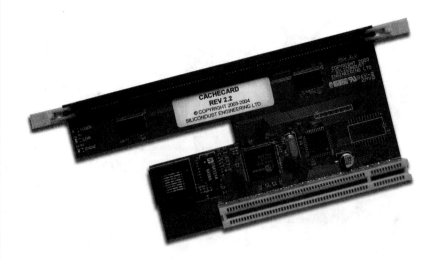

Cold, Hard Cache

This addition of SDRAM allows the entire TiVo database—what TiVo uses to handle all of its operations—to be stored in a cache memory. Normally, every time you ask TiVo to do something (perform a title search, create a Season Pass, and so on), it has to go into its file system on the hard drive and fetch this information. The more bloated your disk is with data, the longer this fetching process can take. Loading all of this database information into a cache means quicker seek times.

To set up the CacheCARD, you need the following:

- The 9th Tee CacheCARD with Network Interface. The card is available for $99.95 from 9thtee.com. It is compatible with both stand-alone and DirecTV DVRs. It is not available for Series 2 machines. The card does not include an Ethernet cable for networking or the SDRAM memory module that is required. You must supply these.

- A 512MB PC133 SDRAM memory module. You're looking for a standard 512MB, unbuffered, PC100/PC133 synchronous dynamic random access memory (SDRAM) module. Any brand will do (though it's ideal to choose a brand that others have had success with).

- A Cat5 Ethernet cable to network with your home Ethernet LAN.

- A copy of the latest CacheCARD drivers (free download at SiliconDust Forum: www.silicondust.com/forum/viewforum. php?f=1).

Tip

Memory Suppliers (www.memorysuppliers. com) offers a suitable module for only $65. That's a really great price, and the module is known to work in the CacheCARD. It also has a lifetime guarantee. Here's the direct address: www.memorysuppliers. com/51pc7ns168pi3.html. You can do a search on Froogle.com for a cheaper module, but you won't likely find one.

You can load the CacheCARD software onto TiVo in three different ways. You can use a serial connection, you can use an Ethernet connection, or you can copy the files from a floppy disk while your TiVo drive is connected to your PC. If you plan to use a serial connection, you need to attach a serial cable between your PC and TiVo, as described in Chapter 10, "Quick n' Dirty Serial Networking." You also have to follow the steps outlined there for getting a Linux Bash prompt over the serial line (if you haven't performed this hack already). If you want to use an Ethernet connection to copy the files, read the section "Talking to TiVo via Ethernet" in Chapter 14, "Accessing Your TiVo's Linux Bash Prompt." If you want to go ahead and load the CacheCARD drivers into TiVo while you have its drive(s) connected to your PC, follow the instructions provided on the SiliconDust Forums (www.silicondust.com/forum/viewtopic.php?t=2) for creating a disk image on a floppy disk and loading the driver from there. We don't discuss the latter method here.

> **NOTE**
>
> As mentioned in the previous chapter, accessing the Bash prompt over a serial network cannot be done on a S1 DirecTiVo without "flashing the PROM," a process we do not discuss in this book. Search on dealdatabase.com/forums for DIY details.

Installing the CacheCARD: The Software

The first thing you need to do to get started on the software installation is to download the latest version of the CacheCARD software. We didn't bother to put the software on the book's CD-ROM because we thought having the most recent version of the drivers (for all the 9th Tee edge connector cards) from the website made more sense. The CacheCARD driver is available from http://www.silicondust.com/forum/viewforum.php?f=1.

Note that two versions are listed: nic_install_pc and nic_install_tivo. For either the serial comm or over Ethernet installation, you want to download nic_install_tivo. If you plan to install the CacheCARD drive while your TiVo drive(s) is connected to your PC, you'll want nic_install_pc. For that installation, you'll also want to follow the PC Installation Instruction given on the SiliconDust Forums. We don't cover that procedure here.

> **NOTE**
>
> cpio stands for copy input/output and is a ubiquitous copy utility program. It can be found among the Linux tools installed on TiVo, and it is useful especially if you haven't already installed the utility files detailed in the "Bash's Little Helpers" section of Chapter 14.

Over a Serial Network

With the latest nic_install_tivo Zip file on your PC and your PC connected to your TiVo over a serial line (and the Bash prompt talking to the serial port, as described in Chapter 10), do the following:

1. Unzip the nic_install_tivo file onto your PC (it will be called
   `nic_install_tivo.cpio`).

Tip

If typing rz in your term window is not the trigger you need to pull to launch the dialog box for selecting and sending files, consult the help docs that came with your terminal program.

2. Launch your terminal window program and establish the connection to your TiVo (as described in Chapter 10).

3. Move to TiVo's /tmp directly and clean it out, like so (at the Bash prompt):

```
cd /tmp
rm *
```

4. Now use your terminal window program to transfer the cpio file on your PC to the /tmp directory on your TiVo. This is usually done by issuing ye old ZMODEM command rz in the terminal window. This will likely pop up a Select Files dialog box where you can find the cpio file on your PC and upload it to TiVo.

5. Extract the cpio file by entering the following command:

```
cpio -i -F nic_install_tivo.cpio
```

6. Now it's time to run the unarchived program to install the driver:

```
./nic_install_tivo cachecard
```

7. In the main menu, configure the network setting for the Ethernet port on the card by entering a static IP address based on the other IP addresses on your network. If you're unfamiliar with IP addressing and how to create an appropriate IP address, see the section "Setting the IP Address Method" in Chapter 15, "Home Media Feature." Also, before leaving the nic program, make sure that Daily Call is set to Network so that, from now on, TiVo uses your LAN to log on to TiVo Inc.'s servers to download guide data.

8. To exit the program, press 0. When asked whether you want to clear the log file, say Yes.

9. Reboot TiVo by unplugging it, waiting a few seconds, and then plugging it back in.

10. Make sure the lid of your TiVo is off and that you have a view on the side of the CacheCARD facing the TiVo's mobo (so that you can see the status light indicators on the card).

Over an Ethernet Network Connection

To install the drivers over an Ethernet connection, you follow the same procedure as with a serial connection, except that you use a Telnet program to access the Bash prompt. You issue the same commands:

```
cd /tmp
rm *
```

Then you transfer the driver file using an FTP command. We discuss Ethernet connections to TiVo in Chapter 14.

Installing the CacheCARD: The Hardware

 The installation of the CacheCARD hardware is very straightforward:

1. Open your TiVo using the hardware blessing instructions in Chapter 8, "Upgrading Your Hard Drives."

2. Insert your SDRAM into the slot on the CacheCARD. You might have to rock it back and forth a bit to make sure it's well seated. With it in place, engage the locks on either side of the module.

3. Insert the CacheCARD into the edge connector slot following the same instructions given for the similar TurboNET card in Chapter 9, "Networking Your TiVo." If you have a Series 1 DirecTV DVR, you need to remove the hard-drive bracket to gain access to the edge connector. As explained in Chapter 9, if your TiVo has a strip of rubber underneath the edge connector, you might have to untwist the motherboard locks on the edge connector end of the mobo to raise the board enough to socket in the CacheCARD. Make sure the card is fully seated on the connector.

4. Plug in the Cat5 Ethernet cable that you're going to use, and run it out of the TiVo box. See Chapter 9 for tips on different ways of running the cable out of the case.

5. Leave the cover off the TiVo for now. When you get the network connection established and the drivers for the CacheCARD loaded into TiVo, you'll want to check the activity lights on the card (labeled Link and Cache), to verify that the installation was successful.

Caution

Because you will be loading new files onto your TiVo, it's a good idea to do a backup of the existing software. Follow the instructions in Chapter 8 for removing TiVo drives and making a backup on your PC. If you did a backup when expanding drive space in Chapter 8 and you want to risk losing shows if something goes wrong, you can skip the process of yanking the TiVo drive(s) and doing a PC backup.

6. With the drivers loaded into TiVo and the CacheCARD attached to the mobo (with the memory and Ethernet cable installed), it's time to run a little test. Power up your TiVo. The green Link light should be glowing to indicate a network connection. The red Cache light should be on as well, indicating that TiVo is properly accessing the memory chips.

With the CacheCARD running, you should see a definite improvement in TiVo's performance. If you have trouble with the installation, post the nature of your problems on the SiliconDust Forums for help.

Chapter 12

Dark Hardware Hacking Arts

It is not within the scope of this book to get too deeply into the arcane and often dark (as in dreary, nightmarish, life-sucking) art of deep hardware hacking. Plenty of other books and websites get into such things, from replacing the motherboard-mounted modem on a Series 1 TiVo to completely rolling your own DVR using standard computer parts and open-source DVR software. In this chapter, we mainly survey what sort of basic things you can do, give you some idea of what technical skills and tools are involved, and then point you in the direction of the resources you need to do the work yourself. Sound like a plan?

If a Modem Fries in Cyberspace, Does Anybody Hear It?

One of the most common breakdowns on TiVos, especially Series 1 machines, involves the modem circuits. As described in Chapter 6, "Touring Your TiVo: The Hardware," TiVos, both Series 1 and Series 2, use embedded modems on their motherboards. This is a series of chips and support components, the main parts being a modem chip and a modem controller chip (a little computer that bosses the modem around and tells it what to do). Besides failure simply due to cheap components, a common reason for the modem going kaput is a power spike over the phone line. As we mentioned in Chapter 1, "Which TiVo Is Right for You?," it's always a good idea to get a surge suppressor (or ideally, an Uninterrupted Power Supply) for your TiVo (and other media components), and such a suppressor should have jacks for the phone line (and coax cable, if you can get it). The reason for this is that power fluctuations/spikes can cause damage, and those spikes can enter through your phone line and coax cable (from either a cable service connection or a DirecTV satellite connection).

Gareth On...

Note to self: Always practice what you preach. As we were working on Chapter 1 and I wrote the bit about getting a surge protector with phone and coax protection, I was thinking to myself, "Gee, *I* should really do this." I have an old APS model that's served me well (without phone input/output), up until recently. We had a particularly active electrical storm a few weeks back. No bolts touched down anywhere near us, but in the wake of it, our phone lines started acting all screwy. After one incoming ring, the phones would die. I started doing basic troubleshooting by taking each phone offline and calling our number (from my cellphone). The problem persisted. I realized I would need to take my two DVRs that were still using their internal modems offline, but I decided to go outside the house first and check the network interface device (NID), the phone company box on the house. I figured that if the problem existed there, it was in *their* lines, not mine. Same single ring, then nothing. When the Verizon linewoman showed up, she checked the NID, came into the house, and asked, "Do you have a TiVo hooked up to the phone?" She unplugged my S1 TiVo's modem, and everything was fine. She had just come from another call with the exact same problem. A spike during the storm had apparently fried my modem and was shorting out the phone system. Luckily, I was just about to get the S1 onto my LAN via the 9th Tee AirNET card (see Chapter 9, "Networking Your TiVo").

These are the most common modem-related problems, as told through their error messages, with a few suggested fixes in parenthesis:

- Modem Not Responding (may be dead, may just be locked up, try rebooting TiVo and unplugging/replugging in phone cable)
- No Dialtone (likely dead in the water, but you can try rebooting TiVo, or turning off dial-tone detection [under "Change Dialing Options" in "Phone Connection"])

- Failed to Connect (the modem chips may still be okay, but some of the support electrics in the modem circuit may be blown)
- Service Not Answering (service may be down, or TiVo is not making and holding a proper connection, try making the daily call later)

Basic Troubleshooting

The first thing you always want to do when your TiVo is misbehaving is to "hard boot" it by unplugging it, leaving it unplugged for a few seconds, and then plugging it back in. The modem controller is a little computer, and like all computers, it can hang. A reboot can get it back on track. Also, unplug your RJ-11 phone jacks from the back of TiVo and from the wall, and plug them back in firmly. When we do this, we always blast the plugs and the jacks with a little Dust-Off for good measure. Don't forget too, that you can always check the wall jack itself to make sure it's working by plugging a regular phone into it and listening for a dialtone.

After a reboot and line check, try to make another daily call. If TiVo still can't establish a connection, your modem is probably damaged or dead.

Options for Modem Replacement and Repair

If you're on a Series 1 machine, there are two ways to go about fixing these problems. If you're on Series 2, you basically have one modem-fix solution.

Series 1 Modem Fixes

If you're handy with a soldering iron—and we mean *really* handy, as in motherboard and surface-mounted parts that you can barely see with the naked eye sorta handy—you can actually troubleshoot where the problem is within the modem circuit and order the specific modem components you need from 9thtee.com. The company offers a series of inexpensive kits put together by TiVo hardware hacker ElectricLegs. At the 9th Tee site, you'll find a page describing the kits and a link to an image with troubleshooting instructions. Besides the fact that you need to be a master solder-jockey to handle this project, you need to know enough about electronics and TiVo's mobo to figure out what's going on with the poor documentation provided. The multicolored text on the repair diagram will make your head hurt! You'll find the Modem Repair page at http://9thtee.com/tivomodemrepair.htm.

Tip

A few other issues to consider: Is your phone cable overly-long? That can introduce line noise. Try a shorter cable, if possible. Also: try turning off "Dial Tone Detection" and "Phone Available Detection" (under "Change Dialing Options" in "Phone Connection"). On DirecTV DVRs, you can also slow the modem transfer rate down by entering the Dialing Prefix ,#019 (also under the "Phone Connection" menus).

Tip

When we're talking about the solutions here, we're assuming that you want to stay with a modem-connection scheme. If your modem dies, your *other* option is to take this as a sign from the binary gods that it's time to enter the 21st century and drive your TiVo onto the Information Superhighway via a wired or wireless network connection. See Chapter 9 for all the gory details.

Caution

It goes without saying that flubbing up the modem chip soldering is bad, really bad for TiVo. Toast the mobo with your soldering iron and your lifetime TiVo subscription (if you have one) is toast too.

Tip

Since modems are one of the weakest links in the TiVo hardware chain, knowing that there's a simple external fix (via a prepared kit) can be a comfort. If your granny calls 'cause her TiVo isn't downloading the schedule for "her stories" anymore, you can buy a modem kit from weaKnees that grans can plug in and be downloading her weekly lineup of *Haze of Our Lives* and *The Young and the Libidinous* in no time.

You'll find the modem-repair diagram at http://9thtee.com/images/E-Legstivomodem.jpg.

You can also remove your motherboard and send it to ElectricLegs, and he will replace the appropriate parts for you. The cost ranges from $40 to $60 (plus shipping), depending on what parts are broken.

The other method of "fixing" a broken Series 1 modem problem is to install a new modem, an external one. You can either buy a prepped kit (already set up for plug n' play installation on your TiVo) from weaKnees.com for $79 or hack one up yourself, if you have an old 33.6 or higher external modem taking up space in your techno-junk drawer (and who doesn't?).

DIY Modem Replacement

To do this hack on a Series 1 machine, you need the following parts:

- 33.6 or higher external modem (and power adapter)
- A 25-pin male to 9-pin female serial adapter
- The serial control cable that came with your stand-alone TiVo (you'll have to buy one if you have a DirecTiVo unit)
- A standard serial modem cable (that likely came with your modem) To be able to use a standard Hayes-compatible analog modem over TiVo's serial connection, you need to prep the modem first. This involves hooking up the modem to your PC's serial port and using a terminal emulation program (see Chapter 10, "Quick n' Dirty Serial Networking") to send commands to it.

1. Plug the modem's regular serial cable into your modem and your PC (with the power off, of course).

2. Power up the modem and computer and then open your terminal emulation program. Establish a connection with your modem (make sure you're talking to the correct COM port, which is likely COM1).

3. Type in the following command string and press Return:

   ```
   AT&D0&H0&I0M0&R1&W0
   ```

4. Type in the same string, but ending in W1 instead of W0:

   ```
   AT&D0&H0&I0M0&R1&W1
   ```

The WØ is a command to write (W) your command string to a configuration file (Ø). The Ø file is the command profile that is loaded (from an on-board RAM chip) upon powering up the modem. Writing a copy of the file to the secondary profile space (1) is simply insurance. Table 12.1 details the commands in the string.

Table 12.1	Ye Ol' Trusty Hayes Modem Commands and What They're Good For
Modem Command	**What It Does**
AT	Attention! The universal modem wake-up call.
&DØ	Asks the modem to turn off Data Terminal Ready (DTR).
&HØ	Asks the modem to turn off Clear to Send (CTS) and Xon/Xoff flow control.
&IØ	Disables Receive Data (RX) flow control.
MØ	Shuts up that freakin' modem handshaking sound. Who wants to *ever* hear that sound again?
&R1	Turns off Ready to Send (RTS).

The & in these commands refers to the Extended Hayes Command Set.

Those are zeros in the commands.

It's not worth going into the details of what DTR/CTS, Xon/Xoff, and RTS are all about. Basically, they deal with "handshaking" and maintaining data integrity between two modems (both using the same protocols) and are not needed for your TiVo connections.

5. With the modem properly configured, you're ready to set it up on TiVo. All you have to do is plug in TiVo's serial cable (assuming that you still have yours) into TiVo's Serial Out port, plug the 9-pin to 25-pin serial adapter onto the end of it, and then plug the adapter into the modem.

6. Plug in the modem's power adapter, and don't forget to plug the phone line into the proper jack on the modem and into your wall jack. Turn on the modem.

7. The last thing you have to do is set a dialing prefix in TiVo that will tell it to use the serial port for modem communications. Go to Messages & Setup -> Recorder & Phone Setup -> Phone Connection -> Change Dialing Options. Look on this menu for the Set Dial Prefix option. Enter one of the following dialing strings, depending on how fast of a connection speed you want. You can always start with

When looking for a suitable modem, try to find a US Robotics model. WeaKnees says that they've tested dozens of brands, and USR works the most reliably, by far.

Only Series 1 and S2 stand-alone TiVos include the serial control cable. If you didn't get one with your TiVo (or you can't find yours), you'll need to buy one. weaKnees.com sells them for $11. These cables are unique to TiVo, with special pinouts, so you can't just use a standard serial cable.

a higher baud rate and then crank it down a notch if TiVo and the modem are having trouble making and maintaining a connection:

```
,#396 (9600 baud rate)
,#319 (19,200)
,#338 (38,400)
,#357 (57,600)
```

What speed works for you will have a lot to do with your phone network, how much noise is usually on the line, and so on. Obviously, you can't go higher than the speed of your modem, so if you have a 36.6, don't bother trying to get the 56.6 speed (listed as 57.6) out of your box. It ain't gonna happen. Because the phoning happens behind the scenes, in the middle of the night, there's really no reason to rush it. A common happy-medium transfer rate is 19,200.

8. With the modem hardware set up and TiVo's software tweaked to use the serial port for comms, you're ready to see if everything's working properly. Go to Phone Connection under Recorder & Phone Setup, and ask TiVo to make its daily call. If all went according to plan, you should again be happily connected to your TiVo service.

Troubleshooting

If TiVo and your modem are not working, try the following:

- Check all connections—serial cable, pin adapter, phone cable—to make sure they're all plugged in well. Make sure you plugged the miniplug on the serial cable into Serial Out on TiVo, not IR Out.

- Make sure you plugged in the modem's power adapter and turned on the modem (Do you see little twinkly lights? Good).

- Are you sure you entered the dial prefix properly?

- If all this fails, you might have to try hooking the modem back up to your PC. Try replacing the &H and &I commands with AT&K0. If that seems to take, enter AT&W0 to amend it to profile 0, and then do ATK0W1 on another line to change profile 1. This command is like a global shut-off valve for all flow-control functions and works on some modems.

- If you hook the modem back up to TiVo and you're still having trouble, you might want to ask yourself whether you're sure this modem was working in the first place. Maybe there's a reason why it was in the techno-junk drawer (besides the fact that you now have a high-speed connection in your home).

- At this point, you might just want to break down and buy a modem upgrade kit from weaKnees.com, or maybe ask around and see if friends have old modems to spare. (Who doesn't? We've got half a dozen you can have.) As noted earlier, if the modem you're using is not a US Robotics, you might want to try and find one.

Series 2 Fixes

If you have a Series 2 TiVo, you have fewer options for repair/replacement than with Series 1, in that nobody has come out with a modem repair kit for S2. That's the bad news. The good news is that Series 2 machines have a better-quality modem chipset on them, so especially if you have your TiVo on a surge suppressor with phone line protection, you won't likely need a repair or replacement. If you do end up with a bum modem, check the next two sections to see what you can do about it:

Buy a Replacement Kit

weaKees.com sells a kit for $79 that includes a US Robotics Sportster modem, preconfigured for use with TiVo. All you have to do is plug it into your TiVo's serial port and set a dialing prefix in TiVo setup. Besides the modem kit, you might have to buy a serial control cable (for $11) if your TiVo didn't come with one. Series 1 TiVos came with such a cable, but not all S2 TiVos do. See Figure 12.1.

FIGURE 12.1

The US Robotics Sportster, the modem of choice for external TiVo modem replacement.

DIY Modem Replacement

If you have an old 33.6 or 56K analog modem lying around your basement doing nothing but serving as luxury apartments for dust mites, you can recycle it into a TiVo external modem if your internal one goes bad.

The instructions for setting up an external modem for a Series 2 TiVo are exactly the same as for a Series 1 TiVo (see the Series 1 "DIY Modem Replacement" section earlier in this chapter). The only thing that's different is that you might have to buy a TiVo serial cable if your S2 TiVo didn't come with one, and the path for getting to the dial prefix is different: Messages & Setup -> Settings -> Phone & Network Settings -> Edit Phone or Network Settings -> Phone Dialing Options. The prefixes you can try entering are the same as for Series 1, as are the troubleshooting tips offered earlier in this chapter.

Pump Up the RAM (Stand-Alone Series 1 Only)

When curious TiVonauts began crackin' the cases on their stand-alone Series 1 TiVos, they were intrigued by the two pads on the motherboard that were obviously for adding extra RAM chips. Series 1 TiVos came with a measly 16MB of RAM, and given the sluggish performance of the software, especially when doing things such as creating Season Passes or searching for content in the database, everyone assumed that more RAM would greatly amp up this process (as it would on a PC). It took soldering on chips for hackers to realize that the performance increase was only marginal (which made them look elsewhere for solutions and, eventually, to the CacheCARD concept). See Figure 12.2.

There really isn't a compelling reason for most Series 1 users to add two 8MB RAM chips to their mobo, especially if they spring for the CacheCARD, but if you're an ace with surface-mount soldering and a command prompt, why not? The chips are only around $20, and it does help overall TiVo performance, especially if you're loading and running a lot of additional open-source apps on your box.

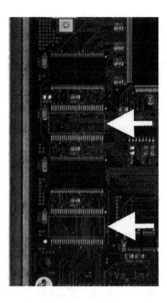

FIGURE 12.2
The RAM solder pads found on the mobo of a Series 1 stand-alone TiVo.

Again, it's TiVo hardware hacker extraordinaire ElectricLegs to the rescue. He buys the chips in quantity to keep the price down. The chips he uses are the Micron MT4LC4M116R6TG-5. These are the same chips that come in the Series 1 stand-alones. The upgrade kit is sold through 9th Tee at 9thtee.com/tivomemory.htm.

After installing the chips, you'll need to use your serial network connection (see Chapter 10) to access TiVo's PROM menu to tell TiVo to recognize and use the new memory. Instructions for doing this are on the TiVo Memory Upgrade Kit page.

As with the modem repair kit, ElectricLegs will install and configure the chips for you for $50. If you're sending in your mobo for modem repair (see earlier in this chapter), maybe you can have him toss some new RAM in there, too. But at $100 for the upgrade/repair, plus shipping, you have to ask yourself whether it's really worth it, when new 40-hour Series 2 boxes are currently going for $129 (maybe even less by the time you read this) .

Enabling Caller ID in Hardware

Owners of Series 1 DirecTV DVRs can load a program onto their TiVos that allows caller ID information to be displayed onscreen (assuming that service is subscribed to from the phone company). But what about other

Tip

If you're serious about hacking the RAM on your S1 Tivo, check out this discussion on Tivocommunity.com: archive.tivocommunity. com/tivo-vb/showthread. php?threadid=25231.

If you have an S1 DirecTiVo and subscribe to caller ID, check out the section on elseed, the caller ID program, in Chapter 17.

TiVo models? Well, hardcore hardware hacker types have reported some success with enabling the caller ID function built into the modem circuit on the S1 stand-alone TiVo. Basically, the hack involves attaching a wire (called "jumpering") to a couple of pins on the Krypton Isolation chip on the mobo marked K2952C and adding a 47K-ohm resistor between another pin on the chip and transistor Q3 on the motherboard. Soldering on these two parts allows you to then make use of elseed, the caller-ID program created by TiVo hacker Greg Gardner (see Chapter 17, "Other TiVo Apps," for more details). If you're interested in taking a look at this hack, here's the link to the posting about it on Tivocommunity.com (and, hey, look, it's Mr. ElectricLegs again! That guy gets around): http://www.tivocommunity.com/tivo-vb/showthread.php?postid=488985#post488985.

Note that he got his pin assignments incorrect on this post. Read the rest of the thread for more information. And here's a link to a (correct) circuit diagram of the hack that another TiVo Community member drew: http://www.tivocommunity.com/tivo-vb/showthread.php?postid=500155#post500155

The Don't Call It *Hard*ware for Nothin'

And that concludes Part II, "Hardware Hacking." If you're tired of yankin' your TiVo out from under the big-screen TV and hauling it to the dining room table to add the hardware we discussed in this section, you can rest a little easier now (and put some ice on that lower back). With a serial or Ethernet connection (on Series 1, anyway) you'll be able to log in to TiVo whenever you want from your PC to load some of the software we'll be discussing in Part III, "Software Bashing." And with the wired or wireless connection you made on your Series 2 stand-alone TiVo, you'll be able to do all sorts of cool things over your network, from beaming shows between TiVos to streaming tunes from your host PC to your TiVo/home stereo. In the next chapter, we take a closer look at TiVo's software components, from its underlying Linux OS to its media filing system (MFS), to its menu interface program.

Part **III**

SOFTWARE BASHING (PLAYING WITH YOUR PENGUIN)

Chapter 13

Touring Your TiVo: The Software

In Chapter 6, "Touring Your TiVo: The Hardware," we got all heavy on you and looked at the physical side of TiVo: the metal, silicon, and plastic that makes TiVo work (and weigh about eight pounds). Now we're going to take a look at TiVo's softer side, the dancing electrons that make TiVo smart (but not so smart that it refuses to record such mind-scrubbing guilty pleasures as a *Joe Schmo* marathon).

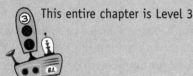 This entire chapter is Level 3

From Ones and Zeros to Tickles and Gooeys

Like all computers, TiVo is built upon a hierarchy of computer languages, from the lowest level machine language of 1s and 0s to higher-level, easier-for-us-mortals-to-cope-with coding and scripting languages, and finally, graphical user interfaces ("GUIs," pronounced "gooeys") that even a child can navigate (see Figure 13.1). Obviously, we won't travel too deeply down this complexity pyramid, but we'll go as far as we need to, which takes us to the level of the Linux operating system (OS).

FIGURE 13.1

TiVo's software suite— from Linux to the myworld GUI—and a gross approximation of their basic functional relationships.

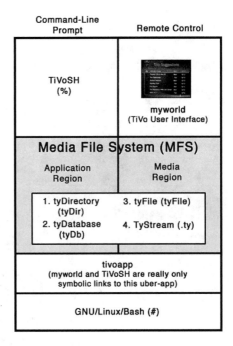

Tip

This chapter is mainly here for those who are curious to pry open TiVo's brain to see how it fires its neurons. For the average user, there won't be much utility here. For those interested in actually touring TiVo's software firsthand and in loading third-party programs (Series 1 users, especially), this chapter will help give you some idea of how TiVo's OS and support software works and what you'll be able to do within it.

Mini-Tutorial on the Linux OS

(or "You'll be a Penguinhead in no time!")

It's amazing to think that Linux has almost become a household name. This happens to us all the time: We're talking to someone who's an obvious non-geek, we use the term Linux and begin to explain what that is, and the non-techie says (a hint of indignation in his/her voice): "I know what Linux is!" So, at the risk of miffing you off, we're going to tell you what Linux is.

Linux is a "Unix-like" computer operating system. For the uninitiated, things can quickly get confusing because Linux is actually part of a larger operating system known as GNU/Linux (though people usually just say "Linux," much to the chagrin, we're sure, of GNU's principal author Richard Stallman).

The story goes something like this: Stallman was working on parts to a free Unix-like OS called GNU. He hadn't created a kernel for it (the heart of the OS, the link to the hardware), just the core utilities and libraries (helper code), a complier (used to translate higher-level languages to lower-level ones), and a text editor. An upstart programmer whiz kid from Finland named Linus Torvalds, tired of dealing with Windows crashes and other annoyances of existing OSes, coded up a kernel, bolted on the existing GNU components and dubbed it Linux. The open source revolution—of collaboratively, freely available, modifiable, and distributable software—had begun. GNU/Linux is called Unix-like not only because its command set, component structure, and other features are similar to Unix, but much of it also "interoperates" with Unix and other "Unix-like" OSes. A number of the utilities used in TiVo hacking are actually Unix commands/programs, such as *ls* (list files in directory), head (show the first few lines of a file), *tail* (show the last few lines of a file), and *touch* (used for dating and time stamping files).

Linux is beloved by computer programmers, and ever-increasingly by the enterprise market, because it is so robust (some users report years without a system crash), so powerful, has fewer security problems, and is freely distributed. Developing nations are embracing Linux with a vengeance because they can keep the costs of systems down, since there's little-to-no software costs (and that software is open and hackable). The component structure of Linux allows it to be scaled to fit different computing environments, which has also made it popular in the handheld market and for embedded systems (like TiVo!).

Similar to the DOS/Windows arrangement, Linux is increasingly becoming known to a wider user-base through its GUIs, programs like X Window and GNOME that run "on top of" Linux and present the user with a graphical/"desktop" interface. In TiVo, the GUI used is called *myworld* and it constitutes all of the menus that you see when accessing TiVo through your remote control. When you access TiVo through the mini-Linux distribution on this book's CD-ROM, through a serial connection, or through an Ethernet/Telnet connection over your LAN, you have to use the command-line interface (CLI) to navigate through TiVo's OS.

NOTE

How to pronounce "GNU" and "Linux" is something of an enigma for many people. GNU is a recursive acronym for "GNU is Not Unix" (that Stallman, what a party animal!). It is pronounced with the "G" (like *G* in "garage," not *G* in "gnome") and then the "NU" like "new." So, two syllables: "Gah-NEW." "Linux" is one of those words that everybody seems to want to pronounce differently. Years ago, hardcore geeks insisted on pronouncing it "Lee-Nooks," after an audio file surfaced with Linus pronouncing it himself (in his thick Swedish/Finnish accent). But that quickly gave way to more western tongues, and today, it's more often pronounced as "LIN-ux (as in the "lin" in "linen" and the "ux" in "tuxedo").

Gareth On...

And now let's play a little game of where's the interface. For those who are new to command-line interfaces like the one that Linux's Bash prompt offers, it can be intimidating at first. "Throw me a bone here, Linux!" you might find yourself thinking as you stare at a bland command prompt. It may be a silly analogy, but I like to think that for such "interface-poor" environments, most of the interface lives in your head, not on the screen. Once you learn the underling logic and command syntax, and how to look things up using the man command, online, and in reference books, more and more, the interface starts to come alive for you; it gets richer. To use another geekly analogy, it's like playing a paper, pencil, and dice game like *Dungeons & Dragons*. The "interface" may be extremely limited, but knowing the rules and background, and filling the blanks in your head, the game can suddenly become as rich and exciting as, say a film, where everything is pre-digested for you.

TiVo and Linux, Sittin' in a (Directory) Tree

Here's a question we hear a lot: If TiVo uses Linux and Linux is open source, how can the TiVo software be proprietary? Ahhh…good question, Grasshopper. It gets back to that component aspect of Unix-like systems. Just as Linus Torvalds combined his Linux kernel with the libraries, utilities, and support apps of GNU, TiVo developers used the Linux kernel and some of the GNU components and added their own parts, namely their Media Filing System (MFS) databasing program, their tyStream media storage format, their TiVoSh shell, and their tivoapp program. It is all these components that are proprietary. Any GNU/Linux components used are not TiVo, Inc.'s to copyright, and all TiVo manuals come with the GNU General Public License (GPL) in the back to clarify the open source licensing of their GNU/Linux components. You can also download their modified Linux kernels and the open source support apps and libraries that they use from this page on the TiVo site: www.tivo.com/linux.

Before we get into the specific Linux apps used in TiVo and the TiVo-specific components, such as the Media File System (MFS), we should run through some of the basic operating principles underlying Linux.

Linux can be broken down into five basic parts:

- **The Kernel**—The heart of the OS, the low-level programs and processes that everything else runs on top of. The essential background components Linux could not operate without are compiled in the kernel. The kernel serves as the essential link between the machine's hardware and all other software in the system.

- **The Utilities**—All of the support programs, device drivers, and other applications and data files that provide support for the OS and the software and hardware installed on the system.

- **The Programs**—The software the user loads onto the system to do whatever it is he or she wants to do: word processing, website building, media recording/playback, accounting, email, games, and so on.

- **The Shell Interface**—The command-line interface/interpreter (CLI) between the user and the rest of the system. The most environmentally-poor but feature-rich means of communicating with the OS. Underneath every GUI is a good shell. In TiVo, the shells are Bash (common to most Linux systems) and TiVoSH (a TiVo-specific shell program for interpreting Tcl, a scripting language that TiVo uses).

- **The GUI**—The Graphical User Interface. In Linux, this is usually the X Window GUI. Riding on top of X are often found desktop environments, such as GNOME and KDE. On TiVo, the GUI is called myworld, and it's the program that most TiVo users interact with. Myworld is often called the TiVo User Interface, which we guess makes it a TUI (Tooey).

Like most computer systems, Linux is organized into a directory tree-type filesystem. Table 13.1 lists some of the common directories found in Linux, and a few unique to TiVo.

Table 13.1   Common (and a Few Not-so-common) Linux Directories and What They're All About

Directory	Full Name	What It's All About (Alfie)
/	Root	The topmost directory in a filesystem tree.
boot	Boot Loader Files	Files used for booting up the system. The kernel is housed here. Visit the kernel!
bin	Binary Files	Where the system's program are stored (usually binary files). This is where common programs such as bash, cat, mv, rm, and umount can be found.
dev	Devices	Drivers and other files related to hardware interfacing. TiVo's serial port drivers live here.
etc	Etcetera	Configuration (conf) files and other miscellaneous stuff.
lib	Libraries	Libraries of codes used by various programs in the system. In TiVo, contains the two lib files that all of the programs within TiVo use.
mnt	Mount Points	Directories that provide access to the temporary mounting of disks for access to them.
proc	Currently-running Processes	The processes being currently used by the operating system.

Table 13.1   Continued

Directory	Full Name	What It's All About (Alfie)
sbin	Superuser Binary	Programs that can only be run by those with root access, so called superusers. Essential OS binaries live here.
tmp	Temporary File	A work directory for temporary storage of programs and files.
usr	User	Location of shareable, read-only data available to users on the system.
var	Variable Files	Log files, administrative data, and other temporary files.
tvbin	TV Binaries	TiVo's programs reside here: myworld, tivosh, modem, switcher-start, and the mother of all TiVo programs: tivoapp.
tvlib	TV Libraries	All of the data used by the programs in the tvbin directory can be found here, from the font files that TiVo uses onscreen to the database information for directors, actors and keywords.

Tip

Geek Lexicon Alert: For the newbie, seeing phrases like "reads from standard input" and "the command writes to standard output" can look extremely gnarly, but they're not as incomprehensible as they sound. "Standard input" usually just means keyboard input; ya know: typing. "Standard output" means to display to your screen. This will sometimes also be referred to as "print to screen" or "printing standard output." You may also run into "standard error," which are error messages that are "printed to screen," on a line by themselves.

Of course, these are simply the directory types. Directory paths can thread through a number of these types, so you could have the directory path:

```
/etc/rc.d/rc.sysinit
```

The etc directory contains a number of files and subdirectories related to system configuration and command execution, along with some miscellaneous junk. Within that directory, there are a number of other files and subdirectories, including rc.d. One of the files within this directory is the system initialization file known as rc.sysinit. This is a document we will become more familiar with as we add some utility programs to our TiVo (Series 1 units, only) and ask TiVo to remember to start up these utilities whenever we reboot TiVo.

Another directory path we'll be working with here is one that we'll actually create in the next chapter:

```
/var/hack/bin
```

This is where we'll stash our additional TiVo applications. Whenever TiVo is running, it will either have dev/hda4 or dev/hda7 mounted as its working partition. It will also have hda9 mounted as the /var directory. When one adds hacks to TiVo, there is no guarantee that they won't be overwritten when TiVo, Inc. updates the software. The good news for Series 1 owners, those who are doing most of the unsupported hacks, is that TiVo, Inc. is not likely to be updating the S1 software anytime soon (if ever), so you should be okay. And in the meantime, stashing hacks in the /var directory on hda9 (which is automatically mounted by TiVo on startup) is as safe a place as any on TiVo, since it's partitions 4 and 7 that can get swapped back and forth (as active and backup partitions) by TiVo. Partition 9 is usually left unscathed.

Gareth On...

You couldn't actually call them household names, but a few Unix terms have made it into the mainstream, or the "side-stream," at least. One of the most well traveled sites in cyber-space is Slashdot: News For Nerds. It gets its name from the root directory path (/), which is called a slash. In the beginning, lots of people got confused by the name, thinking it was http:///..com or www.slash.com. It's actually Slashdot.com. Another Unix term that became popular, at least in brainy households, was thanks to our very own Leo Laporte. He was the man behind the curtain breathing life into "Dev Null," a wise-crackin' tech guru come life-size real-time computer animation on MSNBC's original tech show The Site. Dev Null was a great inside joke for computer geeks, as dev/null is a device address on a Unix machine that discards all data written to it, so Dev Null was basically a black hole of computer wisdom.

To move around Linux successfully, and have some idea of what you're looking at and what it can do, there are a number of things you need to understand. We've now discussed the basic component parts of Linux and some of the filesystem/directory conventions. In a minute, we'll discuss the Bash shell, the common Linux command line interface that is used on TiVo. But before we do that, let's take a look at a full filename print out and talk about what it means. Armed with the information we've already covered here, the list of common Linux commands found in Appendix B, "Common Linux Commands," and the details of a full file output, you should start to get some idea of how Linux and TiVo work.

The first thing we might want to do from the Bash prompt (which will be at the root level when we boot into TiVo's Linux) is to move into a sub-directory just to get the experience of moving around the file system. To see what directories are available from root, type in (at the Bash prompt):

```
ls
```

NOTE

If you're playing around inside your TiVo's Bash interface, you won't have access to even basic Linux navigation tools such as the ls command. To get your feet wet, boot up, through your PC's CD-ROM drive, the mini-distro of Linux that came with this book. It has all of the components discussed here. In Chapter 14, "Accessing Your TiVo's Linux Bash Prompt," we'll explain how to move the Linux Utilities bundle that came with this book onto your (Series 1) TiVo.

Tip

Of course, we don't have to move through the directory hierarchy one level at a time. If we know where we want to go, we can change into that directory directly from root by entering the whole path: cd etc/rc.d

Tip

Don't forget that this book comes with a bootable copy of Linux (referred to as a "mini-distro"). By setting up your PC to boot from the CD-ROM drive first (see Chapter 8, "Upgrading Hard Drives," for details on how to do this, if you're unsure), you can instantly have a Linux OS running on your PC and can use that to try out what you learn here and try the commands listed in Appendix B.

This is the List command and it will "print" all of the contents of the directory level you're currently on, without any details, to the screen. From this list, we'll see the etc directory, which holds various startup, configuration, and profile-type files. To move into that directory, we enter this command:

```
cd etc
```

You'll notice that all we get in return here is another Bash prompt. We have no clue that we actually moved into the etc directory. Issue another ls and it will list the contents of this directory. With this information, we see another subdirectory, called rc.d ("rc" stands for "run commands," btw). Change directories and move into it. Issue another ls.

Within this directory, you'll likely see a number of configuration files that begin with rc; one of these will likely be called rc.sysinit. This is a run command/config file we'll be editing in the next chapter and anytime we make changes to TiVo that we want reflected after a reboot.

To see the complete information on the rc files in this directory, issue the ls command again, but this time adding the –l option, which will reveal the long-format details of the file:

```
ls -l
```

Each of the lines displayed will look something like the following:

```
-rwxr-xr-x 1 root root 20600 Jul 23 14:18 rc.sysinit
```

That junk at the beginning may look odd, but it tells a lot about the file. The leading (-) indicates that this is a file, not a directory (which would be a d). This is followed by three groups of three read (r), write (w), and execute (x) indicators, for system owner, users, and others, respectively. If a group doesn't have a permission, it's indicated by a (-). So, in the previous example, the users and others do not have "write" permissions to this file. The number after the permission string refers to the number of hard links for this file (see the ln command in Appendix B for what this means). The owner and users/others are then named. On a single user system where you're the "superuser," these'll likely be listed as "root." These IDs are then followed by the size of the file (in bytes), the date/time stamp for the last modification, and finally, the name of the file itself.

The Bash Shell

The traditional user interface for Unix and other command-line interface OSes is called a shell program. It's called a shell because it forms a delicious outer candy coating...er...layer between the user and the innards of the operating system. The original Unix shell was called *sh* (or the "Bourne Shell") and was created by programmer Stephen Bourne. "Bash," a newer, widely extended Unix/GNU/Linux shell stands for "Bourne-Again Shell." Bash is the default shell program on most GNU/Linux systems, on Macintosh OS X's CLI, and on TiVo. If you want to muck around in TiVo, you'll need to know the basic syntax and commands of Bash. Shell programs usually have their names (and version numbers) in the command line prompt itself to clue you in to what set of commands are available to you. The Bash shell you'll find on TiVo looks like this:

```
Bash-2.02#
```

All of the Linux commands we discussed previously in this chapter, in the next chapter, in Appendix B and in chapters where we install applications on TiVo or amend configuration files for hardware additions, commands are all entered at the Bash prompt.

TiVoSH

The developers of the TiVo OS created their own flavor of CLI called *tivosh* (for "TIVoSHell"). Tivosh is actually a custom-built interpreter for the *Tcl* scripting language (see next entry) that allows TiVo developers and technicians to have command-line access to Tcl, and through Tcl, to the inner workings of their proprietary Media File System (MFS), the heart of TiVo's audio/video content (as well as all of the scheduling information, actor/director/keyword data, ToDo Lists, and so forth). Most of what tivosh is good for as far as we're concerned is its ability to grant us access to MFS content. To invoke tivosh, you simply type it at TiVo's Bash prompt. It will return the following:

```
%
```

That's the tivosh prompt. From here, you can navigate the MFS hierarchy. See the section later in this chapter for information on MFS and how to get around inside of it.

Tip

To learn more about how to use Bash, see Chapter 14 and Appendix B. Other useful sources are the Bash tutorial at the HypeXR site: www.hypexr.org/bash_tutorial.shtml and "The Linux Terminal—A Beginner's Bash:" http://linux.org.mt/article/terminal.

Touring Your TiVo: The Software

More Deep Geek Tech Talk: In getting deeper into the inner workings of TiVo's OS, you'll hear the terms "compiled" and "interpreted" (or "compiler" and "interpreter") a lot. These refer to two different ways of handling computer instructions. Complied code is written in languages like C and C++ and then translated (the "compiling" part) into the lower-level languages that the machine itself "speaks" (a.k.a. "machine code"). Compiled code, being up close and personal with the machine level, executes very quickly. Interpreters and/or scripting languages are more abstract, living higher in the code hierarchy. They execute slower, but are easier for us mortals to code in, and they are capable in turn of gaining access to the lower-level complied functions.

Tcl (and iTcl)

Tcl (which originally stood for "Tool Command Language," but is now known simply as "Tcl," pronounced "tickle") is a powerful scripting language that is often used for rapid prototyping, building graphical user interfaces, and for software testing. It may have been all three of these that attracted TiVo developers to the language. One of the unique things about Tcl is that the interpreter is customized for the application you're using it with, so you can create your own commands in the lower-level (compiled) language (C/C++ in TiVo's case) and then access those commands through Tcl scripts (and through a custom shell like tivosh) to make calls to the compiled program.

A variant of Tcl, called iTcl (or "incr Tcl") is an extension to Tcl that adds object-oriented-like data structures and procedures to make Tcl even more powerful and for easier coding of more complex scripts. TiVo's OS utilizes both Tcl and iTcl scripts.

Delving into the depths of Tcl scripting is beyond the scope of this book. If scripting languages are your cup of java, er...so to speak, you can find plenty of info about Tcl online. For Tcl specifically as it relates to TiVo, we recommend Jeff Keegan's book *Hacking TiVo* (ISBN# 0-7645-4336-9), which has an excellent general Tcl tutorial and information on the command set unique to *tivosh*.

Both Tcl and iTcl are open source software projects, and guess where you can find them? At Sourceforge, of course, that bastion for bitchin' free software development. The Tcl pages can be found at sourceforge.net/projects/tcl. The project pages for iTcl are located at incrtcl.sourceforge.net/itcl.

Media File System (MFS)

The soul of TiVo is its proprietary Media File System (MFS). Obviously, TiVo is a single-purpose embedded system designed to find, record, store, and display television programming (and increasingly, other digital media). The heavy machinery to do all of this is found in the MFS. In Table 13.1, we detailed some common features of the Linux filesystem. TiVo's custom-built system is very different. First off, there are two distinct file regions. The Application Region stores all of the applications that TiVo uses, such as the uber-app, tivoapp, and the myworld GUI. It is also here that all of the database components are stored, from the details of your TiVo's account configuration to all of the show information you have access to onscreen, to the IDs and locations of all your recorded shows stored on the Media Region (the other region of the MFS). Refer back to Table 13.1. It's an interesting structure because it does double-duty as both a filesystem and as a database program. All contents of the MFS constitute one of four datatypes:

- **tyDir**—The tyDirectory objects represent the paths in the MFS directory tree structure.

- **tyDb**—All of the data elements that MFS uses are stored as discrete objects via tyDatabase entries.

- **tyFile**—The various sound and image files that TiVo uses for the myworld GUI, search indexes, and other components are stored as tyFiles.

- **tyStream**—As has been discussed in previous chapters, the actual recorded programs, with their MPEG-2 audio and MPEG-2 video components, are written to the MFS Media Region as tyStreams (in the .ty file format).

So now that we've gotten your curiosity up, wanna take a look at some of this stuff? We figured you might. To start with, you'll need to get to TiVo's Bash prompt, using whatever method you have available: serial network (Chapter 10, "Quick n' Dirty Serial Networking") or telnetting in over an Ethernet connection (Chapter 14). With the Bash glowing away on your screen, enter tivosh (by typing *tivosh*). You'll get the tivosh prompt (%). At this prompt, enter

```
mls /
```

This command is tivosh's answer to the Unix/Linux ls (List). We're guessing that it's short for "MFS List." Note that it's followed by the forward slash (/). Unlike the Unix filesystem, in tivosh, you always have to tell it what directory you want to list, even if it's the one you're already in. Pressing enter will show you the first 50 entries on the root level of the MFS database. To see more, or to start at a certain entry point in the directory, use the following syntax:

```
mls /SeasonPass/
```

Caution

Don't make us have to say it again! If you want to spelunk inside of TiVo's MFS, you want to be darn careful, and it's a good idea to have a backup of your OS on your computer in case you do something that turns your beloved TiVo into a high-tech boat anchor.

Tip

It's even possible to run the mls MFS listing command from this book's CD while your TiVo drive(s) is hooked up to your PC. Just boot up through the CD (as described in Chapter 8) and set the following variable (at Bash): export MFS_HDA=/dev/hd*X* (where *X* is the drive letter of your attached TiVo drive on your PC's IDE cable). If you have two TiVo drives attached, also use MFS_HDB=/dev/hd*Y* (where *B* is your second drive and *Y* is its location on your PC's IDE). Now you're free to explore the MFS.

Tip

When navigating MFS, all directory paths must begin with a leading slash (/MenuItem, /ShowcaseIndex, /User, and so on).

This will reprint the list starting at SeasonPass and showing us the next 50 items. If you actually wanted to look *inside* of the SeasonPass directory, you'd drop the slash from the end of the command line, like so:

```
mls /SeasonPass
```

As you can see when you use the mls command, tivosh prints a long form of the file listings (similar to adding the –l option in a Unix ls command). Let's look at one of these listings:

```
Name    Type    FsID    Date       Time    Size
----    ----    ----    ----       ----    ----
Genre   tyDir   78      07/24/03   04:55   1752
```

The first item is the name of the file; the second is the file type (tyDir, tyFile, tyDb, or tyStream); the next column is the Filesystem ID (FsID), a unique number assigned to all MFS data items; the date and time of the last change to the item follow; and finally, the size (in bytes) of the item. As you might guess, this item is a directory of genre definitions for TV programming that TiVo uses.

The next fun thing to play around with is tivosh's dumbObj command. This is used to print the contents of a database (tyDb) item. As a simple example, we'll use the LocationConfig object in the tyDir /State/. Let's crack that nut open and see what's inside. Type in (at the % prompt):

```
dumpobj /State/LocationConfig
```

What you'll get back looks something like this:

```
LocationConfig 40092/10 {
    DaylightSavingsPolicy = 2
    IndexPath  = /State/LocationConfig
    PostalCode = 22204
    TimeZoneOld  = 1
    Version    = 1
}
```

Tip

When you're done touring TiVo's magnificent filesystem, don't use a Ctrl-C to leave tivosh. You exit a shell by using the exit command.

This object describes your physical location, namely your ZIP code, and your location's policy toward daylight savings time, maybe in case you live in parts of Indiana, Arizona, or Hawaii where DST is not observed. The number following the db item name (LocationConfig), before the /10, is the FsID for this item (in this case 40092). If you know an object's FsID, you can dump it by using its ID instead of its name to print its output (for example, dumpobj 1080149). Database objects can have links to other objects within them (indicated by other FsIDs in the object's print out). Adding the "–depth 1" to the dumpobj command will reveal the contents of those linked tyDb objects (one level deep) within the requested object's output.

By using the mls and dumpobj commands, you can learn a lot of interesting and curious things about the inner working of the MFS. And it's not just for geekly curiosity, either. If you're handy with Tcl scripting (or willing to learn), you can write scripts to do such things as print out lists of your SeasonPasses, with their recording priorities (share 'em with your buddies online!), and create your own Showcase banners, replacing the ones that appear on the main Showcases menu (C'mon, you know you want to make one that changes "Cinemax" to "Skinemax"). Details on these types of Tcl scripts, as well as docs for many more of the MFS/tivosh shell commands, can be found in Jeff Keegan's book *Hacking TiVo*.

myworld

When you turn on your TV and set TiVo as its input source, the set of screens you're looking at is called myworld (see Figure 13.2). This is the graphical user interface that sits on top of the GNU/Linux OS, the Bash shell, tivosh, the Media File System, and all the rest of TiVo's soft bits (refer back to Figure 13.1). Myworld is actually put together via Tcl scripts (as we noted in the Tcl section, this is a frequent use for Tcl). There's little you can do of general interest with myworld from the command line. It's just instructive to know that this is where TiVo puts it all together, displaying content drawn from the Application and Media regions of the MFS into a visual form that you can navigate via remote control.

Tip

If you want to play around with the MFS and commands like *mls* and *dumpobj*, but don't want to bother with accessing a Bash prompt over serial or local telnet, fear not young propellerhead, the MFS Module for the TiVoWeb project (Series 1 only), described in Chapter 16, "TiVoWeb," allows you to surf your MFS from the Web!

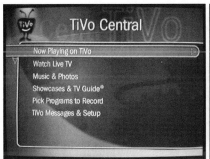 

FIGURE 13.2

myworld (and welcome to it). Where you and TiVo meet on either side of the TV screen.

tivoapp

The mother of all TiVo apps is...well...tivoapp. In fact, the other TiVo applications, myworld and tivosh (and a number of other supports apps), are actually symbolic links to tivoapp. "One app to rule them all and in the darkness..." Wait, that's something else. Sorry. Anyway, all symbolic links point to this single application. These various programs started out as separate components, but over successive releases of the software (2.x and up), they started to get gobbled up into one monster application. As a user and TiVo hobbyist, your interface to tivoapp is through tivosh and myworld.

Too Much Information!

This chapter probably separated the hardcore data cowpokes from the bucolic townsfolk. If your mind kept wandering off to think about such weighty issues as whether Ryan and Trista from *The Bachelorette* are still together, or you spent the time you *should* have been carefully reading this chapter obsessively pressing the TiVo button + 0 on your remote to watch the opening animation over and over again, this chapter probably wasn't for you. If you couldn't get the book's CD into your PC fast enough so you could start crusin' around Linux, and your idea of fun is now browsing the Linux *man* (manual) pages (www.hmug.org/man/), then this chapter likely only piqued your curiosity. If you want to delve deeper into TiVo's OS and Linux in general, we recommend checking out the books and websites listed in Appendix A, "Resources." If you're on a Series 1 TiVo, you'll also have plenty of opportunity to futz around with Linux in forthcoming chapters, as we look at TiVoWeb and/or other third-party TiVo applications.

Chapter 14

Accessing Your TiVo's Linux Bash Prompt

As explained in earlier chapters, TiVo uses Bash, the command-line "shell" program commonly found in Linux, Unix, and other Unix-like systems. If you're going to do anything on the "other side" of TiVo's myworld GUI, you're going to have to gain access to the Bash prompt. From here, the inner workings of TiVo are your oyster.

Serial Bashing

We've already discussed accessing Bash through a serial port connection in Chapter 10, "Quick n' Dirty Serial Networking." This is a perfectly reasonable means of periodically logging in to TiVo, for just pokin' around to see what's going on in there or for loading a few "bootstrap" support apps, or whatever (which we'll do a bit of in this chapter). But, in using serial networking, you'll quickly realize that this thing moves slower than a paid-by-the-hour contract worker. Besides being an acceptable access method for the periodic Basher, it's also an okay solution if you have the luxury of leaving your PC and TiVo connected through their respective serial ports.

If you want to make a serial network connection between your PC and TiVo, get thee to Chapter 10. There you'll find out how to assemble the appropriate networking cabling and how to amend your TiVo's startup script (the sysinit file) to accept serial calls from your PC.

Tip

As we've mentioned earlier, you can get a Bash prompt on a Series 2 TiVo and do some fun hackin' and slashin' (if that's your idea of fun). Since the hoops to jump through are numerous (with many of them on fire), we won't cover these procedures here. We recommend William von Hagen's book, which not only has the instructions, but also has useful Series 2 hacking tools on its CD. That means that this chapter is pretty much limited to Series 1 owners (unless you've found how to access the S2 Bash prompt elsewhere). For the rest of the chapter, assume we're talking about Series 1 standalone TiVos. For S1 DirecTV DVR, you can access Bash over serial after doing a procedure called *flashing the PROM*, which we don't discuss here. Do a search for the details at dealdatabase. com/forum. After the PROM hack, you'll be able to do what's covered in this chapter.

Talking to TiVo via Ethernet

If you've set your TiVo up for Ethernetworking, you can use this connection to create a faster and more multi-purpose connection with your PC. The speed and reliability of this type of connection allows you do such things as load larger third-party apps onto TiVo and transfer tyStreams from your TiVo to your PC, to either watch them there in their native format, using programs such as TiVo MPlayer, or for editing or format-conversion using a program like TyStudio (see Chapter 17, "Other TiVo Apps," for more information on these programs).

We have another one of those TiVo chicken and egg problems here though (we'll run into this more than once in this chapter)—to get TiVo to return our calls, we need to set up TiVo to talk to us through the Bash prompt over our Ethernet connection, but we can't get into TiVo to amend the rc.sysinit file to make this request. So, it's back to our life-saving serial network.

Opening TiVo to the Net via Serial Network

If you did the serial networking hack described in Chapter 10 and amended TiVo's rc.sysinit file to connect Bash over TiVo's serial port, you're all set for this. Make any necessary cable connections, open up your terminal program on your desktop computer, and make the connection to TiVo.

Once you have your trusty Bash prompt (#) in your terminal window, you'll want to amend TiVo's rc.sysinit file so that it will open TiVo up to telnet access and system-wide logins by entering the following:

```
mount -o remount,rw /
echo 'tnlited 23 /bash/bin -login &' >>
/etc/rc.d/rc.sysinit
mount -o remount,ro /
```

The purpose of this command set is to send the `tnlited 23 /bash/bin -login &` instruction to the end of the rc.sysinit file from the command line, without having to open the file in a text editor to make the changes there. If you're curious, here's exactly what's going on:

The first command string, `mount -o remount,rw /`, tells Linux to remount the root directory (/) using the –o, which qualifies the nature of the mount. Here, we further qualify the command using the remount option with the rw option. This is, in essence, saying: We want to remount the root directory so that we have full read/write privileges 'cause we're about to write to a file.

The second string, `echo 'tnlited 23 /bash/bin -login &' >> /etc/rc.d/rc.sysinit`, asks Linux to take the startup telnet-related command line `tnlited 23 /bash/bin -login &` and write it to the end of the rc.sysinit file located in the /etc/rc.d/ directory (using the >> redirection operators).

The third command line is simply another remount, this time, to reset things back to the default state, which is read-only (ro).

With these commands issued over the serial net, you're ready to restart your TiVo to allow them to take effect. Hardboot your box by unplugging it, waiting a few seconds, and plugging it back in. Your TiVo is ready to connect to the network via telnet.

Opening TiVo to the Net via a Hard Drive Connect

If you don't already have a serial network established, the only other way of getting one is to yank your hard drive(s) from TiVo and do an installation on your PC, as described in Chapter 8, "Upgrading Hard Drives." To go this route, you would

1. Perform the hardware blessing to open your TiVo case, remove the drive(s), set the jumper(s) for proper PC installation, install the drive(s) in your PC, and set the PC up to boot from the CD-ROM included in this book. All of this is described in Chapter 8.

   At the Linux Bash prompt you get via the Linux distribution on the CD, we'll issue the same commands as in "Opening TiVo to the Net via Serial Network" earlier in this chapter. But first, we need to mount the correct hardware (our TiVo drive) so that we can "talk" to it from the Linux OS in the CD drive. Issue the following commands:

   ```
   mkdir /mnt4
   mount /dev/hdX4 /mnt4
   cd /mnt4
   ```

   In the preceding code, replace the X with the letter of your TiVo drive as it's connected to your IDE chain on your PC (either hdb, hdc, or hdd). Also, if you get an error while trying to mount partition 4, make and mount a partition 7 (mnt7) directory.

Tip

There are actually three ways of "shelling in" to TiVo. There's the serial method, discussed in Chapter 10; the Ethernet telnet method discussed in this chapter; and a way called PPP-over-Serial, which makes use of the venerable Point-to-Point Protocol. We're not going into the latter method here. We think, if you want to be networking with your TiVo with any regularity, you're going to want the speed and permanent connectability of Ethernet. But if you want to know how to use PPP with it, check The Dummy's Guide to PPP Over Serial for Win 9x (http://black-widow000.150m.com/TiVo-PPP).

Caution

As always, you want to be mindful of the fact that you're monkeying around inside of TiVo and a mistake could cause havoc. If you don't have a backup of the TiVo OS, you should either make one, or proceed with extreme caution.

Tip

If you're unsure about what's going on here, it might be a good idea to reread the Mini-Tutorial on Linux in the previous chapter and refer to the Common Linux Commands table in Appendix B.

NOTE

In case you were wondering, tnlited is a telnet daemon that operates through port 23 of your TiVo's Linux OS. In version 3.x of the OS, tnlited is built in. *Geek Etymology Moment*: "Tnlited" takes its name from *telnetd*, a popular open source telnet client (making *tnlited* a truncated version of *telnet-lite-d*). "Daemon" is a computing term for a class of programs that run in the background. "Port" in computing gets its name from "seaport," and refers to a numbered interface point for data to come in and out of the system. Port 23 is generally the "port of call" (er...if you will) for telnet access.

With partition 4 (or 7) successfully mounted, you're ready to issue the commands as given in "Opening TiVo to the Net via Serial Network" earlier in this chapter.

3. When you're done making the changes, issue the Linux shutdown command, which will power down your PC.

4. Reinstall the drive(s) in your TiVo (making sure the jumper settings are correct for TiVo), reconnect TiVo (including your Ethernet cable, if you disconnected it from your network), and power it up.

Your TiVo is ready to connect to the network via telnet.

What's That IP Addy Again?

To be able to access the Bash prompt over your Ethernet connection, you're going to have to know what the IP address of your TiVo is. Series 1 TiVos with OSes 3.0 and up have unofficial drivers installed in them for Ethernet networking. If you installed the 9th Tee TurboNET card (see Chapter 9, "Networking Your TiVo"), you didn't have to do anything to set up the network connection. When you plugged the Ethernet cable into your TiVo and PC and powered everything up, the DHCP server on your LAN gateway/router assigned your TiVo an IP address. But unlike Series 2 stand-alone networking, where you simply have to go to the Settings menu to see what IP address got assigned when you networked your box, there's no menu on Series 1 machines showing you your TiVo's address. Bummer, dude. So to be able to talk to your TurboNET-connected TiVo, you have to know the address. That pokey, but oh so trusty serial network comes to the rescue again!

Using the serial connection (see Chapter 10 for details), at the Bash prompt, issue the following command:

```
sbin/ifconfig eth0
```

This asks Linux to use the interface configuration program stored in the sbin directory to take a poke at the Ethernet line and to tell us what it finds. In the returned data, you'll see a line that starts with:

`Inet addr:192.168.1.102` (your IP address will obviously be different).

Write this number down. This is your IP address. You'll need this to be able to telnet into TiVo over the network.

As a side note, keep in mind that if you installed the install_nic drivers for the 9th Tee CacheCARD, then as part of the running of the installation program, you were asked to assign a static IP address. You hopefully wrote this number down and can now use that from now on to establish a telnet session with TiVo.

Pinging Our Song

To check to make sure that our Ethernet connection is working properly, we can issue a ping command from our desktop machine. Ping is a good resource to know about so that you can bounce a signal off of your TiVo at any time to make sure things are connecting properly.

On a Windows PC, click Start, Run to open up the Run dialog and type in cmd to open up a command (DOS) prompt window. At the DOS prompt, type ping followed by your IP address (see Figure 14.1). So we would type

```
ping 192.168.1.102
```

FIGURE 14.1

The Ping's the thing. This is what a ping return looks like on a Windows Telnet utility.

Telnetting into Bash

With your Ethernet hardware installed, the amendments made to the rc.sysinit file to allow for remote logins over the network, and your TiVo's IP address in hand, you're ready to get serious about treating your TiVo as a full-fledged network destination. Open up NetTerm, SecureCRT, minicom, Mac's Terminal utility, or your favorite terminal program. Nearly all such programs support both modem-type connection (as with our serial networking) and TCP/IP telnet sessions.

Tip

Your DHCP server used with your router/gateway will most likely dynamically assign the IP address to your TiVo. This makes things a lot easier in that you don't have to remember static IP addresses for all of the devices on your network, but can be a hassle if you have to reboot your system and TiVo gets assigned a new addy. A lot of DHCP servers will just keep assigning the same numbers (unless you install new devices to the net), so the address you get from the serial login may remain for a while—or forever. But if you want to ensure that it stays the same, you can instruct your DHCP software to assign TiVo a static address. Consult the docs that came with your router to see how this is done with your box.

Enter the IP address of your TiVo in the appropriate manner for the program you are using and log in to your TiVo. In the terminal window, you should see TiVo's Bash prompt. That's it! You now have a way of using your home network to gain access to TiVo.

Setting Up an FTP Server on TiVo

While the Web and HTTP are the main ways in which we access and upload/download data these days, you're still likely familiar with the ol' FTP (or File Transfer Protocol). In fact, you most likely have an FTP program on your desktop machine already. Wouldn't it be cool if we had one of these programs set up on our TiVo too so that we could easily connect FTP to FTP and transfer files between TiVo and the rest of our network? Imagine finding a cool new TiVo program online and being able to nearly instantly download it and send it from your PC over to your TiVo to install it. Well, you can, thanks to tivoftpd, an FTP server you can install on TiVo. With this baby in your box, you can move files back and forth to TiVo using standard FTP commands. The utility tivoftpd is included in the Series1/Utilities folder on the CD. But unfortunately, once again, we're faced with the TiVo hacker's chicken and egg dilemma: How can we transfer a file from our PC to a TiVo when we don't have the proper file transfer tools on the TiVo end to receive the file transfer tools? There are several workarounds.

Sending It over Serial

If you still have your serial connection handy, you could open up your terminal window program, issue the rz command at the Bash prompt to bring up a file transfer dialog box, select the file, and send it on over that way. That's one low and slow method. Once the app is installed, all you have to do is invoke it (see "Executing TIVOFTPD" later in this section).

Transferring It While Upgrading Hard Drives

You can use the opportunity of having your TiVo drive(s) connected to your PC to move the tivoftpd app to the appropriate directory on TiVo (see Tip). Once the app is installed, all you have to do is invoke it (see "Executing TIVOFTPD" later in this section).

It May Already Be Installed!

You may be closer to file transfer freedom than you realize. If you installed the install_nic package as part of your 9th Tee CacheCARD or AirNET installation, it installed tivoftpd (along with tnlited) during that process. If this is the case, you are ready to invoke it (see "Executing TIVOFTPD" later in this section).

Get It the Way TiVo Does

Okay, if you're just too damn tired of dragging out that serial cable to make a pokey serial connection or the thought of pulling out your TiVo drive and hooking it up to your PC again makes steam shoot out of your neck bolts, there's an interesting, kinda cool (in an uber-geeky sorta way) hack you can use.

Here's the deal: TiVo itself has a built-in app called http_get that it uses to download files over its dial-up connection. You can use this same program to download a little binary goodness of your own. Follow these steps:

1. First off, to make things easier, transfer tivoftpd to your PC's desktop (why will become clear in a moment).

2. Determine the IP address of your desktop computer (by entering `winipcfg` in the Run window of your Win9x machine, clicking on Details in the Network Connections Control Panel on XP, or looking under the Network icon in System Preferences on a Mac).

3. Now telnet into TiVo by entering *its* address in your telnet program (not your PC's), and at the Bash prompt, enter

   ```
   http_get -T 0 -C 0 -D /var/hack/bin –U http://192.168.1.
   ➥105:80/tivoftpd
   ```

   Of course, you would enter the URL for your PC, not ours. This command will use http_get to fetch tivoftpd from our PC desktop and move it to the /var/hack/bin. We're assuming you've already created this directory. If not, use the mkdir command in Bash before you use http_get to create this destination directory.

   In case you're curious, the -T 0 and -C 0 (those are ZEROES, by the way) are where TiVo would normally have your machine's serial number and call ID in the outgoing call. Zeroing them out works just fine. The –D flag refers to the following directory and the –U indicates what follows is a URL.

4. You're done with transfer. Tivoftpd is now in your var/hack/bin directory.

You can actually use http_get to grab anything off the Web and move it to your TiVo (it doesn't have to be a local net fetch as we did here). The only problem is that you have to know the exact IP address path. There is no

Tip

Regardless of which program you're using to make your telnet connection, you'll need to make sure that you have the IP address entered in the proper place, have port 23 selected, and have chosen TCP/IP as the connection method.

Tip

Folks who are going to be adding apps to their TiVos should create a special directory under /var on TiVo's partition 9 (dev/hda9) to store them. To do this, use the mkdir command and say `mkdir /mnt9/hack`. As you move apps from your PC to TiVo, stash 'em here. You'll also want to create a /bin subdirectory within /hack to store all of your program files.

To web serve content on your desktop computer, you're going to need to have a web server app running. This can be any ol' server, such as MS Personal Web Server, or a freebie found at download.com, tucows.com, or elsewhere. All you have to do is make sure the server is running on your computer and that you've told it (in the appropriate preferences menu) where your files to be served are going to be stored (and then, of course, make sure the files are in there for TiVo to be able to fetch them).

domain name resolution, and because of the common use of "virtual hosting" where several domain names share the same IP address, which one you get sent to has to do with the domain name you entered in the first place. Since you are using only IP addresses in http_get, this can be a problem. But luckily, we don't have to worry too much about this after we get our FTP server set up on TiVo, 'cause then we'll be able to download whatever we want, wherever we find it, to our PC and then use our PC's FTP program to connect to TiVo's FTP server and transfer files at will.

Executing TIVOFTPD

With the application now moved over to TiVo via http_get, you're ready to telnet into TiVo and to set permissions for who gets to use and then to execute it. This is done by launching your telnet program, logging in to TiVo, and at the Bash prompt, entering

```
chmod 755 /var/hack/bin/tivoftpd
/var/hack/bin/tivoftpd
```

The first line uses the Change Mode (chmod) permissions command to make the tivoftpd program available to the owner for read/write/execute (7), to users for read/execute (5), and to "others" as read/execute (5). Of course, since you're likely on a fairly open home system and you're the owner/"superuser," you are all-powerful [Cue maniacal mad scientist cackle]. If you want, you can also use 555, which will deny write permissions, since you're not likely to want to write to this executable.

The second line executes the program itself. You are now ready to try logging in to the FTP server to see if it's working okay.

Using Your Built-In Command-Line FTP

If you're on a Windows machine and don't have an FTP app, you can use Microsoft's built-in FTP DOS program to access TiVo's FTP server. To launch it, open up the Run window from the Start menu and enter Command. At the Command prompt, type

```
ftp [Your TiVo's IP Address Number]
```

Press Enter to bypass the login procedure and you're in! Tivoftpd is a daemon (that's what the D in the name is for). It runs in the background just dying to hear from another FTP client. After the login, you'll see the common FTP command prompt:

```
ftp>
```

Transferring a File

Once you have your FTP connection established, it's just a question of choosing the source file and the destination directory. You can go ahead and choose another utility app from the Series 1/Utilities folder on the CD, move it over to the C:\ directory (for convenience) and get ready to FTP it over to TiVo. If you're on a graphical FTP app, you'll use buttons and windows to navigate and issue commands. If you're on a command line, a typical session would look something like Table 14.1. On a command line FTP, all of the commands in bold would be entered at the ftp> prompt, and the non-bold text is how the server should respond.

Tip

To find out more about FTP and all of the common (and not so common) transfer commands, take a look at this tutorial: www. tombraider4u.com/ ftptutorial.shtml.

Table 14.1   Common FTP Session Commands and What They Mean

FTP Command/Response	What it Means
lcd C:	We're asking FTP to make C: the local directory to watch
local directory now C:\	FTP responds to verify the change
cd /var/hack/	On TiVo, we're moving into the /hack/bin directory that we made (see earlier Tip)
Directory change successful	FTP responds to verify the change
bin	We're asking FTP to transfer the upcoming as a binary file
Type set to I.	FTP responds to verify the change
put [name of app]	We're asking FTP to transfer (put) the requested application
PORT command successful	FTP responds to verify transfer is ready to roll
File transfer complete	The program has been moved to the /var/hack/ directory on TiVo
Quit	We're asking FTP to close our session

Backgrounding TIVOFTPD

One last thing we should do is once again amend our rc.sysinit file so that it launches the tivoftpd daemon whenever we restart TiVo. We do this the same way we set up the tnlited (see "Opening TiVo to the Net via Serial Network" earlier in this chapter):

```
mount -o remount,rw /
echo 'var/hack/bin/tivoftpd  /bash/bin -login &' >>
➡/etc/rc.d/rc.sysinit
mount -o remount,ro /
```

Now you'll always have FTP access to TiVo from our PC.

Installing Bash's Little Helpers

The CD-ROM that came with this book has a number of Linux/Unix utility programs that will make your work within TiVo much easier and more enjoyable. As we said before, TiVo's built-in GNU/Linux tools are minimal because TiVo, Inc. only cares about those apps that can help them during manufacturing, testing, and service. They never expected that you'd have your greasy little digits inside their file system. Subsequently, some of the most basic, and extremely useful, Unix/Linux components, such as ls, head, tail, and dd, are not installed, but we can quickly fix this.

1. First thing you need to do is to use your preferred FTP program to move the compressed gzip utilities file called tivobin.tar.gz from the CD-ROM (located in the Series1/Utilities folder) to the /var/hack directory on your TiVo.

2. Next you need to expand the contents of the file like so (via Bash, over your telnet connection):

```
cd /var/hack
gzip -d tivobin.tar.gz
cpio -idu -H tar < tivobin.tar
```

This procedure takes us into the var/hack directory, uses the gzip utility to decompress the program bundle, and then uses the cpio utility to unarchive the "tarball."

3. We end up with a subdirectory called tivo-bin. Let's keep things clean and tidy and move this into our existing hack/bin directory by using

```
mv tivo-bin bin
```

4. Next we need to assign permissions so that all of the programs are executable. We can do a global chmod through use of a wildcard:

```
chmod 755 /bin/*
```

5. Having the utilities raring to go is all well and good, but they can't do much if the system itself doesn't know where to find them. To do this, we need to tweak Bash's PATH variable so that it knows to add our var/hack/bin as a place to look for executables. Enter the following command at Bash:

```
export PATH=$PATH:/var/hack/bin
```

This tells Bash to add the contents of the var/hack/bin to its list of executable directories. To check it, after you've entered the above, type

```
echo $PATH
```

Your screen should print something like

```
/bin:/sbin:/tvbin:/devbin:/var/hack:/var/hack/bin
```

6. Okay kids, we're almost there! We should have use of all of the utilities now, anywhere within the Bash shell. But we have one problem. The PATH variable amendment will only stick until the next time you reboot TiVo, then it will go back to its original PATH statement, losing the links to our precious utilities. To prevent this from happening, we need to amend the .profile, another type of configuration file where things such as PATH variables are stored. To add our var/hack/bin directory to this document, we need to remount the root directory for read/write permissions, send the changes to .profile, and then put root back into read-only mode. This is how it's done:

```
cd /
mount -o remount,rw /
echo "export PATH=\$PATH:/var/hack/bin" >> /.profile
mount -o remount,ro /
```

That's it! Now, whenever you "shell in" to TiVo you should have access to all of the same basic Bash commands and utilities you would on most other Linux systems. To see a listing of all of the utility apps that we just installed and what they do, check out Appendix C, "About the CD-ROM."

Learning More About Bash

If you read carefully through Chapter 13, "Touring Your TiVo: The Software," consulted Appendix B, and cavorted around inside your TiVo and or the mini-Linux distribution that came with this book, you've likely come to one of two conclusions: 1) Linux is freakin' cool, I want to know more! I can't wait to see what other nifty apps and hacks are available to me, or 2) I haven't been in this much anguish since I had a root canal while being forced to read the Federal Tax Code. If you're the former, there are plenty of resources online for learning more about Bash, your TiVo's gateway to Linux (and, of course, tons of material on Linux proper). One good place to start is "The Linux Terminal—A Beginner's Bash" (http://linux.org.mt/article/terminal), which is a decent tutorial for a newbie, at least one who's gotten as far as you have. If you're the latter kind of person, don't sweat it, the Penguin ain't that cute to everybody. Get yourself a Series 2 TiVo and network it using the Home Media Feature (if it's stand-alone) and you'll be able to do most of the stuff the Series 1 folks can do, minus the tedious bit-twiddling.

Chapter 15

Home Media Feature

In Chapter 9, "Networking Your TiVo," we detailed how to set up the hardware and software for a wired or wireless connection between your TiVo and your home network. In this chapter, we'll discuss the TiVo Home Media Feature, some of the third-party products you can use with HMF, and some of the open source alternatives to the HMF server software, especially JavaHMO.

What Is the Home Media Feature?

As we discussed in Chapter 1, "Which TiVo Is Right for You?" the Home Media Feature (or HMF) is a free service and software offered by TiVo, Inc. that allows you to connect your Series 2 stand-alone TiVo to your home computer network. The HMF currently offers the following features:

- **Multi-Room Viewing**—If you have more than one Series 2 stand-alone TiVo and have subscribed to the HMF service for all of them, you can share programming between DVRs over your network. Any program recorded on any TiVo can be viewed by any other (S2) TiVo on the network.

- **Web-Based Scheduling**—HMF allows you to schedule programs for your TiVo(s) over the Internet using any web browser.

- **MP3 Music Playback**—Your entire digital music library (in the MP3 format) on your Windows PC or Mac can be made available to your home stereo system via your TiVo.

In the "Future of TiVo" section in the introduction, we covered a number of the new or promised HMF features and third-party add-ons. Refer back to that list to see what else may be in store for HMF.

As previously discussed, the Home Media Feature is available only on stand-alone Series 2 TiVos and on DVD/TiVo combo units. It is not available for Series 1, DirecTV DVRs, or HD DirecTV DVR, and currently, there are no known plans to change this. Our Tech Editors, the weaKnees.com boys, have talked to TiVo directly, and they have *NO PLANS* to network DirecTiVos, so: *STOP CALLING WEAKNEES!* They haven't a clue about when or why not or if ever!

- **Digital Photo Viewing**—You can view individual digital photos or run photo slide shows on your TiVo/TV that are actually stored on your PC or Mac.

- **Daily Call via the Internet**—With your TiVo connected to a LAN, you can set it up to place its daily call via the Internet instead of over the built-in modem and phone lines. This ability is actually available even if you aren't running the TiVo Desktop application (see later in this chapter), but have your TiVo connected to your network.

These are just the current offerings from TiVo, Inc. They will be offering other services soon, likely by the time you read this (such as TiVoToGo, which we'll discuss in a moment). Also, there are a number of third-party commercial offerings available now (see "Commercial Third-Party Applications," later in this chapter) and some that have been announced for the near future. Mainly, these new apps are additional tools for manipulating your digital music and photo files for display on your TiVo, but at least one partnership, with XM Satellite Radio, is substantial, offering HMF users the ability to use the TiVo interface to navigate XM radio.

Who Needs HMF?

Whether you want to set up HMF or not has a lot to do with how you use your TiVo or how you'd *like* to use it. Here are some of the sorts of users that might find HMF worth the investment in network gear and the setup time:

- **Music Junkies**—If you have an extensive collection of MP3 files on your computer and can't be away from the tuneage for very long without starting to break into song, scaring the daylights out of housemates and housepets, HMF may be worthwhile. If you don't have a decent home stereo system on the receiving end of your TiVo, it's probably not worth the effort, but then, if you're a music freak, you probably invested more in your stereo than you did on the family car.

- **Family Photo Freaks**—If your idea of a rip-roarin' good time is to sit around with a captive audience of family members and friends, regaling them with tales of your thrilling Carnival Cruise with Kathy Lee Gifford, complete with a moment-to-moment slide show ("This is the beef tongue they served at the all-you-could-eat buffet. Marvelous."), then the digital photo feature is definitely for you.

Leo Laporte's Guide to TiVo

What Is the Home Media Feature?   Chapter 15

Personally, these types of tedious travelogues make us want to crawl under the couch with the Roomba robo-vac, but your mileage may vary.

Gareth On...

One cool use I found for the slideshow feature was as an additional bit of ambience for our annual Tiki/Luau party. I downloaded a bunch of Shag art (www.shag.com), and used the HMF Desktop Application to serve the images to TiVo. I used the slideshow feature, slapped on the ol' Martin Denny CDs, blended up some devastating Mai Tais, and the party was good to go. The colorful Shag art really added to the rest of the party decor.

- **Impulsive Schedulers**—One of the coolest features of HMF is the ability to schedule programs over the Web, from any browser. This is very handy if you're at work and forgot to record something, or if someone at the water cooler starts yammering on about a show you simply *MUST* see: You can set up a recording request for it immediately, before it slips your mind.

- **Multi-Room Couch Potatoes**—If you find yourself asking the blank-eyed teen clerk at Circuit City if they offer bulk discounts on multiple TiVos, you're likely the kind of mediaphile who wants to connect all of your home's computers, DVRs, and digital stereos into on big network. And you likely have the disposable income to do it. You, my vegetative friend, are a prime candidate for HMF.

If you are any of the above user types, or a heady mix of several, then you might want to consider setting up the HMF. If you don't have a huge jones for digital music at your home media center (or already have a digital sound system there), are not a big slideshow-off, can wait until you get home to schedule shows, and don't plan on networking TiVos together, you can probably skip the HMF. You'll probably want to keep your eye on Home Media developments though, because TiVo, Inc. seems to be moving aggressively to add features that make your TiVo DVR more of a central media appliance. Some may not be that impressed with what HMF offers now but will be ready to pony up when the TiVoToGo service allows you to watch recorded programs on other PCs, laptops, and DVD players. Before you decide *not* to set up a network connection and HMF, you might want to also take a look at the JavaHMO section later in this chapter. This free open source program offers a number of nifty features (like streaming Internet radio and movie listings on TiVo that HMF does not yet offer).

Getting HMF

With a physical network connection established via a USB-to-Ethernet adapter card or a USB wireless network adapter (see Chapter 9) you have all the hardware (at least on the TiVo end) for installing HMF.

When the Home Media Feature was first introduced, as the Home Media Option, it cost a one-time fee of $99 for the first TiVo and $49 for each additional unit you register. In mid-2004, TiVo began offering it for free and changed its name to the Home Media Feature. It is now already available on your stand-alone Series 2 TiVo; all you have to do is set up the networking hardware and then download and install the TiVo Desktop application (see the following section).

FIGURE 15.1

TiVo Central screen with HMF loaded (which is now done automatically).

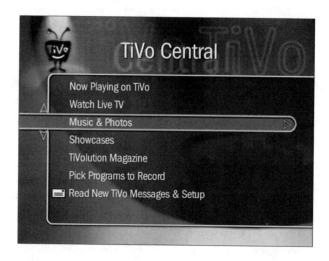

NOTE

You don't actually need to download the TiVo Desktop app if all you're going to be doing is scheduling shows over the Web and/or using your LAN to place TiVo's daily calls. TiVo Desktop is only required to serve music and photos to your TiVos.

When you register your new TiVo (or when you go back to tivo.com to set up HMF), you'll be given a link to the TiVo Desktop application. This is the software that you'll need on your host computer to be able to serve music and photos over the network to your TiVo. On a Windows PC, you need to be on Windows 98 or higher, or on the Mac side, you'll need OS X 10.2 or higher (along with iTunes 3.0 or higher and iPhoto 2.0 or higher). Windows NT and Mac OS 9 are not supported.

Setting Up Your TiVo on the Network

TiVo, Inc. has made it fairly easy to set up the HMF desktop software so that your home network will recognize your TiVo(s) and so that you'll be able to use all of the HMF features. How you set up this connection depends on a number of things, the most significant being what type of network connection you have: wired or wireless. Let's look at both.

Wired Network (via Ethernet)

If you set up a wired network in Chapter 9, using a USB-to-Ethernet adapter and Ethernet Cat5 cable, the first thing you'll need to do is go to the "TCP/IP Settings" found at TiVo Central -> Messages & Setup -> Settings -> Phone & Network Setup -> Edit Phone or Network Settings -> TCP/IP Settings (see Figure 15.2).

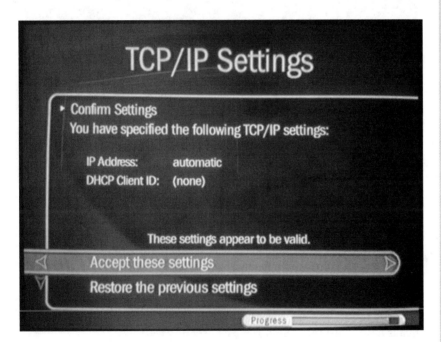

Setting the IP Address Method

From here you have to choose the method your network uses to assign IP addresses. As you likely already know, IP (Internet Protocol) addresses are either dynamically assigned (by the network) or "static," meaning they're fixed addresses that you have to enter manually during a network setup (see

Tip

After you install either a wired or wireless adapter, you'll need to restart your TiVo so that TiVo's software can recognize the adapter.

FIGURE 15.2
The TCP/IP Settings screen.

Figure 15.3). Most likely, your LAN router or gateway uses DHCP (Dynamic Host Configuration Protocol), so unless you know for certain that it does not, choose this menu item ("Obtain the IP Address Automatically") from the TCP/IP Settings menu (by making sure it is highlighted and then pressing the Select button).

FIGURE 15.3

The Obtain the IP Address Automatically screen.

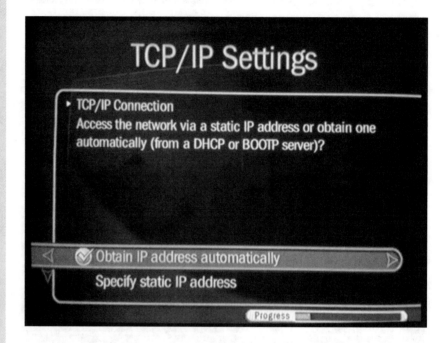

Tip

On a Windows 98 PC, you can usually find all of the information required for a static IP address setup (IP address, router address, subnet mask, and DNS) by choosing Run from the Start menu and typing in winipcfg. This will launch the IP Configuration utility. On Windows XP, go to the Network Connections Control Panel and double-click on the Local Network Connection icon (or other icon, depending on your configuration). Then click on the "Support" tab. On a Mac, this information can be found in System Preferences, under the Apple menu (click on the Network icon).

If you know your IP address is static, or you try auto-assignment and it doesn't work, you'll need to choose "Specify a Static IP Address." You will be taken to screen with four number-entry boxes. The IP number you enter will be created by you, but based on your computer's IP address, as assigned by your Internet service provider. This static IP address, like all current IP addresses, is what's called a "dotted quad." This refers to the fact that the address has four parts separated by periods, or "dots." These quads have up to three numbers each (see Figure 15.4).

In the static address for your PC and home network, the first three quads will always be the same. The last quad refers to each device on your network and should be unique. So, for example, if your host PC's address is 192.168.1.1, and your laptop's is 192.168.1.2, then you'd want to enter 192.168.1.3 for your TiVo's IP number. Once you've decided what number to enter, use the number keypad on your remote to enter it onscreen and press Select (which will save the input and take you to the next menu). See Figure 15.4.

FIGURE 15.4
The "Specify a Static IP Address" screen with boxes for entering the four "quads" of the address.

Other Static Address Settings

For static addressing, you also need to know your subnet mask, gateway/router address, and a Domain Name Server (DNS) address. Now don't go gettin' all sweaty. These aren't as geeky as they sound and are easily found on your computer.

The *subnet mask* is simply a number that tells the network which part of the IP address of a given device is shared by the whole network and which part is specific to that device. The dotted quad for the mask will usually be 255.255.255.0. This tells the network that the first three quads belong to the network and the last quad identifies each unique device (or "subnetwork"). You will find your subnet mask number in the information your ISP gave you when you registered, or by entering the IP address of your router/gateway. What this address is will usually be listed in the router's installation guide. With the subnet mask number in hand, enter it using the number keypad on your remote (as shown in Figure 15.5) and press Select to go to the next menu (Gateway/Router Address).

NOTE

In IP addresses, when there are leading zeroes (such as 192.168.**001**. **001**), they do not have to actually be entered. In this example, the IP address could be also expressed as 192.168.1.1.

FIGURE 15.5

The Subnet Mask screen.

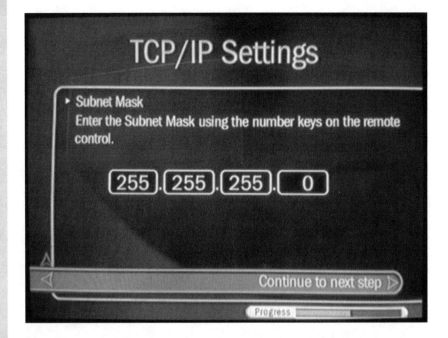

The gateway/router address is just what it sounds like: the IP address assigned to your home router. It is usually provided by your ISP or router manufacturer, or it can also be found by looking at your host computer's network configuration information (as described in a previous Note). Once you've found the number to enter, use the number keypad on your remote to enter it and press Select (see Figure 15.6). You will be taken to the next screen (DNS Address).

You will also need the Domain Name Service (DNS) number. This is the IP address that points to the Internet server whose job it is to resolve IP address numbers into domain names. All of the Internet domains you are familiar with: google.com, ebay.com, yahoo.com, and so forth, are actually numbers, not names. But since it would be impossible for you to remember that Google's home in cyberspace is 216.239.39.99, the Domain Name Servers of the Internet allow you to type in google.com and they then link that name to Google's IP address. The number that you'll enter in the DNS Address screen will be the one provided by your ISP. You will also be able to find this address by going to your Network Control Panel/IP Configuration screen as described earlier in this chapter. When you enter the DNS, press Select. You will be taken to a final TCP/IP Settings screen and asked to confirm your settings. Once selected, you're done with the TCP/IP setup.

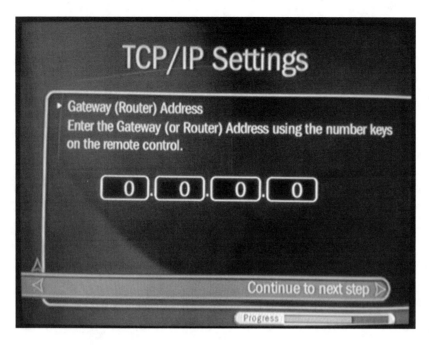

FIGURE 15.6
The Gateway (Router) Address screen.

Final Wired Setup

After you press Select on the final TCP/IP Settings screen, if TiVo detects that you're currently accessing its remote servers over a phone line, it will ask you if you want to change your connection type. Choosing "Connect via the Internet" will mean that TiVo will no longer use your phone line making its daily calls. If you plan on doing remote scheduling from a Web browser, you'll have to be connected via this connection type, too. Obviously, you should only do this if you have an always-on Internet connection (as opposed to a dial-up connection).

Wireless Network (via WiFi)

If you set up a wireless network in Chapter 9, using a USB-to-wireless adapter, the first thing you'll need to do is go to the "TCP/IP Settings" found at TiVo Central -> Messages & Setup -> Settings -> Phone & Network Setup -> Edit Phone or Network Settings -> Wireless Settings (see Figure 15.7).

Tip

If you're not sure about the local address for your router and can't find the info, the address is often 192.168.1.1 or 192.168.0.1 entered into you browser.

FIGURE 15.7

The Wireless Setting screen

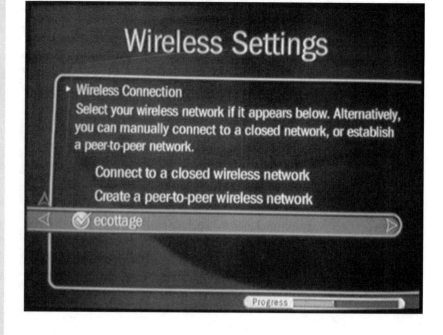

When entering your network name, you must use the proper case. If your network is called "The Electronic Cottage," you'll have to enter it exactly as that, spaces, caps, and all. Use the Thumbs Up/Down on your remote to toggle between upper- and lowercase letters.

Choosing Your Network Type

The Wireless Settings screen will ask you to choose what type of network you have: open or closed. An open network means that the network's ID (called an "SSID," or "Service Set Identifier") is broadcast in the open. If your network was called "The Electronic Cottage," for instance, you'd see its name in a list (and all open wireless network SSIDs within wireless range). Choose your network's name and press Select.

If your network is not open, and therefore not detected by the HMF software, choose "Connect to a Closed Wireless Network." This will bring up a screen where you can enter your LAN's SSID using the arrow keys on your remote to choose letters/numbers from the Ouija screen.

When you're done entering your network's name, if TiVo detects that your network has no password protection, it will ask you to verify the setup (by pressing Select). If it *does* detect a network password, it will ask you to select the password type (hexadecimal or alphanumeric), as shown in Figure 15.8. If you have set up your wireless network yourself, you should know which type of password security you used. If you didn't, consult the person who did do the setup to find out. If you choose alphanumeric (the likely password type), you'll then be asked to select the level of security the password provides (40-, 64-, 104-, or 128-bit encryption). Again, this is something you would already know if you set up your network, or something you can get from the person who did.

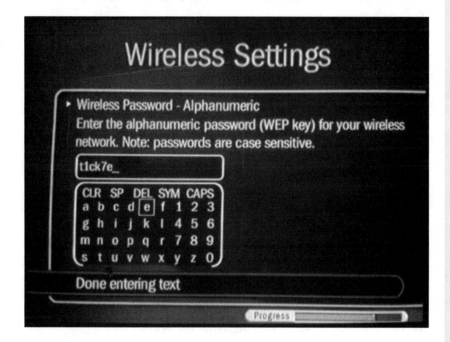

FIGURE 15.8

The Wireless Encryption screen.

Although there are the previous four different encryption levels supported, there are only two menu choices ("40 or 60-bit Encryption" and "128-bit Encryption"). If you have 104-bit on your network, select 128-bit. As of this writing, 256-bit encryption is not supported by Series 2 TiVo software. See Figure 15.9.

With the encryption level chosen and the Select button pressed, you'll be taken to a Wireless Settings confirmation screen. Confirming the settings will then take you to a final screen asking if you want to change your connection type (from the built-in dial-up modem to an Internet connection for making TiVo's daily calls). You likely will want to make this change. It will mean you no longer need to tie up the phone with TiVo modem connections, and it will allow you to use the HMF remote scheduling feature (see later in this chapter).

You are now done with the wireless network setup procedure. The next thing you'll need to make sure of is your DHCP (Dynamic Host Configuration Protocol) settings.

If You Have DHCP and *Do Not* Have a DHCP Client ID

You likely have DHCP onyour router/gateway, a feature that automatically assigns IP addresses to devices on the network so you don't have to. If you have DHCP and do not have a DHCP Client ID (most people do not), you're done! TiVo will automatically complete the network setup for you.

If You Have DHCP and You *Do* Have a DHCP Client ID

Go to the TCP/IP Settings menu (TiVo Central -> Messages & Setup -> Settings -> Phone & Network Setup -> Edit Phone or Network Settings -> TCP/IP Settings), choose "Obtain IP Address Automatically," and then enter your DHCP Client ID onto the screen that you're taken to. Your DHCP Client ID would have been provided to you by your ISP. Enter it now by using the arrow buttons to move around the Ouija screen. Client IDs are case-sensitive, so use the Thumps Up/Down buttons to toggle between caps and lowercase. Choose "Done Entering Text" and press Select when you're done. At the Confirm Setting screen, choose Accept the Settings. You're done!

If You Do Not Have DHCP on Your Network

If you have a static IP addressing scheme on your network (not likely these days, but possible), you'll have to enter your TCP/IP settings manually. Go to the "Setting the IP Address Method" and "Other Static IP Settings" sub-sections in the Wired Network screen (via Ethernet section earlier in this chapter). Follow the instructions relevant to static IP addressing. When all the appropriate address information has been entered, accept your entries via the "Confirm Your Settings" screen, and you're done!

Networking TiVos for Multi-Room Viewing

To use the multi-room viewing option to record a program on one Series 2 TiVo and then view it on another Series 2 TiVo, you have to have the following:

- More than one S2 TiVo (duh).
- Each TiVo needs to have a service account in good standing.

Tip

TiVo.com has some decent network troubleshooting information. For more information, check out:

http://customersupport.
tivo.com/tsg.asp?LEVEL=
3&L1=63&N1=
Networking&L2=64&N2=
Wireless&L3=67&N3=
Connect+My+DVR+to+a+
Wireless+Network

- Each TiVo needs to be subscribed to the Home Media Feature ($99 for the first unit, $49 for each additional unit).

- Each TiVo needs to be on the same home network (or on a TiVo-to-TiVo connection, covered later in this chapter).

With all of this, the hardware for a network established (as covered in Chapter 9), and the network setup complete (as described earlier in this chapter), you'll need to turn on the Multi-Viewing Option via your account page on tivo.com. To activate, go to tivo.com/manage, and log in to get to the "Manage My Account" page. From the navigation menu on the left side, choose "DVR preferences," as shown in Figure 15.9. At the bottom of the screen, you'll see a list of your registered S2 TiVos with check boxes in front of each. Check the units you want to share programs between. Hit "Save Preferences." It will take up to 24 hours for changes made on the website to take effect, and multi-room viewing will only be available on each unit after each has made its daily call and been updated with this newly requested feature.

NOTE

If you have a Series 2 SA unit (TiVo-branded) and a Pioneer DVD/DVR combo unit on the same network, you can't use HMF to burn a show from the TiVo-branded unit onto the Pioneer. Quite unfortunate.

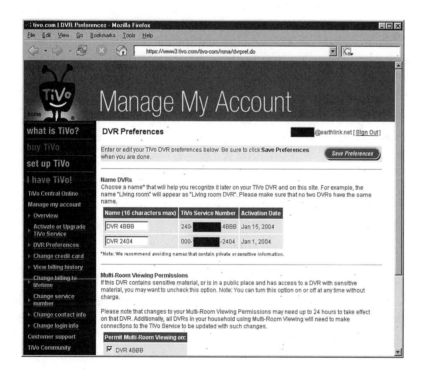

FIGURE 15.9

The DVR Preferences screen on TiVo.com with all S2 TiVos selected for file sharing.

Once your TiVos are hooked up and the multi-room viewing feature is turned on, you'll know it because the other TiVos on your network will show up onscreen on the Now Playing menu. You'll see a DVR icon and the name of the TiVo(s) on the network.

To view a program stored on another TiVo, all you have to do is select the remote DVR from the Now Playing menu. The Now Playing recordings from this remote TiVo will be displayed. When you choose a desired program, you'll see a Program screen for the selected show and be given a choice ("Watch on This TV" or "Don't Do Anything"). If you choose "Watch on this TV," the program will begin transferring to the TV/TiVo you're watching. If you watch the program *during* the transfer, you may experience delays (similar to the sort of buffering you see when viewing Internet streaming video). Once you start the transfer, you can either watch as it's being transferred or wait until it's done. As you might imagine, buffering show content is much faster on a wired (Ethernet) connection, so if you have the option of going wired for multi-room viewing, do it!

Remote Scheduling

To us, this HMF feature is the most useful. It allows you to schedule TiVo recordings from any web browser. Once your HMF account is activated and your network has been set up as described earlier, all you have to do is go to TiVo Central Online (tivo.com/tco), and enter your user ID (your registered email address) and password. You'll be taken to the main TiVo Central Online screen (see Figure 15.10).

From here, you can search on a show Title, Description, or Actor/Director, or search via Channel/Date/Time. Clicking on the Advanced Search link takes you to a page where you can enter Title AND/OR Description AND/OR actor/director. You can also choose from the same categories/subcategories you find on your TiVo (see Figure 15.11).

Once you have your search results for your show, clicking on a results link takes you to a Program Info page. From here, you can select either a one-time recording or a Season Pass. After choosing one or the other, you'll be taken to a Schedule It! screen that offers the same options as the Record Options menu on your TiVo. The screen also allows you to select which TiVo (if you have more than one S2) and if you'd like to get an email confirmation on the scheduling.

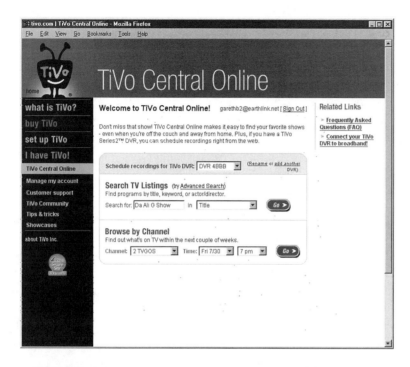

FIGURE 15.10
The TiVo Central Online
screen.

FIGURE 15.11
The Advance Search
screen, with options
similar to TiVo's unof-
ficial Advance WishList
feature.

At this time, the TiVo
Desktop is not available
for Linux—ironic since
TiVo is built on Linux! To
use HMF and a Linux
server, see the JavaHMO
section under "Free
Third-Party Applications"
later in this chapter.

Installing TiVo Desktop Application

To use the digital photo viewing and MP3 music playing features of HMF, you'll have to download the TiVo Desktop application. It's available at tivo.com/desktop. Here you'll find versions for both Windows and Mac OS X. The installation is different depending on what platform you're on.

Windows

To install the TiVo Desktop on Windows, all you have to do is download the application, double-click on it, and follow the setup Wizard screens. When the installation is complete, click Finish.

The Wizard will install two applications, the TiVo Publisher and the TiVo Server, and a background utility: the TiVo Connect Beacon. TiVo Publisher is the program you use to load both photos and music you want to "publish" to your TiVo. The TiVo Server/Connect Beacons always run in the background after you install them (and are automatically re-launched whenever you restart your computer) and make available, or "serve," all of the images and music you load into the Publisher. You can tell that the TiVo Server/Beacon is running or not by looking for the TiVoGuy icon in your Windows Taskbar.

Macintosh

On a Mac, you'll need to double-click on the TiVoDesktop_Mac_1.8.dmg icon that you've downloaded. This unpacks the disk image (.dmg) and leaves you with a TiVoDesktop volume to open. Within the volume, double-click on the TiVoDesktop.pkg and follow the onscreen installation instructions. When the installation is complete, click "Close."

The TiVo Desktop app is now installed but has not been turned on yet. Go to the "System Preferences" under the Apple menu and click on the TiVo Desktop icon in the "Other" section of the Preferences menu. Click on the "Start" button.

Working with Music and Photos on TiVo

With everything set up for making full use of the Home Media Feature, you're ready to start your own narrowcasting media empire, serving music and images across your network.

"Publishing" Music on the HMF Music Player (Windows)

The TiVo Publisher program is extremely easy to use. It has two tabbed sections, one for music publishing, one for photos. To publish music for listening to on your TiVo, click on the Music tab (see Figure 15.12). The top left pane displays the contents of your computer in a typical Windows Explorer format. Navigate through your directories to find your My Music folder, or other folders in which you have your music stored. If you have already created MP3 playlists, you can make your way to those and just load a list. The music files/playlists that you select will appear in the right pane. Click on the ones you want to publish and hit the Publish button along the top of the program. The "published" music will appear in the bottom pane and are now available on your TiVo. The TiVo Publisher supports the common playlist formats M3U, PLS, ASX, and B4S. You can also drag and drop folders of tunes or individual MP3 files into the bottom pane of the TiVo Desktop. Files within folders will be played in alphabetical order.

NOTE

If your TiVo Publisher app is on a computer with separate profiles for different users, each user will have to launch the app and "publish" their own files. Only the files of the currently logged in user will be served to the TiVo.

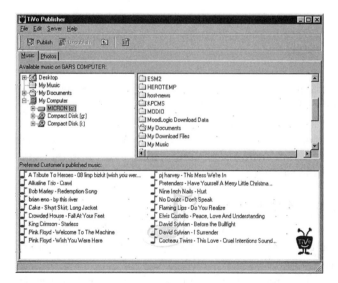

FIGURE 15.12

The Music tab on TiVo Desktop. The available files are in the upper pane; the selected music files and playlist are on the right. "Published" music appears at the bottom.

"Publishing" Music on the HMF Music Player (Mac)

The TiVo Desktop program for the Mac is extremely easy to use. To launch it, go to System Preferences under the Apple menu and click on "TiVo Desktop" (in the Other section of the System Preferences window).

The TiVo Desktop has two sections, accessed by tabs: Music and Photos (see Figure 15.13). To serve music to your TiVo, click on the Music tab and then select either "Publish My Entire iTunes Library" or "Publish Only These Playlists." If you choose the latter, you can check the list you want to play on TiVo. You can also enter the name of the music library as you want it to appear on TiVo.

FIGURE 15.13

The Music tab of the Mac TiVo Desktop. Requires music files to be stored in your iTunes library.

Tip

If you have multiple Windows and Mac machines on your network, they can all serve content to your TiVo(s). You simply need to install the appropriate version of the TiVo Desktop app to each of them and make sure each is running. Their music and image content will show up in HMF as separate folders on the top level of the HMF directory. Nifty!

As of this time, the current version of the TiVo Desktop for Mac does not support AAC (Advanced Audio Coding), the data compression scheme used for Apple's iTunes Music Store offerings. AAC is an audio compression standard that is intended to replace MP3. The TiVo Desktop will only serve content from your iTunes library that is in the MP3 format. It will ignore AAC files.

Playing Music on Your TiVo

Once you have your TiVo Desktop application loaded with the music you want to serve, it's time to head on over to TiVo to spin some tunes. To play the music you "published" to the TiVo Desktop, go to TiVo Central -> Music & Photos. Once selected, you'll see your computer login name and the name of your host computer in the onscreen list. So, if your computer's name is Beulah and your name is Blake, you'll see an item called "Blake's Music on Beulah." Selecting this folder displays all of the tracks, folders, and/or playlists you loaded onto the TiVo Desktop (see Figure 15.14).

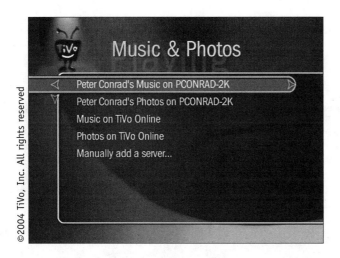

FIGURE 15.14
The Music & Photos
screen showing the available
music and photos
found on the network.

Tip

You can easily make *non-commercial* AAC files
available to the TiVo
Desktop by converting
them to MP3. iTunes has
a built-in converter. Go
to the iTunes menu,
select Preferences, and
then click on the
Importing button.
Choose "MP3 Encoder."
Go to your iTunes library,
select the track(s) you
want to convert, and
then choose "Convert
Selection to MP3" from
the Advanced menu.
Songs bought from the
Apple Music Store cannot
be converted this way.

NOTE

The Options choices
offered from the Song
screen apply to all playback,
not just the particular
song or folder
you're accessing the
Option screen from.

To play tracks, simply scroll up and down within the main Music menu (or subfolder) to choose the track you want to hear and then press Play. You'll be taken to a screen for that song, just as you'd be taken to a Program screen for a TV show. From here, you can play the selection or change various playback features (set playback to shuffle through tracks, repeat, and play through subfolders) by selecting Options.

When you choose Play from the main Song screen, the track begins playing (it may take a few seconds to start) and a Music Banner (see Figure 15.15), just like the TV Channel Banner, pops up (showing song title, artist, album, and other info). When the selected track finishes, the following selection in the list begins. TiVo will continue to play each successive song. When it's done playing all of the files in a folder or playlist, it starts back at the top. If you've selected "Include Subfolders" within the Options, TiVo moves on to any subfolders you have within the folder it's currently playing.

To control music play, you can use the Play, Pause, Fast Forward, and Rewind buttons just as you would with a TV program. Hitting "Instant Replay" takes you back eight seconds in the song. Hitting the "Advance/Skip to Tick" button jumps you forward to the closest tick mark on the Status Bar, just as it would when watching a show. If you've turned on the unofficial 30-second Advance feature (see Chapter 3, "DIY Network Programming"), hitting the "Advance" button jumps you 30-seconds into the track.

FIGURE 15.15
The Music Banner will look familiar to you. The screen displays and main remote features work the same way in Music (here shown using the JavaHMO Server, described later in this chapter).

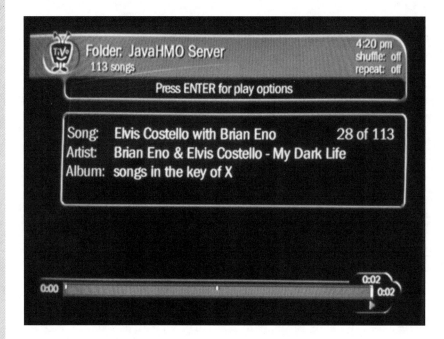

While the music player that comes with TiVo's HMF is okay if you're a casual music listener, if you're a real digital music aficionado, with giga-bytes worth of MP3 files apparently reproducing on your hard drive, you probably want to use an application that's a little more sophisticated. See the section on MoodLogic in "Commercial Third-Party Applications" later in this chapter for one popular solution.

Using The HMF Digital Photos Viewer (Windows)

Photo publishing works almost exactly the same way as music. You simply launch the TiVo Publisher, click on the Photo tab, and navigate through your computer using the directory tree in the left-top pane. When you find the folder that you want to get pictures from, the pictures in that folder appear in the top-right pane. Click on the ones you want to publish and then click the Publish button. Your selected pictures will appear in the bottom pane and are now available for viewing on your TiVo (see Figure 15.16).

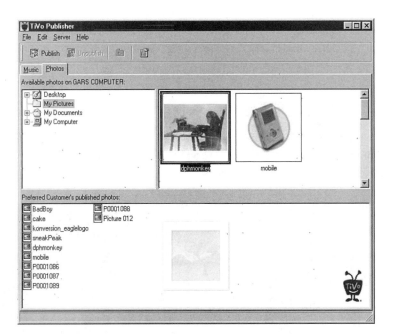

FIGURE 15.16
Publishing photos with
the TiVo Publisher.

Using The HMF Digital Photos Viewer (Mac)

Photo publishing via a Mac works almost exactly the same way as music.
You simply launch the TiVo Desktop app in the System Preferences, and
click on the Photo tab. You will be presented with the contents of your
iPhoto libraries. If you want to publish the entire contents of your Library,
select that radio button. If you only want to select specific albums, you can
check the ones you wish to publish (see Figure 15.17).

FIGURE 15.17
Publishing photos with
the Mac TiVo Desktop.

Viewing Photos on Your TiVo (Windows and Mac)

To see the images you "published" on your TiVo, go to TiVo Central -> Music & Photos. Once there, you'll see your computer login name and the name of your host computer in the onscreen list. So, if your computer's name is Ulro and your name is Urizen, you'll see an item called "Urizen's Music on Ulro," as shown in Figure 15.18. Selecting this item in the list takes you to the Photos page containing all of your published images (and folders of images). TiVo HMF can display images in the JPG, GIF, BMP, TIF, and PNG formats.

FIGURE 15.18

The main Photo page on TiVo.

Tip

If you publish content to the TiVo Desktop and it does not show up on the Music & Photos screen, it's not getting properly served over the network. It probably means that the TiVo Desktop server is not on. On a PC, launch the TiVo Publisher and choose Start/Resume server from the Server pull-down menu. On a Mac, go to System Preferences, launch the TiVo Desktop, and make sure the button on the screen says Stop. It may even be a good idea to hit Stop and then Start again. And for both platforms, restarting your computer is always a good idea.

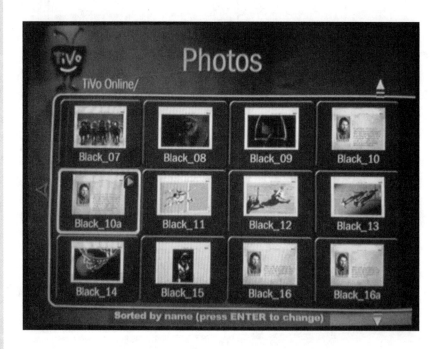

To view a slideshow of a folder, click the Play button on your remote while the folder is highlighted. The slideshow will begin. If you want to view the contents of the folder individually, hit the Select button, navigate through the images within the folder, and press Play for the image you want to view. The remote control's main media navigation buttons (Pause, Fast Forward, Rewind, Play) will move you through the slideshow or folder's contents. The Instant Replay button will jump you back one image, while the Advance button will "skip to tick," taking you a set number of slides forward in your show (relative to how many images you have in the slideshow folder).

Each photo available on your TiVo has its own information screen, similar to a Program screen for TV recordings (see Figure 15.19). This screen contains a thumbnail of the image, a title, dates related to the image (date taken, date imported, date modified), a menu selection to rotate the image 90-degrees clockwise, and some slideshow viewing options. The slideshow options let you set the speed of the show (from two seconds to five minutes), whether to shuffle through the show folder at random, and whether to include any subfolders. These slideshow options apply to all slideshows, not just the one you're currently on. They will stay in effect until you change them.

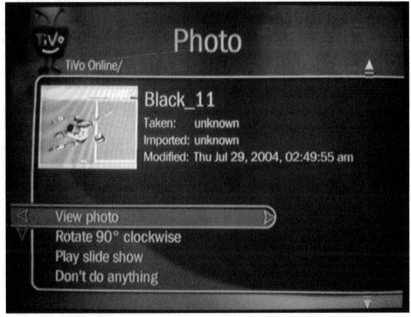

FIGURE 15.19

An individual Photo information screen.

While the photo viewing feature in TiVo's HMF is good enough for what it does, industrious hackers have created open source alternatives to the TiVo Desktop app that use the photo publisher feature for such novel uses as displaying images of local movie listings, weather maps, and Webcam images. See the JavaHMO section later in this chapter for one stellar example of such a freely available third-party application.

Commercial Third-Party Applications

As we mentioned in the introduction, TiVo, Inc. is aggressively signing deals with other hardware, software, and media service providers to extend the capabilities of their Home Media Feature. Here are a few of the current offers you may want to consider test-driving.

MoodLogic

If you have larger numbers of MP3 files and lovely crafted playlists, party mixes, and so on, it won't take long before you hit the wall with TiVo Desktop's music serving capabilities. Enter MoodLogic, a popular digital music program that works with TiVo's HMF (see Figure 15.20). Not only does MoodLogic offer the same basic features as TiVo Desktop, but it adds cool capabilities, such as the SmartMix choice, available on TiVo's Music screen, which will choose tracks in your music libraries based on a track you are currently listening to, so if you're playing Moby and choose SmartMix, it will automatically make a playlist of other similar electronica. You can also create on-the-fly mixes based on mood, so if you find your living room filled with an impromptu party, you can choose "Get Up," and MoodLogic will kick out the jams. Baby left you? Life's so unkind? Choose "Blue" and head for the Scotch and cigarettes (we're kidding about the booze and cancer sticks part).

FIGURE 15.20

MoodLogic, a very versatile MP3 jukebox that works both on your desktop and publishes to your TiVo.

MoodLogic retails for $29.95. You can download a free 14-day trial version at moodlogic.com/tivo.html.

Picasa Digital Picture Organizer

What MoodLogic is to MP3 serving on HMF, Picasa is to digital photos. It has a gorgeous interface, easy-to-use operation, and many built-in picture editing tools. Like MoodLogic, it's not just a TiVo HMF tool, but serves as a full-featured image editor on your desktop PC. The program offers all sorts of ways to organize albums of images, to search on images, build image timelines, and publishing images directly to email and Web logs (on the desktop, not via TiVo). One awesome new feature in Picasa 1.6 is the ability to publish slideshows to your TiVo with an MP3 music file attached (see Figure 15.21). You can create a soundtrack to accompany your slides, or record a narrative on your PC, save it in MP3 format, and attach it to the show. Now you can really bore the bejezuz out of your dinner guests with a complete audio/visual presentation about your spiritually renewing trip to Six Flags.

FIGURE 15.21

Picasa Digital Picture Organizer. A new audio feature allows you to attach soundtracks to slideshows. Oh joy.

Picasa retails for $29. You can download a free 15-day trial version at picasa.net. Picasa is only available for Windows machines (Win98, Me, 2000, XP).

If you're a programmer and want to try your hand at creating applications for TiVo's Home Media Feature, you can download the relevant developer's resources at tivo.com/developer.

Adobe Photoshop Album

Adobe's photo organizer is similar to Picasa, but more expensive ($50), not as user-friendly, and it lacks the ability to attach MP3 files to slideshows. They also don't even offer a trial version. Hey, it's your money: www.adobe.com/tivo.

Free Third-Party Applications

TiVo, Inc. has made the specs for its HMF available to developers so that third-parties can create applications that work with the service. This has allowed programmers to create applications that can be used with HMF, and to offer these applications free of charge.

JavaHMO

By far one of the best of the free HMF apps available is JavaHMO (www.javahmo.com). It is meant as a replacement to the TiVo Desktop (see Figure 15.22). It not only allows you to publish MP3 music and digital photos to your TiVo, but it also adds such useful features as local movie listings, weather maps, and streaming Internet radio on TiVo. Some of these added features are so welcomed by TiVo users that it has convinced more than one to subscribe just so they can use JavaHMO. This program is worth going into some detail about, as we think you might want to seriously consider using it in place of the TiVo Desktop.

FIGURE 15.22

JavaHMO. It ain't pretty, but it has a number of cool features that TiVo, Inc. will hopefully someday add to the TiVo Desktop.

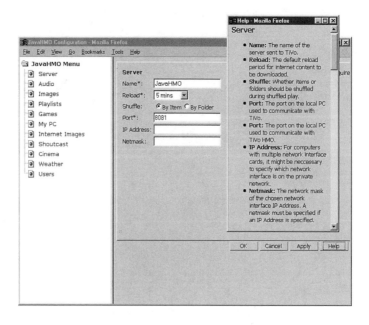

Installing JavaHMO

One of the great things about JavaHMO is that, because it was created in the Java language, it is cross-platform compatible. It can be run on Windows machines, Macs, and on the Linux OS. Installation is a little different on each platform, so let's look at the specifics.

Windows XP

1. To install JavaHMO on your Windows XP, the first thing you'll need to do is download JavaHMO-1.2.exe from javahmo.sourceforge.net/download.html. This version of the download contains the required Java Runtime Environment (JRE) and Java Advanced Imaging (JAI) packages.

2. Before you install JavaHMO, you'll need to either completely uninstall the TiVo Desktop applications or at least disable the TiVo Publisher and the TiVo Connect Beacon (the part of the TiVo server that runs in the background and talks to your TiVo). To shut down the Publisher, simply make sure it's not running. To shut down the Beacon, right-click on the TivoGuy icon in your Taskbar and choose "Exit." To make sure the Connect Beacon doesn't automatically load on reboot, go to Control Panel -> Administrative Tools -> Services. Right-click on the TiVo Connect Beacon icon and choose Stop from the menu. Then under Properties, choose either Manual or Disable in the Startup Settings.

3. Double-click on the javaHMO-1.2.exe file that you downloaded to launch the installation wizard. As part of the install, it will check to see if you have current versions of JRE and JAI installed, and if you do not, it will install them. When you're done, press Finish and restart your PC.

4. On your desktop, you'll see a JavaHMO IE browser page shortcut. Clicking on this takes you to http://localhost:8081/configure. This is the interface page for the JavaHMO service. You can also type this URL into any browser on your desktop to launch the JavaHMO services page (refer to Figure 15.25).

Tip

If you have any problems installing JavaHMO on any platform, go to the JavaHMO project page (www.JavaHMO.com) and check out the FAQ files.

Windows 98

JavaHMO was designed on an XP machine and wasn't optimized for use on Windows 98. That said, it's fairly easy to tweak it so that it will work on Win98. Here's how:

1. Follow the same instructions as Steps 1–3 in the Windows XP installation.

2. When your computer restarts, use the My Computer applet to go to the JavaHMO directory (default path: C:\Program Files\JavaHMO). Click on the bin folder. Inside, you'll find a program file called run.cmd. Change this to a batch command file by changing its name to run.bat.

3. With the run.bat file renamed, double-click on it. This launches Java via MS-DOS. You will need to launch this file each time you want to run JavaHMO, so you may want to create a shortcut on the desktop for easier launching.

4. While the MS-DOS window is onscreen, check to make sure that Java has enough DOS Memory Environment to run properly. Click on the Properties icon at the top of the DOS window and then click on the Memory tab. Make sure it has at least 2816 assigned to its Initial Environment. You can select up to 4096. Click Apply.

5. With the run file renamed and launched, the Memory Space increased (if needed), you're ready to launch JavaHMO. On your desktop, you'll see a JavaHMO IE browser shortcut. Clicking on this takes you to http://localhost:8081/configure. This is the Java interface page for the JavaHMO service. You can also type this URL into any browser on your desktop to launch the JavaHMO services page (refer to Figure 15.25).

Macintosh

1. To install JavaHMO on your Mac (OS X 10.3.1 or higher), the first thing you'll need to do is to download the Java Runtime Environment (JRE) version 1.4.2, Java Advanced Imaging (JAI) 1.0, and JavaHMO-12.dmg, all available or linked from javahmo. sourceforge.net/download.html.

2. Install the JRE and JAI applications first. These should already be part of your Mac system and will only be installed if you don't already have the needed versions.

3. With the Java components installed, double-click on the JavaHMO-12.dmg disk image. When it's unpacked, double-click on the JavaHMO.mpkg. This installs the JavaHMO program and support files (in the usr/share/javaHMO directory). During the installation process, an auto-startup utility is installed (so that JavaHMO auto-loads whenever your reboot your Mac). If you don't want this utility installed, deselect it by using the Customize button on the installation screen. A program called JavaHMO Control is also installed (in your Applications folder). This is basically a "start/stop" button for JavaHMO, to be used if you chose to not install the auto-startup utility (or if you want to turn off TiVo serving for some reason).

4. With the JRE, JAI and the JavaHMO components installed, and your Mac restarted, all you need to do is launch the JavaHMO Control app, and then enter the URL http://localhost:8081/configure in any web browser. This launches the Java interface page for the JavaHMO service (refer to Figure 15.25).

Linux

1. Make sure you're using the root account.

2. Download the Java Runtime Environment (JRE) version 1.4.2, Java Advanced Imaging (JAI) 1.1.2, and javaHMO-1.2-3.i386.rpm, all available or linked from javahmo.sourceforge.net/download.html.

3. Install the JRE and JAI first, accepting all of the default settings offered by the installation wizards.

4. Use the version of RPM (Red Hat Package Manager) that came with your Linux distro to install javaHMO-1.2-3.i386.rpm files.

5. If you're running Red Hat, you can start JavaHMO by running /etc/rc.d/init.d/JavaHMO. If you're on another version of Linux, you can run jhmo start.

6. With the JRE, JAI and the JavaHMO components installed, and your machine restarted, all you need to do to launch JavaHMO is to enter the URL http://localhost:8081/configure in any Web browser. This will launch the Java interface page for the JavaHMO service (refer to Figure 15.25).

NOTE

JavaHMO for Linux assumes you're using the current version of X Window (X11) and that you have set your DISPLAY environment variable. If you are not using X Window, you'll have to edit your wrapper.conf file. See the details of what to edit at javahmo. sourceforge.net/install. html (in the Other section).

Using JavaHMO (The Desktop Side)

Once you have JavaHMO installed, operation is fairly straightforward. The interface is not the prettiest in cyberspace, and some of the operation is not extremely intuitive. But once you learn your way around, you'll begin to see what makes JavaHMO so exciting as a TiVo HMF alternative app. JavaHMO has a lot of features. We won't go into how to use them all here. Clicking on the Help button within each menu item will describe the function of each text entry field, window and button. Here's a list of the main features that JavaHMO offers:

- **Server**—For specifying various behaviors related to JavaHMO's service to TiVo. Contains such controls as how often Internet content (see "Internet Images" below) should be refreshed and whether shuffled content on TiVo should be shuffled based on individual items or folders. If you used a static IP address and subnet mask for your TiVo, you'll also have to enter those numbers here.

- **Audio**—Just as with the TiVo Desktop, only MP3 audio files and playlists are supported. The playlist formats supported are M3U and PLS.

- **Images**—Allows you to publish images to TiVo just as you would with the TiVo Desktop. In JavaHMO, more formats are supported: JPG., GIF, TIF, BMP, PNG, PNM, and FlashPix.

- **Playlists**—A separate area for loading your MP3 playlists.

- **Games**—Currently, JavaHMO offers one game, a very tedious version of tic-tac-toe. Wonderful teaser though for the possibility of future HMF-delivered games. Is this game TiVo's Pong?

- **My PC**—Publishes a screen capture of your PC's desktop to the Photo area on TiVo. There must be some way to use this to find out if the kids (or hubby's) are on their PC downloading Net porn.

- **Internet Images**—Big Brother-esque surveillance comes to TiVo. Enter the address of any Internet Webcam (or any other Internet image) and it will be sent to TiVo's Photo area. The rate at which these images are refreshed is set at the Server menu item.

- **Shoutcast**—Internet streaming radio on your TiVo/home stereo system via shoutcast.com. Select from a scrolling menu of genres and all of the "stations" available in that genre will be available on TiVo. To change genres, you have to make the change in the Shoutcast area of JavaHMO; you can't do it from within TiVo.

- **Cinema**—Entering in your city, state, and ZIP code will let JavaHMO find your local movie listings and send them as images to TiVo.

- **Weather**—Entering in your city, state, and ZIP code will let JavaHMO find local weather maps and send them as images to TiVo.

- **Users**—Allows you to set permissions, with user names and passwords, for who gets to have access to JavaHMO's media/server configurations.

Using JavaHMO (The TiVo Side)

Using JavaHMO on TiVo works exactly the same as with the Music & Photos feature of the TiVo Desktop (see Figure 15.23). You gain access to all of the music, images, and other features you "published" by going to TiVo Central -> Music & Photos. With JavaHMO, the list of available services will be much longer.

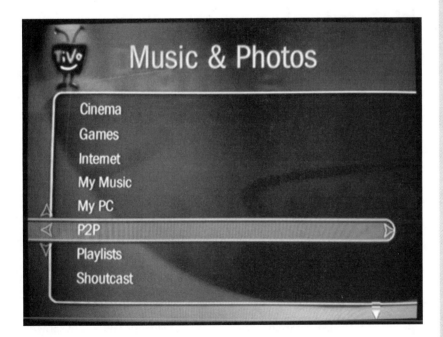

FIGURE 15.23
JavaHMO on TiVo. Look at all those nifty offerings!

Navigating around in JavaHMO on the TiVo works exactly the same as with TV programming and with the music and images using the TiVo Desktop. Refer back to the "Playing Music on Your TiVo" and "Using the HMF Digital Photo Viewer" sections earlier in this chapter for more information on getting around inside of Music & Photos.

What follows in Figure 15.24 and 15.25 are a few screen captures of some of the unique features offered in JavaHMO. The images (and the captions) speak for themselves.

FIGURE 15.24
Hey look, ma, it's the five-day forecast on my TV! Well, I never...!

FIGURE 15.25
And you thought Tic-Tac-Toe was dull on a paper!

Other Free Third Party Apps

There are a number of HMO-related applications out there. A good place to look for applications is at sourceforge.net. Many TiVo related open source projects are hosted there.

Portable Open TiVo HMO Project

If you're on a Linux machine and not using JavaHMO, you can still serve music and images to your TiVo with HMF via the Portable Open TiVo HMF Project, found at sourceforge.net/projects/ptivohmo.

Seeing and Hearing Your Email

If you know your way around the Perl scripting language, you can use the how-tos on Tobias Hoellrich's website, Kahunaburger (www.kahunaburger. com), to turn incoming email on your PC into PNG formatted images for viewing or into MP3 files for playing. The instructions on the site show the scripts he used, what Perl modules you'll need, and what other apps, such as a text-to-speech synthesize program.

Chapter 16

TiVoWeb (Series 1)

As we've already made clear, Series 1 TiVos were never designed for home networking and, certainly, were never designed to join the global virtual community of cyberspace. Their only official link to the outside data world was through a pokey 36.6 analog modem that was wired to a single destination: Tivo, Inc. Hardware such as the 9th Tee TurboNET solved the physical connectivity problem, but what could you do with a Net connection without software that offered the same sorts of remote TiVo control that Series 2's Home Media Feature offers? Enter the TiVoWeb Project.

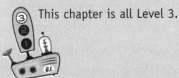
This chapter is all Level 3.

What Is TiVoWeb?

Created by Josha Foust, TiVoWeb is more than just a remote scheduler, a la TiVo, Inc.'s official web-based feature (called TiVo Central Online). It offers nearly the entire workings of your TiVo over the web (plus some awesome added features). We've said throughout this book that Series 1 boxes are popular among tech hobbyists mainly because of their openness and hackability. But for many, the powerful features

Tip

For more about the Tcl scripting language, see Chapter 13, "Touring Your TiVo: The Software."

NOTE

We assume that you already have your S1 TiVo networked, that you've already absorbed the basic networking and Linux intel from earlier chapters (namely, Chapters 9, "Networking Your TiVo"; 10, "Quick 'n' Dirty Serial Networking"; 13, "Touring Your TiVo: The Software"; and 14, "Accessing Your TiVo's Linux Bash Prompt"), and that you've already created a /hack directory in /var. If you haven't already masticated these fine paper-pulp offerings, go back and get ta chewin', or this chapter won't make much sense.

of TiVoWeb are also a big draw. You can do such cool things as read your TiVo messages (or send a message to your TiVo over the Web), cancel programs in the To Do List, organize Season Passes, and even *undelete* programs! You can do all this from a location as close as the web browser in your home office (why get up and go *all* the way into the family room?) or as remote as an Internet cafe in Jakarta. One of the many appreciated features of TiVoWeb is that you can do two things at once (besides watching a show while recording another). You can be reorganizing your Season Passes (over the web) while a show is being recorded and someone is watching a previously recorded show on TiVo.

TiVoWeb is yet another open-source project. Josha Foust is the primary author, but others have chipped in with key components, bug fixes, and useful utilities. TiVoWeb also is set up for plug-in modules that add new functions created and contributed by other TiVo hackers. TiVoWeb is coded entirely in Tcl (starting with version 1.9.4), the same scripting language that TiVo developers used to build myworld, the TiVo user interface. This enables anyone who is proficient in Linux hacking and Tcl scripting to create their own TiVoWeb hacks (and share them with the world over the Internet).

How to Install TiVoWeb

The first thing you need to do is to get TiVoWeb onto your TiVo. A compressed version of the program is included on the book's CD-ROM (in the directory Series 1/TiVoWeb). Using a serial connection and a terminal file transfer (via the rz upload command) or via Telnet/ Ethernet with the tivoftpd server installed on your TiVo (see Chapter 14, "Accessing Your TiVo's Linux Bash Prompt"), move the file tivoweb-tcl-1.9.4.tar.gz into the /var/hack directory.

If you're at the TiVo Bash prompt and want to use TiVo's built-in http_get utility to fetch TiVoWeb from cyberspace (instead of using one of the earlier local transfer methods), enter the following at the command line:

```
http_get -T 0 -C 0 -D /var/hack -U
➥http://199.240.141.102:80/tivoweb-tcl-1.9.4.tar.gz
```

This is the same procedure we used to get tivoftpd onto our TiVo in Chapter 14. See the "Get It the Way TiVo Does" section in that chapter for more information on this command string.

With `tivoweb-tcl-1.9.4.tar.gz` safely moved into the /var/hack directory on TiVo, start unpacking it with the following commands (at Bash):

```
cd /var/hack
gzip -d tivoweb-tcl-1.9.4.tar.gz
cpio -H tar -i < tivoweb-tcl-1.9.4.tar
```

With the tivoweb-tcl program now expanded within /var/hack, you have one more piece of business. The current Genre information that TiVo, Inc. uses is not compatible with TiVoWeb. To deal with this, Josha scripted a fix to the user interface iTcl script (`ui.itcl`). Before you try to launch TiVoWeb, you'll want to replace the existing script with the new one (included in the TiVoWeb folder on this book's CD-ROM). Move it over to your TiVo using your preferred method of transfer. With it in your /var/hack/tivoweb-tcl/modules directory (which was created when you unpacked TiVoWeb), change into that directory and issue this command:

```
mv 00ui.itcl.txt ui.itcl
```

That should do it. You should now be ready to start the TiVoWeb server and log into it via your web browser.

Using TiVoWeb

TiVoWeb offers many cool and useful features (see Table 16.1). Luckily, the developers have done a great job of emulating TiVo's user interface and otherwise creating an extremely easy-to-use remote TiVo control tool. You can pretty much figure out how everything works without requiring any help (it's all the input field, hyperlinks, and buttons you're used to seeing on the web). We're not going to go through all the TiVoWeb features here; we cover just a few of the main ones and a few truly unique ones (such as the capability to undelete programs).

Firing It Up

To use TiVoWeb, you obviously need a connection established between your TiVo and your home network (as detailed in previous chapters). You also need to know the IP address of your TiVo (see Chapter 14 if you don't already have this information). Before you can access TiVoWeb, you need to start it up. At your trusty Bash prompt, enter this:

```
/var/hack/tivoweb-tcl/tivoweb
```

Tip

If you're on a net-connected, dual-tuner-enabled DirecTV DVR, you might want to consider using TiVoWeb Plus (tivo.fp2000.org/twp/). It is a mod of TiVoWeb that offers control over both tuners for program scheduling (TiVoWeb 1.9.4 does not), and a bunch of other cool features.

A bunch of startup information scrolls by. When you see the status line `Accepting Connections`, you know that TiVoWeb is ready for Net access.

Moving over to your web browser, enter the IP address of your TiVo. What you should see on your screen will look similar to Figure 16.1.

FIGURE 16.1
TiVoWeb's "home page" as it appears in your browser window.

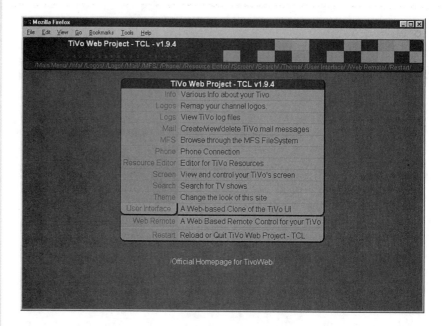

Tip

After you launch TiVoWeb from the Bash prompt, it will serve its pages to the web until you reboot TiVo. If you want the TiVoWeb server to relaunch each time you restart TiVo, see the "TiVoWeb on Startup" section later in this chapter.

TiVoWeb is loaded with features. Table 16.1 lists the Main Menu items and what each is all about.

Table 16.1:   Look at All Them Nifty Features and TiVo Tools

Menu Selection	What It Does	Notes
Main Menu	Acts as TiVoWeb's front page and your gateway to TiVoWeb.	From here, click on text links across the top or in the menu.
Info	Displays information about your TiVo, from what channel it's currently on, to its internal temperature, to which Linux kernel you're running.	This is handy for such excuses as: "Sorry, boss, I gotta get home, my TiVo is overheating!"
Logos	Allows you to assign logos that are stored in TiVo to the Channel Bar and the Now Showing list. You can also create and import your own custom channel logos.	Those of us with actual lives can just hit the Automatically Assign Logos link at the top of the page and be done with it.

Table 16.1:   Continued

Menu Selection	What It Does	Notes
Logs	Displays all of TiVo's log files. Clicking on a logfile link takes you to that log.	The result is the same as if you used the C-E-C ThumbsUp code (see Chapter 4, "Remote Control Freak").
Mail	Allows you to read your TiVo messages from afar and even to send messages to your TiVo, either to the typical Messages menu or as a "pre-TiVoCentral" message.	This is great for ragging on your house-mates: "Leo, you've been watching too much women's beach volleyball. May we recommend more PBS?"
MFS	Acts as a web way into your TiVo's Media File System.	The result is the same as using the `mls tivosh` command over a local Net connection.
Phone	Gives details about your TiVo's phone calls (last call, next call, and so on).	You can use this feature to make daily calls.
Resource Editor	Lets you edit elements within TiVo resources.	You can do such things as change the names of menu items.
Screen	Enables you to view what menu is currently active on TiVo—and change it.	Use it remotely to scare the stuffing out of housemates.
Search	Acts as the program search screen.	Functionality is similar to Search by Title on TiVo itself.
Theme	Uses different looks for the TiVoWeb interface itself.	Stylesheets (CSS) are used to enable you to change the look of your TiVoWeb screens.
User Interface	TiVoWeb's answer to the TiVo GUI.	Contains Now Showing, SeasonPasses, To Do List, and so on.
Web Remote	Acts as a virtual remote for controlling TiVo. Can be used with a wireless keyboard, too.	This actually displays an appropriate remote control image for your model TiVo/remote.
Restart	Restarts TiVoWeb or quits out of it.	This is useful when you are making changes such as resource editing and you want to see those changes implemented.

Searching, Scheduling, and Recording Shows

As with TiVo, Inc.'s Remote Scheduling feature, available to Series 2 stand-alone users, TiVoWeb enables you to search on the upcoming two weeks of programming to look for shows you might want to single-record or to create Season Passes for (see Figure 16.2).

FIGURE 16.2
The TiVoWeb search page.

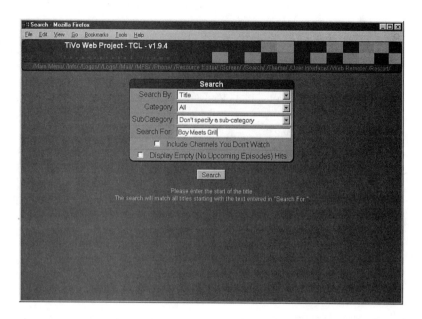

TiVoWeb's search engine is similar to TiVo Central Online. It enables you to search on show title, or keyword, title keyword, actor, or director. Entering a search term and pressing the Search button returns a page similar to the one shown in Figure 16.3.

FIGURE 16.3
TiVoWeb's expanded Search page with results listed and hyperlinked below.

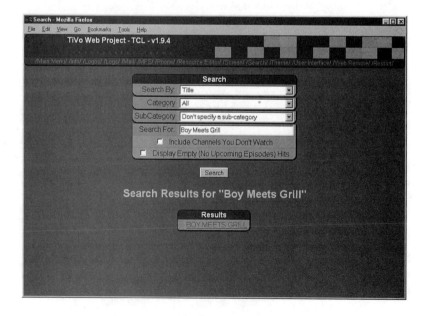

By clicking on the link for an item you're interested in, you're taken to the page for that program. One nifty thing about TiVoWeb is that, if you click on a link to, say an upcoming *Boy Meets Grill*, and you've already recorded episodes of this show, they're listed on the program's page (in a Now Showing list) above the list of upcoming shows (see Figure 16.4).

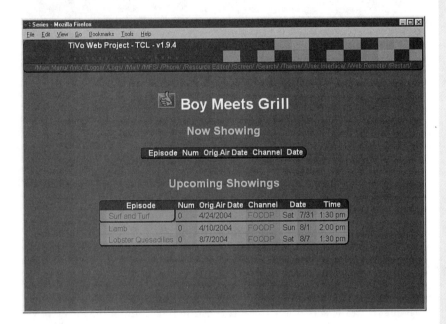

FIGURE 16.4
Boy Meets Grill, and Now Showing meets Upcoming Showings.

Clicking on a program you're interested in recording walks you through a series of screens similar to what you would encounter scheduling TiVo directly (or on Series 2 using TiVo Central Online). You can choose a single recording, create a Season Pass, select recording quality, use Keep at Least, and so on. One other welcome feature of TiVoWeb is the Conflicts button. When you're done setting up your recording and you hit the Conflicts button, TiVo tells you if there are recording conflicts right away (see Figure 16.5). This is how things work if you're setting up a recording directly on TiVo, but if you're on an S2 stand-alone and are scheduling through TiVo's website, you don't know whether there's a conflict until you get robomail in your inbox pointing them out. Because TiVoWeb is served directly from TiVo itself, it alerts you to conflicts before you ask it to record a show.

Tip

One of the funny, tweaky features of TiVoWeb is the capability to edit recording description information in Now Showing. To do this, go to the Now Showing list, click on the link to the show, and then click on Edit Program. There, you can change everything from the title of the show to the description, actors, guest stars, directors, and more. These changes stay with the recorded show until you delete it.

FIGURE 16.5

Chill out. "No Conflicts," mon. You're free to record.

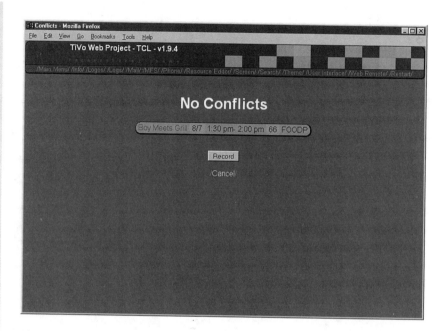

Canceling Scheduled Recordings

Another useful feature that TiVoWeb offers (and TiVo Central Online does not) is the capability to delete recordings that are queued up in either the Scheduled Suggestions list or your To Do List. Along a column on the right side of the screen for these two listing types, you'll see check boxes. All of the items in the list are autochecked, 'cause TiVo has them queued up to record (see Figure 16.6).

When you've selected all the shows you want to kill, by deselecting them, you hit the Cancel button. You'll be asked if you really want to do this. Click Yes, and, vamoose! Becker and Ted Danson are history faster than you can say "Gulliver's Travels."

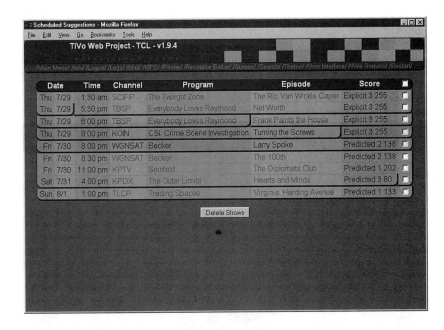

FIGURE 16.6
Schedule Suggestion list ready for recording. If you don't take action, several episodes of *Becker* are slated for TiVo. Make it stop!

Undeleting a Recorded Program

As with any computer, when you delete a program on TiVo, it doesn't actually get sent to bit oblivion right away: The space where it is stored just becomes available to be overwritten with new data. This makes it possible for you to use the recovery utility programs on your PC to sometimes reclaim content you've sent to the trash and removed from access. On a PC, the longer you wait, the less likely recovery is possible. This is even more the case on TiVo because it is frequently writing large media files. But if you delete a program by mistake, TiVoWeb offers the chance to bring it back from the dead.

To use the Undelete feature, go to the Delete Shows menu from the User Interface link. If the screen says "No Shows Available for Undelete," you're out of luck; your show has already been paved over. If there are shows still intact, you'll see a list of recently deleted programs (see Figure 16.7). To undelete a show, simply click on the Recycling icon on the left side of the listing. You'll be asked to confirm. When you press Yes, your previously deleted show is placed back onto your Now Showing list. Nifty!

FIGURE 16.7
TiVoWeb's show reanimator. Undeleting brings shows back from the dead.

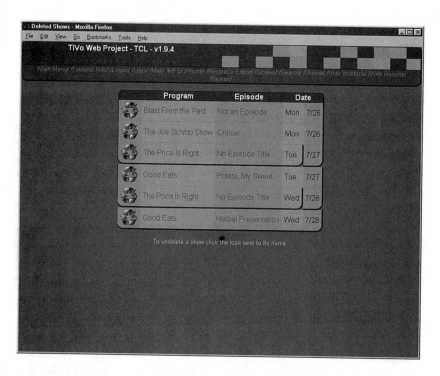

Adding Other TiVoWeb Modules

TiVoWeb is an open-source software project, and, as with most such projects, there are many hands at work. Besides those who've contributed to the creation and improvement of the program itself, there are those who've created additional modules to plug into the program. Because TiVoWeb is all done with Tcl scripting, it is relatively easy for other programmers to code up a script and load it into TiVo.

To add a module, here is what you would do:

1. Grab the module that you want (there's a list of some popular ones on The TiVoWeb Project page, tivo.lightn.org, and more at alt.org/wiki/index.php/TiVoWeb%20Modules) and download it to your PC.

2. Using your preferred method of transfer, move it into the directory at /var/hack/tivoweb-tcl/modules.

3. Go to your TiVoWeb home page and choose Restart and then Quick Reload. The TiVoWeb server restarts, and the new module is loaded into the appropriate menu.

That's it. It's actually that easy.

Given the ease of adding functions to TiVoWeb, it's a shame there aren't more modules available. A few of note:

- **Movie Search**—A module that's optimized for specifically rooting out films of interest from the TiVo guide data.

- **DisplayText**—This module enables you to enter text, along with color options and screen placement, and send it to pop up on top of whatever TiVo is currently displaying. Send messages to your kids from work: "Turn off SpongeBob and do your homework!"

- **Now Showing with Sort and Folders**—One of the features that Series 2 software offers that S1 does not is the capability to organize programs in Now Showing into folders. This Tcl modules brings that functionality to Series 1 (see Figure 16.8).

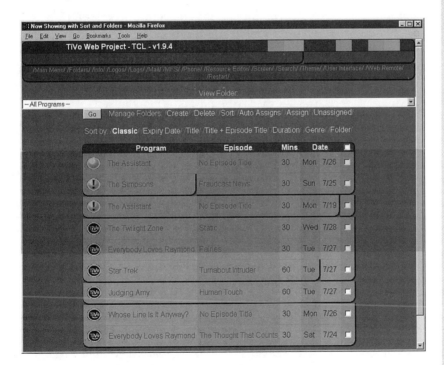

FIGURE 16.8
The Now Showing with Sort and Folders TiVoWeb module, ready for action.

TiVoWeb on Startup

As we mentioned earlier, launching TiVoWeb from the command line as we did at the beginning of this chapter keeps it running only until you reboot your TiVo. Fortunately, you don't have to restart your TiVo very often (they are Linux boxes, after all), but eventually, you will, and you don't want to have to restart the TiVoWeb server from Bash every time you do. This is easily dealt with by amending the `rc.sysinit` file in a similar manner to what you did to keep your Telnet and FTP daemons at work after a reboot. At the Bash prompt, enter the following:

```
mount -o remount,rw /
echo "/var/hack/tivoweb-tcl/tivoweb" ¦ cat
➥/etc/rc.d/rc.sysinit
mount -o remount,ro /
```

Now TiVoWeb should always be available as long as your TiVo is powered up and your home network is running.

The Future of TiVoWeb

The future of TiVoWeb is obviously tied to the future of Series 1 TiVo itself. As the competition heats up in the DVR market, with big players such as Comcast and Time-Warner assailing little ol' TiVo, TiVo, Inc. is throwing everything at consumers to try to get them to buy new (Series 2) TiVos. When we started this book, the Home Media Option cost $100 (for the first TiVo—$50 for each additional TiVo), and TiVo's monthly service fee was $13 per box. As we finish up the book, HMO is now free (and called Home Media Feature), and if you have more than one TiVo, additional boxes are only $7 per month. The prices of Series 2 stand-alone TiVos have fallen dramatically as well. As we type this, TiVo, Inc. is offering 40-hour reconditioned S2 TiVos for $49! Pretty soon, they might be giving 'em away. For real.

For those interested in getting down 'n' dirty with TiVo hacking, this presents a great opportunity. As less tech-savvy users upgrade to Series 2, they're giving away their Series 1 machines or unloading them dirt-cheap on eBay. Score, dude! If you're looking to play around with the Series 1 hacks in this book, even if you already have a Series 2 machine, ask around. You might find friends with Series 1 boxes now gathering dust. We know of two Penguinheaded friends who were "gifted" with S1 machines in the last week alone (at the time this was written). When they get in there and start rearranging the furniture, who knows what wonders they might code up? TiVoWeb and other open-source TiVo projects could enjoy a spike in development, thanks to this likely increase in hand-me-down DVRs. That said, it's just a matter of time before S1 TiVos are as antiquated as Ataris and the Commodore 64, so get while the gettin' is good.

Tip

The modules listed on the TiVoWeb Project page (tivo.lightn.org) are not nearly up-to-date. There are numerous other modules floating around out there, and new ones show up all the time. Do Google searches and keep your eye on tivocommunity.com for the latest (such as ChannelGrid, a module that brings the *TV Guide*-style grid layout to guide data).

Chapter 17

Other TiVo Apps

In this chapter, we look at some of the third-party applications that
have been written for use with TiVo. The bad news for Series 2 users
is that most of these apps are for Series 1 TiVos (both stand-alones and
DirecTV DVRs). The good news is that much of their functionality
can be found in either the official Home Media Feature software or
third-party HMF apps, such as JavaHMO (see Chapter 16, "Home
Media Feature"). For each application in this chapter, we'll tell you
which versions of TiVo it works with (if we know). We'll also tell you
which apps are available on the included CD-ROM.

All apps in this chapter should be considered Level 3 unless
otherwise noted.

elseed

The chips used on most DirecTV DVRs have a built-in caller ID function. This small program, created by Greg Gardner, can be used in
conjunction with a caller ID phone service to display caller ID information on your TV screen through TiVo. You don't need a home network connection to use it; you just need to have your TiVo hooked up
to your home phone line (and have caller ID on it). It's known to work
with DirecTiVo models Phillips DirecTiVo DSR6000, Sony

Tip

Before you undertake
the installation of any
of the software in this
chapter (or on this
book's CD-ROM), do a
search for discussions of
the same on
tivocommunity.com and
dealdatabase.com/
forum. Computers are
like little ecosystems:
They all have their own
unique character, vulner-
abilities, and so on.
With TiVo, there are
many different models,
software versions, different hardware compo-
nents used, and so on.
The software you're
interested in will likely
have a topic (or several)
detailing the successes
or failures of installation
on different types of
TiVos. You can also ask
questions if they aren't
already answered in the
topics. The TiVo users on
these forums are gener-
ally very helpful. Also
visit the sites of the
developers (listed here)
for new versions, bug
fixes, FAQs, and more.

DirecTiVo SAT-T60, and Hughes DirecTiVo GXCEB0T. It might work with others. It also might *not* work with one of the previously mentioned boxes if different modem components were used. Apparently, different components have been used in the same model TiVos, causing problems for this hack. The README file that comes with the app has some suggestions for troubleshooting problems you might encounter. elseed is included on this book's CD-ROM.

JPEGWriter

This little app enables you to display images in the JPEG format on your TV through TiVo. Images appear in 256 colors and are autoscaled to 1/2, 1/4, or 1/8 of their actual size to fit-to-screen. This application is especially useful (and required) as a support app in programs such as TiVo Control Station (see later in this chapter) for displaying things such as weather maps. A copy of JPEGWriter is included on the CD-ROM (in the Series1/TCS folder). It works only on Series 1 machines, both stand-alone and DirecTV DVR.

GAIM

If the host PC on your home network is a Linux box, you might want to take a look at GAIM, an instant-messaging (IM) app that, with a TiVo support app called gaim2tivo installed, will send IMs from AOL's IM program, ICQ, MSN Messenger, Yahoo! Instant Messenger, and even IRC accounts. When a message comes in to any of the running apps, it gets sent over your LAN to your TiVo and pops up in a text box. Just think, all of that deep, witty, real-time IM chatter can now interrupt your riveted viewing of *Who Wants to Marry My Dad?*! There is a Windows version of GAIM, and TiVo users have installed it with varying degrees of success. If you're up to the challenge and you just can't *think* about living without IM overlaying your favorite shows (now that you know it's possible), you might want to give it a try. You can download GAIM (Readme docs, users forum, and so on) at sourceforge.net/projects/gaim/. You can get the TiVo plug-in (and read about the ins and outs of using it) through this topic on the DealDatabase Forums: http://www.dealdatabase.com/forum/showthread.php?threadid=14453.

TiVoVBI

To use Closed Captioning on your TiVo, you *can* use the CC feature on your TV set, but it's a hassle to switch back and forth between the TV control menus and TiVo. TiVoVBI is a little app that puts Closed Captioning capability onto your TiVo (even for older TV displays that don't have CC), and it enables you to create log files of CC data. It can also keep up with TiVo's fast forward and rewind features. If you've ever watched Pat and Kenny on the *Late Show with David Letterman* reading *Oprah* transcripts and wished that you could play along at home, now you can (you go, girl-friend!). TiVoVBI works on both Series 1 stand-alone and DirecTV DVRs. You need to install a kernel modification to use TiVoVBI that's different depending on whether you're on a stand-alone or DirecTiVo. Here are the respective links:

> http://tivo.samba.org/download/mbm/bin/tvbi.o (for SA S1)

> tivo.samba.org/download/mbm/bin/tvbi-dtv.o (for DirecTV DVRs)

One of the many cool things about TiVo Control Station is that it enables you to turn TiVoVBI on and off from your remote. Otherwise, you have to issue Bash commands (or one of the earlier TCL scripts you can find online that will do the same thing) to use it. If you have TCS installed, after installing TiVoVBI (and the appropriate kernel mode), you can press the Clear-5-Clear buttons on the remote to toggle it on, and you can press 5-5-Clear to toggle it off. A copy of the TiVoVBI is available on the CD.

TiVo Control Station (TCS)

TiVo Control Station is a sort of uber-application (hence the name) that can control a number of TiVo software hacks that bring web-based content to your TiVo. Currently, TCS offers stock quotes, sports scores, and weather forecasts and maps. In all cases, the information is laid over the TV signal in colored text (except for the weather maps, which display as, well, maps). All of the apps and content in TCS are controlled by the remote, so, for instance, to see the day's baseball scores while watching *The View* (oh, the humanity!), you would press 6-1-Clear on your remote.

If you want to take a peek at stock indexes and particular stocks while you're watching *The Apprentice* (to see if "You're fired!"), all you have to do is press Clear-7-Clear. You can even configure the indexes and stocks you want to watch by editing a configuration file. You can learn more about the workings of TCS at www.zirakzigil.net/tivo/TCS.html.

A copy of the program and the README file are included on the CD. To run TCS, you need a couple of support applications as well:

- newtext2osd (needed for onscreen display [OSD] of text)
- ps command (for clean TCS startup, shutdown, and processes killing)
- JPEGWriter (for displaying onscreen weather maps)

Copies of all these apps are also included on the CD-ROM. See Figures 17.1, 17.2, and 17.3.

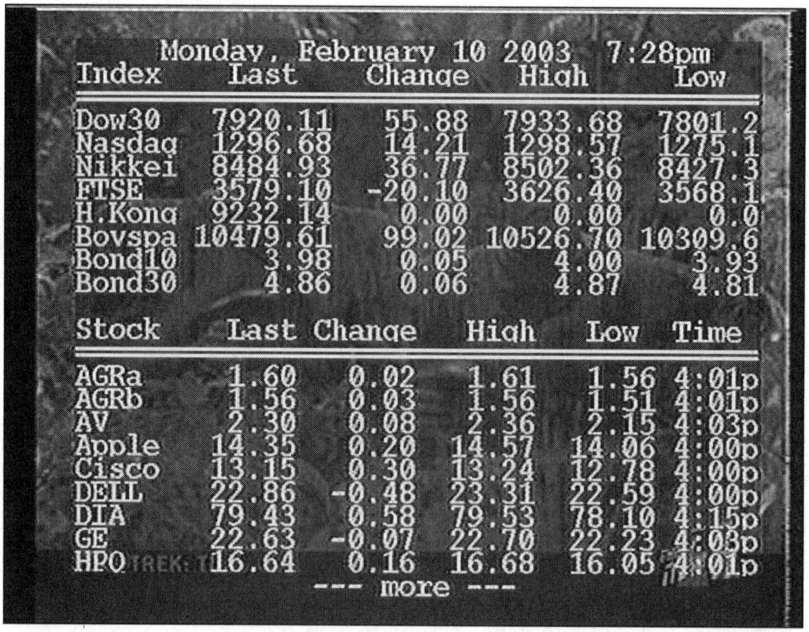

FIGURE 17.1
Stock quotes displayed onscreen via TCS (watch the market act as unruly as Donald Trump's hair). This image is the property of www.zirakzigil.net.

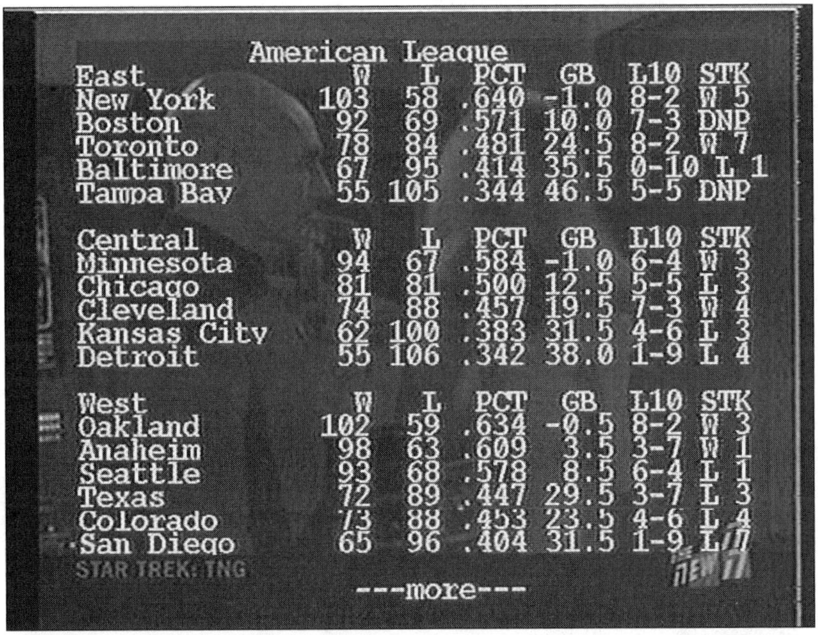

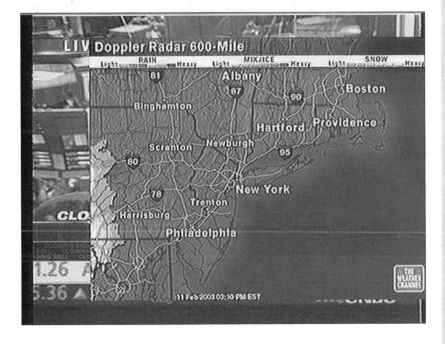

FIGURE 17.2
Sports scores viewable at any time with the click of the remote. This image is the property of www.zirakzigil.net.

FIGURE 17.3
Check out the groovy weather maps you can display with TCS and JPEGWriter. This image is the property of www.zirakzigil.net.

TiVo Control Station works with both Series 1 stand-alone and Series 1 DirecTV DVRs. Some of the components in TCS work on a hacked Series 2 stand-alone, but others don't. The creator is looking for feedback on successes and failures with S2 use, so if you get it working on an S2 machine, contact him via the previous URL. TCS is shareware, by the way, so if you install it, be sure to send the creator his $15 shareware fee (details appear on the website).

TiVo MPlayer

In Chapter 15, "TiVoWeb," we talked about being able to transfer tyStreams (that is, TiVo media content) from your Series 1 TiVo to your PC. If you want to play back .ty files directly, you need a program such as MPlayer to do it. The interface is no nonsense, with your PC's arrow keys used to go forward and reverse in the programs. Versions can run under Windows and can be compiled to run on Mac OS X and Linux/Unix machines. Instructions (not for the weak of heart) and binaries are available at tivo-mplayer.sourceforge.net.

TPOP (TiVo Email)

This handy little app enables you to receive email within TiVo's messaging system, provided that you have the venerable POP3-type (Post Office Protocol) email account. It does not support the newer Internet Message Access Protocol (IMAP) standard. The program is fairly easy to install; after you have installed it, all you have to do is tell it (through a command-line configuration) the IP address of your POP3 account, your username, and your password. Then, when you get email to your Internet email account, you'll see the email icon on your TiVo Central screen, and you can navigate through messages (read, save, delete) just as you would the messages from TiVo, Inc. Of course, you can't respond to the messages; you can just read them. We're not sure whether TPOP works on Series 2 stand-alones (it obviously can't work on Series 2 DirecTV DVRs because they have no network capability). TPOP works on both stand-alone and DirecTV DVR units, as long as they're networked. To download a copy of TPOP, check out this thread on TiVocommunity.com: www.tivocommunity.com/tivo-vb/showthread.php?s=&threadid=69479&perpage=20&pagenuber=1.

There are links to a downloadable copy. Be sure to read through the entire thread and download the latest version, which, as of this writing, is at www.tivocommunity.com/tivo-vb/showthread.php?postid=1977730#post1977730.

Caution

Obviously, a software backup should always precede the installation of any unofficial software on your TiVo. Remember the rule: If you can't afford to lose it, back it up—and you certainly can't afford to risk your TiVo OS unless you have a copy of it stored on your PC (or on your original TiVo HD that you safely saved in a closet someplace after a drive upgrade).

TyStudio

As we're sure you know by now, the media files created, stored, and retrieved within TiVo are called .ty files (or tyStreams). Every dyed-in-the-wool TiVo hacker eventually wants to know how to get access to these "streams," for sending to their PC, for editing, and for converting to other nonproprietary formats. This is what TyStudio is all about. This open-source software project offers a suite of tools to extract, edit, and convert tyStreams. With a Series 1 TiVo on a network, you can grab shows to your PC, edit out commercials, convert to MPEG-2 for burning to CD, and more. There is no Series 2 support for TyStudio yet, but the developers are looking for programmers to make that happen. There is also no version of TyStudio for the Mac, but that's allegedly in the works. What's more, the developers are working on a new version of TyStudio that includes support for creating DVDs, making DVD menus, and so on. To learn more about TyStudio, and to download the appropriate version for your PC, go to dvd-create.sourceforge.net/tystudio.

YAC

YAC (the initials stand for "Yet Another Caller ID") is a little app that uses your PC's analog modem (assuming that you still have one of those in or attached to your computer) and your phone system's caller ID service (assuming that you subscribe to one) to display caller ID information on your computer screen. That's on the PC side. To also show the caller ID information on your TV screen through TiVo, you need to install an app on TiVo called a listener. YAC on the PC works only with analog modems that support caller ID. If you have one of those old and ubiquitous WinModems (let's all give a big raspberry in the general direction of this much-hated piece o' poo), it will likely not work.

Because the program is fairly easy to install (and, yeah, look, it's on our CD!), you can try loading it, hooking up your modem, and then calling your landline (from a cellphone, or get a friend to call) to see if it works. If it does, you can go ahead and install the listener on your TiVo. And don't forget other PCs on your network.

Any Windows PC can also get a listener (available in the software bundle), and caller ID info will simultaneously display on all computers on the net. YAC is compatible with both networked Series 1 and Series 2 stand-alones and Series 1 DirecTV DVRs (see Figure 17.4). For more information, check out sunflowerhead.com/software/yac/.

FIGURE 17.4
YAC-ity yac: It's your mother-in-law—don't talk back!

Tip

If you're on a Linux PC, there's now a YAC client for you, too, called xyac. You can download it at www.bah.org/~greg/tivo/xyac/.

JavaHMO

Just so that owners of stand-alone Series 2 TiVos don't feel totally left out, we wanted to take this opportunity to remind you of the wonders of JavaHMO, the open-source app that can be used to replace the TiVo Desktop program. We discussed this program in detail in Chapter 16. This program, which is relatively easy to set up, not only provides what the TiVo Desktop app does (namely, music and digital photos from PC to TiVo), but it also offers features that even many of the Series 1 third-party apps do not provide, such as local movie listings, Internet streaming radio, and Internet Webcam.

Now that TiVo is offering the Home Media Feature for free, if you're on a Series 2 stand-alone and have a home network, there really is no reason not to install JavaHMO and to plug your TiVo into the mainline media feed of cyberspace. We can guarantee that TiVo Inc. is opening up this channel for free because (besides trying to stay competitive with new players in the DVR market, such as the cable giants) it's also setting us up for all sorts of new and cool features (such as TiVoToGo). The JavaHMO project page can be found at javahmo.sourceforge.net.

Deep Geeks Are Doin' It for Themselves

These are just some of the third-party open-source apps that have been created to work with the different flavors of TiVo. There are many more programs and more in the works. Expect to see additional programs (and easier hacking tools) for Series 2 machines, as more hacker-types get a hold of them. So far, many hardcore programmer types have been clinging to their more hack-friendly Series 1 boxes and have turned up their noses at S2 technology. But with prices for brand-new Series 2 machines getting so temptingly low, and curiosity being what it is, eventually more of these folks are going to start cracking the lids on S2s and coding new apps. So, keep your eyes peeled on sites such as dealdatabase.com, tivocommunity.com, and sourceforge.net. And don't forget to check out tivo.com on a regular basis. The site frequently announces officially supported software and services there. They're working the deals pretty hard these days, so keep an eye out for holiday specials, factory reconditioned machines, and other promotions.

In the next chapter, we'll run down some TiVo-specific and general Linux/Unix utilities that you might want to consider if you're doing any significant software hacking, serial networking, DIY drive prepping, and the like.

Part  IV

Resources

On the Web

Here's a list of TiVo-related resources that can be found on the Web.

TiVo Retailers

You can buy new (Series 2) TiVo units in many local consumer electronics stores, such as Best Buy and Circuit City, but if you want to buy online, here are a few retailers to consider.

Abt Electronics (www.abtelectronics.com)

This consumer electronics company has been in business for 68 years. They claim that they're the largest independent retailer of consumer electronic gear. One of the benefits of buying from Abt is that it's a one-stop shop. While you're buying your TiVo, you can toss an iPod, a plasma HDTV, a home theater sound system, and a Sony VAIO into your cart. Wait a minute, maybe that's *not* such a good thing.

Amazon (www.amazon.com)

This mother of all etailers is always a good place to check for deals. For instance, at the time of this writing they had the 40-hour SA TiVo for ten dollars less than TiVo, Inc.

Resources

DirecTV (www.directv.com)

You can purchase DirecTV satellite systems and service (including DirecTiVos) in a brick and mortar store, but if you want to, you can also buy directly from DirecTV's Web site.

DigitalRecorder.Com (www.digitalrecorder.com)

A full-service supplier of stand-alone TiVos, DirecTiVos, and ReplayTVs. Besides selling new units, they also provide upgrade and repair services, and sell parts and DIY upgrade kits. They have tricked-out TiVos with up to 340 hours of record time. Their upgraded units ship with six months parts and labor warranty and two years warranty on the hard drives.

eBay (www.ebay.com)

Don't forget that eBay as a source of both new and used TiVos (and ReplayTVs). This is especially a great place to look for a used Series 1 box if you want to do a lot of hacking, have easy access to backdoors, and so forth.

TiVo, Inc. (www.tivo.com)

TiVo sells their TiVo-branded SA models (duh) from their website. Besides new units with 40, 80, and 140 hours of record time, they carry factory refurbished Series 2 stand-alones for as low as $99 (after a $50 rebate). They also sell parts and accessories, such as remotes, wireless phone jacks, network adapters, and surge protectors.

TV Authority (www.tvauthority.com)

If you're looking for an online retailer that carries all sorts of cutting-edge A/V equipment, check out this site. TV Authority carries Plasma TVs and monitors, HDTVs, HD tuners, projection TVs, home theater audio equipment, and accessories. Oh yeah, and TiVos, too.

WeaKnees (www.weaknees.com)

Our pals at WeaKnees sell new stand-alone units upgraded with as much as 320 hours of recording time and DirecTiVo units upgraded to 240 hours. They also sell the Toshiba DVD players with TiVo and the Pioneer DVD/TiVo Recorders. They carry a complete line of prepared hard drive kits (no computer required), hard drive pulls (yanked from new TiVos), and accessories and replacement parts. The site also includes some excellent troubleshooting info, FAQs, and more.

Upgrade Kit Suppliers

Upgrade kits allow you to replace your current TiVo hard drive or to add a second drive, often without even having to connect the drives to a PC. You tell the supplier what model TiVo you have and they supply drives with the proper TiVo OS already installed.

DigitalRecorder.Com (www.digitalrecorder.com)

See *TiVo Retailers*

eBay (www.ebay.com)

If you want to find inexpensive used hard drives for a complete do-it-yourself drive upgrade, check out what's available here.

See *TiVo Retailers*

PTVupgrade.com (ptvupgrade.com)

PTV was one of the first vendors to offer upgrading parts for TiVos. They sell prepared upgrade kits (up to a mind-boggling 640 hours of record time), networking parts for Series 1 TiVos, and the TiVo CacheCARD (for adding cache memory to Series 1 SA and DirecTiVos). They also sell software for more easily upgrading your own new HDs (without having to use apps like BlessTiVo) and offer professional installation services.

WeaKnees (weakness.com)

See *TiVo Retailers*

Parts Suppliers

For do-it-yourself TiVo-related projects (such as adding a networking card, installing a multiswitch for a satellite system, or wiring your house for multi-media services), check out these suppliers.

9th Tee (www.9thtee.com)

9th Tee has been selling TiVo parts since 1999. They specialize in networking components, such as the TurboNet and AirNet cards for Series 1 machines, and they're a reseller of PTVupgrade kits. They also carry all sorts of media and computing supplies, from satellite multiswitches to cable organizing components, to tools for doing electronics work.

Hovis Direct (www.hovisdirect.com)

Hovis sells parts for networking a JP1-compliant remote control (see Chapter 4, "Remote Control Freak") with your PC. They sell ready-made JP1 cables as well as the parts to make one yourself. They also have how-to JP1 articles, software downloads, and links to other JP1 sites.

JP1 Cables (jp1.filebug.com)

Another seller of JP1 cables for connecting universal remotes to PCs.

PTVupgrade.com (www.ptvupgrade.com)

See *Upgrade Kit Suppliers*

Radio Shack (www.radioshack.com)

Radio Shack stores are an amazing convenience that many of us persnickety geeks take for granted (in our desire for them to carry even *more* of what we want). Where else can you find, often in your own neighborhood, nearly every A/V accessory mentioned in this book (along with dozens more), electronic components and tools, and computer parts, along with TVs, cameras, phones, and dozens of types of batteries? Sure some things are overpriced and the do-it-yourselfer section is shrinking faster than America's marshlands, but it's the convenience that'll keep you coming back.

SmartHome (www.smarthome.com)

A small tribe of TiVo devotees are also home automation enthusiasts. These are the folks who like their homes to talk to them, sense their movements (or the unauthorized movements of others), keep a constant mechanical eye on the yard, and automatically dispense dinner for the dog. For these gadgeteers, TiVo, a media computer for their TV, fits perfectly into this early-adopted automated, Jetsonian lifestyle. So where do they get those wonderful toys? At online shops like SmartHome. SmartHome carries every type of A/V and home automation component, from full-blown home theater systems to all types of media wiring, in-wall and out. If you're thinking of putting together a media center, complete with a distribution panel (where all of your services come into [and out of] a central control box), SmartHome has all the parts you're looking for. They sell the full line of Leviton Integrated Network products, which can handle all of your coax, cat5, phone, A/V cables, and even backup power supplies.

TiVo, Inc. (www.tivo.com)

See *TiVo Retailers*

TiVo Parts (www.tivoparts.com)

Yet another supplier of refurbished TiVos, hard drives, parts and support gear, such as cables, splitters, adapters, etc.

WeaKnees (www.weaknees.com)

See *TiVo Retailers*

Tutorials

If you want to learn more about the Linux OS, programmable universal remotes, and various aspects of TiVo hacking, there are plenty of tutorials available online. To track down more, try a Google search on what you want to learn, plus "how-to" or "tutorial."

Bash Programming—Introduction How-To (www.tldp.org/ HOWTO/Bash-Prog-Intro-HOWTO.html)

If you're new to the bash shell, this online tutorial will get you up to speed pretty quickly (assuming you already have some familiarity with Linux/Unix or at least working with a command-line interface).

Hi-Fi Remote (www.hifi-remote.com/ofa/)

This site has all sorts of articles, how-tos, reviews, tips and tricks, and discussion related to JP1 remotes (especially those from Radio Shack and One-for-All). A great place to read up about this popular type of hackable remote before buying one.

The Hindsdale How-To (www.newreleasesvideo.com/hinsdale-how-to)

Before there were books about hacking and upgrading your TiVo, there was the Hindsdale How-To. It takes you step-by-step through the process of turning a new, unformatted hard drive (or drives) into a TiVo drive. It shows this process using popular TiVo utility programs such as Mfs Tools and BlessTiVo. BTW: In case you're wondering, Hindsdale is not a person; it's a place, as in Hindsdale, IL.

Interactive TiVo Upgrade Instructions (tivo.upgrade-instructions.com)

If you're looking for a set of customized upgrade instructions that will ask you questions about your TiVo model and upgrade desires, and then produce a set of steps for your specific situation, you'll want to check out this website. After answering three short screens of questions, you get all of the instructions you need for a DIY storage upgrade.

Linux HowTos (howtos.linux.com)

Part of the Linux Documentation Project (www.tldp.org), this site offers dozens of how-tos on every aspect of Linux installation and operation. The entire linux.com site is a great resource for anyone interested in this powerful OS.

TiVo Network Hack How-To Guide (tivo.stevejenkins.com/network.html)

Site author Steve Jenkins does a fantastic job of explaining the process of networking your Series 1 SA or DirecTiVo using the 9th Tee TurboNet card (for connecting your TiVo to an Ethernet network).

TiVo Wiring Guide (www.electrophobia.com/tivo)

Wiring up a home media system can be confusing. It's actually rather straightforward when you think about it—as we tried to explain in Chapter 2, "Getting the Most Out of Your TiVo"—but looking at all those snakey wires can make you go a little funny in the head. This site offers dozens of simple wiring diagrams showing many common hookup situations. Even if your exact configuration is not found here, you should be able to figure out your situation from what is.

Discussion Groups, Blogs, Portals

There is a very active community of TiVo users online. Sites like the AVS Forum and the TiVo Community Forum are great places to learn about every aspect of TiVo, from up-to-date tips on buying units, to working through software or hardware problems, to installing user-created apps and other deep hacks.

AVS Forum (www.avsforum.com)

This site, the Audio-Visual Science Forum, is one of the must-visit online watering holes for TiVo and A/V enthusiasts. Unlike the TiVo Community Forum (see below), this bulletin board covers all aspects of home media, including PVR tech. It's a good place to go to put this one part of your media system into a larger context. People often confuse AVS Forum with the TiVo Community Forum because they used to be one and the same before the TiVo part became its own discrete entity. For that reason, the most up-to-date TiVo info is usually found on tivo-community.com, though you'll be rewarded with plenty of great insights and intel by including the AVS Forum in your regular online travels.

Darkwing's DTiVo Links (www.angelfire.com/darkside/wanker)

A recommended site for links to dozens of software hacks and applications for Series 1 DirecTiVo. Also includes two lengthy tutorials on using versions 2.x and 3.1 of the DirecTiVo software, including info on using many of the apps and mods linked to on the site. Caution: Pop-ups Ahead.

DealDatabase Forums (www.dealdatabase.com)

As the name implies, this website is about getting good deals on consumer products, even how to get all sorts of freebies. Want a free sample of "tushy wipes" or Tiffany perfume? DealDatabase will hook you up. But getting that clean, fresh feeling for free is not why we're listing it here. DealDatabase has a very active TiVo hacking forum. Because it's not associated with TiVo, Inc. (as the TiVo Community Forums are), users are free to discuss such forbidden topics as extracting video from TiVo.

Linux Online (www.linux.org)

All roads to Linux start on this website, or they should, at least for those new to the OS. The site does an excellent job of introducing newbies to Linux and keeping every penguinhead informed about what's happening in the world of open source software. Their Linux 101 courses are a great way to get you started.

PVRblog.com (www.pvrblog.com)

Bookmark this weblog and it will keep you up to date on all of the news, new product announcements, how-to articles, and reviews related to the whole field of personal video recorders (not just TiVo). The blog is run by Matt Haughey, creative director at Creative Commons (creativecommons.org), with contributions from Raffi Krikorian, author of *TiVo Hacks*, and others.

Tcl Developer Xchange (www.tcl.tk)

If you want to learn how to use the Tcl scripting language for creating your own TiVo apps, this site is a recommended resource. Includes The Tcler's WiKi, a collaborative collection of Tcl tutorials, tips and tricks, and links to many other Tcl-related sites and resources.

TiVo Community Forums (www.tivocommunity.com)

If you bookmark one site from this list, this should be it. This active community of TiVo users discusses every aspect of TiVo, from how to get started, to more "power user" concerns such as TiVo networking and drive upgrading, to hardcore hardware hacking. One cool thing about the TiVo Community is that they just don't talk about the technology of TiVo, they talk about TV itself, making it a great place to get a heads up on new shows to record, returning shows, and schedule changes (which can mess up your scheduled recordings), as well as to debate the medium in general.

JP1 Users Group on Yahoo! (groups.yahoo.com/group/jp1)

A place to discuss interfacing a JP1-enabled universal remote to your PC for customizing the button functions. When you find yourself talking about "shift-cloaking" and "toad-toggling" your remote buttons (don't ask), you'll know you've become a true A/V geek (and you might be in need of professional help).

TV-Related Web Sites

Sometimes, TiVo hackers get so enamored with tweaking their units (er...so to speak) that they seem to forget that what this is really all about is motion pictures, the boob tube, the telly, the idiot box, the electronic babysitter, the square-headed girlfriend, you know: TELEVISION! We're card-carrying media citizens and we not only like TV, we like other media *about* television. Here are a few recommended sites.

Lost Remote (www.lostremote.com)

Run by a couple of TV executives, this site covers the business, politics, technology, and culture of the TV industry, with an emphasis on the cutting-edge.

TVBarn (www.tvbarn.com)

Aaron Barnhart has been the TV critic of the *Kansas City Star* since 1997. He got the gig thanks to the popular e-zine, "Late Show News," which he mailed out for years before that. Aaron was also a true DIY publishing pioneer—he self-published his own *Barnhart Guide to TV* for several seasons, selling copies over the Internet. The TVBarn site contains Aaron's columns, links to his TV discussion forum, and entertainment news headlines. His weekly mailing list (which you can sign up for on the site), contains guest line-ups for the coming week's talk shows. This list is a great tool to have in-hand when creating auto-record WishList items so you can catch your favorite actors, musicians, and politicians as they make the talk show circuit.

TV Tome (www.tvtome.com)

This ambitious volunteer-built site is sort of like TV's answer to the Internet Movie Database (www.imdb.com). The site's creators are trying to build a comprehensive guide to every episode of every TV show ever broadcast. So far, they have 1,700 completed show guides and 2,800 partial guides. They also have pages devoted to over 180,000 people associated with TV (actors, directors, and producers), with pictures, bios, and so on. An awe-inspiring labor of love.

TV Week (www.tvweek.com)

This web edition of the weekly TV industry newspaper covers all forms of broadcast, cable, and interactive media. Their "Converging Media" section will be of particular interest to TiVo fans. It is here that you'll learn about such lovely "innovations" as RipeTV's "TiVo-proof" advertising model where 30-second commercial skipping is counteracted by overlaying ad logos and animations on top of the shows themselves! You thought those on-screen station logos and stupid animated preview overlays were obnoxious—just wait until you have to watch an entire episode of *Alias* while being reminded that Cialis is available "for when the time is right."

Books

We don't need no stinkin' paperless revolution! We still love books. We'd like to take this opportunity to recognize all of the trees that have been sacrificed to help fire our neurons. You did not die in vain. We promise to use our increasing brainpower only for good, and to figure out how to grow you faster (or replace you with hemp) so that we can buy, read, and collect even more analog storage devices made out of your pulverized carcasses.

Hacking the TiVo, William von Hagen, Premier Press

All of the hardcore TiVo hacking books reviewed here have their strengths and weaknesses. This one, by long-time Unix/Linux programmer and tech writer Bill von Hagen, is not as dizzyingly technical as *Hacking TiVo* (see the following review), but has more useful details and covers more territory than the O'Reilly *TiVo Hacks* book (also reviewed in this section). *Hacking the TiVo* is well laid out, design-wise, with clear pictures and screen captures, and numerous code examples. It also does a decent job of covering hacking both Series 1 and Series 2 systems (the other books focus on Series 1), as well as using both PCs and Macs to do it. The book has, however, been criticized for poor content organization (and rightly so), some technical errors, too many typos, and for being outdated in some areas. Unfortunately, all of the TiVo hacking books have holes in them, or poorly explained procedures that can seriously trip up all but the most experienced hacker. If you decide you really want to go to town on your TiVo, hacking it beyond the scope of our book, you're really going to want to get all three of the hacking books covered here, read the details in each on the procedures you're interested in, and hopefully, you'll get a clear enough picture of what to do. The best thing about this book is the comprehensive (as of its publication date) CD of TiVo-related apps and utilities and relevant Linux tools. If you're interested in hacking a Series 2 TiVo, you definitely need this book. It's the only one that goes into any detail (and includes hacks on the CD) for S2 machines.

Hacking TiVo, Jeff Keegan, Wiley

Longtime fixture on the TiVo Community Forum, software engineer Jeff Keegan, pulls out all the stops in trying to provide enough details about TiVo hacking, especially on the software side, so that those with an interest in programming and development can write their own TiVo hacks (using the Tcl scripting language). Jeff himself is responsible for the *email*, *search*, and *log* modules for the TiVoWeb project (see Chapter 16, "TiVoWeb"). This book should have been more clearly identified as a Series 1-focused guide. Rumor has it that Keegan initially had more S2 hacks in the book and on the CD, but legal concerns from the publisher forced their removal. If you have a Series 1 machine and are serious about tricking out your box with many add-on apps, learning more about TiVo's software, and maybe trying your hand at some scripting, this is a great book to have. One criticism of the production is that the paper it's printed on is so cheap (basically one grade above newsprint) that some of the pictures are poorly reproduced and the pages can easily tear as you're thumbing through it. Also includes a CD with many of the tools and apps described in the book, as well as a bootable Linux distribution.

Hardware Hacking, Joe Grand, Ryan Russell, et al, Syngress

This isn't a TiVo book, but after assembling the tools and doing the projects in our book, you might want to branch out into hacking more of your consumer electronics hardware. The best thing about this book is that it assumes you have the desire for hardware hacking but little to none of the expertise, so it starts off with a crash course in basic electronics, soldering, hacker tools, reading schematics, and more. The book covers a wide range of hacks, from how to replace a dead iPod battery to how to turn an old CueCat proprietary barcode reader (which companies like Radio Shack used to give away for free) into a generic reader that allows you to build a sophisticated library database simply by swiping the barcodes on the books you own. Hacking your PS2, building a WiFi antenna, and adding more RAM to your Palm PDA are all covered. There's a lengthy section on creating your own PC- or Linux-based home media PC (with PVR function, DVD and MP3 playing, CD-ripping, and more). The authors are good about pointing out that building such a box is time-consuming, can be difficult, and to do it well, can cost more than commercial gear (such as a TiVo and a DVD player). Whimsical hacks include re-casing an old Mac SE entirely in Mega Bloks (think: Legos) and adding UFO lights to a USB mouse.

Hardware Hacking Projects for Geeks, Scott Fullam, O'Reilly

This handsomely designed book is written in the same spirit as the Joe Grand title, but it includes completely different projects. It too starts out with some electronics basics, and has more basic hardware tutorials throughout. Projects include turning a Primestar satellite dish into a WiFi antenna, building your own two-to-six hour laptop battery backup from standard D-size batteries, and how to hack a Furby doll so that it is completely programmable. It too includes a built-it-yourself PVR project, but it is not nearly as full-featured as the one in the Grand book. Some of the stranger projects include turning the lights/windows of a building into an 18 x 8-pixel display (eighteen windows wide by eight floors high) and how to turn an old all-in-one Mac into an aquarium.

Linux in a Nutshell, Siever, Figgins, Weber, O'Reilly

If you use Linux on a regular basis, or after reading our book and playing around in the TiVo Bash shell, you want to learn more, this book deserves a spot in your software toolbox. You know that Linux is not for the weak of geek when you see that the "nutshell" that contains it is nearly a thousand pages long. But since Linux takes so many forms and has so many components, covering many of them (as this book does), requires serious amounts of tree meat. A lot of the book's content can be found in the Linux man (manual) pages, and on various online Linux repositories, but having such a succinct and comprehensive volume handy can save a lot of time (and you can take it to the john).

Linux Toys, Christopher Negus, Chuck Wolber, John Wiley & Sons

Yet another hardware hacking book, this one focusing on what the heck you can do with that old PC gathering dust in the corner. Thirteen projects are detailed, using the Linux OS and free Linux applications. Projects include turning your PC into a MP3 jukebox, a home video archiver, a digital phone answering service, a game box, and a home network server. It also includes a chapter on turning a PC into a PVR, though to do a decent job of it, you need a rather high-end PC. This book and accompanying CD are centered around the Red Hat Linux distribution. Red Hat can be downloaded for free over the Net (ftp.redhat.com).

TiVo Hacks, Raffi Krikorian, O'Reilly

Like *Hacking TiVo*, this book is really best suited for owners of Series 1 TiVos. It isn't surprising that hacking books would focus on Series 1, since it's infinitely more hackable than Series 2, but the hacks books do a poor job of pointing this prejudice out. If you do have Series 1 and want to go a few steps beyond what's covered in our book, this offers such things as a crash course in Tcl scripting, how to create custom channel logos for TiVo, streaming video from your TiVo over your home network, and more. The book is done in the straightforward, succinct style that has made the Hacks series so popular. This brevity makes for a handsome and handy little guide, but can be a little too lean on details for the less-than-expert reader.

Software

Besides the software included on this book's accompanying CD, and what may have been mentioned throughout the text, here are a few specific titles and TiVo/Linux-related repositories you might want to know about.

Beyond TV 3 (www.snapstream.com)

A slightly more user friendly (and Windows-based) PVR is the Beyond TV 3, offered by Snapstream. This commercial product includes many of the features found on TiVo (pausing live TV, time-shifting, commercial skipping, and Web-based program scheduling) and a few that aren't (free TV guide data, ability to export shows in different compression formats, skipping commercial blocks in a single click). BTV3 only works with TV cards that do hardware encoding of MPEG-2 (most of them use software-based encoding), so you likely need a new TV card (if you don't already have one) to use this program. Snapstream sells BTV3 as a software product for $70 (download direct for $60) and in kits bundled with various Hauppauge TV tuner cards. Although BTV 3 is marketed as a plug 'n' play consumer product, it still has a few bugs to work out and requires a high-performance-minded machine (with lots of RAM, a giant hard drive, video card with at least 16MB, Windows XP, and the proper TV card). Still, at $140 for a kit with the software and the low-end Hauppauge card, this is a great way to add a PVR to your desktop PC.

Freevo (freevo.sourceforge.net)

An open source software project offering a free home theater PC platform built around Linux and many open source applications. As with all such projects, they're more for tinkerers than average users looking for a robust and full-service PVR. But these projects are under constant development and improvement, even as the hardware to make them work well continues to drop in price. Eventually, these free applications will become a reasonable alternative to a TiVo, or at least a relatively inexpensive way to add a second PVR to the family.

MythTV (www.mythtv.org)

Another home media PC project popular among penguinheads. Not really ready for prime time, but if you have a spare PC lying around, and spending the weekend troubleshooting Linux "issues" is your idea of a good time, check out MythTV.

Sourceforge (sourceforge.net)

This site is the premier portal for all things related to open source software development. The site provides free hosting services for thousands of open source software projects, with collaborative development tools, news of project updates, discussion groups, e-lists, and other nifty features. There are dozens of TiVo-related software projects hosted on the site. Just do a search on "tivo" to scoop them all up.

TiVo's Linux Files (www.tivo.com/linux)

In the spirit of the GNU Public License (GPL) for open source software, TiVo has posted the source code for the components of the TiVo OS that are open source. This does not include the proprietary TiVo components, such as myworld and the software that controls the TiVo Media Switch. The files do include the Linux distros used in TiVo, the development libraries, some of the drivers, and some modules.

TiVoUtils (tivoutils.sourceforge.net)

A useful list of Linux utilities for working inside of Series 1 and Series 2 TiVos. Also includes links to datasheets for various TiVo hardware components, online versions of the TiVo manuals, and some other misc. docs.

Misc. Resources

But wait, there's more!

Hacking the TiVo FAQ (tivo.samba.org)

A gigantic document covering most every aspect of Series 1 TiVo hacking. Unfortunately, the site hasn't been updated since 2001, so some of the information, especially in discussing what other software and hardware is available, is out of date. If you make use of this FAQ, you'll want to also read related topics on the TiVo Underground Forum on tivocommunity.com.

JP1-Equipped Remotes (jp1.filebug.com/remchart.htm)

This basic chart lists all of the remotes manufactured by UEI with JP1 capability. One of the things you need to understand about the JP1 interface is that some remotes have the JP1 jack already built into the circuit board, and some have just the pads for soldering on the jack. This chart details this, along with what processor the remotes use, how much EEPROM (erasable programmable memory) they have, whether they are compatible with popular remote customizing programs, and more. Unfortunately, the chart doesn't appear to be updated that often, so many of the most recent Radio Shack and One-For-All remotes are not listed.

Linux Man Pages (www.hmug.org/man/)

This site is an online, searchable version of the man (manual) pages maintained by the Huntsville Macintosh Users Group (HMUG) as part of their Mac Unix project.

PVRCompare (www.pvrcompare.com)

This site provides extremely comprehensive information that compares TiVo to other digital recorders, namely the ReplayTV and the Comcast/Scientific Atlanta DVR. We don't think there's really any contest between TiVo and these other recorders, but if you're the type of consumer that wants to make informed buying decisions, you'll want to check out this site.

TiVoHelp.com Knowledge Database (www.tivohelp.com)

This site is an attempt at building an extensive TiVo knowledge database through volunteer contributions. There aren't as many articles here as you'd find on a commercial knowledge database, but most of the common software and hardware problems and upgrades are covered.

Common Linux Commands

What follows is a rundown of some of the basic commands you'll need to make your way around the Linux OS (and therefore the command-line side of TiVo). These are only a few of the most commonly encountered commands. Most of them can be found within TiVo (if you access the TiVo OS via a serial connection, as described in Chapter 10, "Quick n' Dirty Serial Networking," or via telnet and Ethernet, as described in Chapter 14, "Accessing Your TiVo's Linux Bash Prompt"), but others cannot. TiVo only includes Linux components that it needs to function, or that TiVo, Inc. technicians need to test and fix machines. Many of the missing applications are included in the Linux Utilities package found on the CD. Most of these commands can also be invoked on your PC by booting into the mini-distribution of Linux also found on the CD (details for booting into this disc can be found in Chapter 8, "Upgrading Your Hard Drives").

For more background information on Linux, its basic file structure, the Bash command-line shell (where you'd enter these commands), and more can be found in Chapter 13, "Touring Your TiVo: The Software."

Appendix B   *Chart of Common Linux Commands*

Command	Full Name/Meaning	What It Does
&	Background job	Placing the ampersand symbol at the end of a command-line string causes that command to be run in the background.
cat	Concatenate file(s)	The most basic Unix file viewer. Displays specified file(s) to screen. Since most files are longer than the display, the `less` or `more` commands (see below) are often more useful. While the uber-geeky name implies the stringing together of data for output, `cat` is most commonly used for outputting (printing to screen) a single file.
cd	Change Directory	Establishing the current working directory by entering: `cd [name of destination directory]` Using `cd` anywhere in the shell with no destination specified takes you to your home directory (which on a stand-alone PC is likely root).
chmod	Change Mode	Sets access permissions for files and directories. Permissions are read-only (r), write (w), and execute (x).
cp	Copy file(s)	Copies a single or multiple files. Use of the -p option copies the file(s) with all permissions, timestamps, and owner and group information. -i will prompt you before overwriting any existing file(s).
dd	Disk Dump	Copies an entire disk partition, or selected files, to a backup.

echo	Prints its arguments to the screen	Prints simple text to standard (read "screen") output. So, at Bash:
		`echo Are we having fun yet?`
		would return:
		`Are we having fun yet?`
		Is there an echo is here?

exit	Exit	Exit out of the shell program.
grep	Global Regular Expression	A powerful Unix search utility that uses the Regular Expression (RegEx) syntax rules. A beginner's tutorial can be found here: www.regenechsen.de/regex_en
gunzip	GNU Unzip	Decompresses files using the GNU version of the popular PC compression utility Zip. Compressed files have the .gz file suffix.
gzip	GNU Zip	Compresses files using the GNU version of the popular PC compression utility Zip. Compressed files have the .gz file suffix.
head	Head of a file	Prints the first 10 lines (by default) of a specified file. -N will print the *n* number of lines you indicate.

Command	Full Name/Meaning	What It Does
--help	Help	Prints help info for specified command: `cd --help` would show help information on the cd command.
ifconfig	Network Interface Configuration	Command for configuring or viewing the configuration of your network interface.
kill	Kill process	Terminates a running process, specified by a process ID (PID) or via use of the `kill pidof [program]` command.
less	Less file viewer	File viewer that prints only one screenful of data at a time. Enter will move you through one line at a time; Spacebar: one screenful. ^B or b take you back a screenful.
ln	Create Links to a file	Creates either a "symbolic" link to another file (think "shortcut" in the PC world or "alias" on the Mac), or a "hard" link that is basically a second name for the same file (so that the file will only be deleted when all links to it are). The default is hard link, so use the -s option to create a symbolic link. BTW: Symbolic links can be established across partitions, but hard links cannot.
ls	List files in a directory	Displays attributes of directories and files. Use the options –l to display full file information and –F to show file attribute symbols (e.g. / = directory, * = executable).

man	Manual pages	Built-in documentation system. To get info on a specific command/program, enter:
		`man [command  of interest]`
		For topic help, type:
		`man -k [topic of interest].`

more	More file viewer	Displays the specified files to the screen, one screenful at a time. Enter will move you through one line at a time; Spacebar: one screenful. ^B or b takes you back a screenful.
mkdir	Make Directory	Creates one or more directories.
mount	Mount drive(s)	Makes the content of a storage device (that is, a drive) available for use.
mv	Move a file	Moves a file (or files) into a destination directory. Use of the –i option will prompt you before overwriting an existing file.
ps	List processes	A process is a unit of work within the OS. Every running Linux program involves one or more processes (represented by a process ID, or PID).
pwd	Print Working Directory	Prints to the screen the full (absolute) path of the current directory.

Chart of Common Linux Commands

Command	Full Name/Meaning	What It Does
rm	Remove a file	Removes specified file(s). Use of the −i option will prompt you before overwriting an existing file.
rmdir	Remove Directory	Deletes one or more empty directories that you name. With the −r option, deletes non-empty dirs, and with −ri, it will ask you before deleting each item in the directory.
shutdown	Shutdown Linux	This command will cease all operations and turn off the hardware. Use of the -r option will reboot the system.
tail	Tail of a file	Prints the last 10 lines (by default) of a specified file. −N will print the *n* number of lines you indicate.
tar	Tape Archive program	Originally designed as a means of writing (and reading) files to (and from) tape backup drives. Now a common means of packaging (and archiving) collections of files on Linux/Unix systems. Uses the suffix .tar. A tar package is also known as a tarball.
umount	Unmount disk	Remove a mounted disk so that it is no longer available (mounted) to the system. Always unmount disks after use. Note that the command drops the "n": umount.
vi (or vim)	"Visual Interface" text editor. "VIM" is "Vi Improved."	Vi is the most common text editor found on Unix (and Unix-like) machines. VIM is often found on Linux boxes as well. There are many features available here. Use the :help command to get more info. Vim even has its own homepage: www.vim.org.

Control Characters

Command	Full Name/Meaning	What It Does
^Z	Suspend	Suspend the currently running foreground job. It doesn't kill the job; it just suspends it. Type bg if you want the job to continue in the background, and fg if you want to bring it to the foreground again.
^C	Kill Current command	Terminates the current foreground command.
^D	Terminate the shell program	Same as the exit command.

Wildcards

Command	Full Name/Meaning	What It Does
*	Set wildcard	Represents any set of characters except for a leading period.
?	Character wildcard	Represents any single character.

Command	Full Name/Meaning	What It Does
		Input/Output Redirectors
¦	Pipe	Redirects the standard output from one command to the input of another command.
<	Input from file	Input for the specified command is drawn from the file that's pointing to said command: `command < file`.
>	Output to file	Output from the specified command is sent to the file pointed to: `command > file`.
>>	Append to out file	Use of double >> appends to the file pointed to rather than creates/overwrites it as in a single >.

About the CD-ROM

The CD that accompanies this book contains a number of useful utilities used in upgrading and hacking TiVos, as well as a number of third-party programs that can be used with TiVo. In this appendix, we'll run down what's on the disc, how to load these programs onto your home computer and/or TiVo (as appropriate), and what to do with them once they're installed. Many of these programs have already been discussed in the main text. When we come to those, we'll point you back to the chapter where you can find more information.

CD Organization

The CD-ROM is divided into four main sections:

- **Linux**—This folder/directory contains all of the components used in booting into the mini-distribution of Linux from your home computer's CD-ROM drive. This Linux OS is used for DIY TiVo drive upgrading on Series 1 and Series 2 machines (as discussed in Chapter 8), Series 1 network software installation (Chapters 9, 10, and 11), and for installing software on Series 1 TiVos (Chapters 14, 16, 17). You can also use this fully functional Linux distribution to explore and learn more about this powerful and fascinating operating system (that your TiVo, among other things, is built upon).

- **Series1**—This folder contains third-party applications for the Series 1 TiVos. Programs of note include MFS Tools 2.0, used in various hard drive hacks, and TiVoWeb, the open source Web-based interface for networked Series 1 (both stand-alone and DirecTiVo).

- **Series2**—Unfortunately, there aren't as many third-party programs for S2 machines as S1 (though much of S1's add-on functionality is already built in). This directory contains JavaHMO, the Java-based network server for standalone S2 machines, and Hexedit, the utility program that can be used for hacking the hash code on S2 machines to gain backdoor access.

- **Support Docs**—This is where you will find some PDF files related to various TiVo technologies, as well as the GNU General Public License, the license that covers all of the open source applications contained on the disc. ReadMe/Installation files related to the applications on the CD can be found in the folders for the respective programs.

Contents of the Disc

On the enclosed CD-ROM, you'll find the following digital goodies.

- **Linux**—The CD contains a bootable version of Linux, called isolinux, built on the distribution known as Slackware. This copy of Linux can be used for all of the hardware and software hacking discussed in the book that requires access to Linux (for drive formatting, file copying and backup, and file installation onto TiVo drives attached to your PC). See "Installing and Using the CD" later in this appendix for details on how to boot into Linux from your PC.

- **Unix Command Suite**—Besides the bootable Linux distro found in the Linux directory on the disc, there is also an archived (in .tar.gz format) collection of useful Unix/Linux commands. These are common commands found on nearly all Unix/Linux-based systems, but they do not come with TiVo. To navigate inside of your TiVo using the built-in Bash shell, you'll want to install these commands. Table C.1 lists some of the more important commands found inside of the tivobin.tar/gz archive. We're only listing the ones you're likely to make use of right away in exploring TiVo (or that you might just want to try for fun). There are other commands already built into TiVo's Linux, or are in the archive, but were already discussed them elsewhere, especially in Appendix B. Refer to that for an explanation of additional commands. You can look up others found in the archive (but not discussed in the book) online via the Linux man pages (hmug.org/man). See "Installing and Using the CD" later in this appendix for details on how to copy this archive onto your TiVo.

Table C.1   Miscellaneous Useful Unix/Linux Commands Contained on the CD-ROM

Command	Name	What It Does
wc	Word Count	Prints out a count of bytes, words, and lines in a file.
uname	Uname	Print out info on your system: kernel version, hardware and processor type, OS name, and so on. -a option prints out full details.
tty	Terminal Device	Prints name of terminal device associated with current shell.
touch	Touch	Allows you to change the time/date stamp on files.
ls	List	Lists the attributes of files and directories. -l to see long-form listings.
tr	Translate	Will translate one specified set of characters into another set.
su	Superuser	Gain root access by entering su -l and then entering the system/su password. You don't have to log in on this book's Linux. It automatically logs you in as root.
split	Split File	Splits specified file into multiple files of equal length. Keeps original and labels split files: filenameaa, filenamebb, and so on. Default split size is 1000 lines.
rmdir	Remove Directory	Removes one or more specified empty dirs. -r option removes non-empty dir and all contents (caution!).
fgrep	Fixed-String GNU Regular Expression	Same as grep -F (see grep in Appendix B)
egrep	Extended GNU Regular Expression	Same as grep -E (see grep in Appendix B)

Table C.1	Continued	
Command	**Name**	**What It Does**
`tail`	Tail	Prints out the last ten lines of a specified document.
`head`	Head	Prints out the last ten lines of a specified document.
`ps`	List process	Displays information on running processes.
`sort`	Sort	Displays lines of text by rules that you specify (such as alpha order).
`dd`	Data Doubler?	Makes a copy of a specified file and sends the copy to an output file. Origin of command abbreviation unknown (so we made "data doubler" up).
`chgrp`	Change Group	Used to change the status of group ownership of files and directories
`chown`	Change Owner	Changes the ownership of files and directories
`pathchk`	Path Check	Determines the validity of filenames and directory paths. Checks to make sure directory paths are searchable and filenames are acceptable.
`dir`	Directory Contents	Lists the current contents of the directory (same as issuing `ls` command).
`nl`	Number Lines	Prepends line numbers to specified file copied to standard output.
`od`	Octal Dump	Copies a file to standard output and displays the file in octal (eight bytes per line) and other specified formats (hexadecimal, decimal, ASCII).
`md5sum`	MD5 File Checksum	Computes a checksum using the MD5 algorithm. Checksum is a means of ensuring the integrity of data by calculating and comparing a sum based on the value of the data being checked. If the newly calculated value differs from the original value, the data has somehow been corrupted.

Series 1

In the series1 directory on the disc, there are two main folders, one for applications and one for support utilities.

Applications

We included only the best and most sought-after S1 applications on the CD. There are many more programs that can be found online at places such as sourceforge.net, tivocommunity.com, and dealdatabase.com/forum.

- **TiVoWeb**—A web-based interface for networked stand-alone TiVos and DirecTV DVRs that offers many of the same features found on Series 2's Home Media Feature, and a bunch of features not found anywhere else. See Chapter 16, "TiVoWeb" for installation and operation information.

- **TiVo Control Station**—An uber-app that brings together a number of program scripts created for networked S1 TiVos and allows them to be controlled via TiVo's infrared remote control. TiVo Control Station is Shareware and is available for download from http://www.zirakzigil.net/tivo/TCS.html. See Chapter 17, "Other TiVo Apps" for more information.

- **YAC**—"Yet Another Caller-ID" program, a combination application with a PC "server" and a TiVo-based "listener." Uses the caller-ID function of an analog modem (if you still have such a thing) to display caller-ID to your PC, and over your LAN to your TiVo. See Chapter 17 for more information.

- **Elseed**—A caller-ID program for DirecTV DVRs. See Chapter 17 for more details.

- **JPEGWriter**—Allows for the display of images in the JPEG format on your TV via TiVo. See Chapter 17 for more details.

- **TiVoVBI**—Allows Closed Captioning (CC) information to be displayed via TiVo (instead of your TV) and allows the CC information to be captured to file. See Chapter 17 for more details.

Support Utilities

- **MFS Tools 2.0**—If you're planning on backing up your TiVo drive(s) to your PC, formatting your own TiVo disks, or other work with TiVo's drives, you'll want to use the MFS Tools 2.0 program found on the CD. The program comes with a decent set of documents that explains how to do the various backup and restore procedures available through MFS Tools. See also Chapter 8, "Upgrade Hard Drives," for more information on using this utility program for DIY drive upgrading.

- **Newtext2osd**—An open source upgrade to TiVo's built-in text2osd, a utility designed to display text onscreen (OSD = "on screen display"). This utility is used by TiVo Control Station (see "Applications" earlier in this chapter) for onscreen display of text data.

- **MacTools**—There is also a folder of TiVo hacking tools for use with the Mac, including MacTiVo Blesser (which allows you to bless—in some cases—a second drive and add it to the first, without having to remove the existing drive), MFS Browser (for looking through TiVo's MFS database via a Mac), and TiVoPartitionScheme, a program for recognizing TiVo's partition map. Instructions for using these tools are included within their respective folders.

Series 2

In the Series2 directory on the disc, there are two main folders, one for applications and one for support utilities.

Applications

Besides the applications included on this book's CD-ROM, there are new add-on programs planned for networked S2 TiVos. Most of these, such as MoodLogic and Picasa (demo versions of which are included here), are commercial products, but as TiVo hackers move from S1 to S2 technology, expect to see new open source efforts as well.

- **JavaHMO**—This Java-based open source program serves (pun intended) as a replacement to the TiVo Desktop app, the program that sends digital music and images from any computer on your LAN to a networked Series 2 SA TiVo. JavaHMO adds a bunch of cool features, such as Internet radio (Shoutcast) and local movie listings. See Chapter 15, "Home Media Feature" for detailed installation and operating instructions.

- **MoodLogic**—This commercial MP3 server offers many more music manipulation tools than either TiVo Desktop or JavaHMO. A trial can be freely downloaded from http://www.moodlogic.com.

- **Picasa**—This commercial digital image archiving and server software offers many more image manipulation tools than either TiVo Desktop or JavaHMO. Picasa can be freely downloaded from http://www.picasa.com/picasa.

Support Utilities

The disc includes a couple of utilities that will be of interest to the S2 TiVo hacker.

- **MFS Tools 2.0**—See description in Series 1 section earlier in this appendix.
- **Hexedit**—To open the backdoors on Series 2 TiVos, you have to change the hexadecimal code on TiVo's partitions where the cryptographic hash codes are stored for backdoor passwords. No one has figured out the backdoor password for TiVo software beyond 3.0, but finding and replacing the hash values for these codes (via a hex editor) is one workaround. We didn't discuss this process in our book. You can find full details of how to do it in William von Hagen's *Hacking the TiVo*. You can probably find the instructions online as well, by searching forums such as dealdatabase.com/forum and tivocommunity.com.

Installing and Using the CD

To properly install and make use of this book's CD you need to be able to do two things: boot Linux and copy some Unix binary files to TiVo.

Booting Linux

To boot into the Linux distro that came with this book, all you have to do is to set up your Windows PC to boot from the CD-ROM drive. To do this, you'll need to change the startup/boot sequence in your computer's BIOS. The BIOS is entered when the computer is booting up. How to enter the BIOS settings is indicated on the initial DOS startup screen (often F1, F2, or Del). In BIOS, you'll want to look for the appropriate setting for the startup/boot sequence (the name and placement will vary). The sequence will often be set to drive A, C, CD-ROM (and/or other drives). You want to either change it to A, CD-ROM, C, and so forth, or put CD-ROM first. With the sequence changed and saved, shut down your machine and restart it with the CD in the CD-ROM drive. You'll be taken into the Linux mini-distro.

About the CD-ROM

NOTE

A slightly different procedure for moving the tivo-bin files from your PC to your TiVo box via FTP and telnet can be found in Chapter 14: "Accessing your TiVo's Linux Bash Prompt.

It's a good idea to test that the PC does, in fact, boot from the CD before attaching a TiVo drive to the PC. If it boots into a newer version of Windows, Windows will overwrite some critical information on the drive and render the drive largely useless. So to prevent this from happening, test the CD boot process before attaching any TiVo drives.

Copying the Unix Binary Files

In the Linux directory, there's a TAR/GNUZIP archive called tivobin.tar.gz. This package contains all of the Unix/Linux commands that TiVo's Linux-based OS does not include but that you will need (or might want) when mucking around inside of TiVo. To install this archive in TiVo, do the following steps:

1. First you'll need to have your TiVo drive mounted to your PC following the instructions in Chapter 8. If you're hooking your drive up for upgrading/backup, that's a good time to move these programs over as well.

2. For ease of transfer, it's a good idea to copy the tivobin.tar.gz file onto a floppy disk and move it to the TiVo drive from there. In Linux, the floppy drive will be known as fd0.

3. With your TiVo drive attached to your PC, and booting in from your Linux CD (with the tivobin floppy loaded), you'll want to mount the TiVo drive (and the appropriate partition), make a /hack directory, if you haven't already, and copy the tivobin file into it. Here are the commands (at the Bash prompt):

```
mkdir   /mnt9
mount /dev/hdX9 /mnt9
[where X is the letter of the TiVo drive on your
PC's IDE chain: hdb, hdc, or hdd]
mkdir /mnt9/hack
mkdir /floppy
mount -t vfat /dev/fd0 /floppy
cp /floppy/tivobin.tar.gz /mnt9/hack
```

4. Now that the file archive has been moved onto your TiVo drive, it's time to pack up and get ready to move the drive back into your DVR. It is from there that you'll finish the installation. To be able to do this, you'll need to have access to the Bash prompt over a

network (see Chapter 10, "Quick n' Dirty Serial Networking," and Chapter 14, "Accessing Your TiVo's Linux Bash Prompt"). Before we yank the drives, however, we need to unmount our partitions (at Bash):

```
cd /
umount /mnt9 umount /floppy
exit
```

Now hit Ctrl-Alt-Delete, and when your PC begins to reboot, turn it off.

5. With the TiVo drive reinstalled (see the instructions in Chapter 8, and don't forget to change the jumper settings!), and your TiVo's Bash prompt staring back at you, perform the following installation procedure:

```
cd /var/hack
gzip -d tivobin.tar.gz
cpio -idu -H tar < tivobin.tar
mv tivo-bin bin
chmod 755 bin/*
```

6. We're ALMOST there. Now we need to edit TiVo's PATH environment variable so that it knows to run these commands each time we start up TiVo. We need to amend the PATH located in the .profile file. Here's the command sequence:

```
cd /
mount -o remount, rw /
echo "export PATH=\$PATH:/var/hack/bin" >> /.profile
mount -o remount,ro /
```

Whew. That's it. Now you should have access to all of the Linux commands detailed in Appendix B, Table C.1, and elsewhere in this book.

Using MFS Tools

When you boot up the Linux distro included with this CD, MFS Tools is automatically loaded along with it. To utilize this program's functions, follow the instructions on screen for accessing the Series 1 or Series 2 tool sets. See the MFS Tools manual in the Series 1 (or Series 2) Utilities directories on the disc for detailed instructions.

About the CD-ROM

Using the Applications on the CD

The applications on the CD are either described in more detail in this book (such as TiVoWeb, JavaHMO, MFS Tools) or are described in installation/ReadMe files included with them on the CD. To install them, simply insert the CD into the CD-ROM drive on your Mac or PC, navigate to the appropriate folder, and treat them as you would any other application installation. Also, throughout the text, there are links to the websites for the software's developers and popular discussion forums, such as tivocommunity.com, where you can get more information, help, software updates, and more.

Analog In electronics, refers to a continuously variable signal (as opposed to an on/off, digital signal). The easiest way to keep analog and digital straight is to think of an undulating wave (analog) versus a set of stair-steps (digital). One big problem with analog signals is noise (think of the pollution and little critters riding in that wave). A lot of effort is spent (through filtering, amplifying, shielding, special types of connections) to try and keep noise out. See also *digital*.

Aspect Ratio The width of an image divided by its height. The traditional television screen ratio is 4:3 (or 1.33:1). The ratio found on most digital televisions is 16:9 (about 1.78:1). This ratio is also referred to as "widescreen." Wider screens mean that films can make the transfer to television while preserving the original cinematic aspect ratio, and without the need for *letterboxing*, the black masking bars placed across the top and bottom of the screen.

ATSC (Advanced Television Systems Committee) Refers to the digital television (DTV) standard found in the US and Canada. The standard is named after the body that developed it, the Advanced Television Systems Committee. ATSC allows for multiple standard-definition (SDTV) channels to be carried on the same bandwidth as a single analog channel would use. The main benefit of the standard, however, is for the transmission of high-definition television (HDTV) signals. The goal of the standards committee was to develop a global DTV standard that would do away with the incompatibility problems that previous standards—NTSC (North America), PAL (Europe, Asia, Africa, Australia), and SECAM (France, Eastern Europe, Russia)—had created. They had no such luck. New DTV standards, besides ATSC, include DVB (Europe) and ISDB (Japan). See also *NTSC, PAL, SECAM*.

Auto-Correct On TiVo, the name given to the built-in rewind or fast-forward (respectively) modes that are engaged when moving in 2x or 3x FF or 2x or 3x Rewind mode. Also referred to as *overshoot correction.*

Auto-Thumbs The single "Thumbs Up" automatically given by TiVo to any program you record, or for any Season Passes you create. The TiVo software smartly surmises that, if you went through the trouble of recording something, it's probably worth adding it to your Thumb Ratings database.

Bash A Unix/Linux command shell program. The name is an acronym for *Bourne-Again Shell,* referring to Stephen Bourne, the programmer who created sh, the first Unix shell. TiVo has a copy of Bash already installed, and it can be used to access underlying applications. As with all Unix/Linux commands, it is case sensitive and only answers to bash. See also *Linux, shell, Tcl.*

Blessing TiVo hacker-speak for partitioning and identifying a TiVo hard drive. If you upgrade your TiVo HD, or add more storage via a second drive, and you don't use a prepared (already "blessed") upgrade kit, you have to mount the drive(s) on a PC, partition them, and then load on the TiVo software. This is known as "blessing the drive." We wanted to get in on the word coinage, so we nicknamed the popular method of muscling off the top of the TiVo case (by kneeling in front of it and pushing on the back edges) the "hardware blessing."

BNC Connector A type of connector commonly found on coax cable. There are two main types of BNC, a push and twist type and a threaded type (similar to an F-type connector). *BNC* stands for *Bayonet Neill-Concelmann,* the word *bayonet* referring to the type of twist-and-lock connector used, and Neill and Concelmann, referring to the inventors of the technology. See also *coaxial cable, F-type connector.*

Boat Anchor Mode The term "boat anchor" has been used in tech circles for decades. It refers to a piece of hardware that has been rendered useless, usually through operator error. In TiVo, entering the remote sequence Clear-Enter-Clear-Advance makes TiVo think that it has no available guide data and it stops being the TiVo you love. Obviously you do not want to test this out yourself.

Bullwinkle Mode Slang for the AutoTest Mode (Pressing keys 1, 2, 3 while viewing a Now Playing program description and then pressing 4). This useless-to-the-user mode randomly generates key presses until you reboot your box. Probably used in system testing at the factory. Why "Bullwinkle Mode?" Good question. Maybe as in: "Hey Rocky, watch me pull a rabbit outta my hat. Oops. Wrong hat." Though, I am told there was an early, and revered, TiVo employee named Richard Bullwinkle.

Buttonitis A condition that far too many remote controls suffer from. Rather than relying on good design that allows for buttons to have multiple functions under different menus, or to eliminate button requirements with better software interfaces, more buttons are slapped onto the remote. Luckily, TiVo's remote is one of the nicest designed and does not suffer from this unfortunate malaise. See also *remote bloat.*

Cat5 Cable See *Ethernet.*

CATV (Community Antenna Television or CAble TV) The term *community antenna* means that, rather than having an antenna at each home, a series of antenna and satellite dishes are used at a central location (called a *head end*) to bring down local and remote channels, and these are then fed through fiber, coax cables, and signal amplifiers to each individual home. *CATV* is sometimes used to mean *Community Access TV*, but these cable channels, set aside, by law, for community use, are correctly known as *Public Access TV (PATV)*.

Chrominance The part of an analog video signal that contain the color information (including hue and saturation). Abbreviated as *chroma*. See also *luminance*.

Click of Death When a computer (or TiVo) hard drive experiences a catastrophic hardware failure, the drive often makes an ugly clicking sound as it tries in vain to continue functioning. This sound is referred to as the click of death because it almost always means that your drive has moved on to the big storage space in the sky.

Coaxial Cable A type of electrical cable technology where a central conducting wire is surrounded by an insulating material that is surrounded in turn by another conducting material (which is usually further surrounded by an insulating sheath). The technology gets its name from the fact that both conductors share the same central axis. See also *BNC Connector, F-type Connector*.

Component Video An analog video standard that separates parts of the signal and transmits them over three wires: one for luminance information and two for color. Separating the signal to this extent allows for a much better signal than other schemes, such as S-video and composite video. S-video is technically a type of component format, as the signal is divided, but only on two wires, one for color and one for luminance. See also *composite video, DVI, HDMI, S-Video*.

Composite Video An analog video standard where all channels of video information (luminance and chrominance) are combined on a single line. Used for the NTSC TV format and commonly found in analog home media devices (VCRs, game systems, and so on). Composite video is usually terminated with RCA-type jacks. See also *component video, RCA Plug/Jack, S-Video*.

Compression In computing, the processing of data so that it takes up less space for storage, or so that it can be transferred more quickly over a network. One might think that encoding data in this fashion would be difficult, but it isn't, as there is plenty of redundancy available in the compressible world. Look at an average video signal and pay attention to how much on the screen does not change (or changes little) over multiple frames. Compression techniques can be used to throw out the redundant information from frame to frame, thus saving disk space. There are two main types of compression: *lossy* (where some data is lost in the encoding/decoding process) and *lossless* (where the original integrity is maintained through compression and decompression). MPEG-2, the audio/video coding standard used in TiVo, is an example of lossy compression. See also *MPEG-2*.

DBS (Direct Broadcast Satellite) Referring to direct-to-customer satellite services (such as DirecTV and DISH). DBS systems are often also referred to as *mini-dish systems* because of the small 18–24" dish antennas used in contemporary models. See also *LNB*.

Digital A property of discrete, binary values (as in "on/off," high/low, 1/0), rather than a continuous "wave" of values, as in analog. One of the many advantages of digital technologies over analog is that noise is greatly reduced (since all that's being communicated is "ons" and "offs"). One disadvantage is the loss of information, as when an analog signal is "squared off" when being converted to a digital one. How much data is lost depends on the "resolution" of the analog-to-digital (A/D) conversion. See also *analog*.

Distro A bundling, or "distribution," of the GNU/Linux OS and other support components into a "branded" version (such as Debian, Red Hat, Knoppix). Lean and mean versions that have been created to fit onto a CD (or floppy) and run from there, are known as mini-distros. The Linux version on this book is such a creature.

DSS (Digital Satellite System) Another generic term for a direct-to-customer satellite media delivery system. See also *DBS*.

DVI (Digital Video Interface) An all-digital connection standard that allows digital signals to travel to digital displays without being transferred to analog then back to digital. Used on many flat-screen monitors and DTVs. One benefit of DVI is that it can transmit analog signals on the same connector. In HDTV use, DVI is usually combined with HDCP to add copyright protection to the link. Sometimes referred to as *Digital Visual Interface*. See also *HDCP, HDMI*.

Ethernet The most common wired communication technology for the home or local area network. The most common types of Ethernet are 10Base-T and 100Base-T, which have four twisted wires (two pairs) carried on what's called Cat5 (Category 5) cable. Data transfer rates for 10Base-T are up to 10 Mbits/s and up to 100 Mbits/s for 100Base-T. The common connector type for Ethernet is the RJ-45 jack.

Feedhorn In radio electronics, the device used to capture and guide an electromagnetic signal from an antenna reflector (such as a satellite dish) to a receiver. The feedhorn on a DirecTV dish is attach to an arm protruding from the dish and is combined with the LNB converter (often referred to as an *LNBF* (Low Noise Block Feedhorn). See also *DBS, LNB*.

Fort A makeshift cover for an infrared receiving window on an electronic device used to isolate the signal from an IR blaster so that IR signals from other devices don't interfere. In TiVo hookups, the cable receiver provided by the cable company can sometimes misbehave and respond to remote signals it's not supposed to pay attention to. A fort, often made from cloth, wide tape, or cardboard, is used to cover the IR window. Also called a *tent*.

F-type Connector A common form of terminating a coaxial cable used in RF transmission. The connector has a center pin and a threaded bushing that screws onto a matching threaded F-type jack. See also *BNC Connector, coaxial cable, RF*.

Gender Bender Name given to a type of hardware adapter designed to join two cable connectors of the same "gender" (for example, two "female" connectors would require an adapter with male connectors on both sides to join the two female-ended cables together). Also know as a "gender changer," "gender mender," and even "sex changer." It is a long-standing tradition in electronics to use the term "male" to refer to a plug, a connector with pins, or any other technology that gets inserted into a receptacle. The corresponding fitting is referred to as "female." In TiVo, making a serial connection between your PVR and your PC requires a female-to-female gender bender as TiVo's serial cable ends in a male connector and so does your PC's serial port. See also *null modem, RS-232*.

GNU A free Unix-like set of software tools that, when combined with the Linux kernel, became a full-blown operating system distributed under the name GNU/Linux, or often simply as a "Linux distribution." GNU set the standards for open source software development, with the developers' insistence that it remain open to all users "to run, copy, modify and distribute" and with the creation of the GNU General Public License. Pronounced guh-NEW. See also *GNU General Public License, kernel, Linux, open source*.

GNU General Public License TiVo is built upon the Linux operating system, which is built upon GNU components. Some of the software used in TiVo is open source and is therefore subject to the GNU General Public License. The GNU GPL stipulates that you can use, modify, and redistribute the open source software as long as the terms of the GPL license are complied with. A copy of the GPL can be found in the appendix of all TiVo Viewer's Guides. The main software components that drive TiVo, such as the myworld program, are proprietary and are not open source. See also *Linux, open source*.

Hacking Using one's technical expertise to innovate, improvise, and/or cobble together solutions to technical problems. The term *hardware hacking* is often used to refer to altering an existing piece of technology to do something new with it, especially something for which it was never intended. See also *open source*.

Hard Padding See *padding*.

HDCP (High Bandwidth Digital Content Protection) A copy protection technology, developed by Intel, for use with HDTV and DVI/HDMI. The specification uses a dizzying array of "device keys," "content keys," and "session keys" to verify that the devices connected via the DVI or HDMI are allowed to be talking to each other. Without proper verification, the display (for instance) will not work. Once verified, the content is streamed, in an encrypted format, over the DVI/HDMI cable. The HD DirecTiVo uses this new content protection technology. See also *DVI, HDMI, HDTV*.

HDMI (High-Definition Multimedia Interface) An all-digital connection technology that allows uncompressed digital audio and video to be sent over one USB-like cable from a suitable A/V source (such as an HDTV tuner) to a digital TV monitor. HDMI is being developed with HDCP capabilities built into it. See also *HDCP, HDTV*.

HDTV (High Definition Television) The current "high-end" digital TV format that can display up to 1920 pixels times 1080 lines, offering an image that is some six times sharper than standard-definition TV. HDTV screens use a widescreen 16:9 aspect ratio. The video standard for high-definition is MPEG-2 and the digital audio standard is Dolby Digital (known generically as "AC-3"). See also *SDTV*.

He (She) Said "Taped" A phrase used in online and offline geek circles whenever someone makes the mistake of saying "taped" in reference to programming recorded on a digital recorder (where, of course, there is no tape). Often prefixed by the Beavis snicker: "He-he. He-he. He said 'taped.'"

ISO (International Organization for Standardization) An international organization that sets standards for industry and the commercial sector worldwide. The group is comprised of one standards body from each country, as well as representatives from many major corporations. Standards derived from this body will have an ISO number attached to them. One such number, ISO 9660, is frequently seen in computer circles as it refers to the standard for making "disk images," copies of the contents of a data storage device, such as a CD-ROM. The file extension .iso is used for disk images. These .iso files are the most common way by which the Linux OS is distributed. These files are also often referred to as *ISO images*.

Jumping the Shark Hollywood slang for a television program (or anything else) that has lived beyond its prime. The term comes from a Happy Days episode in which Fonzie jumps over a shark while on water skis. Even before the term itself was coined, critics pointed out this episode as an example of what a once-popular show in deep decline looks like. Other jump the shark moments: when Oliver showed up on the Brady Bunch, and when Dick Sargent was replaced by Dick York (without explanation) as Darren Stevens on Bewitched.

Kernel As the name implies, the kernel is the core of a computer's operating system. An OS employs many different component applications that specialize in different tasks and provide various services to the system. The kernel is tasked with how and when these programs can gain access to the underlying hardware components. The kernel also often includes a "hardware abstraction layer," software routines that handle platform-specific details so that programmers can write device-independent applications. See also *GNU, Linux*.

Linux A Unix-like computer operating system built upon GNU components, another Unix-like system. An open source operating system with many different versions available (many of them free of charge), Linux has taken the computer world by storm. Ironically, even though it's been coded collaboratively, by programmers from around the world, it is known for being by far more robust, less crash-prone, and more code-efficient than Microsoft Windows. Because of Linux's efficiency, and its cheap (or free) cost, it is becoming extremely popular in embedded systems, including PVRs such as TiVo. Unix is an OS created by Bell Labs scientists in the early 1970s as "get by" software for handling electronic documentation. They never could have imagined that thirty years later, it (and its offspring like Linux) would be one of the chief software architectures holding together a globe-spanning "cyberspace." See *GNU, open source*.

LNB (Low-Noise Block Converter) A device used for broadcast satellite reception that converts the high-frequency signals being reflected from the dish into lower frequencies, which then travel through coax cable to a satellite receiver. "Low noise" refers to the fact that the device is engineered to minimize the radio noise that can be very damaging to a high-frequency signal. *Block* is another term for a radio band. Also known as a *Low-Noise Block Down Converter*. Dual-LNBs have two converters that can feed two TV tuners or receivers, and a Triple-LNB can accommodate three tuners. In DBS systems, these devices are often referred to as an *LNBF*, or *Low Noise Block Feedhorn*. See also *DBS, feedhorn*.

Luminance In an analog video signal, the part of the signal that conveys information about the signal's brightness (or luminosity). Abbreviated *luma*. See also *chrominance*.

MFS (Media File System) Name for the file system/database scheme developed for TiVo. It is divided into two "regions," or partitions: the MFS Application Region (where information related to TiVos operations is stored) and the MFS Media Region (where the audio/video files are stored). See also *Tivosh*.

MP3 Short for *MPEG-1/2 Audio Layer 3*. The digital audio compression standard that is widely used globally for the encoding of digital music. Series 2 TiVo's Home Media Feature allows one to play MP3 files stored on a PC on TiVo. See *compression, MPEG-2*.

MPEG-2 A digital video and audio compression standard created by the Motion Pictures Coding Experts Group (MPEG) and designated as ISO 13818. MPEG-2 is widely used for cable and satellite signal broadcasting, DVD coding, and HDTV transmissions. See also *compression, MP3*.

Multimedia Timewarping System The actual name for TiVo, Inc's patent on PVR technology. The patent covers the ability to record one program while another is being watched, the particular method used for synchronizing audio, video, and closed captioning information, and some of the storage, playback, and navigation features that TiVo uses.

NTSC (National Television Standards Committee) The organization that sets the standards for analog television in the United States. Also the name given to the standard itself, which has been widely adopted in other parts of the world. NTSC is not known for its high quality, which had led to the joke that the initials really stand for "Never The Same Color." See also *ATSC, PAL, SECAM*.

Null Modem A type of serial/RS-232 cable that connects two PCs together so they can communicate without the use of a modem. A null modem cable can be used to connect TiVo to a computer for access to TiVo's Linux prompt. See also *gender bender, RS-232*.

Open Source A movement in the computer sciences to make computer software source code open to programmers who want to improve upon it and distribute their own versions. In the early days of computing, all code was open to examination, improvement, and tinkering; then most of it became proprietary. Open source proponents want to open it up again. Also called the *free software movement*, but that name implies non-commercial, which "open source" does not (you can still sell it as long as you allow users to make changes and redistribute their own versions). See also *hacking, Linux*.

OTA (Over-the-Air) Refers to the traditional form of radio (including TV) broadcasting where signals are sent out as radio waves through a transmission tower and "brought down" on the receiving end via a small antenna. In contrast with cable and direct broadcast satellite systems. Sometimes referred to as *off-the-air* or *over the antenna*.

Ouija Screen Nickname given to TiVo's text-entry screens (found under the "Pick Programs to Record" menus). The name comes from the fact that navigating through the alpha-numeric grid with the remote is reminiscent of spelling words out on a Ouija board.

Padding Name for the addition of recording time on the beginning and/or end of a program so as to guarantee that the entire program is captured. This feature, officially known as *overtime scheduling*, was added to TiVo in software version 2.0. The introduction of this feature has led to many discussions, some simple hacks, and some hard coding of software to handle different types of padding situations. The overtime scheduler is often referred to as *hard padding*. Negative padding, available to Series 1 users as a user-coded application, allows one to stop a program after its scheduled start time or before its scheduled end time. *Soft padding* is a desired feature that would only record overtime if it didn't interfere with another subsequent program scheduled for recording. *Semi-soft padding* is a get-by hack that uses a combination of prioritized Season Passes and WishList recordings to create something approximating soft padding.

PAL (Phase Alternating Line) The other white meat, or at least, the other principal analog TV encoding standard used throughout much of the rest of the world where NTSC is not. PAL is widely regarded in the TV/video world as being superior to the NTSC standard. Where the joke goes that NTSC stands for "Never The Same Color," PAL is said to stand for "Perfect At Last," though that's a bit of an overstatement. See also *NTSC, SECAM*.

Peanut Nickname given to the TiVo remote because of its curvy, symmetrical peanut-like shape. While the remote is widely praised as an extremely well designed device, some criticize the fact that its symmetry makes it difficult, in the dark, to tell which end is which.

Penguinhead Slang term for a diehard Linux enthusiast (think: "Deadhead"). Refers to Tux the Penguin, the logo/mascot for the Linux OS. See also *Linux*.

Pixelization When an object on a video image is intentionally blurred out to hide something (as in Janet Jackson's breast in the infamous Super Bowl footage). The term is also widely used to refer to loss of information in a video signal leading to visible blocks in the image. This is properly known as *compression artifacts* or *artifacting*. See also *compression*.

PTCMs (Pre-TiVo Central Messages) Name given to the pop-up messages that sometimes occur when you press the TiVoGuy button on your remote to go to the TiVo Central screen. These messages can contain everything from system-related announcements to commercial ads. Many TiVo users are concerned that PTCM ads might increase in frequency and become a real annoyance—a form of PVR spam.

Pull Term used for working (or new) components removed from an existing electronics device to be used as parts for another device. For instance, weaKnees.com sells "hard drive pulls" taken from brand new TiVos. Using such a pull is an easy way of upgrading or replacing a TiVo HD without having to bless the drive(s). See also *blessing*.

RadioCrap Derogatory nickname for Radio Shack. Hardware hackers and audio/video enthusiasts have a love-hate relationship with "the Shack." There's one on nearly every street corner, but the employees are often impressively clueless, and over the years, the do-it-yourself/parts sections have gotten smaller and smaller as cell phones and remote controlled toys spread throughout the stores like frisky Tribbles. Also known as RatShack.

RCA Plug/Jack The ubiquitous plug/jack technology used for composite video and analog audio cables. Developed by RCA, the plug has a male center pin surround by a metal attachment ring. The ring is often segmented to make it easier to plug/unplug. The corresponding jack has a center hole and a metal ring slightly smaller than on the plug, allowing for a snug friction fit. Also referred to as a *phono plug*. See also *composite video*.

Remote Bloat The disturbing profusion of remote controls that seem to reproduce on your coffee table. While the universal remote was designed to cure this affliction, too often, universals can't handle all control functions (or they're too difficult for the average user to successfully program), still requiring several remotes to control all media equipment. See also *buttonitis*.

Reverse Engineering The process of taking apart an already existing device to figure out how it works so you can then make your own copy or an improved version. Hardware hackers reversed engineered the proprietary edge connector found on Series 1 stand-alone TiVos to create networking cards that could use this connector. See also *hacking*.

RF (Radio Frequency) Refers to the portion of the electromagnetic spectrum that can be turned into waves, generated by an alternating current (AC), and transmitted and received via antennas. RF is used for all forms of home media broadcasting, from over-the-air antennas, to the "community antennas" of cable services, to the microwave mini-dishes of direct broadcasting satellite systems. RF signals are usually delivered to the receiver via coaxial cable and either F-type or BNC connectors. See also *BNC*, *coaxial cable*, *F-type connector*.

RS-232 The common standard for serial data communications. The serial port on your PC (if it still has one) is technically known as an RS-232 port. Serial communication is in contrast with parallel communication. Parallel technology allows for multiple streams of back and forth data communications, serial connections only allow one data stream at a time. It might seem that parallel would be the superior, faster technology, but for a bunch of reasons we won't get into here, serial is actually faster. RS-232 is being phased out in favor of the USB serial standard. All TiVos have an RS-232 port and most come with a serial cable. It was meant to allow connection to a serial channel controller (found on some cable and satellite receivers), but this port can also be used for setting up a communications link between TiVo and a PC. See also *gender bender*, *null modem*, *USB*.

SA Short for "stand-alone." Used in TiVo circles to differentiate regular/non-satellite receivers from the DirecTV with TiVo (or DirecTiVo) models.

SDTV (Standard-Definition Television) A digital TV broadcasting standard that is higher definition than analog, but less so than HDTV. SDTV delivers up to 704 pixels by 480 lines. See also *ATSC*, *HDTV*.

SECAM (Sequentiel Couleur avec Mémoire or Sequential Color with Memory) Guess who has their own TV standard? The French. SECAM is similar to PAL, but uses a different technique for encoding the color information. It also has the ability to "remember" color information, which helps eliminate the artifacting found in NTSC. Many countries that use SECAM market TV sets that can display it and PAL (and sometimes even NTSC). Every standard has a joke version of its name. For SECAM it's "System Essentially Contrary to the American Method." See also *NTSC*, *PAL*.

Semi-Soft Padding See *padding*.

Serial Communication See *null modem, RS-232*.

Shell A computer program that allows a user to access operating system functions and services as well as applications and files. A shell can either be a command-line interface (CLI) or a graphical user interface (GUI). TiVo's myworld program is a GUI (pronounced gooey), but the underlying Linux-based OS components are accessed via a CLI. See also *Bash, Tcl*.

Skip to Tick Another name for the Advance button on the TiVo remote or the action that the button performs (if the 30-second advance feature has not been invoked). *Tick* refers to the time interval marks on the Status Bar. If the 30-second advance has been turned on, skip to tick will be disabled in regular playback mode, but will still work for Rewind and Fast-Forward.

Soft Padding See *padding*.

Stopple A hard drive stutter, usually indicative of looming disk failure, where the audio and video freeze for a few seconds while watching a recorded program and fast-forwarding through a show is choppy.

Suggestion Engine What the underlying software that makes the TiVo Suggestions feature possible is commonly referred to as.

SUID Shorthand for "Save Until I Delete," the menu command that allows you to tell TiVo to keep a program until you manually delete it.

Surface Mount An electronics assembly technique (common in computer technology) where components are soldered directly (sometimes called baking) onto the printed circuit board, instead of the older method of soldering on the components via wire leads. Also often abbreviated as *SMT* for *Surface Mount Technology*.

S-Video An analog video transmission technology that improves upon composite video by sending the color and luminance information through separate wires. This prevents crosstalk between the two streams that can degrade the signal. S-Video is terminated with a 4-pin mini-DIN connector. Why four pins for only two data streams? They are two pairs of signal and ground wires. BTW: The "S" in the name stands for "Super." See also *component video, composite video*.

Tcl (Tool Command Language) A scripting language that can be used to create applications. Tcl is relatively easy to learn, with powerful capabilities. Although it is platform-independent (it can be used on Windows, Mac, and Unix/Linux systems), it is most popular among Unix/Linux users. TiVo developers used Tcl when designing TiVo's software. A Tcl interpreter, called Tivosh, can be found in all TiVos. *Tcl* is pronounced *tickle*, and yes, it's supposed to have a lowercase "c" and "l." See also *Bash, Tivosh*.

Tent See *fort*.

Terminal Emulator A program that turns your expensive 21st century computer into a pre-Millennium "dumb terminal." Using such a program, one can log in to another computer on a network (or via a direct modem connection) and move around within the remote system. In TiVo, a terminal program is used on a PC to gain access to the software on a serially-connected TiVo. See also *null modem, RS-232*.

Time-Shift Viewing Roughly translates to: "Never, ever have to watch commercials again and save yourself at least 15 minutes per hour-long show—and use that saved time to watch even *MORE* recorded TV!" Given the fact that the TiVo patent is titled "Multimedia Timewarping System," maybe time-shift viewing could be called *timewarping* as well. Also *time-shifting*. See also *Multimedia Timewarping System*.

TiVo Debt The obligation one can feel to watch all of the programs in TiVo's "Now Playing" list. Particularly common among new users who aren't used to having so much programming available that they actually want to watch.

TiVoed (or TiVo'd) You know your product is a commercial success when your brand becomes a common noun (such as "Kleenex" for tissue) or a verb. The term TiVoed can be heard almost daily by someone on television (or around the water cooler) and is quickly becoming synonymous with "recorded." It is so popular that even people who own other brands of PVRs say: "I TiVoed Six Feet Under last night." See also *"He said 'taped.'"*

TiVoGuy The nickname given to the dancing TV cartoon character seen in TiVo commercials, during the start-up sequence, and depicted on the TiVo remote control. Also sometimes called the *TiVo Dude* and even *sTeeVo*.

TiVoMatic Another term for iPreview, the feature that allows you to quickly jump to the Record Program screen whenever you see the Thumbs Up icon embedded in previews for an upcoming program (and press the Thumbs Up button on your remote).

Tivosh The command-line interpreter created by TiVo, Inc. as a version of Tcl optimized for TiVo development. *Tivosh* is short for *TIVO SHell* See also *Bash, Shell, Tcl*.

Tux the Penguin See *Linux, penguinhead*.

USB (Universal Serial Bus) The serial communications protocol now commonly used on computers and digital media appliances to connect devices. It replaces the earlier RS-232 standard. Besides better transfer rates, USB has a number of other improvements, including the ability to plug/unplug devices while the system is powered up (called "hot swapping"), and USB cables can also carry power to peripheral devices that have low power needs. All Series 2 TiVos have two USB ports. On SA models, USB ports can be used for networking (via wired or wireless adapters) and for the "Content Security Key" that enables the TiVoToGo service. See also *RS-232*.

Vaporware Said of software or hardware that is continually promised but never delivered. TiVo, Inc. has been accused of promoting vaporware with such teasers as the stand-alone HD TiVo receiver which has been shown in prototype form for years but has yet to make it to market.

Whispering Arrows The inexplicable term that TiVo, Inc. uses for the arrows seen on the TiVo interface that allow you to move up and down within a menu or side to side through menus above or below in the menu hierarchy.

WiFi (Wireless Fidelity) The local area network (LAN) wireless radio standard described in the 802.11 specifications. There are several flavors of WiFi: 802.11b, the first to become popular, makes use of the 2.4GHz radio band. This band is crowded with other electronic devices, from portable phones to microwave ovens. To exploit a less populated part of the spectrum, 802.11a was introduced in 2001. It operates at 5GHz and can reach transfer speeds of up to 54 Mbits/second (where 11b can only handle up to 11 Mbits/s). In 2003, a third version was released, 802.11g. Like 11b, it operates in the 2.4GHz neighborhood, but can achieve theoretical rates akin to 11a (though, in practice, both 11a and 11g operate at more like 25 Mbits/s). Since many homes now use WiFi, Series 2 TiVos can be added to a home network via a USB wireless adapter and the optional Home Media Feature.

Index

Q - R

X - Y - Z